Cambridge Imperial and Post-Colonial Studies Series

Series Editors

Megan Vaughan
University College London
United Kingdom

Richard Drayton
King's College London
United Kingdom

The Cambridge Imperial and Post-Colonial Studies series is a collection of studies on empires in world history and on the societies and cultures which emerged from colonialism. It includes both transnational, comparative and connective studies, and studies which address where particular regions or nations participate in global phenomena. While in the past the series focused on the British Empire and Commonwealth, in its current incarnation there is no imperial system, period of human history or part of the world which lies outside of its compass. While we particularly welcome the first monographs of young researchers, we also seek major studies by more senior scholars, and welcome collections of essays with a strong thematic focus. The series includes work on politics, economics, culture, literature, science, art, medicine, and war. Our aim is to collect the most exciting new scholarship on world history with an imperial theme.

More information about this series at
http://www.springer.com/series/13937

T.M. Devine • Angela McCarthy

Editors

The Scottish Experience in Asia, c.1700 to the Present

Settlers and Sojourners

palgrave
macmillan

Editors
T.M. Devine
University of Edinburgh
Edinburgh, United Kingdom

Angela McCarthy
University of Otago
Dunedin, New Zealand

Cambridge Imperial and Post-Colonial Studies Series
ISBN 978-3-319-82731-5   ISBN 978-3-319-43074-4   (eBook)
DOI 10.1007/978-3-319-43074-4

Cover illustration: © Lebrecht Music and Arts Photo Library / Alamy Stock Photo

Printed on acid-free paper

This Palgrave Macmillan imprint is published by Springer Nature
The registered company is Springer International Publishing AG
The registered company address is: Gewerbestrasse 11, 6330 Cham, Switzerland

Acknowledgements

We are grateful to the Economic and Social Research Council for funding our three-year seminar series on 'Scotland's Diasporas in Comparative International Perspective' (a joint initiative of Angela McCarthy, Tom Devine, and Nick Evans). It was at one of those seminars in June 2015—on the Scots in Asia—that most of the chapters in this book were first presented. They have since been extended and revised for publication here and we are grateful to contributors for their support of the book, their swift communication with us, and their willingness to undertake revisions. We are also appreciative of feedback from two expert commentators at the seminar (Professor John M. MacKenzie and Dr Andrew Mackillop), whose thoughtful reflections fed into the final versions of the chapters presented here. We also thank the Scottish Centre for Diaspora Studies at the University of Edinburgh for providing a venue for the event.

T.M. Devine and Angela McCarthy

Contents

NOTES ON CONTRIBUTORS

Tom Barron is a graduate of Aberdeen and London Universities. He taught in the Department of Commonwealth and American History at the University of Edinburgh from 1965–89, with two periods as a Visiting Fellow, at Peradeniya University and at Colombo University in Sri Lanka. He became Director of the International Office at Edinburgh from 1989–2001. His research interests and publications include work on the history of imperial administration and studies in the British period of Sri Lankan history.

Tanja Bueltmann is Reader in History at Northumbria University. Her research interests are in diaspora and British World history, especially the history of ethnic associationalism and immigrant community life. She is the author of: the award-winning *Clubbing Together: Ethnicity, Civility and Formal Sociability in the Scottish Diaspora to 1930* (2014); *Scottish Ethnicity and the Making of New Zealand Society, 1850 to 1930* (2011); and, with Andrew Hinson and Graeme Morton, *The Scottish Diaspora* (2013). Tanja's current research focuses on her ESRC Future Research Leaders project entitled 'European, Ethnic and Expatriate: A Longitudinal Comparison of German and British Social Networking and Associational Formations in Modern-day Asia'.

T.M. Devine is Sir William Fraser Professor Emeritus of Scottish History and Palaeography at the University of Edinburgh. His main research interest is the history of the Scottish people at home and abroad since c.1600 in comparative and international context. His latest book, *Independence or Union*, was published by Penguin in 2016. Devine was knighted in 2014 for services to the study of Scottish history.

Ellen Filor is a Junior Research Fellow at the Institute of Advanced Studies, University College London. She completed her PhD in 2014 at University College

X NOTES ON CONTRIBUTORS

London. Her thesis examined Border Scots in the East India Company in the 70 years before the Indian Revolt of 1857. Since passing her viva, she has also been a Scottish Studies Fulbright Scholar at the University of Michigan.

Joanna Frew has a PhD from the University of Essex, entitled 'Metropolitan Thought and Practices in the Empire: The Case of Scots and Agricultural Improvement in South India, 1792–c.1814'. The research focuses on Scottish imperial networks in India in the late eighteenth century and asks what effect these persistent networks had on imperial policy at the fringes of empire. After studying history and international relations as an undergraduate, Joanna worked in the NGO sector for ten years, then returned to research after a Master's in International Law at SOAS.

Isabella Jackson is Assistant Professor in Chinese History at Trinity College Dublin. Her research focuses on the history of colonialism in China and the global and regional networks that shaped its treaty ports, and she recently co-edited (with Robert Bickers) a volume on *Treaty Ports in Modern China: Law, Land and Power* (2016). Before taking up her current position, she was a Departmental Lecturer at the University of Oxford and then the Helen Bruce Lecturer in Modern East Asian History at the University of Aberdeen. She is preparing a monograph, provisionally entitled *Shanghai: Transnational Colonialism in China's Global City*, based on her prize-winning PhD thesis on the Shanghai Municipal Council.

John M. MacKenzie has been publishing on aspects of the history of British Empire since the early 1970s. He was general editor of the Manchester University Press 'Studies in Imperialism' series for more than thirty years taking it to more than 100 books. His own books include *Propaganda and Empire* (1984), *The Empire of Nature* (1988), *Orientalism: History, Theory and the Arts* (1995), *The Scots in South Africa* (2007) and *Museums and Empire* (2009). He has recently been the Editor-in-Chief of the four-volume Wiley Blackwell *Encyclopedia of Empire* (2016) and has been co-editor of *Scotland, Empire and Decolonisation in the Twentieth Century* (2015), *Exhibiting the Empire* (2015) and *Global Migrations: The Scottish Diaspora since 1600* (2016). He has travelled and lectured widely in Asia and is currently working on a cultural history of the British Empire.

Angela McCarthy is Professor of Scottish and Irish History at the University of Otago, New Zealand, where she teaches Irish and Scottish history and migration, and migration, race and ethnicity in New Zealand. She is the author/editor of ten books on migration, including *A Global Clan: Scottish Migrant Networks and Identities since the Eighteenth Century* (2006), *Personal Narratives of Irish and Scottish Migration, 1921–65: 'For Spirit and Adventure'* (2007), *Irishness and Scottishness in New Zealand* (2011) and (with John MacKenzie) *Global Migrations: The Scottish Diaspora since 1600* (2016). Angela's most recent monograph is

Migration, Ethnicity, and Madness (2015) and she is currently writing a biography of James Taylor, 'the father of Ceylon tea'.

George McGilvary is an Honorary Post-Doctoral Fellow of the Scottish Centre of Diaspora Studies, University of Edinburgh. His initial work was a biography of Laurence Sulivan MP (1713–86). Further publications deal with Scottish-East India Company connections, patronage and the impact of Scottish nabobs on Scotland. Other works analyse the commercial activities of the Scottish elite in Scotland, London, South-East Asia and China.

Patrick Peebles is Professor Emeritus of History at the University of Missouri-Kansas City, where he taught world history, historical methods, and the modern history of Asia. He is a specialist on the modern history of Sri Lanka (Ceylon), where he was an American Peace Corps Volunteer from 1962–64. His most recent books are *Historical Dictionary of Sri Lanka* (2015) and *Voices of South Asia. Essential Readings from Antiquity to the Present* (2012).

Iain Watson was born in Singapore and raised in the Scottish expatriate environments of Singapore, Kuala Lumpur and Penang. He has pursued a career as a global banker working in the United Kingdom, France, the Yemen, Hong Kong, New Zealand and Australia. Having left the financial services industry, he is currently a PhD candidate at the University of Edinburgh where he is conducting a comparative study of Scottish migrants to Hong Kong and New Zealand since 1945. He holds degrees from the Open University (BA Hons in History) and the University of Edinburgh (MSc in Diaspora and Migration History).

LIST OF FIGURES

LIST OF TABLES

Introduction: The Scottish Experience in Asia, c.1700 to the Present: Settlers and Sojourners

T.M. Devine and Angela McCarthy

The remarkable scale and global reach of modern Scottish emigration has been described at length in recent academic writings. Between 1815 and the Second World War more than 2.3 million people left Scotland for overseas destinations, and this from a country with a population of less than 4.5 million at the census of 1901. When the 600,000 odd reckoned to have crossed the border to England over the shorter time frame of 1841 to 1911 are added to that total, it is easy to see why some regard Scotland as one of the key emigration countries of Europe in the nineteenth and much of the twentieth centuries. Even when out-migration was significantly less, as it was between 1700 and 1815, 80,000 to 100,000 departures from a population of 1.6 million in 1800 have been estimated over that century.[1]

If that great diaspora can be likened to a demographic flood in relation to the base population of the country, Scottish migration to Asia in

T.M. Devine (✉)
University of Edinburgh, Edinburgh, Scotland

A. McCarthy (✉)
University of Otago, Dunedin, New Zealand

© The Author(s) 2017
T.M. Devine, A. McCarthy (eds.), *The Scottish Experience in Asia, c.1700 to the Present*, DOI 10.1007/978-3-319-43074-4_1

the eighteenth and nineteenth centuries seems more akin in numerical terms, to a slow, insignificant trickle. In part, this comparatively small flow accounts for the very thin scholarship on the Scots in Asia compared with the rapidly growing historiography of their migrations to North America, the Caribbean, South Africa and Australasia.[2] Moreover, the research that does exist focuses primarily on India, where issues of patronage, networking and Scottish Orientalism have been to the fore. This, therefore, is a pioneering volume which attempts to establish initial parameters which future scholarship can refine and develop. Its primary focus is on the scale, territorial trajectories, impact, economic relationships, identity and nature of the Scottish-Asian connection from before the Union of 1707 to the present. The book does not therefore seek to be comprehensive in content but rather to utilise the expertise and experience of the small number of researchers who are already active in the field in order to bring out key themes and issues.

Importantly, however, the research in this volume connects with other developments in studies of Britain's empire. On the one hand, the book's engagement with Scottish enterprise fits with the increasing reincorporation in imperial history of economic and trade issues which in recent years has been overshadowed by a focus on empire as a cultural project. Also included is out-of-favour 'high politics' through consideration of the tenure of an influential Scottish governor in nineteenth century Ceylon. But we also attempt to embrace the new imperial history's focus on such issues as colonial knowledge, the construction of identity and cross-cultural encounters.[3]

DEMOGRAPHIC PATTERNS

Before the Union of 1707 and soon afterwards, a few Scots were already active in the East India trade, particularly in the Swedish East Company (Svenska Ostindiska Compagniet: SOIC), the Dutch East India Company (Vereenigde Oost-Indische Compangine: VOC) and, to a lesser extent, the Ostend (Austrian) Company.[4] Their numbers did visibly start to rise within the United English East India Company (EIC), especially from the 1740s, and by the early nineteenth century Scots had undeniably made their mark in that enterprise as civil servants, army officers, physicians and mariners. This was partly a result of the turn to the East (and Australasia and Africa) after the loss in 1783 of the 13 American colonies. Absolute numbers still remained unimpressive, however, in large part because the

Company's administrative cadres were themselves relatively insignificant overall.

Nevertheless, over the 60 years between 1720 and 1780 a minimum of around 2,000 Scots males were recruited to the EIC, or over 33 per year on average, although numbers fluctuated to a considerable extent over time. Data drawn from Company records at a later date in 1806 suggest 21 Scottish writers, 80 cadets and 14 assistant surgeons (115 in all) in its employ at that date out of a total of 644 in these positions across the EIC.[5] One authoritative estimate suggests that even when the EIC's territorial responsibilities had expanded very significantly by the early 1830s, leading to authority over 45 million Indians, it still employed only 895 civil servants and 754 medical officers.[6] By the same period, it is reckoned that there were perhaps fewer than 5,000 additional British males resident in the subcontinent who were not on the Company's payroll. Overall, indeed, in the 1830s, the total number of Britons in India was probably little more than 65,000–70,000 and of these over four-fifths were soldiers in the army of the EIC or in the regular forces of the Crown. Scots tended to be over-represented among the officer class in the military but were much fewer among the rank and file than the Irish and the English. Ship rolls for the years between 1775 and 1781, for example, indicate a total of 4,949 troops sent to the East from Britain. A mere 170 (3.4 per cent) of these were from Scotland.[7]

Scots had a much higher profile by the early 1800s among the 'free' or independent agency houses and shipping interests which linked India to the burgeoning and lucrative markets of South-East Asia. Their activities are examined in Chapter 4. By the early nineteenth century, 50 such enterprises were reckoned to be active in the presidency of Madras alone. These men of business and their successors eventually reached deep into the East by the middle decades of the nineteenth century in the trades of coffee, tea, opium, textiles and raw materials such as rubber and tin. Scots were also to be found throughout the many diverse countries of Asia, including Ceylon, Singapore, Hong Kong, Malaya, Burma, China and, by the 1870s, even in the formerly closed and insular society of Japan. No precise figures are available for the numbers in these pursuits. However, a rough guestimate, based on the 300 odd Scots free merchants and mariners active in the Asian trades by the 1830s, and the likely number of their Scots-born employees and figures for incomers to Ceylon and Malaya, would suggest little more than 2,000 to 2,500 in South-East Asia as traders, managers, planters, physicians, missionaries and ships' commanders by the 1850s, and perhaps somewhat more by 1900. Even by that date the Scottish presence in the East remained overwhelmingly masculine, unlike the white settlement colonies of Canada and the Antipodes.[8]

As outlined in Chapters 8 and 9, Scots had considerable visibility as owners and superintendents in the coffee, and later, though perhaps to a lesser extent, in the tea plantation economies of Ceylon. At one point, indeed, Ceylon could be described as a 'Scotch colony' where the influence of Scots was not only evident in the plantation economy but also in journalism, the law, brokerage, manufacturing and banking. Yet here again, numbers were limited. According to the 1901 *Census of the British Empire*, there were a recorded 275 Irish-born, 2,210 English and 647 Scots in residence at the time the census was taken. In the Indian empire, meanwhile, Scots were 9,325 compared with 9,682 Irish and 77,411 English and Welsh. In Hong Kong, Scots numbered 476 compared with 155 Irish and 1,254 English born.[9] Some caution, however, is needed with these statistics due to the absence or erratic nature of census data for many areas and the temporary nature of much migration. The key point is that any Scottish influence on Asia did not in the final analysis depend on absolute numbers. This is also true of the legacy of Scots in Hong Kong where even today some sojourners think of it as something of a 'Scottish colony', as indicated in Chapter 13, despite them being only a minor part of the total population.

It is reckoned that Scots constituted around one-third of all colonial governors between 1850 and 1939.[10] Needy Scottish aristocrats, lairds and retired military men often sought employment in the colonial administrations and when they achieved influential positions regularly acted as patrons to aid their fellow countrymen to gain employment in other posts. One such example is that of Governor James Alexander Stewart Mackenzie. His attempts to bring Scots to Ceylon are noted in Chapter 9 while his overall career is considered in Chapter 7. Migration from the middle and upper classes also characterised those joining Scottish associations in Singapore and China as outlined in Chapters 11 and 12.

Explanations for the relatively small scale of Scottish migration and that of other nationalities from the British Isles to Asia are not hard to find. One reason was that the EIC was resolutely opposed to colonisation and European settlement in its domains.[11] But also, unlike the Americas and Australasia, the Asiatic world was unlikely to attract family migration of any magnitude. Even British spouses of EIC officials and army officers were uncommon in India until after the 1830s. For the most part, the majority of Scots, as with the British in general who were drawn to the

East over much of the eighteenth and early nineteenth centuries, were young, single men who went out to make money, hopefully as quickly as possible, and then return home with their gains. Only a few stayed on willingly before 1815, once they had survived the many threats to health, although after that date some strikingly different patterns began to emerge in India, as described in Chapter 6. In the eighteenth century, however, the vast majority saw themselves as sojourners rather than settlers. That tradition endured into the nineteenth century with the great Scottish companies of Victorian and Edwardian times, described in Chapter 4, which engaged in the eastern trades, shipping and the plantation business and were usually family-owned. The senior managerial generation gradually ceded power to the kindred at home, be they sons, nephews or cousins, while their elders eventually retired back to Britain. In due course, the same cycle would begin all over again. There was therefore constant movement among family members between their locus in the homeland and their businesses in Asia. This coming and going served to maintain a continuing sense of ethnic identity through the retention of close links with Scotland, bonds which were less likely to be sustained after the first and second generations in the colonies of settlement.

Also, unlike Canada, the USA, South Africa and Australasia, but similar to the Caribbean colonies, Asia was unsuited by climate and environment for mass European emigration. Indeed, like parts of tropical Africa, India in the eighteenth century had the reputation of being the white man's grave. The chances of becoming rich before 1800 were counterbalanced by the very real possibility of succumbing to disease soon after arrival. Thus, between 1707 and 1775, 57 per cent of the EIC's servants died in India. Before the 1760s, two-thirds of those in the writer grade of the Company's administration never came back. A return of casualties of officers and cadets in the army in Bengal between 1770 and 1776 revealed that only six had fallen in action but no fewer than 208 had perished from disease.[12] Into the nineteenth century, Scots in the EIC civil service became more dependent on Company pension provision than immediate riches. As a result, the period of time they were likely to spend in India had to become longer, as Ellen Filor confirms in Chapter 6.

Nevertheless, while Scottish migration to Asia may have been relatively insignificant in number compared to that in other parts of the world, the evidence presented in this book suggests the impact was nonetheless conspicuous and arguably disproportionate in some spheres. This was especially so in the Indian empire from the second half of the eighteenth century and thereafter in Asian trade, shipping, the plantation economies, the scholarly dissemination of ideas about the East and Japan's transformation from feudalism to capitalism in the late nineteenth century. One of the objectives of this collection of essays is to examine these effects and how they might be explained.

IMPACT

Of the global Scots diaspora, only migration to the sugar islands of the Caribbean perhaps invites comparison with the movement to Asia. The West Indies also never attracted much permanent European settlement. Almost all who went there were also young male sojourners and, like their counterparts considered in this book, were intent on making money quickly and then returning home. As in Asia, too, these Scots were a tiny minority among vast non-European populations, though in the Caribbean these were not natives of the islands but black Africans who had been sold into lives of chattel slavery and transported across the Atlantic from their homelands to the Americas. As in India, many young men succumbed at an early stage to the endemic diseases of the tropics and never saw their native land again. In addition, connections with both the Caribbean and Asia benefited the Scottish economy as sources of capital, raw materials and markets, and aided the country's unusually rapid industrial and agrarian transformation from the middle decades of the eighteenth century. Also, both destinations revolutionised the diet of the Scottish people as a result of the consumption of such exotic imports as sugar and rum from the West Indies, coffee from Ceylon and tea from China.[13] As the nineteenth century progressed, the reliance on Chinese tea was circumvented by the successful cultivation of tea firstly in India and then in Ceylon. By 1887, Indian and Ceylon tea consumption in the UK surpassed that from China.[14]

But such comparisons should not to be pressed too far. Scottish sojourning in the West Indies soon fell away after the emancipation of the slaves in 1833 and the associated trading connections swiftly collapsed thereafter. They were already insignificant by the 1860s when only around 2 per cent of export tonnage from the Clyde was shipped to the West Indies, a quite spectacular decline from the share of around 60 per cent of tonnage at the end of the Napoleonic Wars.[15] Indeed, as Tom Barron shows, some Scots émigrés to the Caribbean left the sugar islands after the emancipation of slaves in 1833 and several sailed for Ceylon where they found new opportunities in the coffee estates there and put their skills in plantation management and cultivation techniques to very good use. The immense spatial differences also have to be taken into account. By the middle decades of the nineteenth century, Scottish enterprise in the East stretched over thousands of miles from the Persian Gulf to the Sea of Japan, so enabling the development of the giant corporations in banking, trade and shipping which are described in Chapter 2 and which had few parallels on that scale in the West Indies.

To tease out in detail the implications of these Asian commercial relationships before 1914 for the homeland would require another book. However, some brief preliminary suggestions can be put forward here. Indeed, despite the relatively small scale of Scottish migration to Asia in the eighteenth and nineteenth centuries the impact, not only overseas but on Scotland itself, was significant, as later chapters suggest. It arguably deserves wider recognition in general studies of the empire, the global Scots diaspora and of modern Scottish history than so far received.

The over-representation of Scots in the governance, administration and trade of India from the 1750s until at least 1850, as described in Chapter 2, meant that a minority of sojourners returned home as very rich men earlier in that period. Between 1720 and 1780 there were an estimated 1,600 Scots in EIC service as military officers, mariners, surgeons and administrators. One suggestion by George McGilvary is that at least 124 came home between 1720 and 1780 with 'middling', 'large' and 'small' fortunes, 82 per cent possessed wealth of £20,000 and above, while over a quarter (37) had 'large' fortunes of £40,000 or over.[16] These returning 'nabobs', together with the tobacco and sugar tycoons of the Atlantic trades, provided much of the external capital which was one factor helping to power the unusually rapid industrial and agricultural revolutions in a relatively poor country from the 1760s until the 1830s, after which domestic sources of finance in Scotland for continued growth started to become much more plentiful. Profits seeped home through a number of channels, not only via direct investment from returnees but also as remittances from expatriates to their families in Scotland together with credit often advanced by EIC servants on mortgages to Scottish borrowers.[17]

The precise scale of the stream of Indian wealth which found its way to the homeland in the eighteenth century will probably never be known for certain. The recent bold attempt to provide an estimate which has been described above has already attracted overt scholarly criticism. However, the most recent student of the issue has concluded, 'In no other part of the UK, except London, was the importance of returning personnel and resources as pervasive'.[18] The difference was of course that Scotland was very much poorer in the eighteenth century than London and its hinterland and so funding from overseas was likely to have a greater multiplier effect especially during the so-called 'first phase' of Scottish industrialisation when financial demands for investment across the entire spectrum of manufacturing, agriculture and infrastructural development were most pressing. It was a happy coincidence for Scotland that, as Chapter 6 shows, the influx of great wealth from India died away from the early nineteenth century precisely at the time when the domestic economy was starting to generate internal resources for future investment.

The career opportunities which became increasingly available within the ranks of the EIC bureaucracy, marine and officer classes of the army also had significant implications for Scottish political history in the era of the French Revolution and beyond. Historians of eighteenth century Ireland point to the shortage of colonial posts for the Catholic elites and middle classes up to that point as a crucial factor helping to trigger the social unrest which built up from the 1770s and eventually became one factor in the Irish rebellion of 1798.[19] There were just too many younger sons of these elites in Ireland with frustrated career ambitions who were becoming steadily alienated from the British state.

The patterns in Scotland could not have been more different. As shown in this volume, the Scots were able to exploit imperial opportunities to a much greater extent than the Irish, or indeed the Welsh, not least in Asia before 1800. In 1790, for instance, over a quarter of Scottish constituencies were held by former EIC servants, a rate of political penetration unmatched anywhere in Britain or Ireland.[20] The purchase of landed estates by returning 'nabobs' in several Scottish localities was also often noted at the time.[21] The fact that much of this became possible as a result of patronage and clientage networks within the elites helped to bind most of the smaller lairds and middle classes to the political establishment of the day, reinforced their social position, secured the Union with England and stifled the potential for destabilisation. This was one of several reasons why the radical campaigns in Scotland against the unreformed state disintegrated so rapidly in the 1790s. Only much later, in the Reform Act 1832, were even minor concessions offered within the notoriously unrepresentative Scottish franchise. But even they can be seen as attempts to perpetuate the old order through the provision of limited concessions rather than the surrender of power to any meaningful extent. The hereditary privileges of the landed elite were therefore perpetuated for a much longer time in Scottish society not only through inherited historic authority but also because of new imperial opportunities.

The onward migration of Scots from the career platforms they had built up within the EIC to Ceylon, Singapore, Malaya and as far as China and Japan, also had important domestic repercussions. The great Scottish shipping firms which emerged to service Asian trade regularly awarded contracts to Clyde shipbuilders, while Scottish industry in general gained from the booming markets in capital goods, especially locomotives, railways, machinery, bridges, docks and much else, as Asian infrastructures expanded to manage the massive increase in exports to Europe of primary products, foods and beverages, tea, coffee, rubber, palm oil and raw jute. Even the plantation economies in the East needed equipment, as shown in Chapter 8, and Scottish engineering companies became sources of supply for coffee crushers, pulpers, dryers and turbines as well as sluices and pipes for the development of irrigation works on the estates of Ceylon.

Data for the cumulative tonnage clearing from ports of the Clyde between 1886 and 1911 are instructive in this respect. They reveal that almost a quarter of total volume over that period was destined for India, the East Indies and China. Overall, therefore, Asia ranked second for export tonnage in that period after Europe, above the USA and Canada, and well above Australasia and Latin America. Banks, insurance companies and investment trusts also gained through the Asian connection.[22] Between 1862 and 1914, 76 Scottish investment trusts had interests in Asian tea and rubber plantations.[23] From the 1850s, Scottish Widows, Standard Life Assurance and Scottish Amicable also became active in India and East Asian markets.[24] The most famous industry in Scotland which grew out of these linkages to the East was the processing of Bengal-sourced raw jute in Dundee, a city which soon attracted the soubriquet 'Juteopolis'. At its height in the late nineteenth century Dundee boasted around 60 jute mills and more than 50,000 workers, the majority of them married women. The industry brought great wealth to a small circle of 'jute barons' and their families but those riches coexisted with a regime of poverty, low wages and slum housing for most of their employees.[25]

The expansion of the middle class labour market in the East for Scots officials, engineers, clerks, accountants, physicians, missionaries, journalists, planters, managers, foremen, technicians, administrators, surveyors and bankers was also a striking feature of much of the nineteenth century. This trend not only helped to expand professional opportunities but also sustained the growth of schools, technical colleges and universities in Scotland which helped to train and educate these skilled emigrants. And there was another bonus. The professional émigrés often looked to their homeland for insurance, legal, investment and banking services, so cementing the commercial linkages between Scotland and Asia even further. A striking feature also was the way in which changing economic circumstances in Asia could generate secondary diasporas to other places across the globe. Chapter 8 shows that one result of the decline of coffee production in Ceylon was the dispersal of experienced Scots planters as far afield as Central and South America, Natal, Java, Sumatra and Fiji.

The scale of these Scottish commercial activities both within and beyond the formal empire has on the whole tended to be neglected by British historians. This is not entirely surprising since London and the Home Counties, the heartlands of Victorian economic imperialism about which much has been written, were often bypassed by the big Scottish syndicates as channels of trade and investment to the empire before 1914. The well-known thesis proposed by P.J. Cain and A.G. Hopkins is fairly typical in this respect. They see the drive to British overseas expansion as firmly rooted in the 'gentlemanly capitalism' of the City of London and its affiliates in banking and financial services.[26] Barry Crosbie's work on the Irish in India also highlights the importance of London in the creation and sustenance of professional networks.[27] For all its explanatory power, however, these arguments do not take fully into account the business strategies of companies in the North of England or Scotland. Most Scottish enterprise in Asia as elsewhere after c.1850 emanated directly from the homeland as well as via Scots expatriate firms in India and South-East Asia rather than intermediaries in London. A significant part of British economic activity in the East can therefore easily be omitted from the account when taking a Londoncentric approach.

The impact, however, was not solely confined to commercial activities. Scots were also prominent in the creation of an Orientalist school of thought with a strong Scottish philosophical stamp, particularly evident in previous work on India.[28] Here they were at the forefront of this intellectual endeavour, with Irish understanding of Indian languages and cultures coming through much later.[29] John MacKenzie, in Chapter 3 of this volume, revisits this Scottish cultural and religious effect on Asia, encompassing not just Orientalism, which attracted interest throughout the Scottish universities, but also missionary activity. Joanna Frew, meanwhile, provides a case study in Chapter 5 of the powerful influence of Scottish ideas for agrarian improvement on the Madras presidency in the later eighteenth century. Yet the extent to which Scottish Enlightenment thought or a Scottish background more generally influenced the actions of Scots abroad is still uncertain. Some suggestive comments are made in relation to Governor Stewart Mackenzie's actions in Ceylon, but there is precious little evidence of his overt borrowing of theory and practice from the homeland of the kind demonstrated in Chapters 8 and 9. Ascertaining what ideas shaped his rule—and those of other governors—is an important consideration for future research.

We should also recognise that the adverse social impact of Scottish enterprise on native peoples in Asia ought not to be overlooked or forgotten. The new free-market capitalism which British adventurers brought to the East was red in tooth and claw and their deep-seated determination to make money as quickly as possible ensured that the traditional rights of indigenous inhabitants could often be ruthlessly subordinated to the profit motive. Scots in the EIC were just as deeply involved in the uninhibited plundering of India in the years after the Battle of Plassey in 1757 as English servants and officers, as T.M. Devine shows in the chapter which follows this. They also played a central role in the opium trade to China, with the Scottish house of Jardine, Matheson & Co. becoming the dominant enterprise in a commerce which in the view of many historians had a devastating impact on Chinese society in the nineteenth century, though this view is now contested by other scholars (see Chapter 10). The remarkable expansion of large-scale plantation agriculture for coffee and tea cultivation in Ceylon, charted in Chapters 8 and 9, in which Scots managers and planters were often to the fore, could not have taken place without the dispossession of some peasant farmers, a process which was enthusiastically supported and facilitated by successive colonial governments on the island.[30]

But cross-cultural encounters were not solely negative and relationships were not confined to the diverse peoples of Asia. Superintendents of coffee and tea estates in Ceylon had contact with a range of peoples, albeit from a position of authority, and often learned from them. In some instances they formed intimate ties.[31] Agency houses, as George McGilvary indicates in Chapter 4, similarly needed native support and alliances to achieve success. Scottish ethnic associations, meanwhile, facilitated connections between Scots and other ethnicities though such cross-cultural contact was largely confined to others of white ethnicity. Overall, however, different forms of cross-cultural engagement were sporadic and limited compared with Scottish ties to their own ethnic group. Even in Hong Kong today, as Chapter 13 reveals, Scots reside in distinct expatriate neighbourhoods segregated from local communities.

THE CHALLENGE OF EXCEPTIONALISM

To evaluate the impact of a single ethnicity in relation to others on the historical development of overseas societies is a challenging undertaking as the approach is obviously open to charges of exceptionalism and ethnocentrism. This is perhaps especially so in recent years when global and transnational history has become more fashionable within some circles of the academy. Some recent work highlighting similarities between European and Asian migration flows, such as free migration and networking,[32] also tend to elide consideration of the diversity of those flows and their differential impact. But despite historiographical trends, the findings of this book would suggest that a national focus in imperial and diasporic history remains essential. The distinctive histories of colonialism across different European countries which led to outcomes in Latin America, Asia, Africa and Australasia were in large part dictated by the particular political systems, economies, religious structures and cultures of their metropoles. Nonetheless, trying to bring out national narratives and variables in a convincing manner often requires the use of hard data and the contextualising of numbers by comparison with other nationalities if the pitfalls of exceptionalism are to be avoided in whole or in part.

Perhaps special care should be taken in relation to the presumed impact of Scots migrants. As citizens of a small but historic nation in a political and economic union with a much larger one from 1707, Scots had developed a more assertive and collective sense of national identity by the nineteenth century, not least in relation to the English 'elephant' or 'other' with which they shared the British bed. When abroad this clannishness could and often did result in an outpouring of Scottish self-congratulation, a habit which was common not only in the rituals of Burns Suppers and St Andrew's Day speeches, where boosterism was usually rampant, but also in newspapers, articles and books which celebrated the achievements of Scots as the marks of an exceptional race. Even non-Scots in the empire were prone to praise Scottish contributions as Chapter 9 shows. Such praise was not always based on fact but was sometimes the result of veiled attempts at comparative denigration of the perceived inferiority of the Catholic Irish. Nevertheless, this form of ethnic conceit fashioned mythologies which endured over generations, even down to the present day, as the study of modern Scottish expatriates in Hong Kong conducted in Chapter 13, confirms.

To some extent, too, this parading of Scottish achievement within the empire was an external manifestation of developments in the homeland during the mid-Victorian era. Enormous pride was now taken in the transformation of Scotland over only a couple of generations from a historically poor country to a global powerhouse of modern industry. By the 1870s books were being published in large numbers glorifying this achievement. The Scots were equally conscious of the role they played in partnership with the English in the creation and administration of the greatest territorial empire the world had ever seen. This was always referred to as the *British* Empire, never the *English* Empire. It was publicly reiterated north of the border that the massive growth of empire only took place *after* the Union of 1707 and hence should be considered a joint Anglo-Scottish project from its beginnings. Celebratory publications, hagiographies and speeches made by renowned public figures, ranging from prominent politicians on election hustings to university rectors at graduation ceremonies, heaped praised on the Scots as a special nation of born 'empire builders'.

Earlier in the nineteenth century some among the Scots intellectocracy had expressed real concern about the threat of English cultural assimilation within the union state and the risk that the national status of the country might decline to provincial mediocrity as North Britain. By the mid-Victorian era, however, that anxiety had vanished. Instead, the potent survival and influence of Scottish institutions after 1707 in church, law and education, the limited role of Westminster in routine governance north of the border and the unprecedented economic miracle bred a new self-confidence, sometimes bordering on arrogance, among the Scottish elites. This was the time when heroes like Burns, Wallace and Knox were publicly lionised in print, song and statuary as the historical symbols of a remarkable people. Scottish education was praised as at least a match for any other system globally and the nation's outstanding success in manufacturing proudly showcased to the world in the great International Exhibition in Glasgow in 1901.

Part of this cultural reinvention of Scottish distinctiveness within the union state was the forging of a new middle class identity based partly on laissez-faire ideology in which such traits as hard work, thrift and self-help were presented to the world as intrinsically Scottish values. It was no coincidence that Samuel Smiles (1812–1904), the author of *Self Help* (1859), the great Victorian bible of prudence and personal responsibility, was a Scot from Haddington. Scots had also achieved a much higher profile in the governance of the UK. In the eighteenth century, there had been but one Scots-born prime minister, John, Lord Bute, who provoked hostility in southern political circles during his brief period of office. The later nineteenth century, however, was dominated politically by the figure of W.E. Gladstone of Scottish ancestry, who served four times as premier between 1868 and 1892, while, in the three decades before the Great War, there were three Scots-born prime ministers, Rosebery, Balfour and Campbell-Bannerman, who were then followed by Asquith, who was the sitting MP for East Fife. The celebrity won by the Highland regiments during the Indian Rising (Mutiny) of 1857 and in numerous colonial campaigns after that across Africa and Asia rejuvenated Scottish pride in the old martial tradition. Victoria, the Queen Empress herself, added royal lustre to all this by openly proclaiming her attachment to Scotland as a special place among all her dominions.[33]

A final speculation might be appropriate on this theme. Social Darwinism, the stadial theories of the Scottish Enlightenment and racial writings became of considerable interest among the reading public in Scotland in mid-Victorian times. George Combe's racial analysis, *The Constitution of Man* (1828), became an instant bestseller and Robert Knox's *The Races of Men* (1850), written by one of Edinburgh's best known medical teachers and anatomists, also achieved considerable fame. Both these and other contributions at the time in newspapers and periodicals as well as books praised the racial superiority of energetic and industrious Teutonic Lowlanders over the indolence and sloth of Highland and Irish Celts at a time when Irish Catholic migration to Protestant Scotland had reached unprecedented levels during the Great Famine. It is possible that these new insights into racial differentiation may in popularised form have helped to hone even sharper awareness of the characteristics of different peoples for émigré middle class Scots. Only further research can confirm, refine or deny that suggestion.[34]

Avoiding the intellectual obstacles of exceptionalism can best be achieved through the employment of representative evidence linked to systematic comparison with other ethnic groups. Where possible, contributors in this volume have tried to do just that in order to 'weight' the

Scottish factor by placing it in broader international contexts. Other studies beyond this volume have likewise embraced a comparative approach when studying the Scots abroad, such as Andrew Mackillop's important work on the East India Company, described in Chapter 2, and that of the editors of this book.[35]

Scots were of course not alone in their encounters with Asia. Research on the other three nations of the British Isles has also progressed, though the results are often uneven. It is clear, for instance, from a recent study of Ireland and India that connections with the subcontinent have been underestimated and that, especially in the nineteenth century, a whole range of military, intellectual, political and economic relationships can be traced. Nevertheless, in a comparative sense, the Scottish factor in India remains striking. The Catholic Irish in the eighteenth century were mainly confined to the rank and file of the military, both EIC and state. Those Irish who managed to achieve more prestigious positions at that time were mainly drawn from the middling and upper class Protestant elites. Furthermore, the Irish contribution to Orientalism seems to have been limited until the later nineteenth century and confined on the whole to Trinity College Dublin.[36] Nor is there much evidence in this new work on Ireland and India of the overarching Scottish impact in Asia via the houses of agency, commerce and shipping which is described in Devine's Chapter 2 in this volume. One important similarity, however, is that both Scottish and Irish adventurers drew heavily on contacts and patronage in London, especially during the eighteenth and early nineteenth centuries.[37] The capital was clearly the transitional route for migrants from the non-English nations into empire. By contrast, recent work does point to connections between Ireland and India, especially over issues of nationalism and the struggle for freedom, but also famines and the land question, areas of investigation which find little parallel thus far in the Scottish literature.[38] On the whole, however, the Irish impact on Asia on the basis of current knowledge must be considered much weaker than its Scottish equivalent.

Less consideration is given in scholarly writings to Welsh engagement with Asia, partly because the Welsh apparently moved there in much fewer numbers than the English and the Scots and so were disproportionately under-represented in the historical record. Difficulties in determining Welsh origins also hamper historians' attempts to locate them. The Scots, on the other hand, often developed a significant collective public profile abroad in Scottish-populated colonial militias and St Andrew societies as revealed in Chapters 11 and 12 below on China by Isabella Jackson and Tanja Bueltmann, which render them easier for historians to spot among the mass of British expatriates. When the Welsh have been studied, however, the conclusion is striking: 'Across a diverse range of civil, mercantile and military occupations it is clear that Wales was conspicuous for its lack of engagement with the empire in Asia'.[39] This might have been due to demographic factors in Welsh society where, unlike Scotland, it is argued young men tended to move mainly to careers in England rather than abroad. But the Scots (and Irish) also migrated to England in large numbers. A deeper analysis of the contrasting experiences is therefore needed, preferably through a comparative review of Scots and Welsh societies and their differential links to empire.[40]

Consideration of a *distinctive* English engagement with Asia has attracted even less attention, in part due to a tendency in the wider migration literature which has long perceived the English as 'invisible immigrants'.[41] This is variously attributed to them being the majority Anglophone ethnic group in the places where they settled, the fact that English institutions formed the basis of governance in the colonies and the familiar conflation of 'English' as 'British'. There are indeed some examples of English expatriates establishing ethnic associations and celebrating St George's Day (for instance, as described in Chapter 12) but the number and longevity of such associations not just in Asia but elsewhere is still to be calculated. In general, the English seemingly did not feel the need to loudly proclaim their identity in the same way as the smaller ethnicities of the United Kingdom. They doubtless felt comfortably secure in their demographic, economic and cultural ascendancy.[42]

Throughout the chapters which follow, contributors grapple with perspectives on Scottishness and seek through engagement with the wider literature to identify whether there was a distinctive Scottish experience and if so the effect that it might have had on the East. Did Scots bring different skills to Asia and how far did their educational traditions prepare them in different ways? Were their networks distinctive or unexceptional compared to those of other ethnicities? What was the pull of Asia for them? Did they really punch above their weight, as some contemporaries thought, or was that just exaggerated rhetoric? If there was a distinctive 'Scottish effect' how is that to be explained? These questions and others are discussed in this the first book-length study to consider the role of the Scottish diaspora across Asia from the late seventeenth century to the present.

NOTES

1. Recent studies over the last few years include T.M. Devine, *To the Ends of the Earth. Scotland's Global Diaspora, 1750–2000* (London: Allen Lane, 2011); Angela McCarthy and John MacKenzie (eds), *Global Migrations. The Scottish Diaspora since 1600* (Edinburgh: Edinburgh University Press, 2016); and Tanja Bueltmann, Andrew Hinson and Graeme Morton, *The Scottish Diaspora* (Edinburgh: Edinburgh University Press, 2013). See also chapters by T.M. Devine, Steve Murdoch and Esther Mijers, Douglas Hamilton, Angela McCarthy, and Esther Breitenbach, in T.M. Devine and Jenny Wormald (eds), *The Oxford Handbook of Modern Scottish History* (Oxford: Oxford University Press, 2012), 159–184, 320–337, 423–439, 510–532, 533–552.

2. See, for instance, Celeste Ray (ed.), *Transatlantic Scots* (Tuscaloosa: University of Alabama Press, 2005); Peter E. Rider and Heather McNabb (eds), *A Kingdom of the Mind: How the Scots Helped Make Canada* (Montreal and Kingston: McGill-Queen's University Press, 2006); Douglas J. Hamilton, *Scotland, the Caribbean and the Atlantic World, 1750–1820* (Manchester: Manchester University Press, 2005); John M. MacKenzie with Nigel R. Dalziel, *The Scots in South Africa: Ethnicity, Identity, Gender and Race, 1772–1914* (Manchester: Manchester University Press, 2007); Angela McCarthy, *Scottishness and Irishness in New Zealand since 1840* (Manchester: Manchester University Press, 2011); Malcolm Prentis, *The Scots in Australia* (Sydney: University of New South Wales, 2008).

3. Useful overviews of these issues include Sarah Stockwell (ed.), *The British Empire: Themes and Perspectives* (Oxford: Blackwell, 2008) and Anthony Webster, *The Debate on the Rise of the British Empire* (Manchester and New York: Manchester University Press, 2006).

4. Andrew Mackillop, 'Locality, Nation and Empire: Scots and the Empire in Asia, c.1695–1813', in John M. MacKenzie and T.M. Devine (eds), *Scotland and the British Empire* (Oxford: Oxford University Press, 2011), 60–62.

5. Ibid., 65–71.

6. H.V. Bowen, *The Business of Empire* (Cambridge: Cambridge University Press, 2006), 262, 269–272; George McGilvary, 'Return of the Scottish Nabobs, 1723–1833', in Mario Varricchio (ed.), *Back to Caledonia: Scottish Homecomings from the Seventeenth Century to the Present* (Edinburgh: John Donald, 2012), 91.

7. Andrew Mackillop, 'Military Scotland in the Age of Proto-globalisation, c.1690–c.1815', in David Forsyth and Wendy Ugolini (eds), *A Global Force: War, Identities and Scotland's Diaspora* (Edinburgh: Edinburgh University Press, 2016), 13–31.

8. MacGilvary, 'Return of the Scottish Nabobs', 91.

9. Figures calculated from tables printed in *Census of the British Empire, 1901: Report with Summary* (London: HMSO, 1906), 119, 106, and 134. Online at https://archive.org/stream/cu31924030396067#page/n3/mode/2up (accessed 5 October 2016).

10. A. Mackillop and Steve Murdoch (eds), *Military Governors and Imperial Frontirers c.1600–1800: A Study of Scotland and Empires* (Leiden: Brill, 2003), xxxix.

11. Bowen, *Business of Empire*, 262.

12. Peter J. Marshall, *East India Fortunes* (Oxford: Oxford University Press, 1976), 218–219; T.M. Devine, *Scotland's Empire, 1600–1815* (London: Allen Lane, 2003), 254–255.

13. T.M. Devine (ed.), *Recovering Scotland's Slavery Past: The Caribbean Connection* (Edinburgh: Edinburgh University Press, 2015).

14. S. Rajaratnam, 'The Ceylon Tea Industry, 1886–1931', *Ceylon Journal of Historical and Social Studies*, 4, 2 (1961), 171.

15. Marshall, *East India Fortunes*, 31–32.

16. George McGilvary, *East India Patronage and the British State* (London: I.B. Tauris, 2008), 161, 176, 182–203.

17. Devine, *Scotland's Empire*, 320–345.

18. Mackillop, 'Locality, Nation and Empire', 79–80.

19. Louis Cullen, 'Scotland and Ireland, 1600–1800: Their Role in the Evolution of British Society', in R.A. Houston and I.D. Whyte (eds), *Scottish Society 1500–1800* (Oxford: Oxford University Press, 1994), 237–238. For later Irish recruitment to the EIC see Barry Crosbie, *Irish Imperial Networks: Migration, Social Communication and Exchange in Nineteenth-Century India* (Cambridge: Cambridge University Press, 2012), ch. 3.

20. C.A. Philips, *The East India Company, 1784–1834* (Manchester: Manchester University Press, 1940), 311–312. For the more limited impact on Wales see H. Bowen, 'Asiatic Interactions: India, the EIC and the Welsh Economy, 1750–1830', in H. Bowen (ed.), *Wales and the British Overseas Empire: Interactions and Influences, 1650–1830* (Manchester: Manchester University Press, 2011), 168–192.
21. McGilvary, 'Return of the Scottish Nabobs', 95.
22. Clyde Navigation Trust Shipping Returns, 1886–1911, Mitchell Library Glasgow.
23. Christopher Schmitz, 'The Nature and Dimensions of Scottish Foreign Investment, 1860–1914', *Business History*, 59, 2 (1997), 45–47.
24. Devine, *To the Ends of the Earth*, 232.
25. Bruce Lenman and Kathleen Donaldson, 'Partners' Income, Investment and Diversification in the Scottish Linen Area 1850–1921', *Business History*, 21 (1971), 13–18.
26. P.J. Cain and A.G. Hopkins, *British Imperialism: 1688–2000* (London: Routledge, 2nd edition, 2001). For debate and criticisms on the thesis see M.J. Daunton, '"Gentlemanly Capitalism" and British Industry, 1820–1914', *Past and Present*, 122 (1989), 119–158; A. Porter, '"Gentlemanly Capitalism" and Empire: The British Experience since 1750', *Journal of Imperial and Commonwealth History*, 18 (1990), 265–295; R.E. Dumett (ed.), *Gentlemanly Capitalism and British Imperialism: The New Debate on Empire* (London: Routledge, 1999).
27. Crosbie, *Irish Imperial Networks*, 254.
28. See Jane Rendall, 'Scottish Orientalism from Robertson to James Mill', *Historical Journal*, 25 (1982), 44–69. Also see Martha McLaren, *British India and British Scotland, 1780–1830: Career Building, Empire Building, and a Scottish School of Thought on Indian Governance* (Akron: University of Akron Press, 2001).
29. Crosbie, *Irish Imperial Networks*, 217, 220.
30. Roland Wenzlhuemer, *From Coffee to Tea Cultivation in Ceylon, 1880–1900: An Economic and Social History* (Leiden: Brill, 2008), 303–304.
31. See James Duncan, *In the Shadows of the Tropics: Climate, Race and Biopower in Nineteenth Century Ceylon* (Aldershot: Ashgate, 2007).

32. See, for instance, Adam McKeown, 'Global Migration, 1846–1940', *Journal of World History*, 15, 2 (2004), 155–189.
33. These points are examined at greater length in T.M. Devine, *Independence or Union: Scotland's Past and Scotland's Present* (London: Allen Lane, 2016), 75–91. See also T.M. Devine, 'The Invention of Scotland', in D. Dickson, C. O'Hainle and I. Campbell Ross (eds), *Ireland and Scotland: Nation, Region, Identity* (Dublin: Farmar, 2001), 18–24; T.M. Devine, 'Lost to History', in Devine (ed.) *Recovering Scotland's Slavery Past*, 32–33; for an assessment of the issue across the broader British Empire see John M. MacKenzie and T.M. Devine 'Introduction', in MacKenzie and Devine (eds), *Scotland and Empire*, 9–24.
34. Reginald Horsman, 'Origins of Racial Anglo-Saxonism in Great Britain', *Journal of the History of Ideas*, 37 (1976), 380–387; Colin Kidd, 'Race, Empire and the Limits of Nineteenth-Century Nationhood', *Historical Journal*, 46, 4 (2003), 873–892; Devine, *To the Ends of the Earth*, 116–119.
35. Angela McCarthy, *Personal Narratives of Irish and Scottish Migration, 1921–65: 'For Spirit and Adventure'* (Manchester: Manchester University Press, 2007); Angela McCarthy, *Scottishness and Irishness in New Zealand since 1840* (Manchester: Manchester University Press, 2011); Devine, *To the Ends of the Earth*, especially ch. 6.
36. Crosbie, *Irish Imperial Networks*, 220.
37. Crosbie, *Irish Imperial Networks*, 254.
38. M. Silvestri, *Ireland and India: Nationalism, Empire and Memory* (Basingstoke: Palgrave Macmillan, 2009); Kate O'Malley, *Ireland, India and Empire: Indo-Irish Radical Connections, 1919–64* (Manchester: Manchester University Press, 2008). See also T. Foley and M. O'Connor (eds), *Ireland and India: Colonies, Culture and Empire* (Dublin: Irish Academic Press, 2006). For a summary of recent work see M. Conly, 'Ireland, India, and the British Empire: Intraimperial Affinities and Contested Frameworks', *Radical History Review*, 104 (2009), 159–172.
39. Andrew Mackillop, 'A "Reticent" People? The Welsh in Asia, c.1700–1815', in Bowen (ed.), *Wales and the British Overseas Empire*, 155.
40. Ibid., 162–163.

41. The phrase is Charlotte Erickson's: *The Adaptation of English and Scottish Immigrants in Nineteenth-Century America* (London: Weidenfeld and Nicolson, 1972).
42. See, for instance, Lyndon Fraser and Angela McCarthy (eds), *Far from 'Home': The English in New Zealand* (Dunedin: Otago University Press, 2012); Tanja Bueltmann, David T. Gleeson and Donald M. MacRaild (eds), *Locating the English Diaspora, 1500–2010* (Liverpool: Liverpool University Press, 2012).

CHAPTER 2

A Scottish Empire of Enterprise in the East, c.1700–1914

T.M. Devine

As the Introduction to this volume has acknowledged, there is now a rich historiography on several aspects of the Scottish diaspora. Even for the East, some important contributions have been made, though most of these, perhaps predictably, focus on India. This chapter also begins with the subcontinent but then tries to demonstrate that India eventually became a platform from which Scots traders, planters and ship owners were able to launch into a fresh range of other enterprises as far as China and beyond. These adventurers were few in number compared to the great migrations of their fellow countrymen to North America, South Africa and Australasia. The vast majority who left for Asia during most of the two centuries covered by this chapter were young single men mostly with connections in business, administration, the military and professions. As a result of their own social and education backgrounds and their career choices, some of them were often able to influence the history of the countries where they briefly settled to a much greater extent than simple numbers alone might suggest.

Overwhelmingly, for much of the eighteenth and nineteenth centuries, these Scots came from the small landed and business/professional classes

T.M. Devine (✉)
University of Edinburgh, Edinburgh, Scotland

© The Author(s) 2017
T.M. Devine, A. McCarthy (eds.), *The Scottish Experience in Asia, c.1700 to the Present*, DOI 10.1007/978-3-319-43074-4_2

23

and often achieved positions in Asia as part of family, local and regional networks which endured over long periods of time, often across genera-tions. For the most part they were well educated in the Scottish tradi-tion, sometimes to university level. Few intended to settle overseas but rather aspired to return home in order to live out the rest of their lives in comfortable retirement. Not many, however, are recorded for posterity in biographies or obituaries. For the most part, as individuals, they are lost to history, their only memorials fading names inscribed on gravestones at home or in some of the overgrown and mouldering cemeteries of Asian countries where so many fell victim to the lethal effects of tropical disease at an early age.

This chapter should be seen as complementary to John MacKenzie's which follows it. Here the analysis focuses mainly on economy and busi-ness. The next is concerned with the cultural role and impact of Scottish orientalists, missionaries and administrators in the East.

COLONISING THE EAST INDIA COMPANY BEFORE 1800

The historic failure in the 1690s of the bold initiative at Darien under-taken by the Company of Scotland trading to Africa and the Indies is often seen as the death knell of Scottish colonial ambitions. When considered in the long run, however, the doomed venture can perhaps more accurately be seen as a premature and false dawn in the history of Scottish enterprise in the East rather than in any sense the end of the story. The failure to establish the planned entrepôt in Darien on the Isthmus of Panama in order to link the commerce of the Atlantic and Pacific Oceans had many complex causes. One of them, however, was the resolute determination of the English East India Company (EIC), supported by the crown and gov-ernment in London, to defend its privileges and monopolies in the lucra-tive eastern trades against all comers.[1] Even the Union of 1707 made little difference to this hostile intransigence as far as the Scots were concerned. The new relationship between the two countries legalised Scottish com-merce across the Atlantic with the (now) British colonies in the Americas. By doing so, the Union established the preconditions for the eventual massive growth in the nation's overseas trades of tobacco, sugar, cotton, rum and other exotic and highly profitable commodities.[2] It was a differ-ent story in the East. The year 1695 saw the foundation of the Company of Scotland. But it was also then that the 'old' English East India ensured the exclusion of Scotland as a country from the eastern Empire as a potential competitor. This decision was then institutionalised in the Treaty of Union of 1707. Only Scots as individuals could take part in the activities of the EIC until the abolition of its monopoly of trade with India in 1813, not the country itself or its institutions. No concessions were put on the table of the kind so generously offered in the Atlantic context. As Andrew Mackillop has shown, the agreement within the Union negotiations to grant Scotland substantial compensation for the losses sustained by the Company of Scotland in the Treaty was partly intended to entrench EIC control.[3] In exchange for winding up the Company, Scots subscribers were promised in Article XV of the Treaty a total of £219,094 to cover financial losses as a result of its demise.

While there was a slow drift of Scots into the EIC before 1707, the numbers were tiny and concentrated in niche areas such as medicine and the officer class of the military. After the end of the War of the Spanish Succession in 1713, however, employment problems surfaced for the large numbers of Scotsmen who had served at officer rank in British forces fighting the armies of Louis XIV's France. There is evidence that some of these commanders, now only living on half-pay, were tempted to seek service in the EIC by the early 1720s, though only from the 1730s and 1740s did the Scottish presence in the Company start to become really evident.[4] By the end of the eighteenth century the visibility of Scots in the EIC was already marked. In 1821 Sir Walter Scott could famously write that India had by then become 'the corn chest for Scotland' because of the number of sons of the gentry and middle classes who had found posts there.[5] The invaluable Arts and Humanities Research Council database 'The Scots, Irish and Welsh in Asia, 1695–1813', based on EIC records, shows that by c.1800, Scotland, with around 12 per cent of the UK population, was already achieving over-representation in several key areas of Company service. For instance, in 1806 Scots made up nearly 23 per cent of writers and were especially to the fore in Bengal, the richest of the three presidencies. Free merchants from Scotland accounted for 25 per cent of traders in Madras by 1789. In the last quarter of the eighteenth century 28 per cent of commanders of new East Indiamen were Scots as were one in four of the officers of the royal army on the subcontinent. They were significantly more represented at virtually all levels of the Company than the Irish or Welsh before 1800. In only one area of service did Irishmen vastly outnumber the Scots at this time and that was in the rank and file of the EIC's military forces.[6] As Chapter 6 shows, even when rich pickings in

India became scarcer after 1800, Scots continued to be over-represented across the Company.

Recent research has provided some cogent explanations for this impact. At the heart of the Scottish colonisation of the EIC was the key importance of patronage. Since the Company had been dominated by London financial and political interests from its inception, only personal influence at the higher reaches of the metropolis could enable outsiders to break into the charmed circle of wealth, privilege and monopoly. But not until 1716 was the first Scot appointed to the Court of Directors and he, William Stuart, showed little interest in promoting his fellow countrymen to EIC positions. It was not until John Drummond of Quarell (1676–1742) became a member of the Directorate in 1722 that Scottish colonisation of the EIC started to become significant. His influence on their appointments endured not only until his retirement as a director but even after his death through the range of connections he had fostered earlier.[7]

Drummond was a man with unusually broad mercantile connections both in northern Europe and London. Indeed, such was the significance of his commercial networks and standing that election to the Board of Directors was highly likely, especially because of his continental links and in particular his relationships with the mercantile powerbrokers of Amsterdam. Within ten years of his arrival in the EIC he had sponsored or recommended at least 35 Scots to the service of the Company.[8] His influence soon became legendary north of the border, with perhaps predictable results. As he complained as early as 1731:

> I have told you once again not to recommend any Surgeons to me, for all the East India Company ships have either Scots Surgeons or Surgeon's mates, and till some of them die I cannot, nor will look out for more, for I am made the jest of mankind, plaguing all the Society's of England with Scots Surgeons.[9]

Drummond's importance also has to be seen within the context of the growing crisis in Anglo-Scottish relations in the generation after 1707. Increases in taxation, the failure of the Union to deliver the expected economic dividend and the belief that some in Westminster were intent on the anglicisation of the Presbyterian Church of Scotland all fed into growing turbulence and unrest. The climax came with the Scottish Malt Tax riots of 1725 which threatened to develop into a national insurrection which could destabilise the Union. Such a brazen and widespread challenge to authority concentrated the minds of the government of Sir Robert Walpole (1676–1745) in London. Among other measures taken to combat the problems in Scotland, it was decided to open up the rich vein of Indian patronage to needy elites north of the border and so help to stabilise the Union and draw some of the teeth of Jacobite disaffection. Drummond of Quarell was to be the intermediary of patronage in this strategy because of his superb contacts in the capital and the EIC coupled with his intimate knowledge of political interests and family loyalties in Scotland.[10] The politically skilled administration of the Argyll dynasty in Scotland and Drummond's effective tactics soon helped to build a new stability. They were among the factors that led to the haemorrhaging of support for the Jacobite cause between the '15 and the '45.

This early Scottish bedrock meant that when demand for India posts became insatiable after the plundering of India made possible by the British victory at Plassey in 1757, Scottish interests and networks were already firmly established, not only in the EIC but crucially also in the higher echelons of the mercantile communities of London which had key personal access to the Directorate of the Company. By that date more Scots than ever before had become members of the EIC's governing body and were already major holders of stock. Some of the early eighteenth century generation had also returned to London or Scotland as very rich men and in their retirement maintained a continuing interest and influence in Company affairs.[11] They became important conduits for the distribution of patronage in later decades. The Darien expedition was a frontal assault on the citadel of EIC monopoly and power; unsurprisingly, that tactic failed disastrously. Much more effective after the Union was entryism by stealth and connection. The Scots elites had been taught a bitter lesson in the 1690s which they did not forget after 1707.

Nevertheless, it was an Englishman, Warren Hastings, who eventually started to drive the Caledonian gravy train again from the 1770s. Hastings was governor of Bengal from 1772–74 and subsequently governor general of India from 1774–85. Impeached by Parliament for the alleged criminality of acts committed in these offices, his highly publicised trial lasted from 1788–95. Less well-known than this notoriety, however, was his role as 'Scotland's Benefactor'. It was he, even more than Henry Dundas who later also unashamedly promoted his fellow Scots, who ensured that they attained a greater representation in the civil and military services than ever before. Hastings' policy was not based on Scotophilia but on pragmatism and expediency. Surrounded by enemies in both London and India, he came to rely on the Scottish stockholders in the Company to maintain his position. They were never a majority but they proved their loyalty on several occasions. In return, Hastings was prepared to favour those among their kin and associates who showed potential. His 'Scotch Guardians', as he called them, were always selected for the most important and challenging missions of his governorship.[12] This patronage from above soon created a multiplier effect of chain migrations. When one family member achieved a place, so he often became the principal source of a new network based on an extended kindred of brothers, nephews, cousins and associates. As early death thinned the ranks of the aspiring and as the older rich retired to Britain, openings were always becoming available for the next generation to make its way.

Influence, however, was a necessary but not a sufficient condition for the rise of Scottish prominence in the EIC. The belief that India, despite the possibility of early death, provided a route to easy riches was also crucial: the risks do not appear to have had much of a deterrent effect for the young men of a country which was markedly poorer and had fewer opportunities than England before 1800. Patrons, EIC directors and government officials continued to be inundated with countless requests in the second half of the eighteenth century for places and posts in both the civil and military services. India was not primarily seen as a death-trap by young aspirants at that time but as a fabulously rich society with huge potential for profit and plunder.[13] In this sense, a distinction might be made between India on the one hand and the West Indian and American colonies on the other. To make a pile in the plantation economies across the Atlantic usually required investment in time, effort, money, steady application to business and the management of complex enterprises. Fortunes had to be built up over lengthy periods rather than through a few lucky large windfalls.[14] The alluring image of Bengal, Madras and Bombay at the time was that the chances of massive gains were not only much more abundant but great wealth might come very quickly indeed for the lucky few. Perceptions, of course, are often different from realities. Only from the British victory at Plassey in 1757 until the 1770s was there a veritable bonanza of pillage for EIC servants. But those years were enough to leave an enduring impression on the contemporary mind that India was the place to make a quick fortune. As shown in Chapter 6, however, by the early nineteenth century those expectations were rarely if ever satisfied. The really good times for EIC servants were by then well and truly over.

The formal hierarchy of the EIC consisted of writers, factors, junior merchants and senior merchants. By the standards of their counterparts who worked in public administration at home they were well rewarded, partly to compensate them for the risks they ran, the pain of absence from their families and the higher costs of European lifestyles in India. Yet EIC salaries per se did not provide the road to riches for the Company's servants before 1800. They regarded themselves at that time not only as administrators but also as men of enterprise, trading for their employers, the EIC, but also for their own private benefit. They were able to act as independent and sometimes predatory entrepreneurs. The distances from the Company's headquarters in Leadenhall Street, London, to the East by even the fastest ships were simply too great to permit effective supervision. Servants were therefore allowed a remarkable freedom of action until reforms were imposed on the EIC in the 1780s.[15]

One of the key privileges of the Company's servants before 1800 was the right to trade privately on their own account within Asia. This, rather than their salaries, was the primary source of income for civil servants, army officers, ships' commanders, surgeons and even chaplains. The jealously guarded perquisite was incorporated in a writer's covenant (or contract of employment) and was approved by the Company. Sharp practices flourished. One common procedure was to use EIC funds for private business, so avoiding high interest charges. In the years before reform, some servants sold their own goods to the EIC under assumed Indian names while others charged commission in their role as collectors of rents and dues from the native population living in the Company's settlements. All of this, however, abruptly came to an end as a result of the reforms of Earl Cornwallis and Viscount Wellesley in the last decade of the eighteenth century.[16]

HUMAN CAPITAL

The majority of recruits to these posts were sons of the smaller landed classes, and the middling ranks of Scottish society, merchants, clergy, lawyers and government officials. Of those employed at writer level in 1806, for instance, nine out of every ten were from these social backgrounds.[17] A minority across the spectrum of the ranks of the EIC did come from humbler families in the tradition of the 'Scottish lads o' pairts' (parts) who managed to make their way by dint of innate talent and perhaps also some access to university education. To an extent it might also seem that there was a territorial bias towards the eastern Lowlands as the source of most recruits since those seeking imperial careers in the western Lowlands may have been more drawn to North America and the Caribbean as a result of direct transatlantic sailing routes from the Clyde. But the point should not be overstressed. Indeed, perhaps the most revealing feature of the regional patterns of recruitment to the EIC seen in 'The Scots, Irish and Welsh in Asia, 1695–1813' database is that all parts of Scotland were represented, including the Borders and Highlands.[18]

In large part, the success of many Scots in the EIC and then in other parts of the East reflected the nature of the supply of human and intellectual capital in the homeland. Before the nineteenth century the country may not have been as rich as England, Holland or France but it was not backward. Indeed, even before the Union of 1707 Scotland had developed deep resources of human capital which help to explain both the origins of the Scottish Enlightenment at a later date and rapid modernisation from the middle decades of the eighteenth century. Calvinist ideology which shaped the collective ethos of the society from the later sixteenth century held that life should be centred around discipline, duty and diligence, noble virtues which prepared the individual for the achievement of eternal salvation. These were the precepts enunciated from the pulpit every Sabbath at church services which the entire parish community was expected to attend. Needless to say, this unrelenting inculcation of a strong work ethic over many generations was likely in the long run to have powerful secular as well as spiritual effects. These same religious teachings demanded the need for widespread literacy and learning to ensure common access to the sacred texts. By 1800, therefore, Scotland possessed an enviable nationwide network of parish and other schools. Reading literacy was commonplace among the people of both sexes by c.1800. This could also encourage a tradition of autodictatism among those equipped with the intelligence and interest, including some from humble backgrounds.

The key institution for the education of the sons of the middle classes, on the other hand, that is those who were most likely to achieve imperial careers, was the grammar schools. They taught boys aged nine to 12 to master Latin grammar, composition and speech. The hours were long, nine to ten hours a day followed by homework. These were much more than in equivalent schools in England and France. Corporal punishment was common and deemed essential to good order and the inculcation of academic rigour. Even Sunday was not considered a day of rest. After the service, the boys were marched into the schoolroom to discuss the long sermon which they had just heard. Those who did not have the 'engine' to keep up had to repeat a year or leave the school. Those who survived this draconian regime had the capacity and training to gain entry to university in Scotland, if they so chose, at the ages of 13 or 14.[19]

By 1800, Scotland had more places available in its five universities than any other country in Europe and in consequence produced a surplus of educated young men who could not easily find secure careers at home. Those trained in medicine, philosophy, divinity and the sciences were therefore numerous among the growing band of Scottish intellectual migrants across the empire.[20] Here the needs of educated Scots from genteel but often impoverished backgrounds blended well with the requirements of the EIC. As its trade and administrative responsibilities increased with the expansion of territory in India from the 1750s, so the demand for Company officials with reading, writing and analytical skills rose exponentially. It was a key advantage, too, that Scottish recruits were born into families whose social rank meant they could sometimes tap into the EIC patronage networks to the benefit of their progeny.

These eighteenth century sojourners bore little resemblance to the popular stereotype of migrant Scots as Highlanders dispossessed by clearance or weavers made redundant by technological advance. The migration to India was opportunity-led and those who joined the EIC sought the upward social mobility denied them at home. But personal ambition was not the only factor. The families of these young men, often living in modest circumstances, depended on them sending remittances from the East for living expenses, schooling of siblings, dowries (in Scotland 'tochers') for spinster daughters, annuities for widowed mothers and much else. As one authority has commented of the eighteenth century:

> Few families sent their sons to India if their social and economic position offered a viable alternative. The seemingly avaricious obsession with pay, allowances and the spoils of war exposed in the letters of young Company recruits, reflected not only the greed and ambition of a would-be fortune hunter, but also the anxieties of a youthful breadwinner for the 'clan'.[21]

Against this background, the early death of a son in India before c.1800 was not simply a family bereavement but often a material disaster for them as well.

BEYOND INDIA

The conspicuous Scottish presence in the EIC by the early nineteenth century built a sturdy platform for the expansion of enterprise further east as far as China and Japan. By the late 1820s, the private Houses of Agency had become dominant enterprises in India. Although originally mainly trading concerns they soon developed other functions as bankers, ship-owners, brokers and insurance agents and spread from India into Burma and then to other parts of south-east Asia in the first half of the nineteenth century. In Ceylon, for instance, Agency Houses became an important source of capital provision for the burgeoning coffee plantations on the island from the 1820s. Even before the EIC lost its monopoly of trade with China in 1833, they were already actively engaged in commerce with the Chinese Empire in tea and opium. George McGilvary shows from the *East India Registers* that there were some 214 Scottish-owned or con-trolled Houses of Agency between 1765 and 1834, over a quarter of all those active over that period. He tells their story in detail in Chapter 4.[22]

It might well be also that commercial developments at home could have influenced the rise of these firms to prominence. After the end of the American War of Independence in 1783 the import and re-export of tobacco, which had dominated Scottish trade since the 1730s, went into rapid decline. However, virtually all the leading companies in that enterprise had not only survived the crisis of trade interruption but had derived huge profits from the scarcity prices for tobacco during the war. When the conflict came to an end, the search was on for new overseas opportunities funded from these resources. Modern scholarship has dem-onstrated the development, as a result, of stronger links with British North America (later Canada) and the Caribbean colonies. The connection with Asia, however, is under-researched in this respect. It would be fascinating therefore to discover whether similar patterns can be discerned between Scotland and the East as part of this late eighteenth century process of global diversification.[23]

The coming of these Agency Houses, though deeply significant, was in the long run but the thin end of a veritable Caledonian trading and shipowning wedge which developed more widely in Asia by mid-Victorian times. A striking example was the colony of Singapore, which formally came under British rule in 1819. Of the first 17 trading partnerships set up there, 12 were predominantly Scottish-managed. One of the most powerful to eventually emerge from modest roots was Guthrie and Co., established in 1821 by young Alexander Guthrie from Brechin and managed by his descendants for over a century thereafter. From dealing at first in sugar, spices, vegetable oil and coffee, in 1896 Guthrie's moved into large-scale purchase of Malayan rubber plantations. By 1913, the company owned more than 25 per cent of the land in the colony possessed by British Agency Houses, by far the biggest share.[24] Also significant was the move of the giant Scottish textile firm of James Finlay and Company from earlier specialisation in cotton manufacture at home to large-scale investment in Indian tea and jute plantations, paid for initially from profits made in industry in Scotland.[25]

Other famous names also came to the fore in this period. Thomas Sutherland (1834–1922) from Aberdeen, who had been educated at the city's university, began his career as a clerk in the Peninsular and Orient Steam Navigation Company (P&O), went on to become its vice-chairman and then helped to found the Hong Kong and Shanghai Bank in 1864, with the help of several fellow Scots and English partners. Perhaps, however, Sutherland's role in the early history of the Hong Kong and Shanghai Banking Corporation (HSBC) at this point has been exaggerated, as Iain Watson argues in Chapter 13 below. The bank was also said to be run on 'Scottish principles' with a heavy reliance on joint-stock company formation and as a bank of issue through an extended network of branches, though how distinctive those practices were at the time remains uncertain. Scottish boosterism might well have been at work in Sutherland's story. In 2010, HSBC, long shorn of any Scottish roots, had become both the world's largest banking group and sixth largest business corporation.[26]

Another eminent brand, the Burmah Oil Company, a parent of British Petroleum, developed out of the Rangoon Oil Company and had more Scottish influence in its formation than HSBC. The latter was itself a marriage of two leading Scottish shipowning firms, Hendersons and the Irrawaddy Flotilla Company. Progress was at first slow until, when taken over by David Sime Cargill (1826–2004), born near Montrose before working in Glasgow, the Burmah Oil Company was incorporated in 1886. Two decades later it produced the largest output of oil of any concern in the British Empire.[27]

First in fame (and eventual notoriety) of the Scottish houses at the time, however, was Jardine, Matheson and Co., the subject of Chapter 10. The Company has survived the vicissitudes of war, revolution and economic crisis over nearly two centuries and flourishes to this day, with direct Scottish connections still in place. (The ornamental Chinese junk owned by the company, berthed in Hong Kong harbour, is named *Highland Thistle*.) The enterprise was formally established in Canton under a Saltire Flag in July 1832, though the earliest of the partnerships from which it grew dated back to the 1810s. Known as 'The Firm', Jardine Matheson has had a longer continuous existence than any other British or European business in the China trade and is the only survivor from the period of the Treaty of Nanjing in 1842 which legally opened additional ports in China to foreign commerce. Originally based in Canton, it soon moved after Nanjing to the new colony of Hong Kong and remained the most important commercial enterprise there for much of the nineteenth and twentieth centuries. Until 1864, when it abandoned the trade, Jardine, Matheson & Co was by far the dominant supplier of opium to China, significantly ahead of Dent & Co in second place, another enterprise with some Scottish antecedents.[28]

For the Scots merchants in the East, the opium business was the equivalent of tobacco for their famous predecessors in the eighteenth century Atlantic trades: a route to unimaginable riches. James Phipps, a contemporary compiler of commercial handbooks, took the view that the trade in opium 'can scarcely be matched in any one article of consumption in any part of the world'.[29] For William Jardine (1784–1843) it was 'the safest and most gentlemanlike speculation I am aware of'.[30] The basis of that success came from a traditional problem in the China trade. The East India Company wanted Chinese tea and plenty of it to satisfy the hugely increased demand from the massed ranks of British consumers. But China required little in return other than Indian raw cotton so the Company was forced to pay in bullion to make up the deficit. The discovery of the insatiable appetite of the Chinese for Indian-produced opium changed all that. Between 1800 and 1810, China had gained something like $26 million in its world balance of payments. From 1828 to 1836 that surplus was turned into a deficit of $38 million, such was the impact of the massive increase in opium imports.[31]

Scots private merchant houses in Madras, Bombay and Bengal were key players not only in the development of the China trade but also in the forging of a strong Scottish connection with Ceylon (Sri Lanka) from the 1830s. Partners in some of those firms were attracted by the emerging opportunities on the island from the 1820s for plantation agriculture. The colonial government was starting to sell off land at low cost, sometimes after the dispossession of peasant farmers at a later date, and developing a programme of road building into the interior highlands which had the best climate and soil conditions for tropical agriculture. Moreover, several Scottish owners of sugar plantations in the Caribbean were disinvesting before and after the abolition of slavery in the British Empire in 1833. Several of these former slaveowners put their money (doubtless some derived from post-slave emancipation compensation funds) into coffee estates in Ceylon. They brought with them techniques of soil cultivation from the West Indies which were in advance of those then employed on the island. Agricultural practices from areas in north-east Scotland, such as Aberdeen, Banff and Kincardine, were also applied in modified form to tropical agriculture. Techniques of drainage, weeding and manuring which had evolved over the decades of agricultural improvement from the 1760s on the farms of the North-East were now put to use in the new setting of Ceylon.[32] Many of the pioneering planters and managers were from the north-east counties of Scotland and that connection, once established, endured, though over time many did eventually arrive from other parts of the country. Instrumental in the coffee plantations of Ceylon, Scottish involvement in Ceylon's tea enterprise which followed has probably been underestimated, as Angela McCarthy argues in Chapter 9.

Private family partnerships remained dominant both in the Victorian period and up to the recent past. They depended on a network of recruitment from home which supplied young men who would in time rise to the management of the business. It had been that way for Scots merchants in seventeenth century Sweden, Denmark and Poland and remained so in Asia. The writer Neal Ascherson recalled meeting 'Lofty' Grant, the senior partner in Guthries of Malaya, during his national service there in the 1950s:

> I had been given a taste of the Scottish colonial network which I never forgot. Guthries ... was a private partnership which remained patriarchal: firmly in family hands. Its recruitment, still mainly from the north-east of Scotland which Alexander Guthrie [the firm's founder] had left more than a hundred years before, was operated through a network of friends and relations back in Scotland who recommended likely lads on the basis of intelligence and moral character.[33]

Such systematic nepotism had obvious uses in a volatile and alien environment where trust between trading partners was so crucial and the effective direction of staff thousands of miles from Scotland so challenging. But connections forged through ties of family or friendship in themselves were not enough. Recruits also had to have both ability and reliability. William Jardine warned one correspondent from Dumfries that he had 'a strong objection to extravagance and idleness' which, a warning which he trusted, would be impressed on the minds of his relatives at home: 'I can never consent to assist idle and dissipated characters however nearly connected with me, but am prepared to go to any reasonable extent in supplying such of my relations as conduct themselves prudently and industriously'.[34] So it was that family control in many of these firms proved enduring. The tradition was established that the principals, if they survived the hazards of the East, usually had relatively short careers in the tropics before retiring to Scotland. Their companies were therefore continuously replenished with new blood as opportunities regularly became available for younger men of ambition, ability and loyalty.

Another sector where the Scottish presence was very visible was shipping ownership and management. Until 1914, Glasgow ranked third in the UK after London and Liverpool by the measure of British tonnage registered in UK ports. In addition, Glasgow was the only UK city, apart from the other two, to have a Lloyds Committee located there. At its peak, in 1910, there were no less than 182 management firms in Glasgow and Greenock. The heart of the industry was a core group of 43 companies, each of which managed five or more vessels of over 1,000 tons.[35] Some of the giant firms had a global reach. The most impressive in this respect was the huge conglomerate headed by Sir William Mackinnnon who, in one opinion, could 'lay claim to being the greatest Scottish tycoon of all time'.[36] By 1890, this aggressively entrepreneurial but puritanical Gael from the Kintyre peninsula owned five great shipping companies with a total fleet value of over £3 million.[37] The Mackinnon group straddled a web of inter-related shipping lines which connected London, Lisbon, Sydney, Fiji, Basra in the Persian Gulf, Singapore, Hong Kong, Rangoon and many other locations. The main area of concentration was the immense expanse of the Indian Ocean from east Africa to India and then onwards to Burma, the Indonesian archipelago and as far as eastern Australia. From the Mackinnon companies emerged the Inchcape Group which survives to the present day.

P&O was established in 1840 by Arthur Anderson (1792–1868) from Shetland out of his original firm, the Peninsular Steam Company, which had specialised in trade with the Iberian Peninsula. In due course, the aforementioned Thomas Sutherland helped develop P&O operations to the Far East and then Australasia. In the words of one scholar: 'P&O was effectively the spine of British imperial authority in Asia with Scots in senior management positions both at sea and on shore'. Its Scottish roots in Scottish ownership soon disappeared into the past but as late as 1900 half of the mighty firm's fleet was registered at Greenock.[38] Other notable Scottish syndicates in global shipping included the Anchor Line to the Orient, and the famous Irrawaddy Flotilla Company, its paddle steamers immortalised in the writings of Rudyard Kipling, as they traversed the route from Rangoon to Mandalay. At its peak in the 1920s, the firm's 600 vessels were reckoned the largest fleet of river boats in the world, carrying around 9 million passengers and over a million tons of freight a year.[39]

Doubtless the rise of these major shipping lines reflected in part Scotland's long traditions as a seafaring nation with centuries-old connections to Europe and, in more recent periods, to the Americas and beyond. But there was more to it than that. At its heart was the nineteenth century revolution in commodity trade which resulted in the exchange of European manufactured goods on an enormous scale with the primary producers of the world in return for their foods and raw materials. Scotland, as a global centre of industrialism, needed sea transportation to convey exported goods to all corners of the earth. In addition, because of the Clyde's pre-eminence as the world's largest concentration of shipbuilding and marine engineering by 1900, Scottish shipowners were able to fully exploit the revolution in steamship design at an early stage.[40] The technological lead in marine engineering, hull design and dockside cargo-handling machinery meant they were therefore extremely well placed to exploit the new opportunities in Asia and Australasia when the opening of the Suez Canal in 1869 cut 4,000 miles off the old route around the Cape of Good Hope, so making steam navigation to Asia possible to a much greater extent than before.

The shipping firms of the East therefore became in effect among the best customers of the Clyde yards. The Mackinnon group, for example, was the first to transfer Scottish technology in iron-hulled steamers to the East. Indeed, no shipping magnate ordered more tonnage from Clyde yards after c.1850 than William Mackinnon's five companies. It was also common for the shipbuilders and shipowners to make common cause. William Denny and Brothers had connection with nearly 20 shipping lines and sold over 770 vessels to many of them, valued at more than £20 million between 1880 and 1913. Arguably the most significant shipping innovation in Asian trade came when Mackinnon and his associates established the British India Steam Navigation Company between 1856 and

1862, followed by their acquisition of the Netherlands Steam Navigation Company in 1865. The two firms operated a complex network of coastal and inter-island general purpose steamships in Asian waters of the kind that had been first introduced in the Irish Sea and Clyde estuary. These vessels had the capacity to visit ports of all shapes and sizes across the Java Sea, Indian Ocean and China Sea. They were then followed by the employment of Clyde-built tramp steamers which became the workhorses of Asian trade, shifting coal, rice, timber, sugar, iron and mineral ores to ports large and small over both long and short distances. By the early twentieth century, only in the North Atlantic did Scottish shipping enterprise have such a high profile across the world.[41]

The support of the Asia-wide Scottish diaspora was crucial to this success story. The great steamship companies worked in close association with established Scottish merchant houses, some of which had been in the East since the late eighteenth century. They were vital to the gathering of cargoes for export to Britain and Europe, developing contacts with new sources of supply and the relaying of commercial intelligence. These merchant adventurers of the East in the nineteenth century were following an age-old tradition which stretched back to Scottish traders in medieval Europe. Their counterparts of the Victorian era would doubtless have shared their view that the best prospects for ambitious lads lay outside the homeland. James Lyle Mackay, the formative influence on the formation of the Inchcape Group (and himself created the first Lord Inchcape in 1911), recalled his reasons for leaving Scotland in a speech at his old school later in life. He had worked as a clerk in Arbroath and then for a firm of rope and canvas makers, toiling for a relative pittance from nine in the morning until eight at night. His employer described 'Jeemie' as 'no a bad laddie, but a damned sicht ower-ambitious'. His ambition soon took him overseas. As he put it to the pupils of the new generation when he spoke at the school: 'let me recommend you not to be afraid to go out into the world. There is no scope in Scotland for the energy, the brains, the initiative and the ambition of all the youth in the country ... if there is no prospect for you here, the sooner you get away the better'.[42]

The drive to the East also reflected in large part the advanced condition of the Scottish industrial economy in the mid-Victorian era. By that time, Scotland had, by one measure, become the most industrialised country on earth. According to the UK census of 1851, employment in manufacturing was on average greater north of the border than in the British economy as a whole. At that date, 43.2 per cent of Scotland's employed labour force was in that sector compared to a UK average of 40.9 per cent. There were especially deep concentrations of manufacturing and mining in the western Lowlands, centred on Glasgow and its hinterland, the central Lowlands, Fife and Tayside, with Dundee at the core of the latter. At a time when other European countries and the USA were still overwhelmingly dominated by agriculture, Scotland already possessed a critical mass of world-class shipbuilding, heavy engineering, construction, metal manufacture and the associated array of multiple skills. That provided from the 1840s until the Great War the unprecedented advantages of semi-monopolistic supply of capital goods to primary-producing economies worldwide, including Asia.[43]

The Japanese Connection

When, therefore, Japan became the first Asian state to pursue a strategy of rapid modernisation in the last quarter of the century, Scotland was likely to be one of the advanced economies in the West to which it looked for expertise, advice and ideas. The number of Scots who ventured to Japan as a result of this growing rapprochement was tiny, even by comparison with the small numbers of their fellow countrymen elsewhere in Asia. Yet their influence on Japanese development was immense. The names of the leading pioneers are remembered and revered in Japan to the present day even if they have been mainly long forgotten in the country of their birth.

By the middle of the nineteenth century, under the Tokugawa regime, Japan had pursued for 200 years or so a policy of closing off almost all trade with the outside world. When these prohibitions were abandoned from the 1870s, Japan was still a feudal society. But by the early twentieth century the country had been transformed into a modern economy with advanced industries, finance systems and technologies. A key reason for the remarkable speed of this revolution was the systematic strategy of seeking out foreign expertise and ideas and sending young Japanese students overseas to be trained in foreign centres of technical excellence. The contributions made by Scottish engineers, bankers, educators and merchants to this process were often decisive. The relationship was especially close between c.1870 and 1900 in engineering, finance, iron and steel technology and higher education. The names cited below are by no means an exhaustive list of those involved but are intended only to give a sense of the Scottish influence on this historic transformation.[44]

One of the first and most famous connections came as a result of the continued expansion of the commercial empire of Jardine, Matheson & Co in the eastern seas. Thomas Blake Glover (1838–1911) from Fraserburgh joined the firm at the age of 18 and began his association with Japan in 1859 as a buyer of Japanese green tea for his employers. Glover then went into business for himself as an independent arms dealer supplying the Japanese insurgent movement which eventually came to power as the Meiji government. His support for their cause gave him access in due course to the highest levels of the Japanese state.

He then brought the first steam locomotive to Japan, developed the country's first coal mine, imported its first dry dock and helped to found the shipbuilding enterprise which was later to become the mighty Mitsubishi Corporation of Japan. His most daring exploit was the help given to the 'Choshu Five' to sail for Britain in 1863, disguised as sailors under conditions of deep secrecy as it was forbidden under pain of death until 1866 for native-born Japanese to leave the country. The 'Five' were young noblemen who were intent on studying Western ways in Britain with the aim of returning after a few years to use the knowledge they had gained to bring about the modernisation of their own country. They arrived in London on one of Jardine, Matheson & Co's ships and four of them went on to study at University College, London, under the guidance of their patron and mentor, Alexander Williamson (1824–1904), a distinguished professor of Chemistry of Scottish descent. He subsequently arranged for them to visit Glasgow to study railway engineering, mining, shipbuilding and surveying. The fifth, Yamao Yozo, became an evening class student at the Andersonian Institution in Glasgow while working in the Clyde shipyards by day. Thus were the technical skills of an advanced economy transferred from Europe to the feudal empire of Japan.

On return to their homeland, the five men eventually went on to form the core of a new government which led the formerly isolated state on a rapid journey towards becoming a modern nation. One of them, Hirubimo Hito, became the first and highly regarded prime minister of post-Meiji Japan. Two of the others served as the secretaries of state for foreign affairs and industry in his government. Thomas Glover himself came to be regarded in later years as a central figure in the transformation of Japan. He was honoured by the Emperor with the rare accolade of the Order of the Rising Sun. Today, the Glover Garden House in Nagasaki is reckoned to attract over 2 million visitors a year.[45]

His fellow north-easterner Richard Brunton (1841–1901) is remembered as the 'Father of Japanese lighthouses'. He was a member of the famous firm of lighthouse builders established by the Stevenson family and was appointed by the Meiji government to advise on their construction in Japan as one of the *o-yatoi gaikokujin* or 'hired foreigners' recruited to assist with the strategy of modernisation. Twenty-six lighthouses (known affectionately as 'Brunton's Children') were eventually built in the Scottish style around the Japanese coast and a system of lighthouse keepers put in place modelled on the Northern Lighthouse Board in Scotland. Brunton also helped to found Japan's first school of civil engineering as well as designing Yokohama's sewage, gas lighting and telegraph systems.[46]

Two other 'hired foreigners' from Scotland who had a significant effect on Japanese development were James Alfred Ewing (1855–1935), from Dundee, and Henry Dyer (1848–1918), who was born in Bellshill in Lanarkshire. They both fit the model proposed by Cairns Craig of Scotland's 'Empire of Intellect' by which, from the eighteenth century, many able graduates from the Scottish universities founded institutions of higher learning overseas which were often staffed initially by some of their fellow countrymen and which also followed the Scottish generalist curriculum.[47] But Craig focuses on the intellectual migrants to the Anglophone countries of the USA, Canada, South Africa and Australasia. Ewing and Dyer in contrast made their mark in an Asian society which had long resisted external influences and was devoid of any European settlement when they first arrived.

Ewing was appointed the professor of civil engineering at the Tokyo Imperial University in 1878 and returned to the UK in 1883, where some time later he became principal of the University of Edinburgh. The influence of his former students in helping to create the infrastructure of the new Japan is well evidenced. Similarly, the naval engineer C.D. West, who worked in shipyards in Japan, went on to spend the rest of his life there and for a quarter of a century recruited mainly from Scotland over 100 marine engineers for dockyards, shipyards and shipping companies.[48]

Henry Dyer was educated at Glasgow University and the Andersonian Institution (later Strathclyde University) where he attended classes with the young Japanese, Yamao Yozo, mentioned above. At the age of 24, even before taking his final exams, partly due to Yozo's connections, he was appointed the principal of the Imperial College of Engineering (ICE) in Tokyo in 1872, a post he held until returning to Scotland a decade later. His remit was challenging: nothing less than the establishment of a world-class engineering institution that would train the engineers who would build the new Japan of the future. The courses he designed were based on the principles of the Andersonian and so combined both academic and practical study. To facilitate the approach, Dyer set up the largest engineering works ever built in Japan, which was designed to assist with high-level student training. He also sent a select number of undergraduates to Glasgow for advanced instruction. When he left Japan it was acknowledged that he had more than fulfilled what had been asked of him when first appointed.

Apart from the leadership of Dyer, the Scottish mark on the ICE was impressive. Of the 22 expatriate British staff who held academic posts there in the 1870s, eight were recruited from Imperial College and University College in London, and the rest from Glasgow (mainly) and Edinburgh Universities, to a large extent through the aegis of Lord Kelvin, the great world figure in applied sciences of the time. The philosophy which imbued their teaching was radically new in Meiji Japan where the traditional feudal ethic had stressed a social hierarchy in descending order of warrior, farmer, craftsman and merchant. For the Scottish professoriate, it was engineers, sustained by codes of diligence, duty, innovation and application, who should be regarded as the professional leaders of the modern age.[49] In the words of the historian of science W.H. Brock:

> that the export of Scottish engineers and engineering teachers to Japan in the 1870s aided that country's astonishingly rapid process of modernisation from a feudal to a capitalist society will not occasion surprise or dissent. As the *Japan Weekly Mail* editorialised in 1878: 'in no direction has Japan symbolised her advance towards assimilation of the civilisation of the western world more emphatically than in that of applied science'.[50]

Even after his return to Glasgow, Dyer himself continued to work tirelessly to advance the interests of the Empire of Japan and assist the many Japanese students, engineers and trainee managers who came to learn in the West of Scotland. His name lives on in the country he loved through a biography and a five-volume collection of his writings edited by a Japanese scholar.[51]

CONCLUSION

The expansion of the formal and informal British Empire east of India in the nineteenth century helped to ensure that the nations of the British Isles eventually had both the advantage of open markets as far as China and colonial territories protected by naval and military force in much of Asia. Inevitably, it was the English with their massive demographic dominance at home who were most visible in *Pax Brittanica* abroad. But a somewhat different picture emerges when the sizes of each of the national populations of Britain are taken into account in relation to influential positions acquired and major business ventures established in the East. As shown in this chapter, Scots were significantly over-represented in relation to their share of the total UK population across a range of sectors for much of the period c.1750–1914, much like the patterns already researched for Canada, the Caribbean and the Antipodes. In Asia, their activities extended from the bureaucracies of the East India Company in the eighteenth century to the plantations of Ceylon and Malaya in the nineteenth, from the great shipping companies which traversed the sea lanes of the Orient to the opium trade with China, and finally to the industrialisation of Japan after c.1870. Indeed, because of the relatively small overall size of British migration to the East, it has been possible to identify the Scottish factor in the societies there in more precise terms than can easily be achieved for the countries of major European settlement in North America, South Africa and Australasia.[52] This chapter has suggested that a consideration of some distinctive aspects of Scottish society and economy before 1914 might provide at least part of the explanation for the multifaceted impact of the Scots. Yet a fuller answer will probably only be possible when a sustained comparative examination of the histories of the British nations—the English, Irish, Welsh and Scots—across Asia is undertaken and completed.

In addition, this chapter and several others which follow it reveal that Scottish settlers and sojourners sometimes left a specific stamp on many parts of Asia. That was not always to the benefit of those countries where the rapid growth of plantation economies could lead to dispossession of traditional peasant farmers and their families. More positively, however, the impact could range from the transfer of agricultural and philosophical ideas from the homeland to the application in Asia of Scottish industrial technologies and modes of technical education. This evidence therefore provides strong support for 'a four nations approach' to the study of the British Empire and for the view that a national focus conducted within an international context can reap considerable intellectual dividends when assessing the impact of European cultures on overseas societies in the imperial era.

Many of the Scottish ties to the East survived well into the twentieth century, though the Japanese connection had largely gone by 1914 as the now modernised nation was able by then to grow its own technical talent and expertise. After the Great War, however, the golden age of sustained growth for the great Scottish trading and shipping companies in Asia started to come to an end with the collapse of world commerce in the depressions of the 1920s and massive overcapacity in shipbuilding across the globe as well as growing competition, ironically enough, from Japanese exports across the continent. The aftermath of the Second World War gave some temporary respite with the absence of competition for a time from those economies of Europe and the Far East that had been devastated by the global conflict. Also, decolonisation from the later 1940s did not at first spell the end of commercial hegemony. Yet by the 1970s and 1980s such newly independent countries as Sri Lanka (formerly Ceylon) and Malaysia (formerly Malaya) began to nationalise or acquire British-owned plantation corporations, over 300 of them in Sri Lanka alone. At the same time, Scottish trading and shipping firms started to sell off assets to indigenous interests or merged with larger multinational companies. Though Scots continued to make their careers in Asia, as Chapters 12 and 13 below confirm, by 2000 little remained of Scotland's commercial empire in the East. Only that colossus of capitalism, Jardine Matheson Holdings, continued to flourish and serve as a reminder into the twenty-first century of the old days of Scottish economic prominence in the eastern seas.[53]

NOTES

1. Fully explored most recently in Douglas Watt (ed.), *The Price of Scotland: Darien, Union and the Wealth of Nations* (Edinburgh: Luath Press, 2007). For the period after 1800 until the end of EIC rule in India in 1858 see Chapter 6 in this volume.

2. T.M. Devine, *The Tobacco Lords: A Study of the Tobacco Merchants of Glasgow and their Trading Activities, 1740–1790* (Edinburgh: John Donald, 1975); T.M. Devine and Philipp R. Rossner, 'Scots in the Atlantic Economy, 1600–1800', in John M. MacKenzie and T.M. Devine (eds), *Scotland and the British Empire* (Oxford:

Oxford University Press, 2011), 30–54; Douglas J. Hamilton, *Scotland, the Caribbean and the Atlantic World 1750–1820* (Manchester: Manchester University Press, 2005); T.M. Devine (ed.), *Recovering Scotland's Slavery Past: The Caribbean Connection* (Edinburgh: Edinburgh University Press, 2015).

3. Andrew Mackillop, 'A Union for Empire? Scotland, the English East India Company and the British Union', in Stewart J. Brown and Christopher A. Whatley (eds), *The Union of 1707: New Dimensions* (Edinburgh: Edinburgh University Press, 2008), 116–134.

4. Christopher Storrs, 'The Union of 1707 and the War of the Spanish Succession', *Scottish Historical Review*, 87 (2008), 31–44; Andrew Mackillop 'Locality, Nation, and Empire: Scots and the Empire in Asia, c.1695–c.1813', in MacKenzie and Devine (eds), *Scotland and the British Empire*, 62.

5. T.M. Devine, *Scotland's Empire 1600–1815* (London: Allen Lane, 2003), 251–252; Scott is quoted in Alex M. Cain, *The Corn Chest for Scotland: Scots in India* (Edinburgh: National Library of Scotland, 1986), 7.

6. Reported in Mackillop, 'Locality, Nation and Empire', 65, 69, 71.

7. George K. McGilvary, *East India Patronage and the British State: The Scottish Elite and Politics in the Eighteenth Century* (London: I.B. Tauris, 2008); T.M. Devine, 'Scottish Elites and the Indian Empire, 1700–1815', in T.C. Smout (ed.), *Anglo-Scottish Relations from 1603–1900* (Oxford: Oxford University Press, 2005), 210–214.

8. Andrew Mackillop, 'Accessing Empire: Scotland, Europe, Britain and the Asia Trade, 1695–1750', *Itinerario*, 29 (2005), 22.

9. John Drummond to William Drummond, 18 March 1731, cited in George Kirk McGilvary, 'East India Patronage and the Political Management of Scotland, 1720–1774', unpublished PhD thesis, Open University, 1989, 207.

10. T.M. Devine, *Independence or Union: Scotland's Past and Scotland's Present* (London: Allen Lane, 2016), 36–40.

11. G.J. Bryant, 'Scots in India in the Eighteenth Century', *Scottish Historical Review*, 177 (1985), 23–27; Sir Lewis Namier and John Brooke (eds), *History of Parliament. The House of Commons,1754–1790, Vol. I* (Oxford: Oxford University Press: 1964), 168.

12. John Riddy, 'Warren Hastings: Scotland's Benefactor?', in Geoffrey Carnall and Colin Nicholson (eds), *The Impeachment of Warren Hastings* (Edinburgh: Edinburgh University Press, 1989), 42.
13. Peter J. Marshall, *East India Fortunes* (Oxford: Oxford University Press, 1976).
14. T.M. Devine, 'The Spoils of Empire', in T.M. Devine (ed.), *Scotland and the Union 1707–2007* (Edinburgh: Edinburgh University Press, 2008), 91–108.
15. Marshall, *East India Fortunes*, 234.
16. Devine, *Scotland's Empire*, 257–258: Arthur Aspinall, *Cornwallis in Bengal* (Manchester: Manchester University Press, 1931), 1–39; Bankey B.M. Misra, *The Central Administration of the East India Company, 1756–1834* (Manchester: Manchester University Press, 1959), 240ff.
17. Mackillop, 'Locality, Nation and Empire', 71.
18. Ibid.
19. The above two paragraphs draw on Richard Saville, 'Intellectual Capital in Pre-1707 Scotland', in Brown and Whatley (eds), *Union of 1707*, 45–60; G. D. Henderson, *Religious Life in Seventeenth-Century Scotland* (Cambridge: Cambridge University Press, 1937), 217–225; Gordon Marshall, *Presbyteries and Profits: Calvinism and the Development of Capitalism in Scotland, 1560–1707* (Oxford: Oxford University Press, 1980), passim; Karin Bowie, 'New Perspectives on Pre-Union Scotland', in T.M. Devine and Jenny Wormald (eds), *The Oxford Handbook of Modern Scottish History* (Oxford: Oxford University Press, 2012), 303–319.
20. Cairns Craig, 'Empire of Intellect: The Scottish Enlightenment and Scotland's Intellectual Migrants', in MacKenzie and Devine (eds), *Scotland and the British Empire*, 84–117.
21. Martha McLaren, *British India and British Scotland 1780–1830* (Akron, OH: University of Akron Press, 2001), 27.
22. Alain Le Pichon (ed.), *China Trade and Empire* (Oxford: Oxford University Press, 2006), 6–7; B.R. Tomlinson, 'From Campsie to Kedgeree: Scottish Enterprise, Asian Trade and the Company Raj', *Modern Asian Studies*, 36, 4 (2002), 769–791; Roland Wenzlhuemer, *From Coffee to Tea Cultivation in Ceylon, 1880–1900* (Leiden: Brill, 2008), 306.
23. T.M. Devine, 'Glasgow Merchants and the Collapse of the Tobacco Trade, 1775–1783', *Scottish Historical Review*, LII, 1: No.153

(1973), 50–76; D.S. Macmillan, 'The "New Men" in Action: Scottish Mercantile and Shipping Operations in the North American Colonies, 1760–1825', in D.S. Macmillan, *Canadian Business History: Selected Studies* (Toronto: McLelland and Stewart, 1972), 44–103; Eric J. Graham, 'The Scottish Penetration of the Jamaican Plantation Business', and Stephen Mullen, 'The Great Glasgow West India House of John Campbell, senior & Co.', in Devine (ed.), *Recovering Scotland's Slavery Past*, 82–98; 124–144.

24. John H. Drabble, *An Economic History of Malaysia 1800–1990* (London: Palgrave Macmillan, 2000), 42, 99. For early commercial penetration to Asia in general see B.R. Tomlinson, '"The Empire of Enterprise": Scottish Business Networks in Asian Trade 1793–1810', *KIU Journal of Economics and Business Studies*, 8 (2001), 67–83.

25. Colm Brogan, *James Finlay & Co. Ltd* (Glasgow: Jackson Son & Co, 1951), *passim*.

26. Maurice Collis, *Wayfong: The Hong Kong and Shanghai Banking Corporation* (London: Faber and Faber, 1965), 11–29. See Chapter 13 for a short critique of Sutherland.

27. John Darwin, *The Empire Project: The Rise and Fall of the British World System, 1830–1970* (Cambridge: Cambridge University Press, 2009), 57; Stanley Chapman, *Merchant Enterprise in Britain* (Cambridge: Cambridge University Press, 1992), 26.

28. The most recent and thorough study of the enterprise in this period is Richard J. Grace, *Opium and Empire: The Lives and Careers of William Jardine and James Matheson* (Montreal: McGill-Queen's, 2014).

29. J. Phipps, *A Practical Treatise on the China and Eastern Trade* (London: Thacker, 1836), 2.

30. Cited in Michael Greenberg, *British Trade and the Opening of China 1800–1842* (Cambridge: Cambridge University Press, 1951), 105.

31. Le Pichon (ed.), *China Trade and Empire*, 8–13.

32. Ranald Michie, 'Aberdeen and Ceylon: Economic Links in the Nineteenth Century', *Northern Scotland*, 4 (1981), 69.

33. Neal Ascherson, *Stone Voices: The Search for Scotland* (London: Hill and Wang, 2002), 233. See also Angela McCarthy (ed.), *A Global Clan: Scottish Migrant Networks and Identities since the Eighteenth Century* (London: Tauris Academic Studies, 2006). It is not, how-

ever, being suggested that such networks were in any sense uniquely Scottish devices. See, for instance, Enda Delaney and Donald M. MacRaild (eds), *Irish Migration, Networks and Ethnic Identities since 1750* (London: Routledge, 2007).

34. Cited in Robert Blake, *Jardine Matheson: Traders of the Far East* (London: Orion, 1999), 36.

35. J. Forbes Munro and Tony Slaven, 'Networks and Markets in Clyde Shipping', *Business History*, 43, 2 (2001), 22–23.

36. Michael Fry, *The Scottish Empire* (Edinburgh: Birlinn, 2001), 265.

37. J. Forbes Munro, *Maritime Enterprise and Empire* (Woodbridge: Boydell Press, 2003), 8, 34, 505.

38. Peter L. Payne, *The Early Scottish Limited Companies 1856–1895* (Edinburgh: Edinburgh University Press, 1980), 66; M. Kita, 'Scottish Shipping in Nineteenth Century Asia', in A.J.H. Latham and H. Kawakatsu (eds), *Intra-Aian Trade and Japanese Industrialisation* (London: Routledge, 2009), 210–218.

39. Anthony Slaven and Sydney Checkland (eds), *Dictionary of Scottish Business Biography 1860–1960*, vol. 2 (Aberdeen: Aberdeen University Press, 1986), 274–276, 286–289, 290–292; Gordon Jackson and Charles Munn, 'Trade, Commerce and Finance', in W.H. Fraser and Irene Maver (eds), *Glasgow. Volume II, 1830–1912* (Manchester: Manchester University Press, 1996), 65–70.

40. T.M. Devine, C.H. Lee and G.C. Peden (eds), *The Transformation of Scotland* (Edinburgh: Edinburgh University Press, 2005), 61–62.

41. P.L. Robertson, 'Shipping and Shipbuilding: The Case of William Denny and Brothers', *Business History* 16 (1974), 36–47; Munro, *Maritime Enterprise and Empire*, 493–494: A.J.H. Latham and Heta Kawakatsu, 'Introduction', in Latham and Kawakatsu (eds), *Intra-Asian Trade*, 7–8.

42. Kita, 'Scottish Shipping', 210–218; Stephanie Jones, *Two Centuries of Overseas Trading: The Origins and Growth of the Inchcape Group* (London: Palgrave Macmillan, 1986), 36.

43. C.H. Lee, 'Modern Economic Growth and Structural Change in Scotland', *Scottish Economic and Social History*, 3, 3 (1983), 15–17; Christopher A. Whatley, *The Industrial Revolution in Scotland* (Cambridge: Cambridge University Press, 1997), 35–36.

44. Masami Kita, 'Japanese Acquisition of Maritime Technology from the United Kingdom', in A.J.H. Latham and Heita Kawakatsu (eds), *Intra-Asian Trade and the World Market* (London:

Routledge, 2006), 46–74; M. Kita, *Kokusai-Nippon wo Hiraita Hitoboto* [Scottish Peoples who Contributed to the Modernisation and Industrialisation of Meiji Japan] (Tokyo: Dobunkan, 1984), *passim*.

45. Michael Gardiner, *At the Edge of Empire: The Life of Thomas Blake Glover* (Edinburgh: Birlinn, 2007); Alexander McKay, *Scottish Samurai: Thomas Blake Glover 1838–1911* (Edinburgh: Canongate Press, 1993).

46. Edward R. Beauchamp (ed.), *Schoolmaster to an Empire: Richard Henry Brunton in Meiji Japan, 1863–76* (Westport, Conn.: Greenwood Press, 1991). For the Scottish factor, and especially the major contributions of Alexander Allan Shand in the creation of a modern banking system in Japan, see N. Tamaki, *Japanese Banking: A History, 1859–1958* (Cambridge: Cambridge University Press, 1995), 34–37, 95.

47. Craig, 'Empire of Intellect', 84–117.

48. R.T. Glazebrook, 'James Alfred Ewing,1855–1935', *Obituary Notices of Fellows of the Royal Society*, I (4) 1935, 475; Kita, 'Japanese Acquisition', 57–58.

49. Kita, 'Japanese Acquisition', 57–71.

50. W.H. Brock, 'The Japanese Connection: Engineering in Tokyo, London and Glasgow at the end of the Nineteenth Century', *British Journal of the History of Science*, 14, 3 (1981), 227.

51. Nobuhiro Myoshi, *Henry Dyer: Pioneer of Engineering Education in Japan* (Leiden: Brill Publishers, 2004).

52. For non-Asian comparisons see, for example, Devine, *To the Ends of the Earth*, 1–31, 56–84, 125–172; MacKenzie and Devine (eds), *Scotland and the British Empire*; John M. MacKenzie with Nigel Dalziel, *The Scots in South Africa* (Manchester: Manchester University Press, 2007).

53. Jones, 'Merchants and Multinationals', 121; Devine, *To the Ends of the Earth*, 252–257; 'Return to China: Jardine Matheson', *The Economist*, 4 July 2015.

CHAPTER 3

Scottish Orientalists, Administrators and Missions: A Distinctive Scots Approach to Asia?

John M. MacKenzie

Scots were as active in Asia as they were in other continents. Their numbers may have been smaller than elsewhere, but they exercised a striking degree of influence in promoting the cultural reciprocities and interactions of the time. From Constantinople to Manchuria, from the Levant to Japan, they made their presence felt in a variety of fields.[1] While their principal destination was inevitably India, it is important to remember that individual Scottish missionaries, travellers and writers, as well as Scots pursuing mercantile and other professions, were to be found in many apparently obscure corners of the continent. This chapter is concerned with three areas of Scottish activity: Orientalism, administration and missions. Given their numbers, Scots developed a remarkable prominence in all three of these, not least because so many of them were active writers and publicists, disseminating experiences and ideas to academic, religious, political and wider constituencies. Practitioners in all three fields produced large quantities of published material on Oriental studies, administrative theory and Christian strategies. Missionary journals and the Scottish press carried

J.M. MacKenzie (✉)
University of St Andrews, St Andrews, Scotland

© The Author(s) 2017
T.M. Devine, A. McCarthy (eds.), *The Scottish Experience in Asia,
c.1700 to the Present*, DOI 10.1007/978-3-319-43074-4_3

accounts of missions and their personnel.[2] Sources are indeed extensive and this brief chapter can offer only a preliminary synoptic survey. The chapter's sections will survey the three main themes, with a conclusion assessing the extent to which they offer a degree of continuity and can be seen as genuinely distinctive.

The chapter will chart the emergence of a Scottish school of Orientalists from the eighteenth century, originating in the theories and methodologies of East India Company (EIC) rule. The work of these scholars was influenced by Enlightenment ideas, later by Romanticism, and by intellectual trends in the nineteenth century. The second section will consider the significance of the Scottish administrators in India together with the radical reaction to Orientalism. The administrators' ideas grappled with the views of Orientalists, but were developed and adapted through practical experience. Their influence was geographically specific, but their Scottish training and philosophical upbringing connect them to wider contexts. The reaction to Oriental ideas also came from influential Scots, but forms of intellectual Orientalism continued through the nineteenth century. Meanwhile, the Scottish missionary project, after a hesitant start, developed in scale and geographical penetration during that century. To a certain extent, the missions constituted an extension of Orientalist studies, albeit designed for specific ends, facilitating the spread of Christianity. Moreover, Christian missions can be seen as the means whereby ideas about Asian peoples were spread among a wider population in Scotland and elsewhere. To secure moral and spiritual support, as well as crucial funding, missionaries were in the business of disseminating ideas about the populations whom they sought to proselytise. To a certain extent the activities of Orientalists, administrators and missionaries overlap, offering both intellectual and populist discourses to different publics. They also provided commentaries upon the political events of the age, the extension of British rule, and above all the developing aspects of modernity which were key characteristics of their age. All three represented interactions between Asia and Scotland, taking Scottish ideas into contacts with peoples in many parts of the continent while conveying influences back to Scotland. It may be that we can see here the rise, fall and perhaps rise again of a sympathetic understanding of Asian peoples, although this phenomenon operates in varied ways in different parts of the continent. We can also identify the responses of indigenous people in manipulating contacts with scholars, administrators and missionaries in order to absorb and reject aspects of modernity.

As in many studies of this sort, the question arises: What constitutes a Scot? Scottish missionaries adhering to the Church of Scotland (CofS), the Free (FC) and United Presbyterian (UP) Churches are easiest to classify, though some Scots Episcopalians would have joined Anglican missionary societies. We move into a more hazy area with those who had only one Scottish parent or who were born outside Scotland. A Scottish education can result in the acquisition of Scottish ideas by others who were not Scots. Others may have had their ideas modified by wider experience beyond Scotland. Perhaps the most effective clarification of these complexities is to suggest that for this discussion, Scots should have a Scottish genetic inheritance, should generally have been educated in Scotland, should have displayed distinctively Scottish characteristics, or have identified themselves as Scots.

SCOTTISH ORIENTALISM

Eighteenth century Orientalist ideas are principally associated with the EIC judge of Welsh extraction Sir William Jones (1746–94) and others who founded the Asiatic Society of Bengal.[3] But there were also several Scottish Orientalists who worked for the Company or influenced its policies. The governor-general, Warren Hastings, set the tone for the Company's approach. He would have approved of the notion that 'every accumulation of knowledge, and especially such as is obtained by social communication with people over whom we exercise a dominion founded on the right of conquest, is useful to the state'.[4] That seems to confirm the knowledge is power nexus, but Hastings clearly believed that if the subjects of the EIC could not be persuaded to meet the new rulers on their culturally sympathetic ground, those rulers must meet them on theirs. Under the leadership of Hastings, Jones and others, Company rule was based upon an effort at cultural understanding of the ruled.[5] Scots who adopted this approach were invariably associated with the University of Edinburgh and Enlightenment figures such as William Robertson (1721–93), Adam Smith (1723–90) and Dugald Stewart (1753–1828).

However, the earliest Scot to write about India had no such affiliations. Perthshire-born Alexander Dow (1735–79) worked for the celebrated smuggler John Nisbet of Eyemouth, but escaped to the East after some misdemeanour. There he flourished, joining the EIC army in 1760, learning Persian, and swiftly rising through the ranks to lieutenant colonel. In 1768 he published *Tales Translated from Inatulla of Delhi* and the first part of his *History of Hindustan.* The entire *History* was published in London in 1772 with prefixes 'On the origin and nature of despotism in Hindustan' and 'An Enquiry into the State of Bengal'.[6] Having announced that his history had been compiled from Eastern writers and from European travellers of the previous century, he suggested that Indian despotism resulted from the climate, which made subjects indolent, preferring passive obedience to being free. In any case, living under a despotism was a safer way to a less miserable existence. His was the first history of India in English. Dow was also a playwright, whose works appeared on the stage at Drury Lane.[7] Another Scot associated with Hastings was George Bogle (1746–81), son of a Glasgow tobacco lord, who attended Edinburgh University and, after some time in London, became an EIC writer in 1770.[8] He swiftly became Hastings' private secretary and in 1774 was appointed to conduct a mission to Tibet to open commercial relations on an equal footing. Gordon Stewart writes that Bogle was 'curious, tolerant and open-minded'. Though not an intellectual, he was aware of Enlightenment ideas with an 'ability to move outside his own cultural reference points'.[9] Although the commercial objectives failed, diplomatic and cultural relations were opened with the regions north of India. The journals of his expedition were later discovered and, published in 1876, were influential in forming views of Tibet.

The better-known Orientalists who succeeded Dow and Bogle were all working in the shadow of William Robertson. He never went to India, but his *Historical Disquisition Concerning the Knowledge the Ancients had of India* of 1791, his last work, was very widely read. Stewart Brown's excellent analysis reveals far wider content than the title implies.[10] Robertson was interested in the commercial connections of India from ancient times and wrote sympathetically, even admiringly, of Indian culture and the Hindu religion. Thus, he shifted from the political focus of previous books on Scotland and the Spanish Empire towards commerce, technology and culture, and was influential in demonstrating that the history of other societies should be examined in terms of civil and social structures, legal systems, ethics, as well as scientific and literary achievements. Since commercial societies, particularly in an international context, stood at the top of Robertson's 'stadial' system, it followed that India could be viewed in some respects as on a par with Europe.[11] Inevitably, Robertson, as a Church of Scotland minister, was very much a 'moderate', critical of missions and of what would later be called 'cultural imperialism'. Robertson's work clearly chimed with EIC principles and was influential in the development of Orientalism in Europe. But there were critics, and Robertson's sympathetic ideas about India were soon threatened by the development of evangelicalism (promoted by influential EIC figures like Charles Grant) and utilitarianism.

For the next few decades, however, Scottish Orientalists continued to explore aspects of Indian languages, history and culture. This group included such figures as Alexander Hamilton (1762–1824), William Erskine (1773–1852), John Leyden (1775–1811), Alexander Murray (1775–1813) and Vans Kennedy (1784–1846).[12] Several of these close contemporaries came from humble backgrounds. In the spirit of the age, they were polymaths whose activities and publications spanned an extraordinary range of interests and proto-disciplines. All displayed facility as linguists; most worked for the EIC, almost a Scots speciality in this period; and generally they were sympathetic to Indian cultures. They also adhered to the philosophical history practised by Robertson and other Enlightenment figures, viewing history as a discipline capable of the application of scientific laws. Although their ideas were far from monolithic, a few knew each other, forming a network, and it may be said that after the death of Jones in 1794 they constituted the principal group of Orientalists.[13]

Alexander Hamilton[14] spent some years in India, devoted himself to the study of Sanskrit, and later became a professor at Haileybury, publishing works on Sanskrit in 1811 and 1815 and *A Chronology of the Hindus* in 1820. He argued against what he saw as the excessive concentration of Asiatic Society savants upon Hinduism and argued for a wider approach. William Erskine,[15] on the other hand, wrote about medieval India. He completed John Malcolm's biography of Clive, and translated the memoir of the Mughal emperor Babur. Hamilton and Erskine were from reasonably well-to-do families, but both John Leyden and Alexander Murray were sons of shepherds, respectively from the Borders and Kirkcudbrightshire. Murray met Leyden in Edinburgh and directed him towards the study of Oriental languages, which he took up with a will. He soon claimed proficiency in Persian and Arabic (translating poetry from both), as well as Hindustani and Punjabi. Though licensed to preach for the CofS, he qualified in medicine and went to Madras in 1803. Like many Scots doctors, he also worked as a naturalist, later becoming professor of Hindustani in Calcutta. His great project was to study the languages, literature, antiquities and history of the Deccan, but his death in 1811 prevented its development.[16] His translations of work in Punjabi have recently been rediscovered by the Anglo-Punjabi literature and publishing initiative of the Punjab Cultural Association, and a number of websites extol this work. The text of one expresses surprise that Leyden is not more of a household name.[17] His mentor, Alexander Murray, on the other hand never went to India. Largely self-taught as a shepherd, he succeeded in going to Edinburgh University, qualified as a minister, later becoming professor of Oriental Languages at Edinburgh. His *Outlines of Oriental Philology* (1812), connected European and Asian languages, as Jones had done.[18]

Vans Kennedy[19] reached Bombay as a cadet in the EIC in 1800 and seems to have used *munshis* (Indian teachers) to train him in languages. An avid collector of manuscripts, his aptitude for languages led to his appointment as a Persian interpreter. A serving soldier until 1817, he caught the attention of Mountstuart Elphinstone, governor of Bombay and was appointed translator of the regulations of government in Marathi and Gujerati. Active in the Bombay branch of the Royal Asiatic Society as well as Bombay's Literary Society, he criticised traditional narrative approaches to history, typically arguing for comparative philosophical studies of entire societies. He published a Marathi dictionary in Bombay in 1824, and later (in London) *The Origin and Affinity of the Principal Languages of Asia and Europe* (1828) and *Researches into the Nature and Affinity of Ancient and Hindu Mythology* (1828).[20] The discovery of affinities was a major objective of the Scottish Orientalists, searching for parallels in folklore, languages or social structures.

These Orientalist achievements were remarkable, although Leyden and Murray died young, and as a group they have received relatively little attention. Nonetheless, they carried the standard for the EIC policy of understanding the languages and culture of the people of India and, in the case of Hamilton, Leyden and Murray, influenced others through their teaching positions, while all secured audiences for published works, including articles in contemporary journals and reviews. We should not forget, however, that their munshi teachers and collaborators must have been important in helping with translation and other work.

Administrators, Orientalism and Radical Reaction

The Scottish Orientalists were scholars, soldiers and holders of legal positions, but a more influential group of Scottish administrators initiated distinctive policies in India. Sir Thomas Munro (1761–1827), Sir John

Malcolm (1769–1833) and Mountstuart Elphinstone (1779–1859) represent the practical and instrumental wing of Scottish Orientalism. Their social backgrounds were diverse: Munro was the son of a Glasgow merchant and secured a university education, at Glasgow. Malcolm's father was a poor tenant farmer in Eskdale, while Elphinstone was the well-connected son of a peer. Munro and Malcolm both took up cadetships in the EIC army and rose rapidly, participating in contemporary Indian campaigns, notably against Tipu Sultan of Mysore and the Marathas of the Deccan. Elphinstone joined the Bengal civil service, but was also involved in the Maratha campaign. All worked under Governor-General Wellesley and some of their ideas were derived from their roles as agents to princely rulers. Elphinstone was an early envoy to Afghanistan while Malcolm became a notable diplomat, particularly in respect of Persia. Elphinstone and Malcolm both mastered Indian languages. Munro became governor of Madras in 1820. Elphinstone was governor of Bombay from 1819–27 and Malcolm succeeded him from 1827–31. Elphinstone turned down the governor-generalship, preferring his scholarship, and both he and Malcolm published extensively.

In a notable study, Martha Maclaren saw all three as applying ideas derived from both Scottish Enlightenment and civil society.[21] Taken together they had a striking influence on Indian administration. Munro was a leading proponent of the *ryotwari* system of land revenue assessment, based on individual peasant holdings rather than through landholding zamindars, known as the permanent settlement, introduced by Cornwallis in Bengal. Other notions shared among them included the need for indirect rule and the maintenance of indigenous social systems; an early formulation of the 'dual mandate' (that India should be ruled for the benefit of the EIC and of Indians); and the need for 'forward' diplomatic relations with states adjacent to India. These were to be influential for at least a century. All three promoted the traditional Scottish concern with education, Elphinstone founding a college in Poona. To a certain extent they were conservative and pragmatic figures, with Malcolm's focus being framed by his critique of the French Revolution. It may be that after 1818 he was influenced by the Tory romanticism of Sir Walter Scott, becoming more wedded to indigenous power structures and less committed to an assertive and dominant role for the British.[22] Malcolm's writings were remarkably extensive, with nine major books, including his *Sketch of the Sikhs* (1811), *Sketch of the Political History of India* (1811), *The History of Persia* (1815), and *The Political History of India* (1826), as well as an examination of the government of India (1823) and many pamphlets and articles. Elphinstone published on his mission to Kabul and, most significantly, his two-volume 1841 *History of India*, analysed below.

Before Scottish Orientalism had relinquished its influence in India, the EIC approach was under fierce attack. This was led by a Scot and, by descent, a half-Scot. Angus-born James Milne (1773–1836), the son of a shoemaker, was educated at Edinburgh University, where he was taught by Dugald Stewart, though he was later to criticise Stewart's philosophy. In 1798 he became a minister, like several of the Orientalists, but the life of a Scottish cleric was not for him. In 1802 he left for London, where he reinvented himself as James Mill.[23] One may speculate that this name change was symbolic of his abandonment of Scottish origins.[24] After all, Mill's date of birth, so close to that of Erskine, Leyden and Murray, his humble upbringing, his education at Edinburgh University, his connection with the CofS, would all seem to imply that he might have become another Scottish Orientalist. Was it the encounter with Jeremy Bentham, founder of Utilitarianism, or his contact with the London literary community, or simply the fact that he lacked linguistic ability which directed him otherwise? At any rate, he became editor of the *Literary Journal* and a passionate disciple of Bentham. A political and philosophical radical, his multi-volume *History of British India* (1818) established him as the chief denigrator of Indian customs and religion and diametrically opposed to the views of Robertson. In 1819 he joined the EIC's London administration as assistant examiner of correspondence, becoming examiner in 1830, years in which he published on political economy and philosophy.[25] There is some debate about how influential Mill really was among later Indian administrators, but he has certainly become notorious among modern historians for the ferocity of his Indian denunciation. In many ways, the approach of Mill was given administrative respectability by T.B. Macaulay. He was half Scots, son of Zachary, but was born and educated in England.[26] Although Mill never visited India, Macaulay famously spent the years 1834–38 there and, like Mill, was dismissive of Indian languages and culture. He decreed that the language of education, government and the law should be English and that elite and educated Indians should in effect be brown Englishmen. The age of transculturation, as advocated in their different ways by Scottish Orientalists, seemed to be over. Perhaps Mill and Macaulay were aware that the age of commerce, which had seemed to imply equality between India and Europe, was over, giving way to the age of industry, with new technologies creating a greater gulf between the two continents.[27] But it is possible that another Scottish sympathetic history of India, by Elphinstone, was more influential than Mill's critical one.[28]

Elphinstone was well aware that he was writing against Mill. In his preface, he wrote diplomatically that Mill's *History* 'left some room for doubt and discussion' and suggested that direct knowledge of India 'may sometimes lead to different impressions'.[29] In his first volume he examined the laws of Manu, the ancient Hindu code dating from around 500 BC, as well as the Vedas. He pointed out that the laws on marriage were not unfair to women and that material on the protection of widows indicated that 'sati' (the immolation of a widow on her husband's funeral pyre) was a modern invention.[30] He was complimentary about Hindu science, astronomy and mathematics, extolled the beauty of Sanskrit literature, and praised Indian music, painting and sculpture. The second volume consisted of a narrative account of Indian history from the thirteenth to the eighteenth centuries.[31] His projected third volume was incomplete at his death, but was published posthumously, edited by the notable Orientalist Sir Edward Colebrooke.[32]

The 'battle of the two philosophies'[33] was to rumble on through the nineteenth century and modified aspects of the Orientalist position were often upheld by Scots. James Tod (1782–1835) is often seen as the antithesis of James Mill and appears to carry elements of Scottish Orientalism forward into the Romantic age. Tod was of Scots parentage, received some education in Scotland, but spent so much time in London (training as an engineer at Woolwich) and in India that his Scottishness may be questioned, although he certainly fits a Scots tradition. At the peak of his career he was political agent in Gujerat and in Rajasthan, where he developed passionate and sympathetic interests in the Rajputs. Another polymath, he embraced the region's languages, history, cartography, topography, geology and botany. His cultural empathy for the Rajputs led him to place them within a universalist concept of human society, akin to the objectives of the Scottish Orientalists, but overlaid with a pronounced Romanticism. Florence D'Souza's major study of Tod has described him as pragmatic in his forward-looking ideas, avidly pursuing both knowledge exchange and indigenous understanding.[34] Tod disseminated his approach through the Royal Asiatic Society in London after 1823. His major works were *Annals and Antiquities of Rajasthan* in two volumes (1829 and 1832) and *Travels in Western India*, published posthumously in 1839.

Two other careers permit us to shift the focus to South-East Asia, though still within the orbit of the EIC. William Farquhar (1774–1839) from Aberdeenshire participated as an engineer in taking Malacca from the Dutch in 1795. From 1813, he was resident and commandant of Malacca; he spoke Malay and married a French Malaccan woman. In 1819 he succeeded Raffles as resident of Singapore, where he pursued a more sympathetic and laissez-faire approach.[35] His survey of the flora and fauna of the Malay Peninsula led to him commission a magnificent set of paintings by Chinese artists which are the pride of the Singapore museum. His successor as resident was Dr John Crawfurd (1783–1868), from Islay, who studied medicine in Edinburgh. In 1808 he reached Penang and devoted himself to Malay languages and culture. During the British conquest of Java, he was the resident at Yogjakarta and later at the courts of Siam and Cochin China. He published very extensively, including *A History of the Indian Archipelago* (1820), a *Grammar and Dictionary of Malay* (1852) as well as journals of his embassies.[36]

If Tod was a marginal Scot, the Muir brothers were distinctively Scottish.[37] John Muir (1810–83) and his brother William (1819–1905) both pursued careers in India, but developed very different branches of Orientalist scholarship. Born in Glasgow to a prosperous Kilmarnock calico printer, they were educated at Glasgow University. William also went to Edinburgh University and both trained at the EIC College, Haileybury. Mill's *History* was a text there, but they would have read Elphinstone's more sympathetic work later. Both joined the Bengal civil service, John in 1829, William in 1837. John's career embraced the posts of collector and a judgeship and then the principalship of Victoria College, Benares. Returning to Scotland in 1853, he endowed a chair of Sanskrit at Edinburgh University in 1862. This followed major contributions to Sanskrit scholarship which earned him doctorates of Edinburgh, Oxford and Bonn Universities. His work connected well with that of the early Orientalists, particularly his *Original Sanskrit Texts on the Origin and History of the People of India, their Religion and Institutions,* published in five volumes between 1858 and 1870, illustrating his interest in the principal texts of Hinduism and his pursuit of comparative mythology and linguistics. He published many articles and lectures, as well as original Sanskrit verse, invariably seeking Indo-European affinities. He even suggested that Hinduism and Christianity were compatible, while insisting on the superiority of the latter. He had connections with scholars such as Max Müller and with Christian missionaries.

His brother William Muir had a more distinguished career, becoming foreign secretary to the government of India (1865), lieutenant-governor of the North-West Provinces (1868) and financial member of the Viceroy's Council (1874). Like John he was an educationalist, instrumental in founding the Central College in Allahabad which later became the University. On his return to Britain, he became president of the Royal Asiatic Society (1884) and principal of Edinburgh University (1885–1903). Whereas John concentrated on Hinduism and Sanskrit, William was an authority on Arabic and studied the origins of Islam. His principal publications, among many articles, were: *The Life of Mahomet and History of Islam to the Era of the Hegira,* two volumes (1858) and in four volumes (1861), which among other things carefully analysed the Arabic sources; *Annals of the Early Caliphate from Original Sources* (1883); and *The Caliphate: its Rise, Decline and Fall from Original Sources* (1891). In these Muir's handling of Arabic and empirical understanding of sources is still admired, but he has been seen as a classic nineteenth century Orientalist in his condemnation of Islam, which he approached from the standpoint of a devout evangelical Christian. He described Islam as incapable of reform and criticised Muslim approaches to marriage, divorce and slavery, as well as treatment of women. He even suggested that Mohammed had come under Satanic influence, a strikingly pro-Christian view. Nevertheless, he had good relations with elite Indian Muslims, such as Sir Saiyid Ahmad Khan, and he was sympathetic towards the Wahhabis. Like other Arabists, William favoured the simple desert virtues of early Islam over what he saw as the decadence of settled society. Thus, John was perhaps the greater scholar while William was the more committed imperialist and Christian. Nevertheless, the Muirs (particularly John) form a bridge between their eighteenth century Orientalist forebears (with the addition of evangelicalism) and aspects of modern scholarship. But their educational influence ensured that Edinburgh University would remain significant in Oriental scholarship, while their educational institutions in India would prepare Indians to critique aspects of their work and develop modern nationalism.

Edward Said's celebrated work on Orientalism of 1978 stimulated an extensive and often controversial literature, including both passionate support and considerable criticism.[38] But Said and many of his followers have paid very little attention to Scottish Orientalists. Even J.J. Clarke in his book *Oriental Enlightenment* makes no mention of Robertson, any of the early Scots Orientalists, or of the Muir brothers.[39] Yet it should be apparent that the Scottish Orientalists reveal a number of important characteristics about Western studies of Orientalism. There was indeed nothing monolithic about the progression of Western thought on Asia. A succession of works from the eighteenth century examined in often complex and subtle ways the affinities and parallels between West and East as well as the contrasts and differences. Several writers extolled the beauty of Oriental languages and literatures, offering translations of notable texts and poets. It is intriguing to note that German Orientalism (towards which Said was more sympathetic) may well have been influenced by the work of William Robertson, while a succession of Scots carried the work of Jones and Robertson into a new age. Although significant figures with Scottish affiliations—like James Mill and T.B. Macaulay—denigrated the languages and culture of India, others—like James Tod, Mountstuart Elphinstone and John Muir—continued to exhibit more sympathetic views, inevitably influenced by both the Enlightenment and a new intellectual climate in the nineteenth century. The work of Scots (and others) on Orientalism, far from being a side show, requires to be understood in an entirely different framework from the concepts of binary 'othering' pursued by Said. Moreover, Said had nothing to say about the Orientalist interests of missionaries.

CHRISTIAN MISSIONS IN ASIA

Scots clergymen and other religious workers travelled to Asia for various reasons. Some went to minister to Scottish communities settled there or to act as regimental chaplains. They largely preached, inevitably in English, to the converted. The principal problems they faced were to maintain good relations with colonial or indigenous authorities and assert their right to organise in the face of the Church of England's periodic attempts to secure exclusive rights as the Established church of empire.[40] They had to create church buildings and Presbyterian structures: kirk sessions, presbyteries and synods. Sometimes, as in India, the authorities provided funds to help in the building of churches. Scottish churches (usually named St Andrew's) duly appeared in Bombay in 1814, Calcutta and Madras in 1818, while Madras also developed a 'native congregation' with its own minister. These imposing churches survive today, often in choice locations. They reflected the significance of the considerable Scots community in each presidency capital, the arrival of wives and families, and a degree of rivalry with the Anglican Church.[41] St Andrew's in Colombo, Ceylon, was founded in 1842, while Scots churches appeared in Darjeeling (1843),

Penang (1851), Singapore (1856) and Kuala Lumpur (1918).[42] Others were to emerge in the Middle and Far East. Most churches remained affiliated to the CofS, the 1843 Disruption having had little effect upon expatriate communities in Asia, where problems of scale and the absence of patronage discontents militated against breakaway churches. While originally founded for European congregations, they were eventually taken over by indigenous people.

On the other hand, the Disruption had a dramatic effect upon missions. Although missionary societies were founded in Edinburgh and Glasgow in 1795, the power of the Moderates ensured that the CofS only became involved in missions from the 1820s and in 1843 almost all missions went over to the FC. This certainly produced a highly energetic approach to missionary endeavour, together with rivalry between the three Scottish Churches (including the UP). Missionaries setting out to convert Asian peoples faced much greater obstacles and challenges compared with their confreres ministering to expatriates. Whether they aspired to work in major centres (such as Indian cities) or in more remote regions throughout Asia, including China, they faced difficulties of travel, the maintenance of health, local resistance, and physical discomfort. But more importantly they had to learn Asian languages and develop some understanding of the cultures where they sought to work. They often faced disturbed political situations and their lives were frequently at risk from violence and disease. The challenges of communication and cultural understanding led them to become considerable scholars, pursuing translation projects and publishing works about the characteristics and environments of their intended converts.[43]

All this was particularly true of China, a destination for Scots missionaries before they became involved in colonial regions. Robert Morrison (1782–1834), ordained in the Scotch Church in London, was an early missionary sinologist, leaving for China in 1807,[44] followed by William Milne (1785–1822), a self-taught farm labourer's son who, after ordination, reached Macao in 1813. Morrison mastered both Mandarin and Cantonese, dressed in Chinese fashion, became the EIC translator in Canton and published a Chinese grammar and a Chinese translation of the Bible.[45] Milne was expelled from Macao and moved to Malacca to become principal of the Anglo-Chinese College and minister of Christ Church. A prolific writer, he published a great deal on China. The most notable Scots sinologist was James Legge (1815–70), educated at King's College, Aberdeen. Sailing for China in 1839, he spent three years in Malacca's

Anglo-Chinese College before moving to Hong Kong in 1844. Assisted by Chinese associates, he translated Chinese classics while headmaster of Ying-Wa College and minister of the Union Church. He travelled extensively on mainland China and was keen to introduce Chinese people to Scotland, bringing three students with him on furlough in 1846. On his return to Scotland in 1867 he invited his translating colleague Wang Tao to join him. Legge was appointed professor of Chinese at Oxford in 1876 and published many more works in the later nineteenth century. He was thus highly influential in introducing both Chinese classics as well as Chinese people to Europe. Alex Williamson (1829–90), educated at Glasgow University, went to China in the 1850s, travelled extensively to distribute Bibles and Christian books and wrote prolifically on China. John Ross (1842–1915) joined the UP mission to Manchuria, established in 1864, and settled at Mukden in 1872. He met Korean merchants and learned their language, subsequently translating the New Testament into Korean, also writing a Korean primer and histories of the Manchus and of Korea.[46]

The involvement of Scots missionaries in education and language translation is apparent from these examples. It is generally accepted that the Scots missions pursued educational and medical work earlier than others and, despite some doubts, they remained central to their activities. The theory behind missionary education was that the transfer of a generalised Western system of thought would lead to conversion to the Christianity at its heart. Moreover, all Protestant missions regarded the ability to read the Bible as essential for the individual's route to Christian grace.[47] The Scots additionally were often complimented for their industrial missions. Medical missions were based on the vision of Christ as the healer of the world while the prospect of treatment would attract people to the mission.[48] The UP mission in China founded hospitals at each station. The first Scots missionary to Japan was a doctor, Henry Faulds (1843–1930), trained in Glasgow. In 1871 he sailed to India and joined the medical mission at Darjeeling, moving on with the UP mission to Japan in 1874. Faulds founded the Tsukiji hospital in Tokyo, where the large number of patients testified to the apparent appeal of Western medicine.[49]

E.W. Thompson suggested that the Presbyterian churches 'may claim pre-eminence' in education in India.[50] This is confirmed by the three Scottish missionaries who dominated missionary work in Calcutta, Bombay and Madras. Alexander Duff (1806–78), John Wilson (1804–75) and John Anderson (1805–55) all came from farming backgrounds and were educated at St Andrews (Duff) and Edinburgh (Wilson and Anderson). Duff reached Calcutta in 1830, Wilson Bombay in the same year, and Anderson Madras in 1836; all immediately founded schools and institutions of higher education. In 1843, they joined the FC, thereby ensuring that there were two Scots missions and schools in each presidency capital. Duff became highly influential in his rejection of vernacular teaching and insisted both on the use of English and on educating Hindu and Muslim upper classes in what he suggested would produce a downward filtration effect.[51] The wives of Wilson and Anderson were active in creating schools for girls, often mainly for the less resistant lower castes.[52] The colleges in Calcutta and Bombay ultimately became affiliated to the universities founded in those cities in the 1850s and Anderson's became the Madras Christian College. The numbers of CofS and FC missionaries built up during the century, with branch schools and missions founded in many other towns, often accompanied by hospitals. While Duff was influential in English education and in founding FC missions, Wilson was the more distinguished scholar. Acquainted with a number of Indian languages, as well as Hebrew (even founding a Jewish school in Bombay), he published very extensively. He also took an interest in the preservation of Indian antiquities. Madras produced ordained 'native' preachers from 1846.

By the turn of the nineteenth and twentieth centuries, the annual assemblies of the Scottish Churches devoted a good deal of attention to missions. In 1903, the moderator of the United Free Church (the union of FC and UPC), the Rev. George Robson, declared in his address that 'the whole world is open to Christian effort' and that 'this imperialising Christian factor' would be crucial 'for the Christian conquest of the world'.[53] However much scholars have questioned a missionary surge at this time, still the assemblies give the impression of expanding activity in India, Burma, Malaya, China and Japan.[54]

Indian missions have received some scholarly attention, but Scottish missions in the Middle East are less well known. From the 1830s, Scots began to consider the possibility of converting Jews in order to create a new Christian Israel.[55] Such Jewish missions were founded in several European cities, in Constantinople and the Levant. Early efforts were tentative and Jewish mission committees debated the most effective locations for missions. The Bible supplied both geographical knowledge of the 'Holy Land' and the 'geopiety' that infused missionary ambitions.[56] Damascus, Aleppo and Beirut briefly had missions, but they were withdrawn in favour of Tiberias and Safad in Galilee. Missions, characteristically with schools and hospitals, were firmly established there in the 1880s, as well as in Jaffa on the coast. A celebrated missionary doctor, David Torrance, served at the medical mission for almost 40 years, and other Scots doctors and nurses joined him.[57] Although these missions were primarily directed at Jews, a telling remark by the Rev. John Soutar of Tiberias at the 1899 UP Synod encapsulates the objectives of medical mission: 'He described how religious teaching was conveyed to the motley crowd of patients drawn from motley races'.[58] The missions survived the upheavals of the First World War, the inter-war years and even the establishment of the State of Israel with Jewish missions still being considered feasible as late as the 1950s.[59] However, the number of converts was remarkably low and these missions neatly indicate the capacity of intended converts to seize what was available in terms of education and treatment while resisting baptism.

Although the Scottish Asian missions were generally less successful in conversions than those in Africa, still missionaries were important in disseminating Western knowledge and medicine. Meanwhile, many Scots would have derived information about Asia from the lectures and sermons of missionaries on furlough and from articles both in missionary magazines and the press. Any survey of Scottish newspapers indicates the extent to which visits, lectures, and general assembly meetings were reported. In addition, missionary biographies and memoirs constituted a notable part of Scottish print culture. At another level, Edinburgh University in particular developed expertise in Oriental languages and cultures. Obviously, there were parallel developments in England, Wales and Ireland, but a sense of distinctive Scots identity and of specific contributions to education, medical services, as well as proselytisation were conveyed to those parts of the Scottish public who took an interest.

Conclusion

The purpose of this chapter has been to demonstrate the essential continuity of the Scottish intellectual and linguistic grappling with Asia. Despite notable controversies and debates, it can be argued that the Scottish Orientalists of the late eighteenth and early nineteenth centuries, the administrators who searched for methods of rule that would facilitate British power while still recognising indigenous systems, the missionary scholars and translators, and the contemporary nineteenth century educators and Orientalists were all seeking to comprehend Asian cultures and ideas. They each pursued specific ends, whether feeding knowledge into power structures to render them more effective, or advancing European understanding of other cultures to train students for the pursuit of rule, trade and proselytisation. While other scholars and missionaries from the United Kingdom and Europe sought the same ends, the evidence suggests that Scottish activities had some specific characteristics.

These can be divided into personnel, training, and methodologies. First, Scottish participants in these endeavours were greater in number, relative to the Scottish population, than other nationalities. This partly reflected the preponderance of Scots in the EIC and, at least in the officer class, within the army. Many came from humble backgrounds, but were talented enough to secure educations which not only stimulated a predilection for Oriental languages, but also prepared them for intensive studies and publishing activities. Almost all received some training in Scottish universities for their roles in the military, administration, the law and missions, opening up to them the ideas of the Scottish Enlightenment. They were familiar with, and contributed to, the print culture of late eighteenth century reviews and book publishing, which was to expand mightily in the nineteenth, spreading out into specialist journals, including those of missionary societies. Indeed, missionaries were probably the principal means whereby ideas about Asian societies reached a wider public, even if such articles sometimes contributed to the stereotypical 'othering' of Asian peoples. They may also have fostered a sense of imperial identity both in India and at home.[60] So far as the methodologies are concerned, there can be little doubt that Scots often brought linguistic talents to bear, as well as a willingness to work together with indigenous educators, munshies in India, fellow translators in China and elsewhere. Scots were particularly keen to disseminate educational ideas and institutions, together with the Western medicine in which they excelled for key decades. Missionaries and administrators founded schools and institutions of higher education as well as hospitals, promoting all of these with publications (sometimes exhibitions) designed to spread ideas and raise funds.

While much of this activity was essentially imperial in its import, it is apparent that Scottish educational and medical offerings were seized by Asian people even as they rejected the political, social and religious ideas that they supposedly illustrated. In these respects, the project was ultimately about the spread of modernity and peoples in Asia cheerfully picked out what they found valuable in grappling with the modern world and ultimately in defeating imperial power at its own game. Thus we have to distinguish between the shorter-term objectives of Orientalists, administrators and missionaries and the longer-term outcomes. However, Western education was ultimately to destroy the Romantic concepts of traditional rule promoted by some Orientalists. Thus, Scots in Asia were the conduits of elements of modernity and also the often unwitting facilitators of modern nationalism in the new Asia as it developed in the twentieth century.[61]

NOTES

1. Throughout this chapter, original spellings of place names are used since these are familiar from the sources. Modern equivalents are readily available.
2. While the *Scotsman* was used for this study, many other Scottish papers carried missionary reports.
3. Garland Cannon, *The Life and Mind of Oriental Jones: Sir William Jones, the Father of Modern Linguistics* (Cambridge: Cambridge University Press, 1990). See also S.N. Mukherjee, *Sir William Jones: A Study in Eighteenth-century British Attitudes to India* (Cambridge, Cambridge University Press, 1968).
4. This appeared in an 1845 *Calcutta Review* article, when the old Orientalism was under threat. Quoted in Gauri Viswanathan, *Masks of Conquest: Literary Study and British Rule in India* (New York: Columbia University Press, 1989), 28.
5. J.L. Brockington, 'Warren Hastings and Orientalism', in Geoffrey Carnall and Colin Nicholson (eds), *The Impeachment of Warren Hastings* (Edinburgh: Edinburgh University Press, 1989), 91–208.
6. The entire text is available online, running to some 415 pages with nine documentary appendices.
7. There is a 1771 portrait of Dow by Sir Joshua Reynolds in Petworth House, Sussex, with a copy in Gunsgreen House, Eyemouth.
8. In eighteenth century Scotland, students generally attended university courses rather than seeking graduation. This changed with the rise of professionalisation in the nineteenth century.
9. Gordon T. Stewart, *Journeys to Empire: Enlightenment, Imperialism, and the British Encounter with Tibet, 1774–1904* (Cambridge: Cambridge University Press, 2009), 13 and 31.
10. Stewart J. Brown, 'William Robertson, Early Orientalism, and the Historical Disquisition on India of 1791', *Scottish Historical Review*, 88, 2 (2009), 289–312. See also Stewart J. Brown (ed.), *William*

Robertson and the Expansion of Empire (Cambridge: Cambridge University Press, 2008), particularly the chapter by Geoffrey Carnall on 'William Robertson and contemporary images of India'.

11. The 'stadial' system ranked societies on an evolutionary scale through their modes of subsistence, from hunting and gathering to pastoral, agricultural, and commercial.

12. Sir James Mackintosh is sometimes included in this group, but his work was on the fringes. of Orientalist studies, although his daughter married William Erskine. He worked as a judge in Bombay, but his principal significance is as a Whig and radical politician.

13. The distinctiveness of Scottish Orientalists was first considered by Jane Rendall, 'Scottish Orientalism from Robertson to James Mill', *The Historical Journal*, 25 (1982), 44–69.

14. The cousin of his more celebrated American namesake, he arrived in India in 1803 as a lieutenant in the EIC navy.

15. Erskine was educated at Edinburgh University and worked as a court official in Bombay after 1804. He founded the Literary Society of that city.

16. Leyden was interested in the folklore of the Borders and helped Scott in his *Minstrelsy of the Scottish Borders*. He was also interested in the travels of Mungo Park (whom he met) and on the role of Europeans in North and East Africa.

17. www.drleyden.co.uk (accessed 28 November 2015) and a number of related websites that deal with his translations and aspects of his work.

18. Murray, like Leyden, had an interest in African exploration and published a biography of James Bruce, the Scottish explorer of North-East Africa and the sources of the Blue Nile, in 1808 and also produced a new edition of Bruce's *Travels*.

19. Kennedy came from a reasonably well-off family, but his father lost money in the collapse of the Ayr Bank in 1772.

20. Kennedy became judge advocate general of the Bombay army, published on military law and ended his career as a major general.

21. Martha McLaren, *British India and British Scotland, 1780–1830: Career Building, Empire Building, and a Scottish School of Thought on Indian Governance* (Akron, OH: University of Akron Press, 2001).

22. Jack Harrington, 'No Longer Merchants, but Sovereigns of a Vast Empire": The Writings of Sir John Malcolm and British India,

1810–33' (PhD dissertation, University of Edinburgh 2009), published as *Sir John Malcolm and the Creation of British India* (London: Palgrave Macmillan, 2010).

23. Other Scots indulged in this reinvention. An interesting example is John Braidwood of Oldhamstocks, East Lothian. In London he became Broadwood, the most notable piano maker of the age, now invariably referred to as 'English'.

24. In this he seems to have been successful since he is usually described as an English Utilitarian.

25. Eric Stokes, *The English Utilitarians and India* (Oxford: Clarendon Press, 1959); Ronald B. Inden, *Imagining India* (Bloomington, IN: Indiana University Press, 1990) and Javed Majeed, *Ungoverned Imaginings: James Mill's The History of British India and Orientalism* (Oxford: Clarendon Press, 1992).

26. Catherine Hall, *Macaulay and Son: Architects of Imperial Britain* (New Haven: Yale University Press, 2012).

27. Michael Adas, *Machines as the Measure of Men: Science, Technology, and Ideologies of Western Dominance* (Ithaca, NY: Cornell University Press, 1989).

28. Avril A. Powell, *Scottish Orientalists and India: The Muir Brothers, Religion, Education and Empire* (Woodbridge, Suffolk: Boydell and Brewer, 2010), 61–62.

29. Mountstuart Elphinstone, *The History of India*, 1 (London: John Murray, second edition, 1843), ii.

30. Ibid., 88–89.

31. Mountstuart Elphinstone, *The History of India*, II (London: John Murray, 1841).

32. Mountstuart Elphinstone, *The Rise of British Power in the East*, edited by Sir Edward Colebrooke (London: John Murray, 1887).

33. Stokes, *English Utilitarians*, 1.

34. Florence D'Souza, *Knowledge, Mediation and Empire: James Tod's Journeys among the Rajputs* (Manchester: Manchester University Press, 2015).

35. The Singapore national museum is more complimentary about Farquhar, viewing Raffles as dictatorial. Personal observation.

36. Unusually, Crawfurd was a polygenist, arguing that human races had a variety of different origins.

37. Powell, *Scottish Orientalists and India*. Powell has examined in admirable detail the influence of the Muirs' education and of various family networks connected with India.

38. Some of this can be found usefully summarised and excerpted in A.L. Macfie, *Orientalism: A Reader* (Edinburgh: Edinburgh University Press, 2000) and discussed in Macfie's *Orientalism* (Harlow: Pearson Education, 2002). John M. MacKenzie, *Orientalism: History, Theory and the Arts* (Manchester: Manchester University Press, 1995) tested Said's view of Orientalism against its recurrence in the Western arts. The more populist, but powerful, critique by Robert Irwin, *The Lust for Knowing: The Orientalists and their Enemies* (London, Allen Lane 2006) also makes no mention of Scots.

39. J.J. Clarke, *Oriental Enlightenment: The Encounter between Asian and Western Thought* (London: Routledge 1997). David Smith, *Hinduism and Modernity* (Oxford: Blackwell, 2003) contains important sections on 'The European Discovery of Hinduism' and 'Hinduism and Orientalism', but likewise makes no mention of Scottish Orientalists.

40. The *Scotsman*, 27 August 1876, reported on 'The Ceylon Ecclesiastical Difficulty' in which Bishop Copleston of Colombo, the 'boy' bishop, had decided to assert his authority over the Tamil Coolie mission on the plantations. This was mainly funded by Presbyterian plantation owners. The Bishop had to backtrack.

41. Esther Breitenbach, 'Scots Churches and Missions', in John M. MacKenzie and T.M. Devine (eds), *Scotland and the British Empire* (Oxford: Oxford University Press, 2011), pp. 198–199; Esther Breitenbach, 'Religious Literature and Discourses of Empire: The Scottish Presbyterian Foreign Mission Movement', in Hilary M. Carey (ed.), *Empires of Religion* (Houndmills: Basingstoke, Palgrave Macmillan, 2008), 84–110.

42. The churches in Malaya and Singapore were unusual in pulling in Chinese adherents, the Chinese also being expatriates. In 1881, Singapore appointed the Rev. J. Cook, who was fluent in Swatow and South Fujian dialects.

43. The two most recent missionary histories have relatively little to say about the intellectual activities of missionaries: Jeffrey Cox, *The British Missionary Enterprise since 1700* (London: Routledge, 2008); Hilary M. Carey, *God's Empire: Religion and Colonialism*

in the British Empire, c. 1801–1908 (Cambridge: Cambridge University Press, 2011).

44. Stephen Neill, *A History of Christian Missions* (Harmondsworth: Penguin, 1964), 280–281.

45. Christopher Hancock, *Robert Morrison and the Birth of Chinese Protestantism* (London: T&T Clark, 2008). Glasgow University granted him a DD in 1817.

46. A useful source is the *Directory of Protestant Missionaries in China, Japan and Corea for the Year 1910* (Hong Kong: HK Daily Press, 1910).

47. Norman Etherington, 'Education and Medicine', in Norman Etherington (ed.), *Missions and Empire* (Oxford: Oxford University Press, 2005), 261–284. Etherington notes that missionaries were the first to supply free educational and medical services.

48. Medical work was greatly forwarded by the founding of the Edinburgh Medical Missionary Society in 1842, still in existence as EMMS International. Andrew F. Walls, '"The Heavy Artillery of the Missionary Army": The Domestic Importance of the Nineteenth-Century Medical Mission', in W.J. Sheils (ed.), *The Church and Healing* (Oxford: Blackwell 1982), 87–97. The EMMS held exhibitions to advertise its work, for example in Edinburgh in 1898: the *Scotsman*, 25 July 1898.

49. Two Scottish administrators and educators in the Far East, Sir James Stewart Lockhart (1858–1937) and Sir Reginald Johnston (1874–1938), also pursued scholarship and collecting while at their posts. Both, particularly Johnston, published widely.

50. E.W. Thompson, *The Call of India* (London: Wesleyan Methodist Missionary Society, 1912), 210.

51. A.A. Miller, *Alexander Duff* (Edinburgh: Canongate, 1992). A lengthy obituary of Duff appeared in the *Scotsman,* 13 February 1878.

52. The Edinburgh Ladies' Association for the Advancement of Female Education in India was founded in 1837, part of the major women's involvement in missions in Scotland. Lesley Orr Macdonald, *A Unique and Glorious Mission: Women and Presbyterianism in Scotland, 1830–1930* (Edinburgh: John Donald, 2000).

53. The *Scotsman*, 20 May 1903. These sentiments may explain why the Rev. Robert Kilgour of Darjeeling expressed missionary support for Younghusband's expedition to Tibet, hoping the country

would soon be open to Christianity overcoming 'the ignorance of the Lamas'. the *Scotsman*, 1 June 1904.

54. Andrew C. Ross, 'Scottish Missionary Concern 1874–1914: A Golden Era?', *Scottish Historical Review*, 51, 1 (1972), 52–72.

55. Michael Marten, *Attempting to Bring the Gospel Home: Scottish Missions to Palestine, 1839–1917* (London: I.B. Tauris, 2006).

56. George Adam Smith, *The Historical Geography of the Holy Land* (London: Hodder and Stoughton, 1901).

57. W.P. Livingstone, *A Galilee Doctor, Being a Sketch of the Career of Dr D.W. Torrance of Tiberias* (London: Hodder and Stoughton, 1923).

58. The *Scotsman*, 11 May 1899.

59. There is still a St Andrew's Church in Jerusalem, while the rather grand hospital at Tiberias was converted into an upscale hotel run by the Church of Scotland.

60. Philip Constable, 'Scottish Missionaries, "Protestant Hinduism" and the Scottish Sense of Empire in Nineteenth and early Twentieth Century India', *Scottish Historical Review*, 86, 2 (2007), 278–313.

61. In Nagasaki, the 'Scottish Samurai', Thomas Blake Glover (1838–1911), is clearly honoured by the Japanese as the bearer of modernity. Personal observation.

CHAPTER 4

Scottish Agency Houses in South-East Asia, c.1760–c.1813

George McGilvary

INTRODUCTION

This chapter deals with agency houses that were in existence from the late 1760s to 1813 when the monopoly held by the East India Company (EIC) to trade in India ended—and prior to their mass failure of 1833/34. Later, between 1833 and 1847, more firms in India, described as 'managed agency houses', would develop out of these first mercantile agency houses. From 1847 onwards these had become joint-stock companies where 'management was in the hands of professional managers'. By the 1860s agencies were merely the local bureaux for companies operating from Britain.[1]

Over the years, the phenomenon that grew in India commonly referred to as 'Houses of Agency', 'agencies' or 'agency houses' has been examined by scholars from several angles, but not often from a Scottish perspective, even though the entrepreneurial activities of the Scottish elite in South-

The author is very appreciative of two Small Research Grants: one from Carnegie, the other from Strathmartine that partly funded the research needed for this paper.

G. McGilvary (✉)
University of Edinburgh, Edinburgh, Scotland

© The Author(s) 2017   75
T.M. Devine, A. McCarthy (eds.), *The Scottish Experience in Asia, c.1700 to the Present*, DOI 10.1007/978-3-319-43074-4_4

East Asia might be considered deserving of special study.[2] Several authorities do comment on this Scottish commercial presence, but in a rather glib manner. Robert Blake remarked, 'so many eastern traders originated in Scotland, along with their arch-ideologue, the great Adam Smith', and pointed out that the EIC 'could not do without the private English ... although most of them were Scottish'.[3] Michael Greenberg noted they formed part of a defined social group, a 'rising and ambitious mercantile class'.[4] Monsieur Le Pichon thought that over half the partners in agency houses in these years had Scottish names.[5]

Apart from the work of C.H. Philips on David Scott in 1951, only recently have attempts been made to investigate these Scots. Even then, studies such as those of Jim Parker, Tom Tomlinson and Anne Bulley are few in number.[6] Fortunately, these scholars have produced able examinations of what were by any standards an extraordinary group of Scots and the accomplishments achieved through their Agency houses.[7] Several of the major features revealed are impressive and supported here. For example, according to Tomlinson, Scottish multinational business networks (epitomised by those of David Scott and others mentioned) gave coherence to the regional and international trade of Asia by the end of the eighteenth century. He argues that this advance deserves comparison with what had already been developed in the Atlantic economy in previous decades.[8]

It is also claimed that what were essentially private activities helped Britain capture inter-Asian and European-Asian trade in the second half of the eighteenth century and that this created a 'commercial revolution' in the East, centred firstly on British supremacy in Bengal, then in all India. Nineteenth century free trade, it is maintained, relied upon these late eighteenth century private trade developments, much of it the work of men of business and commerce epitomised by the Scots indicated here. The argument asserts that private traders, steeped in free trade ideas, joined the clamour of British manufacturers to end the EIC monopoly in India, which was thrown open in 1813, with China following in 1833; that, in effect, these Scots helped create truly global networks.[9]

Philips pinpointed the activities of David Scott in all this, contending that his connections and business feats explain much of the continuing and expanding Scottish commercial presence in the subcontinent. Scott, he maintained, introduced discussion within the EIC on the rapid growth of foreign trade with India and Canton. According to Philips, Scott's stated long-term ambition was to reorganise Britain's eastern trade along laissez faire lines. Philips adds that in the attempt Scott used technical knowledge that augmented re-exports to India and China. These increased from £650,000 in 1788, to £1 million in 1793.[10]

This chapter aims to consolidate these findings. The intention is to demonstrate the extent of the Scottish contribution and give reasons for an overarching prominence in the Asian commercial world using Houses of Agency. Because the activities of David Scott of Dunninald MP (1746–1805) were central to what happened, details from his career and members of his immediate network are utilised to illustrate developments and show how agencies worked. An attempt at calculating the scale (as apart from actual numbers) of Scots trading via Houses of Agency has also been made. Quite a few filled substantial roles, influencing the flow of events in the eastern theatre over a considerable stretch of time.

The ensuing text attempts to present a comprehensive picture of how things developed. A résumé of the 1757–74 period and of general trading involving EIC servants and free-merchants outwith Company business is followed by an explanation of why agencies appeared. These Houses of Agency and their principal areas of business are outlined and then illustrated with instances of Scottish participation. David Scott's firms, his activities in India and business conducted in Britain are examined, as are his partners and close associates, who were at the heart of a caucus of Scottish agency houses. Additional detail is given of the Scott-Adamson-Tate-Fairlie-Fergusson-Lennox network. Mention is made of the Scottish Houses of Agency in London and spin-offs that benefited Scotland directly. The chapter closes with an assessment of Scott's particular skills and the professionalism he and his compatriots demonstrated. It concludes with suggestions, gleaned from this research, about why Scots were so prominent in this first period of agency houses.

EUROPEAN COMMERCE IN SOUTH-EAST ASIA PRIOR TO HOUSES OF AGENCY

In India, prior to 1760, various nawabs sought independence. Pirates like Angria ravaged the sea lanes; roving bands of mercenaries, such as the Marathas, did the same on land. The weakness of the Mughal dynasty meant it was unable to resist these threats or those of the heavily armed British, French, Dutch and Portuguese companies operating from fortified trading posts. Only the English company's defeat of the French in 1757 at Plassey (temporarily) ended this struggle for supremacy. The scene was set for an uncontrollable commercial free-for-all among the EIC's direct and indirect employees. After Plassey, bribery and intimidation secured immense hoards of presents, gifts and rupees.[11]

Upon arrival in India, and irrespective of ethnic background, the majority of EIC recruits were immersed in trade, becoming merchants and entrepreneurs in both inland and seaborne commerce of every kind. Most used a native intermediary (banians, as they were called in Bengal; dubashes in Madras). Mid-century, the Mayors Courts in all the presidencies reflected their intense business preoccupation as well as that of free traders and mariners now pouring east.[12] The fortunes made were legendary. Clive and the so-called 'Bengal Squad' returned with colossal fortunes as did the Scots-born John Johnstone who amassed around £300,000, almost equal to that of Clive. A Captain Mackenzie, who commanded sepoys, illustrates the actions of many. He used EIC funds for his own use: 'lent money at between 5 and 14 per cent a month, collected extra cesses on the revenue for himself and speculated in rice'.[13]

However, several major changes took place from the mid-1760s and again in the mid-1780s, in the way the EIC conducted its affairs, altering the whole commercial picture in India and wherever the Company operated. They were in response to a feeling in Britain that the EIC was too weak to handle the impressive expansion that followed from Clive accepting the *Diwani* of Bengal, Bihar and Orissa in 1765 (meaning responsibility for the revenues and territorial responsibilities). All was made worse by the terrible Bengal famine of 1769/70, followed by the Company almost becoming bankrupt. Cumulatively, these events helped bring about the 1773 Regulating Act and partial government takeover.

Following the appointment of Warren Hastings as governor-general (via the 1773 Act) immediate improvements were seen, particularly in the inland trade. Accompanying this upsurge, however, were restrictions. *Dastucks* were abolished. These had given EIC servants permission to trade in commodities such as betel nut, tobacco and rice. Licences were now required to control the salt and opium monopolies formerly operated by Company officials.

Governor-General Cornwallis followed Hastings, and in 1787 another pivotal point was reached. To avoid further money haemorrhage, his decrees of that year ended all the private commercial activities of Company servants and stopped the privilege of sending funds home by bills of exchange.

THE NEED FOR HOUSES OF AGENCY

Company servants were not to be put off by the changes that from the 1770s and 1780s now governed commercial enterprise. Being forbidden to trade in so many inland commodities pushed them towards the Houses of Agency that began springing up to execute the business from which they had been banned, and to which many free-merchants had already gravitated. Agencies in turn used their own money and the savings coming from EIC servants and others to service sugar factories, procure ships and indigo plantations and for involvement in banking, insurance and much else. From the profits made, remittances were sent home, salaries paid, fortunes realised, and the business of the EIC enabled. Others moved their money into the burgeoning shipborne trade, as would the new agencies in time. The transformations thus effected would go on to further the flow of funds into booming commercial activities in South-East Asia.[14]

Expansion of Agency Houses was further fuelled by continuing, intense commercial need. Throughout India they would dominate the purchase and export of goods. In their formation, and to give support to the system devised, such Houses absorbed the traditional skills, knowledge and roles of native banians. Thus, even in 1785, although still in their infancy, they had commenced using systemised banking methods utilising such expertise. The development of an embryo banking system using these agencies was especially important. Individuals who dealt with them knew that the interest rates offered would remain acceptable. So, from 1785 onwards, silk weavers and indigo planters were being paid by agency houses, which were even enabled to raise the loans to do so by the EIC. The Scottish firm Alexander & Co went on to establish a Bank of Hindustan in the 1770s—although, like the one in 1819 founded by MacIntosh & Co, it went into liquidation in 1832/33 with the general failure of the first Houses of Agency.

From the mid-1780s, however, agencies proliferated. Every occupation was discharged and every commodity under the sun involving the inland and coastal (also called 'country') trade was conducted through them. The journalistic activity of the Scottish firm Cruttenden & Mackillop was typical of this versatility. Of particular importance for the future was the triangular trading network of opium, silver and tea (involving India–China–Britain) that began expanding ferociously. This created an even greater need for Houses of Agency. So lucrative was the trade with the Co'Hong merchants in Canton (despite the opposition of the Chinese government) that Scots and other traders found it irresistible. Through these Chinese merchants, chests of opium and bales of raw cotton from India were used to buy silver (*sychee*) in Canton. Still using the Co'Hong, this much desired silver in turn bought the cargoes of tea, spices, silk and porcelain that were carried back to Britain and sold in EIC warehouses. The final push came with the Commutation Act of 1784 which effectively trebled the price of tea at Canton, providing a further stimulus to trade between India and China. The EIC came under extreme pressure to satisfy this rapidly growing market. Agency houses, energised by the need for tea, which could only be gained via the Chinese desire for opium, concentrated even more on producing and despatching the drug.

Great numbers, within and without EIC commercial confines, were involved. Company officials were pressurised and greedy private merchants (like the Scots) clamoured, as did traders from every part of Indian society. All were increasingly involved in building, supplying and paying for the ships required to export the opium from India to China, principally to Canton, Macao and Whampoa. Houses of Agency received colossal profits from this trade.[15]

Consequently, country shipping increased fourfold between 1783 and 1791. The result was that the last two decades of the eighteenth century saw the rise to dominance of British interests, which, as well as capturing the carrying trade between Asia and Europe and India's inland commerce, now took charge of most country trade within Asian waters. From the late 1780s the EIC and Houses of Agency were the principal players in determining the course of business and for what evolved both in India and in China. This development, Tomlinson has rightly argued, provided an institutional set-up for private traders and investors.[16] Their predominance lasted until the failures of 1833/34, to be replaced by 'managing' groups imported from the surviving London agencies.[17]

From the outset, agencies abroad used Indian, Parsi and Armenian money (initially, through banians). However, agencies that started appearing in London (largely created by the mid-century changes that were now affecting all Indian commerce) came into their own. Developments were shaped by agencies' proximity to 'City' money and their convenient position for lobbying Parliament in the interest of freeing trade.

Houses located in the metropolis, many connected to agencies in India, became more useful and firms abroad, particularly in Calcutta, gravitated towards granting bills on agencies there for money advanced in India.[18] Business networks centred in London, Calcutta and Canton would remain interconnected from that point onwards.

According to Greenberg, by 1840 more than 200 London agencies were operating out of the Jerusalem Coffee House, where there was a strong Scottish presence. In 1813 at least 19 principal Scots houses were in business and 27 by the late 1820s. From 1793 the most prominent firm was David Scott Junior & Co. Those belonging to Claud Alexander & Co and Forbes & Co were the leading firms going into the 1830s. Many, like Charles Sutherland and Captain John Lennox (and his family), were partners in other Scottish agencies located in the capital. All (home and abroad) supported one another.[19] There were additional benefits: at least 18 firms and agents working from Scotland handled the affairs of Scottish personnel abroad. They dealt with EIC business in general, with Houses of Agency in particular, and acted on behalf of commercial firms and banks.[20]

SCOTTISH-CONTROLLED AGENCIES

Although from early times there were various small settlements in India with a Scots presence, such as Jacobites in Canton and others in the Ostend and Swedish East India Companies, the unusually large number of Scots in this part of the world really dates from the mid-1720s. By virtue of a patronage system initiated by Sir Robert Walpole (with posts provided by the Scottish EIC director, John Drummond) Scots from the privileged classes went out as EIC officials, seamen, surgeons, military men and free-merchants. In exchange, their families pledged political support at elections and in Parliament to the Whig government. EIC patronage was to be distributed in this fashion throughout the eighteenth century.[21] Initially, the bulk of Scottish business people in Asia consisted of such EIC servants who either abandoned their official positions or carried things forward in a dual capacity—people like Claud Alexander, David Anderson, Campbell of Inverneil, and the Graham brothers of Kinross House. The others were mainly free-merchants, such as David Scott and Ramsay Hannay.[22]

Materialising from these commercial networks and numerous agency houses surfacing throughout Asia (particularly in Bombay and Bengal) was a substantial and powerful group of Scottish businessmen. They had begun forming ties with one another through mutual EIC connections. Even closer friendship came with being part of a clique, a close commercial network. Though the absence of adequate materials makes numerical accuracy impossible, some sort of calculation regarding the scale of their presence can be made. From the Houses of Agency itemised in the *East India Registers*, as well as named Scots in Bengal between 1808 and

1809 who were not employees of the EIC, it seems that Scottish personnel averaged over 25 per cent of the total involvement.[23] Also, a *Select
List* derived from researching this topic provides the names of some 214
Scottish-owned or controlled Houses of Agency operating in the East,
mainly between 1765 and 1834, and this again approximates to slightly
over 25 per cent of all named agencies.[24]

Unlike the EIC, agency houses (in this first phase of their development) were not joint-stock companies (that only began in 1847) and
Scots continued to form ever changing, ever fluctuating partnerships that
kept such firms alive. These were readily bought and sold. Ex-owners
would depart for home, though, of course, they kept large deposits in
India where the best return was made. Many firms were permanent fix-
tures, such as Alexander & Co, David Scott & Co, Alex Colvin, Bazett &
Co, Cruttenden, Mackillop & Co, and the several controlled by William
Fairlie. Those of other Scots, such as Alex Adamson, James Brodie and
James Tate, were almost as long lasting.

Agencies with Scottish partners began to spread throughout Asia
and other parts of the world. Their growth in Calcutta was exceptional:
15 in 1790, 29 by 1803, and peaking at 67 in the 1830s. The *East India
Registers* show that in 1813 there were 14 wholly owned Scottish merchant houses in Calcutta, 12 Armenian, 10 English and two Portuguese.
From 1800 to 1820, the seven principal Houses of Agency there were
owned and/or managed by Scots firms like Alexander & Co, D. Scott
& Co, William Fairlie, Alex Colvin, and Cruttenden, Mackillop & Co.
Hong Kong, New South Wales, Australia, and New York had one Scottish
agency each. Batavia and Mauritius had two, Canton and Macao three
each. There were four in Manila, 10 in Madras and 20 in Bombay. In
addition, there were the numerous Scottish-owned London agencies—a
striking Scottish ascendancy.[25]

MAJOR BUSINESS ENTERPRISES

Aside from the ever hectic inland trade, Scots in this era were involved in
developing major fields: insurance, shipping, shipbuilding and the coastal
trade accompanied banking and journalism. Before and after being swal-
lowed up by Houses of Agency, they traded in diverse locations, such as
the Red Sea and Gujarat Peninsula, Canton, Macao and the East Indies
archipelago. Initially they worked alone or in small syndicates, many of
them joint-stock companies. For example, in the 1760s, at Calcutta, Alex

Mackenzie built and leased ships on his own. James Kyd bought docks in Calcutta where 35 vessels were produced. Others were in small partnerships, taking commissions. Although many continued until late into the eighteenth century, such operations would be taken over by agency houses.

Scottish shipbuilding agencies came into their own in the 1780s with the intense commercial demands of the period. The boom meant 77 ships were launched in Calcutta between 1781 and 1802. Soon, around 290 were calling there per annum. By 1802 Calcutta had a home fleet, as did Bombay. Between 1796 and 1797 some 147 ships had called at Madras. They were helped in that Henry Dundas, at government level, and David Scott, working behind the scenes in the EIC Court of Directors, championed the building of ships abroad. Unsurprisingly, therefore, the most important vessels were built, owned or run by Scots. Predictably, Dundas' nephew, Commander Philip Dundas, captain of the East Indiaman *Melville Castle*, was one of them.

The great Scottish shipping agencies before 1813 included Fairlie & Fergusson, which had nine ships, Fairlie Gilmore & Co with five, and Hogue Davidson also with five. Hugh Atkin Reid owned four and an unspecified number were possessed by Lambert & Ross. John Gilmore & Co and Hamilton & Aberdeen, notable Scottish shipbuilders in this Houses of Agency epoch, were involved in joint Indo-European ownership.[26]

In the field of insurance, 1780 witnessed European-style facilities being set up in Calcutta through Houses of Agency. This became more general by 1784. Agency owners acted as representatives for mushrooming companies: six in 1804, eight in 1808, 15 in 1832. Fairlie, Fergusson & Co, Hogue Davidson & Co, Campbell & Radcliffe, and Alexander & Co all acted for small firms like the Ganges Insurance Co and the Asiatic Insurance Co.[27]

The latter part of the eighteenth century was an excellent time for foreign investment. The American War of Independence meant capital was diverted to Asia, the bulk of which was invested via agency houses. In this way, 14 indigo factories had been built in Bengal by 1785. The Scot Thomas Baillie put up three and Charles Grant (a future Chairman of the EIC) funded an indigo plantation. Though later annulled, in 1778 the Scottish free-merchant Archibald Keir was given an agency loan for finding and developing lead and other minerals. Yet another, John Farquhar, was mining iron ore that was cast into shot and cannon for the Company. Using agencies, he was advanced 15,000 rupees (just under £2,000) for experiments. Agencies advanced the finance to build factories for producing silk, sugar and indigo and for items made from iron ore and copper. Funds poured into lead and coalmining.[28]

Infiltration of seaborne commerce by Scots was widespread. It attracted them in great numbers (both in a private capacity and as partners in agencies). One ship, the *Portland*, was even nicknamed 'The Scotch Frigate'. In the 1770s, before and after amalgamation with agency houses, shipowning Scots like Charles Grant and John Robinson were trading to Suez and Jedda. They operated alongside Asians in the Red Sea area, the Persian Gulf and Gujarat Peninsula. Their participation was greatest, however, along the coastal stretches of the Indian peninsula, the East Indies archipelago and in Chinese waters—the Pearl River and Canton in particular.

The EIC's official policy of non-involvement in the country trade and non-transportation of goods between India and China was at the heart of this invasion, providing opportunities that were not to be missed. By the 1780s the bulk of Scots shippers and skippers worked alongside or as part of agencies, carrying opium to Canton. These included John Fergusson, George Smith, Captains David Rannie, William Robertson, John Miller, John Lennox and John Waddell. Of course, each also used his personal cargo allowance to the full. Shipowning agencies, like David Scott's, were deeply involved, working in profitable partnership with Parsi merchants and a multitude of other Asians.[29]

From the mid-1760s, the East Indies archipelago was increasingly exploited by Scots and their fellow-Britons. Deals were done with the indigenous monarchs (still in control of their own affairs) and opium was regularly shipped from Bengal. As appetite for the drug increased, so a syndicate, the 'Bencoolen Opium Society', formed. This 'country' trader collective (consisting of men who were also part of one or other Indian agency) proved to be much better organised and more effective than Indian merchant collectives. Increasingly, ships carrying opium, some manufactures and raw cotton sailed from Bombay, Madras and Calcutta, funded by agencies there. They returned with peppers, cloves, nutmeg and cinnamon. Many continued *en voyage* to Canton with yet more opium, some returning with tea, but more usually bullion.

A great many Scottish merchants and skippers from the subcontinent were involved. Captain William Cleghorn brought 70 chests of opium from Calcutta; Captain McBride from Bombay carried the superior Malwar variety. The same year (1765) saw Captain Crawford and the *Lapwing*, together with Captain David Rannie on the *Success*, with more opium for sale. Rannie was back again in 1767.[30] In the 1770s, James Stevenson, Captain McIntosh, Captain Cathcart and a Mr Nairne made a great deal of money doing this. In 1771 Captain Orrock was operating both as a Bencoolen merchant and shipowner. Francis Light and his friend, the Scots country trader James Scott, were doing business in Phuket in the years 1771–79. Light recounted that he sold opium for four times what it cost him. Acquisition of Penang in 1786 meant India-based firms, such as Fairlie, Fergusson & Co of Calcutta, could more freely export opium to merchants in the archipelago. This agency allied with locals and others, such as the Scottish pepper planter David Brown and another Scot, James Carnegy of Penang.[31]

THE DAVID SCOTT AGENCY AND NETWORK

Any discussion of the early Scottish agency houses set up in Asia would be meaningless without an appreciation of David Scott's career. His activities permeate almost every facet of this commercial world between 1763 and 1813. His importance was enormous. Yet, while regarded as probably the major player involved with Houses of Agency, Scott was also carving out other illustrious niches: in Scottish politics and society, in the history of Parliament, the 'City' of London, and especially in the Court of Directors of the EIC. His exertions within the Company's executive and the roles undertaken on behalf of Prime Minister William Pitt and close ally Henry Dundas were exhaustive, especially during a time of war with the French.

These other roles are not part of this study. Even so, his near daily dialogue and liaison with his mentor Dundas might have affected his agency activities. Working from within India House and as an MP, while a confidant of Pitt and Dundas, Scott was in a position to influence commercial matters in the East that were of equal consequence to the government and to agencies.

This proximity to the nation's leaders and knowledge of their policies might suggest Scott provided central guidelines and had overall control over what took place within agencies abroad and at home. This is rather unlikely and no firm evidence of it has been found. Also, the need to proceed abroad with face-to-face negotiations precluded central control. It would have been too difficult when dealing with Asians over the funding, building and equipping of vessels. The individual arrangements each agency had to make with a skipper and his cargo also spelt out the same 'on the spot' requirement.

Because Scott was at the centre of the whole development of Houses of Agency and because of his enormous impact, it becomes very worthwhile to inspect his businesses and achievements since he and the close associates who acted with him were at the very core of agency work. Their activities best reflect the prominence attained by the Scottish elite in the Asian and Chinese commercial worlds. Also, Scott's career, in particular, illustrates the movement towards free trade and away from mercantilism, both abroad and in the metropolis.

Scott was the fifth son of Robert Scott of Dunninald, Forfarshire. He secured the interest required to proceed to India as a free-merchant through his grand-uncle, Sir John Lindsay (1737–88), MP for Aberdeen Burghs.[32] Although only 17 when he first set foot in Bombay in 1763, he quickly began to prosper and amass a fortune. The most important thing he did, shortly after arrival, was to establish the agency house of Scott, Tate and Adamson, which came to play a leading role in the political and financial affairs of Bombay.

From the start, Scott traded in opium, and he was to become one of the major dealers in that commodity. Though Patna was the most prominent opium station, during his years in India the headquarters of his firm remained in Bombay where the best quality opium (Malwar) was produced. He dealt mainly in the shipping of this drug and of raw cotton and silks to Canton, but also had a foothold in every place of consequence in the East Indies, especially Calcutta. In 1786, after a 23-year business career in India, he returned, the acknowledged leader of the free-merchants he had just left, with an exceptional knowledge of Eastern trade and an unsurpassed understanding of commercial concerns in western India.[33]

In London, despite the distance and time involved, Scott still kept a tight grip on affairs in India and elsewhere. He maintained an unbroken continuity in the handling of overseas business. There were no interruptions to friendships with individuals who had been close to him abroad. He was particularly scrupulous regarding financial matters. Close links were kept with Portuguese and Danish trading houses (which in the subcontinent depended on Scott for finance). It was the same with Parsi and other Asian merchants and owners of Houses of Agency. His own branches received loving attention. There was unshaken faith in his honesty among all who came in contact with him. These friendships and partnerships already made in India paid dividends back in Britain.[34]

For the first eight years following his arrival in the metropolis, Scott conducted business through the new agency he established: David Scott &

Co. (William Fairlie, who controlled the largest agency house in Calcutta, was also a leading partner in this firm.) However, in 1794 Scott, who had become a director of the East India Company in 1788, was forced to relinquish ownership of the London agency to his 12-year-old son and to trustees, because of an attack by the 'old' directors. They were opposed to an EIC executive owning an agency. They were also against Scott's tendency to dissolve trade restrictions, especially regarding shipping. He continued, however, as the driving force of what was now legally his son's business, bringing into his scheme of things able, assorted nephews, such as Andrew and Henry Shank and James Sibbald. The Indian, Portuguese, Armenian and Parsi merchants in India, like the Portuguese Luis Barretto and the Parsi Dady Naserwanji, both in Bombay, were urged to continue communication with himself and partner Alex Adamson, still in Bombay.[35]

The close friendships (involving agency business) that Scott maintained with six fellow Scots (not related to him) who formed the nucleus of his trading network require particular attention. These were very special people, involved in nearly all he did. Their shared correspondence lays bare the thoroughness and sheer professionalism that attended the running of their businesses. Chronologically, the first special association was made in Bombay with Alex Adamson and James Tate (Scott, Tate & Adamson). The next two lifelong amalgamations were both made in Calcutta: with William Fairlie and Alex Adamson (Scott, Adamson, Fairlie) lasting from 1786–1801; and with Scott, Fairlie, Fergusson, which ended in 1793 on Fergusson's demise. He had already returned to his homeland in 1790.[36] The remaining tie was with ship's commander John Lennox (and included his nephew, William Lennox, who became a partner in Scott's agency).

Scott and these men collaborated for most of his adult life. They had numerous joint business ventures. He was forever proposing and conducting schemes, all conveyed in tones of very close friendship and familiarity. With William Fairlie there was an exceptionally special relationship. Scott told Fairlie that when writing to him he felt he was facing a mirror and speaking to himself.[37]

The professionalism exhibited by Scott, in particular, is reflected in these letters. He shared plans and deepest misgivings. For example, in his opinion an agent employed by any one of them formed the weakest link—so had to be good and trustworthy. Scott could be utterly ruthless if the employee was found wanting in some way. Dishonesty was simply not contemplated. He often expressed the fear that everything would become dangerous should the contents of their mail be seen by others outside the privileged circle. He also made it a rule that they all exchange letters, so that there could be no secrecy or misunderstandings. The replies of his friends show a similar disposition towards frankness and cordiality.[38]

On behalf of all members of the group, but mainly for the benefit of Scott and Fairlie, ship's commander John Lennox flitted between Calcutta and Bombay and wherever else he was required. Details from a freight bill of 1782 concerning goods Lennox shipped from Scott in Bombay to Fairlie in Calcutta is a template for countless such transactions. The cargo was financed by a leading Parsi trader in Bombay, Dady Naserwanji, and the transaction had the blessing and additional help of the local EIC official, Rawson Hart Boddam (soon to become governor of Bombay).[39]

Together, the agencies jointly owned by Scott and his close confederates (as well as those each held outright) took the lead in the purchase and export of India goods. It was a concerted and extensive business network with a hub developing in London, though the major partners maintained agencies in Bombay, Calcutta and Canton, and subsidiary branches in Penang, Batavia, Manila, Macao and New York. Their presence impacted throughout India, South-East Asia and China. It was felt in the Persian Gulf, Europe, the USA, London and provincial business centres in the United Kingdom.[40]

Scott's voluminous correspondence shows that he did not spare himself. Effort was involved in making and maintaining an unbroken personal continuity with business partners. Perhaps his ability to build a close personal relationship into each commercial enterprise was the crucial factor in this success. He was very much 'hands on'. Nor did he neglect the commercial activities sustained with a roster of talented Scottish entrepreneurs. Though outwith his own cabal, the majority were involved with him in trading that required teamwork and collective activity. For the most part, these were fellow partners in Houses of Agency or ships agents: men like Boyd and Claud Alexander, Alex Brodie, Alex Colvin, John and Charles Forbes.[41] Almost all had followed Greenberg's two roads (when explaining how Scots reached Canton) of 'Counting house and Quarter-deck'.[42]

WHY SCOTTISH-CONTROLLED AGENCIES IN ASIA WERE SO SUCCESSFUL

Why Scottish free-merchants-cum-agents were at the forefront of this explosion of commercial activity shines through the existing texts. It was noted, for example, that to draw like-minded colleagues together they did not hesitate to generate networks. Many of these were of a social nature, such as Masonic lodges. Such lines of communication were almost a necessity. They augmented existing close-knit bonds and, by connecting Scots throughout India, China and all South-East Asia, brought them closer to one another commercially, creating a formidable force.

That these Scottish entrepreneurs did not confine their activities to fit in with British imperial designs is also indicated. In the pursuit of profit they were ruthless and selective, choosing when to engage with the thrust of empire and when to disengage. For instance, initially the EIC, the instrument used, was pivotal in every way for success. All revolved around the monopoly. Latterly, however, it was circumvented, then ignored; and finally (as far as trade in India was concerned) in 1813 passed over in the pursuit of free trade.

In the examples provided there is ample evidence of a practical approach by these Scots (not that this was unique). What is obvious, however, and seen particularly in the careers of David Scott and his friends, is a genuine friendship with already established cultures, with no apparent wish to upstage or thwart these fellow traders—in fact quite the opposite. Most Scottish entrepreneurs also recognised they must unite, trust one another and yet bond with wealthy indigenous Asians. They had to forge long-term relationships with the peoples they worked among and traded with. A surprising number of Scots surveyed seem to have accepted things largely as they found them, only grafting improvements where obvious and to the benefit of the local population as well as themselves. They also quickly realised that no matter the scale of their own funding, becoming a successful agency depended upon native support and alliance. It was a sensible approach and appreciated by locals.[43]

It can be argued that such commercial expertise was the product of prior centuries of Scottish trading; of hard-won experience from which remarkable levels of determination and a winning mindset had been wrought. It might be the case, therefore, that Scots exhibited qualities more suited for the jobs on hand than those of other ethnic groups. Of course, other facets were also at play. Parker rightly stressed strong ties of kinship among the Scots, and that most firms were almost family concerns, with 'trusted representatives in every port'.[44] The Scottish tongue also lent itself to close bonding. Familiar ways of talking tended to push men into whichever group made them feel most comfortable, especially when spiced with cultural differences. They would have gravitated together naturally, all leading to a deeper level of networking.[45]

Parker also stressed that they had to be able, willing and educated—and the latter was an area where Scots could point to superior schooling and commercial training.[46] They were from a society that had imbued Dutch commercial theory and method. In London a great number had attended what were called 'cypher' schools prior to setting sail. These taught basic arithmetic, bookkeeping and even codes for keeping secrets from prying eyes.[47]

The fact that the Scots owed their presence to a more select band of patrons than their English cousins also counted. Most were almost handpicked. From 1725 onwards they came via John Drummond of Quarrel, followed by Lord Milton and John Mackenzie of Delvine. The patronage baton passed to Henry Dundas and David Scott at the turn of the century. This pattern was in stark contrast to the inconsistent recruitment of most English candidates for posts.[48]

The Scots elite undoubtedly had a greater need than the English: they came from a land with more limited resources. For the Scots, given their poorer background, entrance to openings that betokened glittering wealth was quite irresistible. Of course, it might simply have been that the Scots were much greedier. What can be argued nonetheless is that these men were professionals to the core. They sustained a prominence unequalled in this era through simply knowing how to get things done. Indications of this professionalism emerge in this study, especially so with the David Scott consortium, illustrating why Scots were so central to the many commercial developments in India and South-East Asia in these years.[49]

Finally, it might be said that these representatives of the Scottish elite and bourgeoisie had the desire, tenacity, knowledge and expertise essential to improve and to progress. They searched for self-worth and quality of life. Given the opportunity in South-East Asia to operate on a level playing field would have freed them from long-held frustrations. The development of Houses of Agency certainly suited them, becoming the means by which they were able to bring to bear formidable attributes and to focus these on circumstances they wished to address. What they succeeded in doing proved to be special, a worthy worldwide contribution.[50]

NOTES

1. See Blair B. Kling, 'The Origin of the Managing Agency System in India', *Journal of Asian Studies*, 26, 1 (1966), 27–49.
2. See, for example, W.E. Cheong, 'Trade and Finance in China, 1784–1834', *Business History*, 7, 1 (1965), 34–47. Others are named in the footnotes.

3. Robert Blake, *Jardine Matheson: Traders of the Far East* (London: Weidenfeld & Nicolson, 1999), 12.
4. M. Greenberg, *British Trade and the Opening of China, 1800–1842* (Cambridge: Cambridge University Press, 1951), 44.
5. See A. Le Pechon, (ed.), *China Trade and Empire: Jardine Matheson & Co. and the Origins of British Rule in Hong Kong, 1827–1843* (Oxford: Oxford University Press, 2006), 211–277.
6. See C.H. Philips, *The Correspondence of David Scott 1787–1805*, 2 vols (Royal Historical Society, London: Camden 3rd Series, vol. LXXV, 1951); C.H. Philips, *The East India Company 1784 to 1834* (Manchester: Manchester University Press, 1961), 71–72, passim; James G. Parker, 'Scottish Enterprise in India in the Eighteenth century', in R.A. Cage (ed.), *The Scots Abroad: Labour, Capital and Enterprise* (London: Croom Helm, 1985), 191–219; Anne Bulley, *The Bombay Country Ships 1790–1833* (Richmond Surrey: Curzon Press, 2000); B.R. Tomlinson, 'The "Empire of Enterprise": Scottish Business Networks in Asian Trade, 1793–1810', *KIU Journal of Economics and Business Studies*, 8 (2001), 67–83; B.R. Tomlinson, 'From Campsie to Kedgeree: Scottish Enterprise, Asian Trade and the Company Raj', *Modern Asian Studies*, 36, 4 (2002), 769–791.
7. See also B.R. Tomlinson, '"The Only Merchant in Calcutta": John Fergusson and the Growth of British Private Trade in Bengal, 1775–1790', in Toyin Falola and Emily Brownell (eds), *Africa, Empire and Globalization: Essays in Honor of A.G. Hopkins* (North Carolina: Carolina Academic Press, 2011), 237–252.
8. Tomlinson, 'Scottish Business Networks', 67–83; see also Tomlinson, 'John Fergusson'; Philips, *Correspondence of David Scott*, 1, xix, 104–105, 176–177, 203–204; Philips, *East India Company 1784 to 1834*, 106; A. Webster, *The Twilight of the East India Company: The Evolution of Anglo-Asian Commerce and Politics 1790–1860* (London: Boydell, 2009), 52.
9. See Philips, *Correspondence of David Scott*, 1, x, xii; also P.J. Marshall, *East India Fortunes: The British in Bengal in the Eighteenth Century* (Oxford: Clarendon Press, 1976), 258.
10. Philips, *East India Company 1784 to 1834*, 72; also Philips, *Correspondence of David Scott*, 1, x; S.B. Singh, *European Agency Houses in Bengal, 1783–1833* (Calcutta: Firma K. L. Mukhopadhyay, 1966), 26.

11. George K. McGilvary, *Guardian of the East India Company: The Life of Laurence Sulivan* (London: I.B. Tauris, 2006), 89, 95–97, 138, 146, 148–149, 173–174, passim; Marshall, *East India Fortunes*, 163–167, 217–250, passim.

12. See Parker, 'Scottish Enterprise in India'; Tomlinson, 'Scottish Business Networks'; Tomlinson, 'From Campsie to Kedgeree'; also Marshall, *East India Fortunes*, 26–27; McGilvary, *Guardian of the EIC*, 9–12; George K. McGilvary, 'The Scottish Connection with India 1725–1833', *Études Écossaises, "Empire; Recherches en cours/Research in Scottish Studies"*, 14 (*Éditions littéraires et linguistiques de l'université de Grenoble*, 2011), 13–32; G.J. Bryant, 'Scots in India in the Eighteenth Century' *Scottish Historical Review*, LXIV, 1, 177 (1985), 22–41.

13. P.J. Marshall, 'The Bengal Commercial Society of 1775: Private Trade in the Warren Hastings Period', *Bulletin of the Institute of Historical Research*, 106, 42 (1993), 176, 184; see also P.J. Marshall, *Trade and Conquest: Studies of the Rise of British Dominance in India*, XIII (Aldershot: Variorum–Ashgate Publishing Company, 1993), 276, 300.

14. See A. Tripathi, *Trade and Finance in the Bengal Presidency, 1793–1833* (Calcutta: Oxford University Press, revised edition, 1979), iv–xi, 10–14; also Marshall, *Trade and Conquest*, IX, 191–213; and XI, 252.

15. For more on this trade see Blake, *Jardine Matheson*; H. Furber, 'The United Company of Merchants Trading to the East Indies, 1783–96', *English Historical Review*, 10 (1940), 138–147; Greenberg, *British Trade and the Opening of China*; Singh, *European Agency Houses*. See also Marshall, *East Indian Fortunes*, passim.

16. Tomlinson, 'Scottish Business Networks', 67–83.

17. See Parker, 'Scottish Enterprise in India', passim; McGilvary, 'Research in Scottish Studies', 24.

18. Marshall, *Trade and Conquest*, VI, 55, 56, also II, 289; Singh, *European Agency Houses*, 8, 31–32.

19. Unpublished database created and maintained by the author; Greenberg, *British Trade and the Opening of China*, 35; Philips, *Correspondence of David Scott*, 1; 11, 75; H. Furber, 'Trade and Politics in Madras and Bombay', in Asiya Siddiqi (ed.), *Trade and Finance in Colonial India, 1750–1860* (Oxford: Oxford University

Press, 1995), 66–98; Singh, *European Agency Houses*, 126–7. See also R. Craig, A. Nix, and M. Nix (eds), *Chronometer Jack: The Autobiography of the Shipmaster John Miller of Edinburgh (1802–1883)* (Dunbeath, Caithness: Whittles Publishing, 2008), passim.

20. Unpublished database created and maintained by the author.
21. See A.A. Cormack, *Colin Campbell 1686–1757, Merchant, Gothenburg, Sweden. His will —annotated, A Scoto-Swedish Study* (Aberdeen: Aberdeen Journals Ltd, 1960); George K. McGilvary, *East India Patronage and the British State: The Scottish Elite and Politics in the Eighteenth Century* (London: I.B. Tauris, 2008), Appendix, et passim.
22. See, for instance, British Library (hereafter BL), Add MS, 45424, ff. 1–147, Claud Alexander Correspondence with David Anderson, 1775–1785.
23. *East India Registers*, BL Asia & Africa Studies (hereafter A & A S), O/5/2/26 and O/5/28, 'Europeans not in the East India Company in Calcutta & Bengal 1808–1809'.
24. *Select List* created and maintained by the author.
25. Database maintained by the author.
26. Scottish shipbuilding dominance continued beyond 1813. By 1833, Cruttenden & Mackillop had become proprietors of the New Howrah Docks in Calcutta, Gilmore & Co. the largest ship-owning company.
27. Philips, *Correspondence of David Scott*, 1, 63; Marshall, *East Indian Fortunes*, 24; Marshall, *Trade and Conquest*, Xlll, 295; Singh, *European Agency* Houses, 18–23, 98–99, 108.
28. Marshall, *Trade and Conquest*, Vl, 57, 61–63; Marshall, 'Bengal Commercial Society', 174; Marshall, 'East Indian Fortunes', 153–154.
29. See Furber, 'Trade and Politics', 75–77, 98; Bulley, *The Bombay Country Ships*, passim; Tomlinson, 'From Campsie to Kedgeree', passim; McGilvary, 'Research in Scottish Studies', 21–22; also Craig, Nix and Nix, *Chronometer Jack*, ch. 16, et passim.
30. D.K. Bassett, 'British 'Country' Trade and Local Trade Networks in the Thai and Malay States, c. 1680–1770', *Modern Asian Studies*, 23, 4 (1989), 625–643; D.K. Bassett, 'British Trade and Policy in Indonesia and Malaysia in the late Eighteenth Century' (Zug, Switzerland: Hull monographs on South-East Asia, 1971),

3, 1–2, 22–27; see also McGilvary, *Guardian of the East India Company*, 79–80.

31. A. Webster, 'The Development of British Commercial and Political Networks in the Straits Settlements 1800 to 1868: The Rise of a Colonial and Regional Economic Identity?', *Modern Asian Studies*, 4, 45 (2011), 899–929; see also A. Webster, *Gentleman Capitalists—British Imperialism in Southeast Asia, 1770–1890* (London: I.B. Tauris, 1998), 41, 45, 53–82. Also, Tanja Bueltmann, Andrew Hinson, and Graeme Morton, *The Scottish Diaspora* (Edinburgh: Edinburgh University Press, 2013), 13, 230. They note that the first 17 trading houses in Singapore were Scottish.

32. See R.G. Thorne (ed.), *The History of Parliament: The House of Commons, 1790–1820* (London: Secker & Warburg, 1986); Philips, *Correspondence of David Scott*, vol. 1; James G. Parker, 'The Directors of the East India Company 1754–1790' (PhD, University of Edinburgh, 1977), 145–146, 241–242.

33. See BL, A & A S, Home Miscellaneous Series, MS 729, 283–287, D. Scott to Luis Barretto in Calcutta, 4 January 1794; H. Furber, *John Company at Work: A Study of European Expansion in India in the Late Eighteenth Century* (Cambridge, MA: Harvard, 1951), 210–211, 220.

34. See BL, A & A S, Home Miscellaneous Series, MS 729, 529, Scott to Tate, 2 February 1793. See also Ole Feldbæk, *India Trade under the Danish Flag, 1772–1808* (Copenhagen: Scandinavian Institute of Asian Studies, 1969), 239; Philips, *Correspondence of David Scott*, 1, xix, 29, 104–105, 176–177, 203–204.

35. See BL, A & A S, Home Miscellaneous Series, MS 729, 144–146, Scott to Luis Barretto, 4 January 1794; see also Philips, *Correspondence of David Scott*, 1, ix–xxii, 46; Philips, *The East India Company 1784 to 1834*, 66–67, 71–72.

36. Tomlinson, 'John Fergusson', 237–252.

37. BL, A & A S, Home Miscellaneous Series, MS 729, 151–153, Scott to William Fairlie in Calcutta, 4 January 1798.

38. See BL, A & A S, Home Miscellaneous Series, MS 230, 44, 63–65, Scott to William Lennox, May 1797 and 7 July 1797; MS 729, 83–84, Scott to Alex Adamson, 16 July 1797; 88–90, Scott to James Tate, 16th July 1797; 151–153, Scott to William Fairlie in Calcutta, 4 January 1798; 357–360, Scott to Alex Adamson, 5

September 1799. See also Philips, *Correspondence of David Scott*, 1, 29.

39. See BL, A & A S, Home Miscellaneous Series, MS 730, 44, 63–65, Scott to William Lennox, May 1797 and 7 July 1797; also Tomlinson, 'From Campsie to Kedgeree', 769–791.

40. See Tomlinson, 'From Campsie to Kedgeree', 769–791 for the voyage of the *Southampton* in 1781–85 and evidence of pioneering spirit.

41. See BL, A & A S, Home Series, MS 729, 83–84, Scott to Alex Adamson, 16 July 1797; see also 88–90, Scott to James Tate, 16 July 1797; 151–153, Scott to William Fairlie in Calcutta, 4 January 1798; 281–283, Scott to William Fairlie in Calcutta, 19 April 1799; 340–341, 357–360, 447 for Scott to Adamson on 12 July 1799, 5 September 1799 and 24 April 1800. See also Webster, *Twilight of the East India Company*, 26–27; Tomlinson, 'John Fergusson', 237–252; Tomlinson, 'Scottish Business Networks', 67–83; Philips, *Correspondence of David Scott*, I, 29.

42. Greenberg, *British Trade and the Opening of China*, 44, also 12, 29–32, 34–39, 43.

43. Emily Erikson, *Between Monopoly and Free Trade: The English East India Company, 1600–1757* (New Jersey: Princeton University Press, 2014), 2; also xii, 3, 13–15, 27–28. She too asserts that the EIC and private firms together had a 'decentralized, networked organizational form'.

44. Parker, 'Scottish Enterprise in India', 201–202.

45. See for example BL, Add MS 45424, Anderson Papers, ff.1–147 Claud Alexander, of the E India Co.'s service: Correspondence with D. Anderson: 1775–1785.

46. Parker, 'Scottish Enterprise in India', 201–202. For bookkeeping in Scotland see T.M. Devine, *The Scottish Nation 1700–2000* (London: Penguin, 2000), 26–27, 29, 62, 71, 91–100; also Rosalind Mitchison, *A History of Scotland* (London: Methuen & Co. Ltd, 1970), 297–298, 350–353, 369–370.

47. McGilvary, *Guardian of the EIC*, 127, reference to the 'Academy of Greenwich' providing this preparation.

48. McGilvary, *East India Patronage*, 21, 25–27, 104, 130–133, 146, 151–152, 166. English candidates depended more on EIC contacts and parliamentary friends rather than patronage managers.

49. For Scottish professionalism at this time see Grant Samkin, 'Trader Sailor Spy', Department of Accounting, Working Paper Series, no 85, University of Waikato, December 2005, 1–45. See also G.K. McGilvary, '"Honest John": The Remarkable Career of John Drummond of Quarrel, MP (1675–1742)', *History Scotland*, 15, 4 (2015), 24–30; and 15, 5 (2015), 30–35.

50. For a discussion on Scottish 'exceptionalism' see the introduction to this book and also John M. MacKenzie and T.M. Devine, 'Introduction', in John M. MacKenzie and T.M. Devine (eds), *Scotland and the British Empire* (Oxford: Oxford University Press, 2011), 9–24.

CHAPTER 5

Scots and the Imposition of Improvement in South India

Joanna Frew

In recent years, there has been a growing interest in the identities, mentalities and networks of imperial actors and their families.[1] This has enhanced our understanding of how and why families and individuals became part of the British imperial project. It has also helped explain behaviour in imperial roles, without artificially ascribing a neat set of philosophies to particular people. Rather, what is foregrounded, and more plausible, is how 'home' contexts, the pre-existing networks of family and friends, and the correspondence that persisted between metropole and far-flung corners of the empire, helped those in the empire sustain their identity and beliefs when faced with unfamiliar cultures.

This chapter investigates the influence of Scottish ideas of agricultural improvement on the work of a group of Scots-born administrators in the Baramahal region of the Madras Presidency, c.1790–1800. It suggests that familiar concepts of improvement were implemented in their South Indian collectorate in order to bring about far-reaching changes, based on an understanding of progress which correlated with family experiences in, and continued correspondence with, a fast changing Scotland in the mid-eighteenth century. But, this chapter also argues that, despite the

J. Frew (✉)
London, England

© The Author(s) 2017
T.M. Devine, A. McCarthy (eds.), *The Scottish Experience in Asia,*
c.1700 to the Present, DOI 10.1007/978-3-319-43074-4_5

altruistic rhetoric that surrounded the project, as was the case in Scotland (and many other locations), improvement was imposed by those with the power and capital to implement it.

By way of brief introduction to the subjects, Alexander Read was appointed head collector of the Baramahal in order to create a land settlement when the region was annexed from Tipu Sultan in 1791, after the Third Anglo-Mysore War. Encouraged by another Scot in Madras, he took as his sub-collectors Thomas Munro, William MacLeod and James Graham.[2] Together they worked in Baramahal until 1799 (until the Fourth Anglo-Mysore War), developing what was to become the *ryotwari* system, made famous by one of this group, Thomas Munro, who eventually became governor of Madras. They had all been soldiering for the East India Company throughout the 1780s, and Read in the 1770s, and as with many Scots had sought careers in India due to financial necessity. This was the first administrative position for the group and a chance to impress superiors by creating order in a war-ravaged region at a time when the Company was in need of income from new territory.

The *ryotwari* settlement, a settlement made directly with the cultivators (rather than through intermediaries, such as *zamindars* or village heads), was said latterly by Munro to reflect the land holding traditions of some areas of South India. However, within the *Baramahal Records* (the collectors' correspondence collated by Read), it is clear they were pursuing policies designed to bring deliberate changes to the social structure of the region. Unsurprisingly, this was resisted by a large proportion of society in the Baramahal, and the collectors' continued justifications for the *ryotwari* settlement reinforce the hypothesis that they held to familiar metropolitan concepts as a means to organise the economy of the Baramahal.

LAND SETTLEMENTS IN INDIA AT THE CLOSE OF THE EIGHTEENTH CENTURY

The appointment of these soldiers as collectors in the Baramahal was initially an 'emergency' posting at the end of the Third Anglo-Mysore War. Read was appointed directly by Governor-General Cornwallis as head collector for the Baramahal and Salem. Munro, MacLeod and Graham, his sub-collectors, had all served under him in the intelligence and supply unit and they worked together in the Baramahal from 1792–99 to 'settle' the region.[3] Cornwallis was concerned about the widely reported corruption of the civilian officials in Madras and for this reason, as well as his previous experience briefly managing two other conquered provinces, Read, although a military man, was chosen to manage the Baramahal.[4]

The Baramahal collectors' writings show that they were very much part of the 'expanding cult of nationality' under Cornwallis.[5] They subscribed to the idea that Britain could implement good governance in India, and identified with the imperial mission here. They saw themselves not as soldiers defending a private company, but as servants of Company and crown, working in 'pursuit of the National Objects', remedying the wrongs of the tyrannical Tipu Sultan.[6]

When they arrived in the Baramahal, the collectors primarily saw 'disorder' caused by war, mismanagement and excessive rent gathering.[7] They saw all around them 'heavy taxation, inadequate revenue to the state, administrative inefficiency, departmental corruption and the misery of the *ryots*', and were committed to developing policies that would transform both the situation of the *ryots*, and revenue for government.[8] The sense of purpose with which they approached their role exemplifies the way in which the imperial mission had been cleansed through the scapegoating of Governor Hastings and the appointment of Cornwallis.

Hastings' governorship had been characterised by aggressive conquest and the establishment of the first tax gathering system that the British set up, namely the Farming System. Under the Farming System, Hastings encouraged *zamindars* to bid for the role of tax collector on estates, an arrangement he believed would ensure that bids reflected the utmost value that local people placed on the land. Hastings claimed this system followed Bengali custom, but some Company servants and their supporters in Westminster regarded *zamindars* as landowners, similar to the British landed aristocracy, and believed this Farming System had destabilised their inalienable property rights.[9] It was the Whig defence of private property, manifested through the Supreme Council and Court in Bengal, that garnered support for a permanent settlement with recognisable landowners.

When Cornwallis was appointed governor general, therefore, it was left to him and his associates to prepare for a settlement that would reflect the notion of *zamindars* as a landowning class. A stable tax system would also allow the Company to reap more financial benefit. This culminated in the 'self-congratulatory' code of Permanent Settlement in 1793 (although not without controversy), whereby *zamindars* had their tax burden fixed in perpetuity and were left alone to manage their estates.[10] It allowed both the 'company apologists and government supporters' in Britain to feel satisfied with the Company's governmental role in India.[11] In this age of Whiggism where individual property rights, free from crown interference, were increasingly seen as the bedrock of liberty and progress, the idea of a despotic sovereign deciding at will who could hold land was anathema.[12] It was believed the Company had acted in such a manner, but now Cornwallis' Permanent Settlement allowed for laissez faire and more stable government in India.

In contrast to this laissez faire attitude, Nicholas Dirks has suggested that the possibility of transforming India through surveys, tax assessments and administration in remote areas became an accepted idea for men like Munro, Malcolm and Elphinstone, during their governorships around 1820; a process which would 'reverse the influence of Cornwallis'.[13] Dirks understands this as the next stage in the British process of establishing dominance in India. However, concurrent to Cornwallis' Permanent Settlement, these surveys and modes of management began to take place, albeit without proper authorisation.

Returning to the Baramahal, we find Read and his sub-collectors requesting of the Madras Board of Revenue that he be given time to find a 'just' settlement option before establishing anything permanent. It was assumed that some sort of permanent settlement would be established wherever the Company was acquiring new territory. The Madras Board of Revenue expected Read to be working on this. However, what the collectors' findings from their investigations of the region resulted in was a very different approach to revenue settlements. This was the origin of the *ryotwari* system, the settlement made directly with cultivators.

Although likely to have had some usage under previous South Indian rulers, the *ryotwari* settlement developed by Read, Munro, MacLeod and Graham was their invention and based on their notion of good governance and improvement. At the same time as supporting Cornwallis, Read showed he was aware that the work he had embarked on was unique, as he explained in a letter to his cousin Charles Wedderburn: 'I have taken upon me the devising and establishing of a system of revenue *very different from any hitherto adopted*, and consider the completion of it as a point of honour. Besides, I have pledged to my friend the Marquis Cornwallis not to leave India until that is done unless my state of health absolutely requires it.'[14]

Early in their collectorship the collectors began to participate in and try to control the annual agreements that were made between village heads and cultivators. They understood the existing tenurial arrangements as oppressive upon the *ryots*, who, in the collectors' metropolitan conceptions of ownership, seemed to be disadvantaged without a formal tenancy agreement and, thus, dependent on the favour of their traditional leaders. Thus, collectors believed that only contracts made directly between cultivators and the Company government would free *ryots* from oppression. The introduction of such 'secure' private property, the collectors believed, would bring about increased cultivation, and therefore increased revenue for the Company, as well as wealth for the inhabitants.

At this time, Read asked the Board if he could have funds to undertake a survey to determine the exact value of the land, but before the survey was completed, the collectors had become disillusioned with the Board's policy of permanent settlement, surmising that the poverty and 'oppression' they saw in the Baramahal came from the power of *patels* and *poligars* to extort higher than necessary rent from cultivators, whilst themselves paying little.[15] The collectors believed that often the peasants did not know when or how much rent was due from them and that they were easily exploited by their superiors, who kept them purposefully uninformed for their own gain.

Agriculture in the Baramahal region had suffered under Tipu's tax raising policies and also during the wars between the Mysore kingdom and the British. It was a sparsely populated area of mainly dry land. The social structure therefore was built around access to water, and differed between dry, wet and mixed 'zones'.[16] Stationed individually across the region in remote villages, the collectors carried out much investigation of their region and corresponded amongst themselves to develop their plans. After using the Mysorian system to make land tax collections in that first year, Read relayed to the Board that there were many problems with it.[17] The Board initially obliged Read's request to delay the introduction of a new settlement because they were happy with the revenue he was collecting and an interim five-year lease was set up with village heads, or *patels*, who in turn would create agreements with cultivators for individual farms or fields each year.

However, over the period of the five-year lease, the collectors involved themselves in the organisation of the tenures under the *patels*, effectively creating a *ryotwari* settlement without authorisation from Madras. In 1796, before the end of the five-year lease, Read issued a proclamation that stipulated annual leases made directly with *ryots* would become the mode of settlement. This was carried out without the Board's permission, and thus shows the lengths that Read was prepared to go to in order to establish his settlement.[18]

If this reversal of Cornwallis' influence, then, was not part of a future redefinition of empire, but contemporaneous with the Permanent Settlement, and engineered by men who supported the governor-general, and in contradiction of existing local structures, it must be asked why this divergence occurred.

UTILISING IMPERIAL NETWORKS AND METROPOLITAN IDEAS

The *Baramahal Records* show that the collectors responded with ease to the mandate to 'know' the country, and with apparent confidence set about developing their management structures. Although there do not appear to have been any very large estates in the Baramahal and Salem, this did not stop the government in Madras from expecting Read and his subordinates to organise the region as elsewhere in the Company's territories; for example, organising some areas of the Madras Presidency into *zamindar* estates, a policy that was carried into effect when Read resigned in 1800.[19] However, for the Scottish administrators in the Baramahal, commitment to this policy was conspicuously absent, despite their admiration of Cornwallis.[20] Indeed, there is no evidence that they seriously discussed among themselves the viability of large landed estates as a settlement option. Moreover, unlike other areas of the Presidency that were undergoing 'settlement' processes at the same time, they did not seek to make village heads the people through whom settlements would be established. Instead, their correspondence with regard to proprietorship centres on why organising tenures for individual farmers would be more appropriate, and how this would lead to an improvement in the lives of the majority of the people.

Where this radical departure originated, given the soldiers-turned-administrators' affiliation with Cornwallis, has been a matter of historical debate for some years. Much of this debate is centred on Munro's career, but it is clear from the *Baramahal Records* that the *ryotwari* system was not his own original idea and that the philosophical or ideological foundations can be traced further back than Munro's desire to curtail the power of *poligars* in this next posting.[21]

The detailed consideration of the survey plans in the *Baramahal Records* must be understood as the utilisation of the collectors' knowledge of improvement, inherited from their Scottish familial networks.[22] Not only was the idea for basing rent on soil type and labour innovative, but surveying was a new and booming profession in Scotland as land tenure throughout the country underwent a revolution, and to know the value of land became important information.[23] This was extended into the empire and a larger than average proportion of Scots were employed as surveyors in India from the end of the eighteenth century, which Martha McLaren explains as a result of their technical education.[24] Where Britishness allowed Scots to access the empire, Scottish experiences and training allowed Scots to excel in particular fields, as confirmed in other chapters of this book.

Although James Graham's family history is untraceable, personal papers and collections of family papers for the other three men reveal that they were typical of many young Scotsmen of the late eighteenth century, surrounded by Enlightenment ideas and absorbed in the related phenomenon of agricultural improvement. Contemporaneously to the age of Enlightenment, the pace of agricultural improvement quickened to such an extent in Scotland that historians regard improvement as an important political discourse and an equally discernible 'age'.[25] It was also supported by contemporary Scottish philosophical ideas about the progress of civilisation, namely, the 'four-stage theory of civilisation' which stated that all societies would move from barbarism to civilisation via pastoralism, agricultural production and commercialism.

Due to the volume of Munro's personal papers, an insight into how this era of Enlightenment played out in his family is readily available. His biographer, Gleig, describes Munro as an avid reader when a young man. As a boy, he revelled in stories of war and conquest in history books but, Gleig records, he soon grew interested in philosophy and ideas of government by men like Hume, and continued to have a particular interest in history.[26] Political discussion was an integral part of Munro's family life, and the family correspondence to and from India shows that all its members were familiar with political philosophy.[27] Munro also placed a great importance on philosophy and history, in order to understand the cultures in which he found himself, and to learn lessons for governance and public life.[28] The continued presence of these ideas in his administrative work has been demonstrated by McLaren. From his correspondence we know he read Adam Smith and Alexander Dow, as well as Orme, Gibbon and Turner, among others, whilst in India.[29] And when writing to his brother about his and Read's early plans for *ryotwari*, he almost directly quotes from Adam Smith's *Wealth of Nations*.[30]

Furthermore, both Read and MacLeod's families were influenced by the prospect of the benefits of improvement. MacLeod's experience shows the most obvious connection to improvement. After the disastrous leadership shown by his clan chief, Norman 22nd (1705–72), improvements were begun by the next chief, Norman 23rd (1754–1801). Norman 22nd's grandson was a much more liberal and earnest man, and when he assumed the chieftainship at age 18, MacLeod would have been aged 14. One of the earliest pieces of advice received by young Norman, who had grown up in Edinburgh, was that the abuses of his grandfather were caused by his desire to live among men of greater fortunes than he, as was the case for many Highland lairds. The younger Norman was advised to go and live with his people in Skye, which he did, beginning improvements to increase the revenue of the estates. In the early 1770s forests were felled to sell wood, and by the early 1780s the British Fishery Society was inspecting the area for the purpose of building villages and fishing ports.[31] Moreover, MacLeod and his brother were actively involved in these improvements as adults. William MacLeod bought a farm in the region and his brother introduced sheep walks.[32]

The Read and Wedderburn families were also involved in agricultural improvement.[33] In Scotland, the family was engaged in improvement in their county with George Dempster MP, an enthusiastic supporter of agrarian change. Read's cousin, Alexander Beatson, was a published land surveyor who also served in the Madras Army at the same time as Read, and although it is unclear how closely they worked together, they kept in touch whilst in India.[34] When Beatson returned to Scotland, he and his brother Robert continued to be active in improvement and were friendly with Adam Smith.[35]

Although in London and India for all of his adult life, it is clear that through his familial networks, Read's cultural and political influences were primarily Scottish, and that active 'improvers' made up an important part of that network. In fact, his closest correspondents throughout his time in India (aside from Munro) appear to have been Wedderburn and Beatson. To this end, Read's knowledge of improvement was likely to have been primarily derived through correspondence with family and shared reading. He had access to practical texts about improvement, and corresponded with his Wedderburn and Beatson cousins on such matters.

For Read, Munro and MacLeod, then, the intimacy with which they experienced the changes in Scotland, and the attendant ideas, were a defining part of their early lives. The popularity of 'improvement', as noted, was contemporaneous to the Enlightenment in Scotland but was also part of the process of Scottish integration and the creation of the hybrid identity of Scottishness and Britishness in the British Union. Likewise, Scottish identity took on a new British character for many of the middle classes, summed up in the concept of 'North Britishness', though this was essentially a hybrid of both Scottishness and Britishness.[36] The Baramahal collectors were part of this positive reframing of Scotland, using their North British identity as part of the British Empire.

It should be noted, however, that Protestantism, another important factor in the construction of British identity,[37] does not feature in the correspondence (familial and otherwise) of the Baramahal collectors, either explicitly or implicitly. Alongside commerce and the rule of law, Protestantism was regarded as one of the defining characteristics of Britain's empire. Yet the collectors have little to say about matters of the spirit and, instead, the focus is on 'man and society' or science. This supports Colin Kidd's thesis that the distinction between temporal and spiritual matters remained important for Scots, despite their union with England.[38]

Moreover, it is also a consequence of the actual background of each collector, where there was no committed Protestant heritage in the immediate family background. Read, who spearheaded the new *ryot-wari* system, was from a Catholic Jacobite background but the Read and Wedderburn families were well integrated into 'Britain' by the end of the eighteenth century. Munro's family were religiously moderate, if religious at all, and much more interested in discussing political theory than religion. MacLeod's father remained loyal to his clan chief, who was expected to fight with Bonnie Prince Charlie, but instead brought out 700 men for the Hanoverian cause, suggesting that this family were happy to be identified with the Hanoverians. However, MacLeod makes no mention of his religious views. This reinforces the point that the collectors' inspiration was drawn from the contemporary economic and 'scientific' theories of the day and that these were utilised aspirationally.

Importantly, and evidenced in the archival material, the effects of the Enlightenment in Scotland are no longer considered to have been the preserve of the Edinburgh literati. Mark Towsey has investigated the popularity of reading for self-learning in Scotland in the second half of the eighteenth century. It was not simply a university occupation, but took place across the country; in libraries, manses and homes, a broad cross-section of society engaged with the theories and ideas of the Scottish literati as a way of making sense of society and as a guide for how to live well, in an 'enlightened' or civilised manner.[39] In cities, literary clubs were established by different groups. For example, in Glasgow the Morning and Evening Club, frequented by businessmen, read the newspapers and discussed parliamentary developments over breakfast.[40] Significantly, the Indian empire featured in discussions in these types of clubs across Scotland, where lawyers, businessmen and others had a stake in the Company through bonds and shares and were interested in its development.[41] News from India also figured in the discussions of informal social networks: interestingly, Munro's letters of news from India and his descriptions of the Mysore wars were highly complimented by the various generals and lawyers who came to hear them, according to his father.[42]

The Baramahal collectors did not have the status to connect with the high echelons of 'improvers', political economists or moral philosophers. They did not carry on correspondence with these people whilst in India, nor did they become Orientalist scholars.[43] Yet, as the families of these men were enmeshed in the connected worlds of either the Scottish Enlightenment or agricultural improvement, these worlds provided a shared foundation for the Baramahal collectors as they worked together in India and continued to draw upon their Scottish identity and networks. It should not be a surprise therefore that many of the collectors' ideas resonated with those of Scottish 'improvers' and political economists.

THE IDEAS BEHIND THE *RYOTWARI* SETTLEMENT

The first step for a *ryotwari* settlement was to survey the land and 'know' its value. In his plans to establish a 'just' settlement, Read was eager to survey all the land under his jurisdiction. He believed that the fields and villages of the region 'probably have never been thoroughly examined before unless by private individuals and certainly have never been all formed into a proper system of revenue management'. In an exhortation at the end of this same letter to his assistants he set out explicitly what his aim was:

> As just hinted and as all the registers and reports will more fully indicate, my plan is not confined to a <u>revenue survey</u> of the country but meant to comprehend all the knowledge it is possible to acquire of its geography, populations, stock, agriculture, manufactures and trade, the distinctions among its inhabitants, their various customs, prejudices and conditions of life. In short, it is not merely my aim to ascertain the extent of private and

public revenue, *but in imitation of our Board of Agriculture*—'to examine the sources of public prosperity, and devise a means of promoting the
improvement of the people founded on a <u>Statistical Survey</u> or a Minute and
careful enquiry into the actual state of every district, & the circumstances
of its inhabitants' ... attempting everything that is possible in an undertaking which may bring so much benefit to thousands and satisfaction to our
employers.[44]

The quotation Read used here is taken directly from the plans for a survey of England by Britain's new Board of Agriculture, established by the
Scottish MP John Sinclair, who pioneered and edited the first Statistical
Account of Scotland in 1790.[45] These aims of the Board of Agriculture
for its survey must have been written in the early 1790s, although the
earliest records available are from 1796, raising an important point that,
given the time it took to receive letters in a Presidency outpost, Read had
kept abreast of contemporary plans for agricultural improvement, possibly
through his Beatson cousins, Robert Beatson having written one of the
first surveys for the Statistical Account.[46]

The preference among many Scottish writers, thinkers and practitioners of improvement was for land to be securely leased or owned in reasonably small sized units so that each landholder or tenant farmer could
directly oversee the implementation of improvement schemes from which
they would benefit, and therefore diligently carry them out. In practice,
most improvement schemes were carried out by landowners, who had the
necessary capital and motivation behind them. And although an idealism
fuelled this movement, much of it was necessitated by the insolvency of
smaller landowners and the financial necessity to become efficient.[47] As we
shall see, this disconnect between theory and practice also applied in the
Baramahal.

However, it is not the case that the collectors arrived in the Baramahal
with fixed ideas of what type of settlement they would put in place. As
noted, existing tenures and farming practices were investigated in more
detail than in most other collectorates. Yet the problems that the collectors
believed they diagnosed resulted in a settlement that drew on their own
conclusions about what was, in their view, most appropriate for increasing
the 'comfort' of the *ryots* and extracting revenue for the Company.[48] The,
apparently, sincere conviction that they could achieve both these aims at
once affirms the influence of metropolitan economic theories upon imperial policymaking.

It is clear that the collectors spent much time investigating and learning about Baramahal society. In some senses they displayed a tolerance and openness that Martha McLaren argues, in her study of Munro, was a result of a religiously tolerant attitude.[49] Their lack of explicit religious references in contrast to Munro's family discussions on politics and Read's absorption in the technicalities of rent calculations point to a more secular interest in 'progress'. In fact, the only explicit references to religion show that Read was keen that there should be freedom for the practice of local religions.[50]

At a time when improvement was a popular passion in Britain and when it formed the basis of the Company government's legitimacy, it should not be seen as surprising or contradictory that the Baramahal collectors' settlement differed markedly from the *zamindari* Permanent Settlement. To the understanding of these Scottish collectors, they were fulfilling Cornwallis mandate to provide security of property in South India. It is this presumption that they would provide better security that clashed with the existing understanding of security in the Baramahal and led to the imposition of improvement, so often the case in Britain and its empire.

IMPROVEMENT FROM ABOVE

In the early years of the system, Read was unapologetic that *patels* (village heads) and *poligars* (military chieftains) would inevitably feel a loss in their social and economic status, but under his settlement procedure he nevertheless welcomed (he said) the petitions he received from these traditional upper strata of society. He claimed he was 'Desirous of bringing forward all possible objections to the survey that may appear in the hope that by answering them in full now, no question in regard to the propriety of our measures may remain to be decided on after our time'.[51] Yet, despite allowing for these petitions, he still held that grievances were exaggerated and the complainants were only trying to retain overprivileged and unjust positions.[52] Since the collectors did not believe that these privileged positions were hereditary, they assumed it was possible to remove people from such positions and do away with the roles altogether, despite the changes to the social structure this entailed, if it answered the need for improvement.[53] As well as being told they were no longer responsible for the culturally important roles of dividing shares of land amongst villagers and collecting taxes, *patels* had to accept huge increases in rent as a result of the survey. Read was of the opinion that 'The patels and other superior renters being the class of people, and I hope the only class that will suffer by the survey', it was:

> natural for them to oppose it with all their influence and it is no crime in them doing so; therefore their struggles to preserve their advantages deserve to be treated with every possible indulgence, and in my opinion very liberal allowances should be made to them as compensation for discharging the functions of their official situations, which would make up for the difference they find in the new system.[54]

The indulgence that was to be shown was the offering of a remission on rent due in hard times, but the fixed assessment rates did not change.

The 'struggles' of the *patels*, however, were contestations that had been acceptable under previous governments, and were seen as part of the role of headmen who would act as negotiators between cultivators and government.[55] Read and his assistants, on the other hand, used their position as an outside, imperial power to impose settlements on recalcitrant *patels* and *poligars*. The collectors would hear petitions as the *patels*' 'superiors' and to make some sort of remission to ease the transition, but the principle of 'equalisation' was not to be undone. Although petitioning the collector was still permitted, any further actions, or expectations of major change, were regarded as criminal. Those who accepted the Company's political encroachments and land settlements were favoured, but those who remained outside the settlements were viewed as rebels.

One of the aims of Scottish writers and 'improvers' was to encourage clan chiefs to give up their 'non-economic privileges and the non-economic dependence of their people'. Instead, they were to 'let land to farmers who would provide maximum return, skill, industry and capital'.[56] Indeed, the new settlements in the Baramahal and the responses to them bear striking similarities to schemes for improvement in the Annexed Estates of the Scottish Highlands, where state power was complete.[57] Initial resistance to these schemes was from tacksmen, who occupied a comparable position to that of *patel*, and whose economic and cultural role was similarly attacked as in the *ryotwari* settlement. When the estates of prominent Jacobites were annexed after the Jacobite rebellion in 1745, the power to grant leases for farming on these estates was given to crown-appointed commissioners and factors who pursued a policy of security of tenure for individual farmers on small farms. They carried out a survey to assess the value of land and tried to eradicate subletting, which was thought to make individuals 'dependent' on the favour of the Highland middlemen. The goal of the commissioners was to create an independent class of landholders, not bound by loyalty to tacksmen or lairds, who would therefore be free to pursue improvement in agriculture. Those who did not become landholders would become hired labour, again, it was thought, severing the ties of traditional loyalties.[58]

As for the *ryots*, their economic security was based on the negotiating powers of a village headman, who would negotiate with the tax collecting regime. However, the individual tenures of the *ryotwari* settlement cut away at traditional patterns of social insurance and limited the opportunities for farmers to negotiate down the heavy assessments as they had done in the past, since *ryots* were now landholders with only the government above them. The Baramahal collectors also stood outside the local economy and, despite the still unsettled position of the Company, did not need to find legitimacy for their presence through conciliatory government. Rather, the collectors believed they offered a different type of security based on private property rather than interdependent necessity. Those who defied them were punished and coerced into accepting the Company's authority.

Yet the coercion, nor the incentives, succeeded in encouraging the *ryots* to increase the size of their farms and extend cultivation, as was the great hope of the Baramahal collectors. Therefore, another improvement strategy was developed by Read. As early as 1793, he was seeking advice from medical personnel about what sorts of crops might grow well in the region.[59] Read explained to his sub-collectors that he hoped other Europeans living in the Baramahal would enter into leases for the cultivation of plantation crops, and lead the way as an example to the *ryots*. The purpose of these plantations was not, he claimed, to export produce but to circulate more goods throughout the Baramahal, another mode of encouraging agricultural improvement.[60] When European farmers were not forthcoming, in 1795 MacLeod and Munro proposed to the Board of Revenue that with their own capital they would purchase land and set up an indigo plantation. The Board, albeit after serious consideration, rejected this proposal because Company servants were barred from holding land.[61]

Munro and MacLeod's motives were not altogether altruistic, and it is unlikely that circulation of goods in the Baramahal was the primary concern. Munro's brothers, Daniel and Sandy, were also in India, operating as private plantation owners, and they encouraged Munro in the idea that a plantation would be more lucrative than a Company career, which for Munro's indebted family in Glasgow would have been very helpful.[62]

Moreover, Munro also noted that the reason Read took the Tiruppattur district as his collectorate was because it 'yields about 40,000 pagodas to himself in order to make experiments'.[63] In other words, this was Read's personal income from the Baramahal rents that he was using to create profitable agricultural schemes.

By 1797 Read had invited 'West India planters' to inspect the region for the development of larger sugar plantations to help meet British demand (contrary to his original stated aims for plantations). This was made clear in Read's justification for seeking advice from West Indies planters when he told the Board of Revenue that sugar plantations were especially necessary with the West Indies plantations in their 'present ruinous state … from which they cannot, especially without slaves, recover for some years', and therefore could not meet the British demand for sugar.[64] Presumably he was referring to the rebellions, such as those in Grenada and St Lucia, which had recently occurred. Far from seeking the circulation of goods in the Baramahal, this was Read's plan to draw the region into the global British economy through the establishment of sugar plantations. These schemes were a departure from the local customs and based instead on British assumptions of economic growth, and even the collectors' own wealth, which was unlikely to be circulated in the Baramahal economy.

The collectors offered many incentives for local people to take on the establishment of plantations, such as *tackavi* and providing free plants, but there was little interest from the inhabitants in leasing government land for plantations, or working on them.[65] And this, finally, reveals the most authoritarian aspect of the introduction of improvement schemes to the Baramahal. Without the need for explanation or justification as to its rightness, MacLeod wrote to Read requesting that he be allowed to move prisoners to work on the plantations as his jails were overflowing.[66] Faced with a lack of voluntary take-up of plantation work, the collectors relied on the forced labour of convicts to ensure the success of improvement schemes. Despite the rhetoric of improvement, the manner in which protest or non-compliance with settlements was dealt with was backed up by the force of imperial power.

CONCLUSION

In the imperial setting, as Read recognised, government had all the power at this early stage of East India Company presence in the Baramahal. He and his sub-collectors were, effectively, law maker, judge, jury and executioner. Their ethics were not derived from a strong sense of Protestantism (as noted, they rarely mentioned religion or God) but rather from the contemporary ideas on man and society and the nature of progress. These theories were pioneered by their countrymen and were, thus, popular and formative for many young Scots in the second half of the eighteenth century. Although the Baramahal collectors did not name the four-stage theory of civilisation, for example, their correspondence shows that they believed the Indians of the Baramahal were fully able to progress along the lines of European societies. There was no question that they would not want to; what had been holding them back was Tipu's tyrannical government. Agricultural 'improvement' would allow this to happen, and it is here that the Baramahal collectors make their influences obvious. The writing of Sir John Sinclair and Adam Smith both feature and it is clear that the idealism is drawn from contemporary and quite specific metropolitan influences.

Yet, on the other hand, in this region, as in many others (and most relevantly across Scotland), progress was imposed to create a new more compliant social order. Despite the rhetoric in Scotland and across Britain, improvement was only possible through landowner capital and enterprising tenants who were able to weather the rent hikes and consolidate holdings at the expense of poorer tenants.[67] After the Jacobite rebellion, improvement was imposed directly by agents of the state. This 'agrarianism' also saw a concerted 'move against more complex, shifting or communal forms of tenure' in India.[68] In the Baramahal the collectors had total legislative control and used this to push plans that were alien to the local culture. Concepts from home were, in this instance, translated into the imperial context with a confidence and vigour that allowed the collectors to develop a new settlement, bolstered by Read's continued correspondence with family and the sharing of knowledge across the empire.

NOTES

1. Margot Finn, 'Family Formations: Anglo India and the Familial Proto-state' in David Feldman and Jon Lawrence (eds), *Structures and Transformations in Modern British History* (Cambridge: Cambridge University Press, 2011), 100–118; Angela McCarthy (ed.), *A Global Clan: Scottish Migrant Networks and Identities since the Eighteenth Century* (London: Tauris Academic Studies, 2006); John M. MacKenzie and T.M. Devine (eds), *Scotland and the*

British Empire (Oxford: Oxford University Press, 2011); A. Mackillop and Steve Murdoch (eds), *Military Governors and Imperial Frontiers c. 1600–1800* (Leiden: Brill, 2003); Avril A. Powell, *Scottish Orientalism and India: The Muir Brothers, Religion, Education and Empire* (Woodbridge: Boydell Press, 2010); Jane Rendall, 'Scottish Orientalism: From Robertson to James Mill', *The Historical Journal*, 25, 1 (1982), 43–69; Emma Rothschild, *The Inner Lives of Empire* (Woodstock: Princeton University Press, 2011).

2. Munro to his father, 14 April 1793, in Rev. G.R. Gleig, *The Life of Major General Sir Thomas Munro, Bart.* (London: Henry Colburn and Richard Bently, 1830), 146.

3. Alexander Read to Cornwallis, 14 January 1792, Cornwallis Papers, Public Records Office (hereafter PRO): PRO/30/11/46, 459; Extract from letter to Read from Board of Revenue, 25 June 1793, Reports on the Settlement of the Baramahal, Boards of Control General Records (Board's Collections), India Office Records (hereafter IOR), British Library: Asian and African Studies, IOR/F/4/4/685.

4. Burton Stein, *Thomas Munro: The Origins of the Colonial State and His Vision of Empire* (Oxford: Oxford University Press, 1989), 38.

5. Nicholas B. Dirks, *The Scandal of Empire: India and the Creation of Imperial Britain* (London: Belknap Press of Harvard University Press, 2006), 204.

6. Munro to his sister Erskine, 10 August 1792, Munro Papers, India Office Private papers (Mss Eur), British Library: Asian and African Studies, MssEur/F151/141, 103; Munro to his mother, 10 January 1794, MssEur/F151/142, 1v; Munro's father to Thomas, 29 February 1792, MssEur/F151/147, 115; Munro to his father, 14 April 1793, MssEur/F151/141, 119.

7. See Baramahal Records (hereafter BR): Management, IOR/V/27/46/196 and Land Rent IOR/V/27/46/200, 1792–1799.

8. Nilmanhi Mukherjee, *The Ryotwari System in Madras 1792–1827* (Calcutta: Firma K.L. Mukhopadhyay, 1962), 7.

9. Bernard S. Cohn, *Colonialism and its Forms of Knowledge* (Princeton, NJ: Princeton University Press, 1996), 60–61; Robert Travers, '"The Real Value of Land": The Nawabs, the British and the Land Tax in Eighteenth Century Bengal', *Modern Asian Studies*, 38, 3 (2004), 532.

10. This Permanent Settlement meant that the *zamindars*, in accepting full property rights under the new government, had less need to abide by social customs that protected poorer peasants. Bankimchandra Chattopadhyay, a Bengali nationalist, wrote in 1872 that British rule had destroyed the Hindu moral code, which the middle and upper classes had accepted, but had not replaced it with another 'bond of social union'. Jon E. Wilson, *The Domination of Strangers: Modern Governance in India 1780–1835* (Palgrave: MacMillan, 2008), 183.

11. Robert Travers, 'Contested Despotism: Problems of Liberty in British India', in Jack P. Greene (ed.), *Exclusionary Empire: English Liberty Overseas, 1600–1900* (Cambridge: Cambridge University Press, 2010), 207–209.

12. Robert Travers, 'Ideology and British Expansion in Bengal, 1757–72', *The Journal of Imperial and Commonwealth History*, 33, 1 (2005), 49.

13. Dirks, *The Scandal of Empire*, 240.

14. Read to his cousin Charles Wedderburn, August 1794, Wedderburn Papers (hereafter WP), Dundee City Archives (hereafter DCA): Gifts and Deposits, GD131/Box 30, Italics added.

15. Read's 7th Report to the Board of Revenue, 15 August 1794, Board's Collections, IOR/F/4/4/685.

16. David E. Ludden, *Peasant History in South India* (Princeton, NJ: Princeton University Press, 1985), 82–94.

17. Read to the Board, 24 November 1792, BR: Management, IOR/V/27/46/196, 134.

18. Mukherjee, *The Ryotwari System*, 12.

19. Settlement of the Revenues of Baramahal, Salem and Kistnagharry (Perpetual zamindari), January 1804, Boards Collections, IOR/F/4/149/2515.

20. Stein, *Thomas Munro*, 46–7.

21. Stein believes Munro's aim, as he developed the *ryotwari* system in his next posting, was a system of tenure that would allow a complete military takeover of the Baramahal, reducing every caste and class to renter or revenue servant, and a more distant authority (in other words the British crown) above the population with himself as the representative. Stein, *Thomas Munro*, 51–9, 347–348.

22. Read explained his plans for the calculation of rent to the Board in his *Fifth Report*, June 1793. The other collectors were asked to

respond to this report first, and both Munro and MacLeod contributed thoughts on the question of basing rent on soil type. Read to the Board, June 1793, Munro to Read, 31 July 1793, MacLeod to Read, 18 September 1793, BR: Land Rent, IOR/V/27/46/200, 1–7, 58–59, 65.

23. T.C. Smout, 'Where had the Scottish Economy got by the Third Quarter of the Eighteenth Century', in Istavan Hont and Michael Ignatieff (eds), *Wealth and Virtue: The Shaping of the Political Economy in the Scottish Enlightenment* (Cambridge: Cambridge University Press, 1983), 67.

24. Martha McLaren, *British India & British Scotland, 1780–1830: Career Building, Empire Building and a Scottish School of Thought on Indian Governance* (Akron, OH: The University of Akron Press, 2001), 25.

25. Anand C. Chitnis, *The Scottish Enlightenment and Early Victorian English Society* (London: Croom Helm, 1986), 6; Colin Kidd, 'North Britishness and the Nature of Eighteenth-Century British Patriotisms', *The Historical Journal*, 39, 2 (1996), 367.

26. Gleig, *The Life of Sir Thomas Munro*, 5–9.

27. Munro to his mother, August 1794, MssEur/F151/142, 8, Munro to his sister Erskine, 5 March 1795, quoted in Gleig, *The Life of Sir Thomas Munro*, 86; Philip Flynn, *Enlightened Scotland* (Edinburgh: Scottish Academic Press, 1992), 269; Munro to his mother, 10 August 1794, MssEur/F151/142, 1–2; Munro to his mother, 31 December 1792, MssEur/F151/141, 107.

28. Gleig, *The Life of Sir Thomas Munro*, 7–9.

29. For example, McLaren believes that Munro's style of leadership was heavily influenced by Smith's *Theory of Moral Sentiments* and thinks it is no accident that Munro asked his brother to send a copy of the book when he started his administrative career in 1792. McLaren, *British India & British Scotland*, 196; Account Papers 1814–1820, MssEur/F151/169, 39–76.

30. He states in quotation marks that the government need not worry about the revenue settlement they were establishing with *ryots* because, '[an] equal quantity of labour will always yield the same produce'. Munro to his brother Daniel (n.d.), MssEur/F151/139, 37v. Unfortunately, the remaining pages of Munro's letter to his brother are missing and the description he gives his brother of the *ryotwari* settlement ends after the quotation above.

31. Canon R.C. MacLeod, *The Book of Dunvegan: Being Documents form the Muniment Room of the MacLeods of MacLeod at Dunvegan Castle, Isle of Skye* (Aberdeen: The Third Spalding Club, 1939), 8–10, 13–15.

32. Donald MacKinnon and Alick Morrison, *The Macleods – The Genealogy of a Clan* (Edinburgh: Clan MacLeod Society, 1969), Section 3, 120; Letter from Christina MacLeod to James Grant, Collector of Taxes, Inverness, 28 August 1809, Warrand of Bught Papers, National Archives of Scotland (hereafter NAS), GD23/6/460.

33. Papers regarding new mill (1805), Box 7/Bundle 3; Papers regarding sheep grazing on Catlaw Hill, Box 3/Bundle 7; Papers on barley samples (1810) Box 5/Bundle 19; Extracts from Strathmore Farming Association, February 1820, Box 10/Bundle 20; House plan and grounds plans (1802), Box 25; Read to Charles Wedderburn, February 1796, Box 30, WP, GD131; Richard Torrence, *The Reads of Auchenleck, Balmachie, Cairney, Drumgeith, Logie, Montpelier, Turfbeg and in India* (Edinburgh: printed privately, 1985), 18.

34. Beatson's Appointment as Surveyor of Kistna and Godavari rivers, Board's Collections, IOR/F/4/17/754; Read to Charles Wedderburn, WP, GD131/Box 25 and loose letters.

35. D. Winch, 'Adam Smith', http://www.oxforddnb.com/view/article/25767?docPos=1 (accessed 3 April 2012); McLaren, *British India & British Scotland*, 195.

36. Kidd, 'North Britishness', 361.

37. Linda Colley, *Britons: Forging the Nation 1707–1837* (London: Yale University Press, 1992), 43–54.

38. Kidd, *North Britishness*, 365.

39. Mark R.M. Towsey, *Reading the Scottish Enlightenment: Books and their Readers in Provincial Scotland, 1750–1820* (Leiden: Brill, 2010), 50–57, 164–175, 210–215.

40. Andrew Hook and Robert B. Sher, 'Introduction' in Andrew Hook and Robert B. Sher (eds), *The Glasgow Enlightenment* (East Linton: Tuckwell Press, 1995), 5.

41. Stefanie Metze, *An Imperial Enlightenment? Notions of India and the Literati of Edinburgh, 1723–1791* (PhD dissertation, University of Aberdeen, 2011), 37–40.

42. See, for example, Letter from his father to Munro, 29 February 1792, MssEur/F151/147, 115.

43. For example, Guha is able to connect Alexander Dow to Scottish political economists because he corresponded with Hume and Fergusson. Ranajit Guha, *A Rule of Property for Bengal: An Essay on the Idea of Permanent Settlement* (London: Duke University Press, 1996), 14–15.

44. Read to his Assistants, 10 April 1797, BR: Arrangements, Tamil Nadu State Archives (hereafter TNSA), vol. 160 (18196), 13. Italics added. Underlining in original.

45. Sir John Sinclair (Bart), *The Statistical Account of Scotland. Drawn up from the Communications of the Ministers of the Different Parishes* (Edinburgh: William Creech, 1791).

46. Robert Beatson, *A General View of the Agriculture of the County of Fife, With Observations on the Means of its Improvement* (Edinburgh: George Cawthorn, 1792), 1.

47. T.M. Devine, *The Transformation of Rural Scotland: Social Change and the Agrarian Economy* (Edinburgh: John Donald, 1999), 64–65.

48. Read to Cornwallis, 20 February 1794, BR: Arrangements, vol. 159 (18195), Doc No. III.

49. McLaren, *British India & British Scotland*, 159.

50. Read to French Missionary Abbe Dubois, 12 September 1797, BR: Property, IOR/V/27/46/199, 81.

51. Read to MacLeod, 27 April 1796, BR: Land Rent, IOR/V/27/46/200, 112.

52. Read to the Board, 30 December 1795 and Read to MacLeod, 27 January 1796, BR: Land Rent, IOR/V/2746/200, 68–69, 73.

53. Read to the Board, Appendix 2: Sketch of revenue management in countries north of the Caveri under the Gentu, the Moorish, and the Honourable Company's Government, 24 November 1792, BR: Management, IOR/V/27/46/196, 137–139; Read to MacLeod, 20 March 1798, BR: Land Rent, IOR/V/2746/200, 137.

54. Read to MacLeod, 27 January 1796, BR: Property, IOR/V/27/46/199, 76.

55. Mukherjee, *The Ryotwari System*, 67.

56. Eric Hobsbawm, 'Scottish Reformers of the Eighteenth Century and Capitalist Agriculture' in E.J. Hobsbawm, W. Kula, A. Mitra, K.N. Raj, I. Sachs (eds), *Peasants in History: Essays in Honour of Daniel Thorner* (Calcutta: Oxford University Press, 1980), 11.

57. The Annexed Estates were those that had belonged to lairds who fought for the Jacobite cause in 1745. Their property was confiscated and many of them were hanged.

58. Annette M. Smith, *Jacobite Estates of the Forty-Five* (Edinburgh: John Donald, 1982), 27, 58–59.

59. Read to the Board, n.d., BR: Management, IOR/V/27/46/196, 173.

60. Read to MacLeod, 7 February 1794, BR: Arrangements, vol.160 (18196), Doc. IV.

61. Copies of correspondence between Read and the Board, 1794, BR: Arrangements, Doc. XCVI; 'Proposal of Captain Read's Assistants in the Baramahal to rent a District for the Purpose of introducing & extending cultivation of cotton etc. Rejected', Boards Collections, IOR/F/4/17/752, 12–14.

62. Munro to his brother Daniel, n.d., c.1794, Mss Eur/F151/139, 32–33.

63. Munro to Daniel, n.d., Mss Eur/F151/139, 38.

64. Read to the Board, 1 October 1797, BR: Products, IOR/V/27/46/198, 121–123.

65. Read to Hamilton, 5 March 1797, BR: Products, IOR/V/27/46/198, 84.

66. Read to Board, 2 September 1795, BR: Police, IOR/V27/46/203, 33; MacLeod to Read, 13 January 1798, Board's Collections, IOR/F/4/67/1481.

67. Devine, *Transformation of Rural Scotland*, 62–66.

68. C.A. Bayly, *Imperial Meridian: The British Empire and the World 1780–1830* (London: Longman, 1989), 190.

CHAPTER 6

Death or a Pension: Scottish Fortunes at the End of the East India Company, c.1800–57

Ellen Filor

In Walter Scott's *St Ronan's Well*, Meg Dods, an inn-owner opines, "'Nabobs, indeed! the country's plagued wi' them. They have raised the price of eggs and pootry for twenty miles round—But what is my business?—They use amaist a' of them the Well down by—they need it, ye ken, for the clearing of their copper complexions"'.[1] Scott's vision of the 1820s Scottish countryside as riddled with yellow nabobs, improving their estates and raising prices (of eggs) was one shared by his contemporaries and later historians.[2] However, this vision of imperial wealth runs counter to many Scots' experience of India at this time. While Scottish fortunes in the eighteenth century East India Company have been well studied, this chapter will move into the unchartered territory of the nineteenth century, focusing on the smaller gains of pensions spread between these

This research was funded by a Scottish Studies Fulbright Award at the University of Michigan. Thanks also to the editors of this volume for their astute comments and Margot Finn for sending me back to the archives at a critical stage.

E. Filor (✉)
University College London, London, England

© The Author(s) 2017
T.M. Devine, A. McCarthy (eds.), *The Scottish Experience in Asia, c.1700 to the Present*, DOI 10.1007/978-3-319-43074-4_6

Company servants, their wives and children. As such, this chapter outlines the effects and repercussions of the diminishing economic returns of a career in India during the last 50 years of the East India Company.

P.J. Marshall, Andrew Mackillop and George McGilvary have outlined the large fortunes Britons reaped in post-1757 India.[3] As McGilvary has shown, of the 80 Scottish civil servants appointed between 1765 and 1774, 25 per cent returned with more than £10,000 and 11 per cent with a fortune over £40,000. Indeed, while rare, some Scots returned with £100,000 or more.[4] However, with the reforms instigated by Cornwallis and Wellesley in the 1790s, these fortunes gave way to much more modest pay and pensions.[5] Such reforms meant that British employees of the East India Company were cut off from the private trade and gifts from Indian rulers that had allowed them to generate large fortunes over the preceding 50 years. The effect of these reforms did not immediately discourage Scots from going to India. In the first half of the nineteenth century, Scots accounted for 12.7 per cent of all those who went to India as civil servants, and in some years they made up over a quarter of recruits. This figure was a disproportionate contribution broadly similar to the previous 50 years.[6] English-born recruits made up the highest percentage (53.1 per cent) followed by those born in India (23.1 per cent). Ireland (4 per cent), Wales (1.3 per cent) and those born in Europe or other British colonies (5.8 per cent) made up the remainder of the students. Stripping out the three lowest nationalities, Fig. 6.1 shows the shifts over time of the birthplace of Indian civil servants. The number of English recruits remained largely steady over the period while the number born in India rose as Britons increasingly married and had children on the subcontinent. The proportion of Scots declined but this masks substantial involvement as late as 1844 when 23 per cent of civil servants were born in Scotland. While this data only allows individuals to be grouped by where they were born, by utilising qualitative sources such as letters and wills, those men who were born outside Scotland but considered themselves Scots by ancestry, blood and/or education have also been incorporated into this chapter.

Even though the subject of pensions dominated the letters of civil servants during the beginning of the nineteenth century, the history of pensions is remarkably unstudied in the East India Company context. While, as John Brewer has demonstrated, pensions were the norm in British governmental positions post-1707, and were vital to the creation of a fiscal-military state,[7] it was not until over a century later that the East India Company instigated similar efforts for its servants.

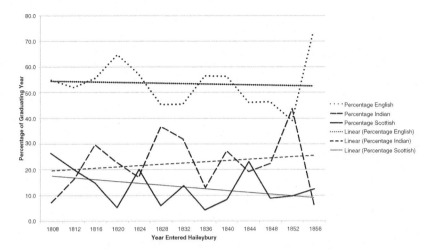

Fig 6.1 Birthplace of Indian Civil Service Recruits by Percentage, 1808–56 (*Source:* Data taken from Committee of College References and Papers, 1808–56, British Library, IOR/J/1/21-90)

The pensions that they did offer from the 1770s to the 1800s were for ill civil servants or deceased servants' widows, and were granted on a case-by-case basis. Appeals could and were refused, whether on the grounds of corruption or failing to meet the necessary level of poverty.[8] As Margaret Makepeace has argued in reference to the East India Company warehouse employees in London, these pensions were part of the Company directors propagating an 'image of paternal benevolence both in India and at home'.[9] The reforms introduced in the nineteenth century guaranteed pensions for all subscribers, positioning the Company less as a benevolent father figure and instead shifting responsibility for retirement onto the individual civil servants in question. Where historians have looked at this new form of pension in India, it has been in relation to the second half of the nineteenth century.[10] By looking at the antecedents of these Raj-era pensions, a thicker narrative of the shifting fortunes of Scots in India emerges.

In the face of diminishing economic returns, why did Scots continue to go to India? Ferdinand Mount, in his study of the Low family from Fife, has suggested that these men were not aware of the declining economic opportunities. Mount recounts that while Robert Low returned to

Britain with a fortune after only 11 years, his sons were not so fortunate in the post-Clive era: 'Undaunted by these changed circumstances or, more probably, not properly aware of them, Robert Low's three sons ... all went out to India and spent much of their adult life there'.[11] However, if the Low boys did not realise that India was less profitable in the 1800s, then they were in the minority. In 1823, for example, William Graham wrote from Bombay that 'The Army is a terrible profession any where in a money point of view and though better in this country than at home is still very bad' and the opportunities for civil servants little better.[12] Instead, India remained a viable option because many of the civil servants' fathers and uncles had been or were in India. As Elizabeth Buettner has suggested, empire was a 'family affair',[13] and these familial connections offered support when navigating life in India coupled with the reassurance that if these uncles and fathers could make money, so could the next generation. Similarly, Scots continued to enter the civil service because the qualifications required for entry and the cost of training were relatively low. Most Scottish civil servants entered the East India training college at Haileybury, Hertfordshire, at the age of 16 with no more than a high school education. Operating from 1806–58, the College ran a compulsory and intensive two-year degree in Oriental languages, law and history.[14] This training was part of a desire to professionalise the Indian Civil Service that ran concurrently with the reforms of pay, pensions and promotion.

This chapter, therefore, offers new angles into the perceptions and reality of India wealth. Through doing so, it can offer insight into the formation of the Scottish middle class. As R.J. Morris has argued, the formation of a British middle class in the nineteenth century was impeded by religious sectarianism and party politics, but that these divisions were slowly overcome by the proliferation of voluntary societies that helped create charitable and cultural union.[15] From another angle, Catherine Hall and Leonore Davidoff's seminal *Family Formations* has highlighted the centrality of the family and gender in the formation of the middle class.[16] This exploration of the East India Company pension seeks to unite Morris' emphasis on charity and Davidoff and Hall's stress on the importance of gender and family in the formation and sustaining of the middle class. Looking at the Company pension adds to this debate the importance of imperial wealth in the formation of the middle class. This research, therefore, will force us to look again at the economic potency of the East India Company and the impact of the pension on the creation and sustaining of the middle class well into the twentieth century.

This chapter is divided into four sections. The first outlines the sources utilised to create a database of Indian civil servants, and examines how contemporaries read these sources. By examining printed lists and hand-written Company records together, a deeper understanding of the pension and the threat of death can be understood. In the second section, I examine in detail what this database can tell us of imperial service in the last 50 years of the East India Company. As the expected monetary reward declined, I follow the other means these men sought to sustain their fortunes. The final two sections explore the two major unintended consequences brought by the introduction of pensions: first, the impact this declining imperial wealth had on the property market in Britain; second, its impact on the marriage market in India. Explicitly, I will examine the increase in civil servants marrying and having legitimate children in India. By looking at a period when a career in India no longer offered a fortune but rather debt, death and modest pensions, this chapter presents a narrative of failure at odds with previous works that have highlighted the economic success of Scots in India.

A QUESTION OF SOURCES

One of the central ways pensions and pay were understood in the nineteenth-century East India Company was through published lists of civil servants' appointments, promotions and retirements. These lists were first distributed by the East India Company in the 1770s and latterly through the burgeoning Indian press and that in Britain dedicated to Indian news.[17] Between 1799 and 1873 a large number of magazines and journals came into existence in India and Britain, often lasting only a couple of print runs before folding.[18] The *Asiatic Journal,* printed in London between 1816 and 1845, was one of the more successful of these new publications. Published monthly, it cost 3s 6d and was (at least according to the editors) a common sight in lending libraries.[19] While many of the pages of the *Asiatic Journal* were taken up with political essays and literature akin to the *Edinburgh Review* (albeit with a distinctive Eastern flavour), one of the most revealing parts of its content was the lists of promotions, deaths, examination results and marriages. Indeed, this mass of information was increasingly how India was understood by those in its service and those interested in the Company. The *Asiatic Journal* was explicit in chasing this audience, stating that '*those who have connexions with India* are furnished, in each month's journal, with a history of trans-

actions there, and a report of all official matters which intimately concern their interest, up to so late a period, as frequently to anticipate the
information communicated by letters'.[20] While historians such as Kate
Teltscher and Sarah M.S. Pearsall have argued persuasively how family
members separated by vast geographical distances used letters to maintain intimacy and share news, the use of printed material to bind families
together has received little recognition.[21] The potential of journals such
as the *Asiatic* has, however, been noted by genealogists, who increasingly
see them as a key source to trace when their ancestors went to India, if
they married there and how many children they had.[22] Following the lead
of these genealogists, much of the data that informs the remainder of this
chapter has been mined from these printed sources: the rate of death and
the rate of marriage, the prevalence of debt and the possibility of fortune,
the chance of promotion and the choice to quit. This variety and mass
of easily accessible (then and now) published information gives access to
the fortunes of Scots during the last 50 years of the East India Company.
Alongside these printed lists, I have utilised the manuscript East India
Company pension registers and the entry records for civil servants held
in the India Office Records, which grant insight into the vast numbers
of men, women and children who were funded by the Company pensions well into the twentieth century. Taking this data, I have traced the
biographical details of civil servants appointed at four-year intervals. This
gives a sample of 452 civil servants to use to examine the impact of this
new regime of pay and pensions.

State statistics have come to be reconfigured in the wake of Michel
Foucault as more than unproblematic facts for the historian to utilise as sources but rather a central means for the state to control and
render legible otherwise illegible social structures. At its most literal,
Foucault's understanding of the order of knowledge as that which 'has
no existence except in the grid created by a glance, an examination,
a language' can be understood in terms of the statistical tables that
proliferated during his Classical era.[23] But those grids of promotion,
death and marriage in the *Asiatic Journal* owed their power only in part
to the state knowledge they conferred. These lists came somewhere in
between the period of Foucault's 'high' enumerative rule and empire
as a 'family affair'. On one level these lists are coldly, cynically about
careers. The lists showed which of a civil servant's contemporaries had
gained promotion or retired or died. They allowed Bengal civil servant
Robert Keith Dick to boast in 1810: 'I have been fortunate in promo-

tion—I have never been superseded—I was the youngest Collector, the youngest Judge & magistrate, & am now the youngest Judge of the Courts of Appeal & Circuit in the Service'.[24] It would be tempting to fit the printed lists of *Asiatic Journal* into Benedict Anderson's narrative of 'imagined community', a colonial newspaper that bound together Britons who had never met under one national and imperial purpose.[25] However, the means by which Dick read these lists defies this analysis. In 1809, Dick wrote from Bengal to his brother-in-law Robert Lindsay in Fife: 'I anxiously look over the list of names by way of Ship or fleet for a Lindsay or a Pringle'.[26] Many of Dick's surviving letters from this period betray this dual reading: the printed lists that told a more or less official story alongside the more personal information he gleaned from family letters.

On another level, therefore, these lists are essentially domestic, mirroring the births, marriage and deaths columns in the British press throughout this period. Considering the distance between family members in the Indian case, these lists took on a far greater potency. These tables informed those at home of the promotions, retirements and deaths of their relatives in India. One S. Gordon wrote of her son-in-law that she was 'greatly vexed to find dear George has not been confirmed in his appointment which I see some other person is named'.[27] Likewise, these lists often conveyed unexpected and often tragic news. Bengal civil servant Pulteney Malcolm wrote in his diary in 1851: 'After dinner I received a sheet of the Bengal newspaper ... amongst it I read by accident "amongst the Obituary is the name of Sir Char Malcolm." Great God! I could not believe it, to see so casually so abruptly the death of my loved Father'.[28] These shocks and dislocations show how Indian careers and familial intimacy were not just mitigated and maintained through familiar letters. These printed tables were often read alongside (or indeed before) manuscript, personal letters. The ubiquity of these publications is demonstrated by their presence in the inventoried libraries of retired Indian servants in Scotland. At Bowland House in Selkirkshire, retired Indian army officer Alexander Walker had the *Oriental Herald* and the *Army Lists* next to the *Scots Magazine* and the *Edinburgh Review*.[29] Hoarding long outdated imperial publications was a memorial to imperial service, an aide-mémoire to the retired Company servant, and a potent reminder of such publications' power in the colonies and the metropole. It is among these ephemeral texts that the function and dysfunction of the end of the East India Company can be perceived.

THE RISK OF LIFE IN INDIA

Most importantly, these lists can tell us about the fate of nineteenth century civil servants: whether they died on the subcontinent or emerged with a pension. The high death rate among civil servants in India has long been recognised. P.J. Marshall has shown civil servants in the 1760s and 1770s had an average mortality rate of 56 per cent, suggesting that the only time possible financial gains outweighed the risk of death was in the 1770s.[30] However, little has been said about mortality after the 1770s.[31] Tracing the careers of civil servants who attended Haileybury between 1807 and 1858 allows these figures to be carried through to the end of the East India Company. The better records for the first half of the nineteenth century not only allow the mortality rates among civil servants to be tied down much more precisely but also let us mark the number who came out of the service with a pension. Of my sample of 452 civil servants, some 47.5 per cent lived long enough to gain a pension, while 42.9 per cent died in India or in Europe while still civil servants. The remaining 9.7 per cent quit, because of ill-health, accusations of corruption, or inheriting a fortune. The overall total disguises change over time (see Fig. 6.2). Up until the 1820s, the mortality rate remained above 50 per cent. Of those who entered Haileybury in 1812, 72 per cent died on the subcontinent. As the century progressed, the likelihood of death did decline, though it was not an entirely steady downward trajectory: the high death rate among the Haleyburians who graduated in 1848 was largely due to a number subsequently being killed in the Indian Revolt of 1857. Such occasional violent events demonstrate that death remained a pressing concern well into the nineteenth century. As mortality rates began to decline among civil servants who entered the East India Company from about 1830 onwards, these men increasingly survived the 'two monsoons' that had finished off their predecessors. Instead, civil servants increasingly died in their 40s in India, occasionally in their 70s and 80s.[32] These men were dying, if not of old age, of oldish age. The need to stay in the country for at least 25 years, normally more, meant that the civil servant was no longer the youthful man of the previous century.

If the mortality trend in the first half of the nineteenth century was a downward one, it had its mirror in the rising trend of those coming out of the service with a pension. For every year after 1828, over half of the civil servants received a pension. This system saw civil servants committing 4 per cent of their pay and allowances towards the pension fund. Those who

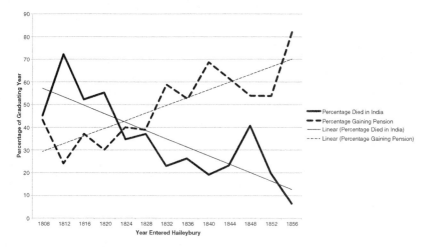

Fig. 6.2 Civil Servants: Death or a Pension, 1808–56 (*Source:* Data taken from *Memorials of Old Haileybury* (1894))

retired on a full pension in 1855 could expect to receive £1,000 annually. In the case of illness, they could retire on a reduced pension. When William Graham remitted money back to Scotland in 1827 despite his debt of £1,500, he reassured his brother 'but as my allowance if I live will probably within 5 years amount to £2000 it is not an object of any great consequence in case of illness I have a pension in the Service'.[33] Regardless of whether married or single, all men had to subscribe to a family pension fund for the widows (£300 a year), sons (£100 a year until they turned 21), and daughters (£100 a year until married) of civil servants.[34] While this support placed limits on the wealth a civil servant could hope to accrue over his time in India, it did offer in exchange a certain amount of stability. For example, the security of a pension meant that it was increasingly viable for these men to marry European women and have children in India, safe in the knowledge that if they died, their family would have a means of support.

If a civil servant entering Haileybury had under a 50 per cent chance of gaining a pension, it should be assessed how far the reward outweighed the risk. While a civil servant could retire on a full pension after 25 years, the reality was that few could afford to live on only £1,000 a year and, as a result, many worked longer to build up their savings. On average, civil servants retired after 30 years in India (see Fig. 6.3). Throughout the period 1808–56, the time to pension increased steadily until, by the 1840s, a man

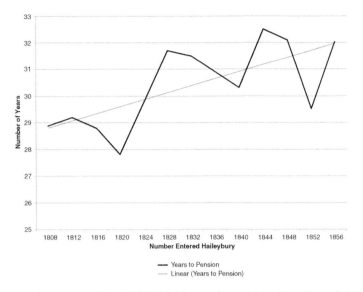

Fig. 6.3   Years to Pension, 1808–56 (*Source:* Data taken from Bengal, Madras and Bombay Civil Funds, British Library, IOR/L/AG/23/5, IOR/L/AG/23/8, and IOR/L/AG/23/11)

could reasonably spend well over 30 years in India before reaching his full pension. In 1857, the longest time a Bombay civil servant had spent in India getting a £1,000 pension was 42 years, in Bengal 56 years, and in Madras one took 60 years.[35] Between 1850 and 1872, only 11.3 per cent of (surviving) civil servants retired after 25 years. Only slightly over half had retired after 30 years of service, and after 37 years some 10 per cent were still working.[36]

When the *Asiatic Journal* began in 1816, the subject that dominated the first year's issue was how to make a fortune in India under these new pressures. This interest was sparked by an article by a retired Company man advising a stranger not to send his son to India for reasons of climate, lack of society and the difficulty of gaining a fortune.[37] One of the most thorough responses was a man who signed himself as 'A Friend to Rational Economy' who demonstrated how a careful civil servant could turn an initial saving of 30,000 rupees into 2,00,000 rupees 12 years later.[38] But mostly, when these letters turned to the question of money and promotion, the tone was one of disappointment and exhibited a narrative of thwarted ambition. A 'Madras Subaltern' who had been in India for ten years wrote dispiritedly in 1817 that he had initially believed that 'a few years after I had obtained the Command of a battalion, I should have had it in my power to have spent the winter of my life in my native country; but my hopes were nipt in the bud at the reforming period of Sir G. Barlow's government. I have long ago discovered with the eastern sage, that in this sublunary sphere there is no rose without a thorn, so that I am now prepared to leave my bones to moulder into Indian instead of British dust.'[39]

The Property Market

The two opposing viewpoints, one optimistic and the other pessimistic, in the pages of the *Asiatic Journal* highlight the need to investigate whether the decline in fortune was actual or merely perceived. Following Scots who retired to Britain allows an examination of their relative wealth versus both their predecessors in the civil service and their contemporaries who had sought a career in Scotland instead of in empire. Of the 57 Scots in my sample, 22 (39 per cent) died in India, four (7 per cent) quit, and 31 (54 per cent) retired on pensions. The wealth these 31 men made in India can be gauged by examining the moveable property (for example, stocks and shares, furniture and money) these civil servants possessed at their death. While moveable property is a slightly crude measure, with wealth potentially concealed in the heritable property or given to relatives before death, it offers the best means to compare like for like income. Against these civil servants, I will use a control group of accountants. Accountants are chosen because they were the brothers, near relations and schoolfellows of many of the civil servants under examination. Not only did accountants have a similar background in education and social standing but, like the Indian Civil Service, accountancy was undergoing professionalisation during this period. The introduction of two-year apprenticeships and the establishing of accountancy associations firmly situated accountancy as a middle-class profession in nineteenth-century Scotland.[40] Taking every fifth member of the 137 founders of the two accountancy associations in Edinburgh and Glasgow, established in 1853 and 1854 respectively, renders a sample of 27 accountants to assess the relative wealth of Indian civil servants against.[41] Probates exist for all but four of the accountants (who appear to have died intestate) and three of the civil servants (one who left a will but no probate and two who appear to have died intestate). The average moveable property at death of the accountants was more than twice that of the civil servants (see Table 6.1). Looking to the median narrows this disparity slightly but not markedly. This analysis suggests how civil servants' wealth increasingly compared unfavourably to other professional, middle class groups who stayed in Scotland.

This data does show that large sums could still be gained in India. James Henderson and David Simson, for example, retired in 1835 and 1872 respectively, both dying with more than £50,000 in moveable property.[42] The difference in the maximum property values between accountants and civil servants is, however, striking: George Auldjo Jamieson's fortune of £188,816 was over three times that of Henderson's £54,900. Stephen P. Walker has suggested that Jamieson was 'enormously successful' and his vast wealth reflected 'a stature … which surpassed that of other Chartered Accountants'.[43] However, two other accountants (Ralph Scott and James Watson) in the sample died with over £100,000.[44] This highlights that the wealth of Jamieson was not an anomaly and that a career in accountancy offered the possibility (if not the probability) of vast fortunes that the Indian Civil Service no longer did. Drilling down into the content of these inventories reveals similarities and differences between the investments of civil servants and accountants. If they possessed over £10,000 in moveable property, accountants and civil servants possessed similar investments in, for example, cotton manufacturers and railways. However, the poorer section of civil servants differed quite considerably from the poorer sections of the accountancy profession: for poor civil servants, pensions were often the largest sums mentioned. In 1885, Francis Anstruther Dalrymple's moveable property of £200 was largely made up of the £149 pension still due to him by the government.[45] Indeed, the £146 pension due to Charles

Table 6.1 Moveable property of accountants and Indian civil servants at death, 1855–1918

	Sample size	Surviving probates	Average year of death	Average property	Median property	Lowest property value	Highest property value
Accountants	27	23 (85%)	1881.0	£34,008.1	£15,843	£705	£188,816
Civil Servants	31	28 (90%)	1881.8	£16,321.8	£8,261.5	−£275	£54,900
Difference	4	5	0.8	£17,686.3	£7,581.5	£980	£133,916

Source: Data Taken from Inventories of Scottish Sherriff Courts, National Archives Scotland, SC1-SC70, 1855–1918, and National Probate Calendar, 1858–79

Grant, who died in 1887 in Inverness-shire, was not enough to cover the small sums he owed shopkeepers and his funeral expenses, meaning he left a debt of £225.[46] These inventories suggest some retired civil servants were living pension to pension without any other investments or savings to act as a buffer in times of hardship.

Of course, moveable property can only tell us about part of the extent of civil servants' wealth in the nineteenth century. The extent of their heritable property, in the shape of land and houses, was the other major part of their wealth. As McGilvary and T.M. Devine have suggested, imperial wealth helped to transform Scottish agriculture and maintain rural estates in the eighteenth century.[47] By examining the investment of Scots in heritable property in the nineteenth century, the shifts in how imperial wealth impacted Scotland can emerge. Where in Britain (or indeed Europe) these Scots returned to is of interest. David Gilmour, for example, has argued that most civil servants chose to settle in the South of England, stating explicitly that 'Scotland was not the usual destination for the Scots'.[48] Utilising the sample of 31 Scots who returned with a pension between 1808 and 1856, and examining where they bought or rented property, shows the falsity of this statement: 17 chose to return to Scotland, 13 settled in the South of England and the situation of one cannot be determined. This drilling down into the property of returned civil servants also demonstrates the kind of property to which these men could hope to return. A number bought small houses on the edges of villages such as Moffat, Melrose and Dumfries. Nine lived in London, in properties ranging from a townhouse in Kensington to a detached house in Ealing. Of the six who lived in substantial rural Scottish estates, all inherited them. Such purchasing power compares unfavourably with that which eighteenth century civil servants wielded, many of whom purchased large country estates on their return.[49]

An illustrative example of the lack of heritable and moveable property owned by civil servants is that of John Adam Loch (1820–92). He was born at the Cape, the son of Scottish Bengal civil servant William Loch (1786–1824) and English Eliza Arrow. After his father's death in Bengal in 1824, John Adam's widowed mother returned to Britain. She lived in the New Town of Edinburgh and all four of her sons were educated at the newly founded Edinburgh Academy.[50] While they spent their teenage years in the urban surroundings of Edinburgh, the boys were kept connected to the countryside by estates owned by their relatives, many of which had been purchased using East India Company fortunes. John Adam was appointed as a Bengal civil servant and sent to India in 1839. His time in India, however, was blighted by debt and ill-health. In 1847, he took out a loan of £1,400 from the Delhi Bank to buy four guns and two rifles.[51] When Loch retired in 1868 on a partial pension because of blindness, he was still repaying the debt. As he did not retire on a full pension, Loch asked the bank to reduce his repayments, and both parties agreed to Loch paying £10 quarterly from his annuity, later increased to £20. By 1883, Loch had paid back £2,020 of the loan. However, the sum Loch owed had increased to £31,644.[52] Even while the bank did not pursue Loch for this sum in the courts during his lifetime, after his death in 1892 they sued his widow unsuccessfully in the Scottish courts for £6,000.[53] While Loch repaid the original debt multiple times during his lifetime and on his death the original claim was found to be erroneous, this debt seriously undermined Loch's ability to acquire property. A landed estate like those he had visited during his youth was out of the question. Instead, he lived in a villa in the south of Edinburgh and his will records that not only the house but also the majority of the furniture was rented.[54] Indeed, the largest sums of his £6,285 inventoried estate came not from his own savings and investments but rather the £5,650 he had inherited from his brother Charles, who had been a reverend in England. Without this inheritance, Loch would have died £1,185 in debt.[55]

Nor was Loch alone in living in Edinburgh's suburbs. Using the census to map his neighbours' imperial careers suggests a large number of the inhabitants of nearby houses had also served in India (see Fig. 6.4). This square of Edinburgh suburbia contains 91 houses, 31 of which, between 1861 and 1891, were lived in by those who had made their money in the East Indies. For example, Ann Isabella Macdonnell, the widow of a Madras colonel, lived at 30 Greenhill Gardens on her husband's pension in the 1860s.[56] After her death in 1871, the house was occupied by Captain William Wilkie, retired from the Bombay Army.[57] The consecutive occupancy of this house suggests the vibrancy East India Company money injected into this part of Edinburgh. Widows renting (and occasionally buying) suburban villas off the back of an Indian annuity suggests how Company pensions spread imperial wealth from the gentry and country estates to the burgeoning Scottish urban middle class. By the 1901 census, however, the number of returned Indian servants living within this square had declined markedly. This could have been a result of the decreasing worth of an Indian pension: the £1,000 pension did not increase in line with inflation. This factor forced the returned civil servant to look to

Fig. 6.4 Map of Edinburgh Suburbs with East Indian Company families marked in black (*Source:* Data taken from 1861–91 Census. Ordnance Survey, Edinburgh Town Plan (Southampton, 1877), Town Plan 1:1056)

smaller houses further out in Morningside or, indeed, to the Edinburgh tenements that had proliferated in the 1890s.[58] By the beginning of the twentieth century, the Indian pensioner was priced out of the suburban villas that his predecessor had helped develop. This shift mirrored that which his predecessor had experienced in the nineteenth century, finding himself no longer able to afford country estates. If, as McGilvary and Devine have suggested, imperial wealth helped to transform Scottish agriculture and maintain rural estates in the eighteenth century, by the nineteenth this (declining) wealth came to effect in very meaningful ways another transformation: the expansion of the Edinburgh suburbs and the urban middle class. As the wealth an Indian career offered dwindled, these suburbs increasingly came to replace the country house to which their fathers had returned.

THE MARRIAGE MARKET

If looking at the moveable and heritable property of civil servants gives a pessimistic view of the economic reward of a career in India, then turning to the other beneficiaries of Company pensions (namely, widows and children) tells a more auspicious story. In late eighteenth-century India, the numbers of Europeans marrying remained low. Civil servant Alexander Pringle, for example, echoed a widely held belief when he wrote from Madras in 1779: 'I am of a very domestick turn and sometimes think I could make a very sober decent kind of married man tho' I am resolved not to try the experiment on this side of the water'.[59] Whereas, previously, interracial relationships with Indian and Eurasian women were usual, by the 1830s they were decreasingly common.[60] As Durba Ghosh has demonstrated, Company pensions aimed to exclude Indian wives and mixed-race orphans from claiming them as early as the 1770s.[61] The provision of pensions for Company servants instead encouraged many to begin a legitimate white family in India. This saw marriages increase in Madras from seven in 1780 to 665 in 1860.[62] In 1857, Sir Charles Trevelyan reported to parliament on the impact pensions were having: 'In India, a civilian was commonly reputed to be worth 300l. a year dead or alive, and a military officer something less, which had a great effect in encouraging early marriages'.[63]

This unintended consequence of the implementation of pensions in the East India Company was swiftly spun as an advantage in order to recruit the best applicants for the Indian Civil Service. In 1856, the

Indian civil servant John Muir argued of the effect: 'We hope and believe that among the successful competitors will frequently be young men who have obtained the highest honours of Oxford and Cambridge. To many such young men a fellowship, or a tutorship, which must be held on condition of celibacy, will appear less attractive than a situation which enables the person who holds it to marry at an early age'.[64] Muir went on to stress not only the sexual benefits of an Indian career but also the superior monetary reward in comparison to an academic career. The easy shift from intellectual prowess to sexual gratification demonstrates how swiftly marriage to (white) women and the raising of children were incorporated into the domestic life of the Indian Civil Service. In 1850, the number of unmarried or widowed (239) and married (240) civil servants subscribed to the Bengal Civil Fund was nearly equal.[65] By 1873, these two numbers had diverged: the number of widowed or unmarried increased 29.7 per cent to 310 while the number of married men had more than doubled to 510.[66] The coming of the pension, therefore, had the unintended (but nonetheless welcomed by the East India Company directors) consequence of encouraging marriage and having (white) children in India.

This increase of marrying in India in a period when the death rate remained high saw a subsequent increase in the number of widows and children relying on Company pensions to sustain themselves in Britain. Such a move led to a dispersal of the relative wealth a pension brought among a wider cast of actors. The recognition of this diffusion of imperial wealth builds on work by H.V. Bowen, who has demonstrated that women made up a significant proportion of those who invested in East India Company stock.[67] Even relatively small annuities of £100 for the unmarried daughters of retired or dead Indian civil servants could ensure economic freedom for the women concerned. While the sons of Indian civil servants received an annuity only until their 21st birthday, the daughters' annuity was guaranteed until they married or earned over £100 a year from other sources. An illustrative example is Robert Keith Pringle, a Bombay civil servant who retired in 1851 and died in his villa in London in 1897 with effects totalling £1,993.[68] He had five daughters who spent a combined 283 years on the fund, equivalent to a total of £32,130.[69] Only one daughter married, the rest remaining on the fund until their deaths. In 1938, Margaret Joanna, the last daughter to die, left £18,151 in effects.[70] That she died with over nine times the wealth of her father highlights the sizeable economic impact Company pensions could have on women's lives well into the twentieth century. While civil servants may have suffered under the new regime of pensions, their daughters profited.

CONCLUSION

The common misconception that India was still a hunting ground for fortunes was one that continued to seduce Scots in the early nineteenth century. Such a conclusion was backed up by the physical proofs this second generation were surrounded by in their youth: their fathers and uncles had raised them on estates bought and sustained by East India Company money. But, if they went to India, their letters sought to dispel this myth with bitter zeal. This chapter has offered a picture of Scottish fortunes in India at odds with that proposed by George McGilvary and Andrew Mackillop.[71] Instead of being driven by a fortune as his counterpart of the second half of the eighteenth century had been, the servant of the last 50 years of the East India Company found himself bound up in the bureaucracy and comfort of a pension. Such stability, however, was paid for by much longer periods in India. A civil servant could now expect to spend 30-plus years on the subcontinent. This Company man, bound between the fear of death and the comfort of a pension, was more inclined to marry and start a (white) family in India and had the reassurance of steady money in old age.

Such a decline in fortunes meant that Indian civil servants were increasingly no longer members of the landed gentry. Instead, civil servants swelled the ranks of the Scottish middle class, buying or renting in the urban suburbs of Edinburgh. Indeed, the sums they accrued compared unfavourably to their contemporaries such as Scottish accountants. The diffusion of wealth that pensions offered to widows and unmarried daughters meant that such urban property was not just the purview of married Company men. Indeed, the middle class collective spirit engendered by subscriptions traced by R.J. Morris is evident in the Company pension system and the printed tables that proliferated alongside these pensions.[72] Moreover, my analysis of the Company pension demonstrates that altruistic charitable subscriptions were not the only economic reason for the unification of the middle class. The subscription of individuals and families to East India Company pension funds illuminates how diffused imperial wealth was central to the expansion of this class. Tracing the impact of Company pensions shows that the making of the Scottish middle class was intrinsically bound up in the British Empire.

This lack of riches, increasingly enclavic white spaces that limited the chance of (interracial, sexual) adventure, and diminished quality of life on return to Scotland all go some way to explaining why Scots increasingly turned their attentions away from India over the course of the nineteenth century. One answer to the puzzle of why Scots continued to go to India is that they did not by the 1850s. As seen in Fig. 6.1, the first half of the nineteenth century saw a downward trajectory until Scots made up about 10 per cent of the total number of civil servants, a proportion in keeping with the 8 or 9 per cent (and occasionally lower) Scots constituted for the second half of the century.[73] This downward trend is too large to be solely ascribed to more civil servants being born to Scottish parents in India. The relatively steady numbers of English recruits should instead point to a narrowing of the background of recruits to the Indian Civil Service. Indeed, the Indian Civil Service in the 1850s can be seen as beginning to conform to P.J. Cain and A.G. Hopkins' description of the British Empire as 'enabl[ing] the mainly southern, professional and public school culture to reproduce itself abroad'.[74]

Highlighting this shift away from India is not to argue that Scots turned their backs on the British Empire. Just as Scots sought their fortunes in the North Sea zone during the sixteenth century, were at the forefront of the West Indies trade during the mid-eighteenth, and were prolific in India after 1757, in the second half of the nineteenth century they moved on to Africa, perceiving it as a fruitful new market to replace the stagnated one of India.[75] Taking account of this shift by Scots from India to Africa (echoing earlier patterns in the seventeenth and eighteenth centuries), the argument can be made that the end of the East India Company marked the end of Scots (relative) dominance of the subcontinent—and, indeed, their wish to be in India at all. The more unregulated frontiers of British colonies in New Zealand, parts of Africa and Ceylon looked more tempting than to moulder in the increasingly bureaucratic India of the 1850s.

NOTES

1. Walter Scott, *St Ronan's Well*, vol. 1 (Edinburgh: Archibald Constable and Co., 1824), 40.
2. George McGilvary, *East India Patronage and the British State* (London: I.B. Tauris, 2008), 184–202.
3. P.J. Marshall, *East Indian Fortunes: The British in Bengal in the Eighteenth Century* (Oxford: Oxford University Press, 1976);

Andrew Mackillop, 'The Highlands and the Returning Nabob: Sir Hector Munro of Novar, 1760–1807', in Marjory Harper (ed.), *Emigrant Homecomings: The Return Movement of Emigrants, 1600–2000* (Manchester: Manchester University Press, 2005), 233–261.

4. McGilvary, *East India Patronage*, 209–229.
5. H.V. Bowen, *Revenue and Reform: The Indian Problem in British Politics, 1757–1773* (Cambridge: Cambridge University Press, 1991).
6. Andrew Mackillop, 'Locality, Nation, and Empire: Scots in Asia, c.1695–c.1813', in John M. MacKenzie and T.M. Devine (eds), *Scotland and the British Empire* (Oxford: Oxford University Press, 2011), 65.
7. John Brewer, *The Sinews of Power: War, Money, and the English State, 1688–1783* (Cambridge: Harvard University Press, 1990), 69–73.
8. See, for example, J. Webbe to Thomas Snodgrass, 7 March 1801, British Library [hereafter BL], IOR/F/4/139.
9. Margaret Makepeace, *The East India Company's London Workers: Management of the Warehouse Labourers, 1800–1858* (Woodbridge: Boydell Press, 2010), 73.
10. Bradford Spangenberg, *British Bureaucracy in India* (Delhi: South Asia Books, 1976), 50; Mary A. Procida, *Married to the Empire: Gender, Politics and Imperialism in India, 1883–1947* (Manchester: Manchester University Press, 2002), 15.
11. Ferdinand Mount, *The Tears of the Rajas: Mutiny, Money and Marriage in India 1805–1905* (London: Simon & Schuster, 2015), 18–19.
12. William John Graham to Robert Cunninghame Bontine, 3 July 1823, National Archives of Scotland [hereafter NAS], GD22/1/333.
13. Elizabeth Buettner, *Empire Families: Britons and Late Imperial India* (Oxford: Oxford University Press, 2004), 4.
14. Bernard S. Cohn, *An Anthropologist Among the Historians and Other Essays* (Oxford: Oxford University Press, 1990), 526–546.
15. R.J. Morris, 'Voluntary Societies and British Urban Elites, 1780–1850: An Analysis', *The Historical Journal*, 26, 1 (1983), 95–118.

16. Leonore Davidoff and Catherine Hall, *Family Fortunes: Men and Women of the English Middle Class, 1780–1850* (London: Routledge, 1997).

17. 'Preface', *The Commonwealth Relations Office List* (London: Her Majesty's Stationary Office, 1964), iii.

18. *East India Periodical Publications, and Licensed Printing Presses* (Cambridge: House of Commons, 1831).

19. 'The Asiatic Journal', *Quarterly Literary Advertiser* (November 1834), 4.

20. Emphasis in original. Ibid., 4.

21. Kate Teltscher, 'Writing Home and Crossing Cultures: George Bogle in Bengal and Tibet, 1770–1775', in Kathleen Wilson (ed.), *A New Imperial History: Culture, Identity and Modernity in Britain and the Empire 1660–1840* (Cambridge: Cambridge University Press, 2004), 281–296; Sarah M.S. Pearsall, *Atlantic Families: Lives and Letters in the Later Eighteenth Century* (Oxford: Oxford University Press, 2008).

22. Ian A. Baxter, *Baxter's Guide: Biographical Sources in the India Office Records* (London: FIBIS, 2009), 1.

23. Michel Foucault, *The Order of Things: An Archaeology of the Human Sciences* (London: Routledge, 2004), xxi.

24. Robert Keith Dick to Robert Lindsay, 29 August 1810, National Library of Scotland [hereafter NLS], Acc. 9769, 30/1/33.

25. Benedict Anderson, *Imagined Communities: Reflections on the Origin and Spread of Nationalism* (London: Verso, 1983), 37.

26. Robert Keith Dick to Robert Lindsay, 3 November 1809, NLS, Acc. 9769, 30/1/32.

27. S. Gordon to Eliza Loch, [c. 1820s], NLS, MS 19417/235–238.

28. 29 July 1851, Diary of Pulteney Malcolm, Volume 9, NLS, Acc. 12150/56.

29. Catalogue of the library at Bowland House, c. 1830, NLS, MS 14053B.

30. Marshall, *East Indian Fortunes*, 218.

31. For soldiers' mortality rates, see Philip D. Curtin, *Death by Migration: Europe's Encounter with the Tropical World in the Nineteenth Century* (Cambridge: Cambridge University Press, 1995), 1–39.

32. *Memorials of Old Haileybury* (London: Archibald Constable & Company, 1894), 551.

33. William John Graham to Robert Cunninghame Bontine, 19 April 1827, NAS, GD22/1/333.
34. L.S.S. O'Malley, *The Indian Civil Servant, 1601–1930* (London: John Murray, 1931), 70.
35. Return of Number of Covenanted Civil Servants of Bengal, Madras and Bombay, House of Commons Sessional Papers, 1857–8 (32), XLIII.61.
36. William Sutton, *Report on the Bengal Civil Fund* (London: Charles and Edwin Layton, 1879), 17.
37. 'The Contrast: Or, Opinions on India', *Asiatic Journal and Monthly Miscellany*, 1 (1816), 537–539.
38. 'To the Editor of the Asiatic Journal', *Asiatic Journal and Monthly Miscellany*, 2 (1816), 550–551.
39. 'To the Editor of the Asiatic Journal', *Asiatic Journal and Monthly Miscellany*, 4 (1817), 213–214.
40. Stephen P. Walker, *The Society of Accountants in Edinburgh, 1854–1914: A Study of Recruitment to a New Profession* (New York: Garland Publications, 1988).
41. Their names and biographical details are taken from T.A. Lee, *Seekers of Truth: The Scottish Founders of Modern Public Accountancy* (Oxford: Elsevier, 2006).
42. Inventory of James Henderson, 1870, Aberdeen Sheriff Court Inventories, NAS, SC1/36/67; Inventory of David Simson, 1891, Edinburgh Sheriff Court Inventories, NAS, SC70/1/298.
43. Stephen P. Walker, 'George Auldjo Jamieson—A Victorian "Man of Affairs"', in T.A. Lee (ed.), *Shaping the Accountancy Profession: The Story of Three Scottish Pioneers* (London: Routledge, 2014), 74.
44. Inventory of Ralph Scott, 1887, Edinburgh Sheriff Court Inventories, NAS, SC70/1/258; Inventory of James Watson, 1890, Glasgow Sheriff Court Inventories, NAS, SC36/48/129.
45. Inventory of Francis Anstruther Dalrymple, 1885, Dumfries Sheriff Court, NAS, SC15/41/20.
46. Inventory of Charles Grant, 1887, Inverness Sheriff Court, NAS, SC29/44/23.
47. McGilvary, *East India Patronage*, 184–202; T.M. Devine, *The Tobacco Lords: A Study of the Tobacco Merchants of Glasgow and Their Trading Activities, c.1740–90* (Edinburgh: Edinburgh University Press, 1990; first pub. 1975), 18–51.

48. David Gilmour, *The Ruling Caste: Imperial Lives in the Victorian Raj* (London: Pimlico, 2007), 313.

49. Clive Williams, *The Nabobs of Berkshire* (Purley on Thames: Goosecroft Publications, 2010), 141–379; Marshall, *East Indian Fortunes*, 216.

50. Thomas Henderson and Philip F. Hamilton-Grierson (eds), *The Edinburgh Academy Register* (Edinburgh: T&A Constable, 1914), 32, 52, 61, 80.

51. John Adam Loch to Eliza Loch, 17 December 1848, NLS, MS 19416/113–114.

52. 'Delhi and London Bank Limited vs Loch', *The Scottish Law Reporter*, 32 (1895), 658.

53. Ibid., 659.

54. Inventory of John Adam Loch, 1893, Edinburgh Sheriff Court Inventories, NAS, SC70/1/319.

55. Ibid.

56. Will of Ann Isabella Macdonell, 1872, Edinburgh Sheriff Court Inventories, NAS, SC70/1/160.

57. Inventory of William Wilkie, 1876, Edinburgh Sheriff Court Inventories, NAS, SC70/1/176.

58. James Kingsmill, 3 Bruntsfield Terrace, Census 1901, NAS, 685/05 111/00 001. On these 'enclaves of returned colonials' in the second half of the nineteenth century, see Buettner, *Empire Families*, 208–238.

59. Alexander Pringle to Susanna Pringle, 6 June 1779, NAS, GD246/46/3.

60. Durba Ghosh, *Sex and the Family in Colonial India: The Making of Empire* (Cambridge: Cambridge University Press, 2006), 8–10.

61. Durba Ghosh, 'Making and Un-making Loyal Subjects: Pensioning Widows and Educating Orphans in Early Colonial India', *The Journal of Imperial and Commonwealth History*, 31, 1 (2003), 1–28.

62. Statistics taken from Parish register transcripts from the Presidency of Madras, 1780, BL, IOR/N/2/11; Parish register transcripts from the Presidency of Madras, 1860, BL, IOR/N/2/41.

63. *Report from the Commissioners Appointed to Inquire into the System of Purchase and Sale of Commissions in the Army* (London: Her Majesty's Stationary Office, 1857), 316.

64. John Muir, *The Indian Civil Service and the Scottish Universities* (Edinburgh: W.P. Kennedy, 1855), 11.
65. Sutton, *Report on the Bengal Civil Fund*, 11.
66. Ibid.
67. H.V. Bowen, *The Business of Empire: The East India Company and Imperial Britain, 1756–1833* (Cambridge: Cambridge University Press, 2006), 104–109.
68. Entry for Robert Keith Pringle in the National Probate Calendar (1897).
69. Bombay Civil Fund List of Pension Recipients, BL, L/AG/23/11/18, 37.
70. Entry for Margaret Joanna Pringle in the National Probate Calendar (1938).
71. McGilvary, *East India Patronage*; Mackillop, 'The Highlands and the Returning Nabob', 233–261.
72. Morris, 'Voluntary Societies and British Urban Elites, 1780–1850', 95–118.
73. C.J. Dewey, 'The Education of a Ruling Caste: The Indian Civil Service in the Era of Competitive Examination', *The English Historical Review*, 88, 347 (1973), 276.
74. P.J. Cain and A.G. Hopkins, *British Imperialism, 1688–2000* (Harlow: Longman, 2002), 286.
75. See, for example, Bryan S. Glass, *The Scottish Nation at Empire's End* (Houndmills: Palgrave Macmillan, 2014).

CHAPTER 7

Governor J.A. Stewart Mackenzie and the Making of Ceylon

Patrick Peebles

Of the many Scottish landowning elites who became colonial governors in the nineteenth century, James Alexander Stewart Mackenzie (1784–1843) is one of the least well appreciated. He was governor of Ceylon for only three years and five months, cut short by illness, and he left a negative impression. He is best known for passing the legislation in late October and early November 1840 that made Ceylon's coffee plantation industry viable. He accomplished much more than this, however; his first two years were devoted to humanitarian reforms that may have had a greater impact than his role in the plantation economy.

Mackenzie's reputation is based primarily on the writings of the leading historian of Sri Lanka during this period, Kingsley de Silva. De Silva emphasises Mackenzie's contribution to the spread of education in the colony, but rightly points out that his reforms became bogged down in a bitter dispute with Archdeacon James Moncrief Sutherland Glenie (1784–1847)

Much of the research for this chapter has been carried out under a grant from the American Institute for Sri Lanka Studies.

P. Peebles (✉)
University of Missouri–Kansas City, Kansas City, MO, USA

© The Author(s) 2017
T.M. Devine, A. McCarthy (eds.), *The Scottish Experience in Asia, c.1700 to the Present*, DOI 10.1007/978-3-319-43074-4_7

143

and his son Samuel Owen Glenie over control of the School Commission.[1] He calls attention to Mackenzie's own plantation investments, which he considers a motive for the legislation of 1839 and 1840. Finally, he claims that Mackenzie 'became an enthusiastic supporter'[2] of a missionary campaign to dissociate the government of Ceylon from Buddhism.[3] De Silva unfortunately begins his research in 1840 and pays little attention to the first two years of Mackenzie's administration, although he is careful to point out that Mackenzie's behaviour seems to have changed over the course of his term as governor.[4]

Popular histories tend to ignore these changes and stress Mackenzie's alleged antipathy to Buddhism. A brief biography says 'he held a Christian intolerance to other religions ... It is difficult to think of him by any stretch of the imagination as one of the great among the Governors ... His unpopularity among planters and his own kind is not a surprise for his sanctimonious pretensions were belied by his conduct'.[5] Another account claims incorrectly 'Mackenzie refused to sign the warrants appointing priests to the chief temples'.[6] On the contrary, in his discussion of the dissociation campaign, de Silva carefully notes that the only reference to appointments of priests came in the last two weeks of Mackenzie's term and that the appointments were made difficult by disputes among priests.[7]

It is the argument of this chapter that Mackenzie's role in the transition of the colony from a military outpost to a plantation society is more than that of facilitating the spread of coffee plantations. Despite ferocious opposition, the untimely death of some of his collaborators, ill health, and some personal flaws, Mackenzie initiated humanitarian reforms in his first two years that shaped the future of the colony. His qualification for the office was not just 'a familiarity with classical Latin',[8] but an enlightened view of the future of the colony possibly produced by his Scottish heritage and his experiences as a lawyer, aristocratic landowner and Member of Parliament. Mackenzie may have drawn on the ideas of the Scottish Enlightenment in the tradition of other Scottish governors in India including Thomas Munro (1761–1827), John Malcolm (1769–1833) and Mountstuart Elphinstone (1779–1859).[9] Admittedly, though, he did not have the transformational influence of other enlightened Scottish administrators such as Lachlan Macquarie (1761–1824) in New South Wales or William Farquhar (1774–1839) and Dr John Crawfurd (1783–1868) in Singapore.[10]

Secretary of State Lord Glenelg selected Mackenzie for Ceylon in 1836 specifically to implement the idealistic but belated Colebrooke-Cameron Reforms passed in 1832.[11] These reforms created a united government for the entire island, a Legislative Council to advise the governor, a system of District Courts open to everyone, and a Supreme Court that had appellate jurisdiction on all cases under a Charter of Justice. William MacBean George Colebrooke and Charles Hay Cameron proposed to fashion a colonial government in which the Ceylonese were active participants, as members of the Legislative Council, legal practitioners, and officers of the civil service. A School Commission was intended to promote education for the Ceylonese to prepare them for the new opportunities.

These reforms had their origin in proposals by Alexander Johnston (1775–1849). Johnston was born in Scotland, the grandson of Lord Francis Napier (6th Lord Napier of Merchistoun, 1702–73), and raised in India. He had been chief justice in Ceylon from 1811–19 and in 1809 wrote a proposal recommending reforms that were contained in the Colebrooke-Cameron Reforms and also influenced the 1813 renewal of the East India Company's charter.[12] He also recommended abolishing the elitist Ceylon Civil Service (CCS). He returned to England in 1819 and continued to maintain his interest in Ceylon, sometimes to the dismay of colonial governors—Edward Barnes (1824–31) called him 'a grand Mountebank'.[13] Barnes' successor, Robert Wilmot Horton (1831–37), also resisted implementation of the reforms; Horton resigned on 28 July 1836 owing to what he considered harassment from Lord Glenelg.[14]

Mackenzie had to contend with widespread resistance to reform from the British civil community, many of whom wanted the government to promote the nascent coffee plantation economy to the exclusion of other policies. The export of coffee was rapidly increasing in the late 1830s, most of it grown by villagers, but by 1837, the West Indian plantation system had been introduced.[15] The sale of crown land for coffee plantations increased greatly in 1837, and a handful of European-owned plantations was beginning to produce coffee when Mackenzie arrived.

In his third year in Ceylon, Mackenzie passed legislation that provided the legitimisation for the West Indian-style coffee plantation industry that was emerging. There is a contradiction in the two periods: in the first two years of his term he aggressively pursued liberal reforms that differed greatly from the notoriously illiberal measures that fostered the plantation economy. The reasons for the change in policy are controversial, and seemed to be a consequence primarily of his ill health.

Mackenzie's Career

James Alexander Stewart was born into the Scottish nobility, the nephew of the 7th Earl of Galloway and the son of Vice-Admiral Keith Stewart (1739–95). He married Mary Frederica Elizabeth Mackenzie (1783–1862), the widow of Admiral Sir Samuel Hood and heir to the Seaforth estate on 21 May 1817, taking his wife's family name. Mary Mackenzie, known as Lady Hood Mackenzie, was more famous than her husband and was his closest adviser. She has been called 'a most outstanding person and probably the ablest of the Mackenzies'.[16] She was the leader of Colombo society. For example, she started a female education society called the 'Chinese and Indian Female Education Society'.[17] She also encouraged a student at the Colombo Academy, James Alwis (1823–78), who became a lawyer and the intellectual leader of the Sinhalese elite. Alwis wrote that Lady Hood served him snacks with her own hands, examined his books and introduced him to the governor.[18]

Mary Mackenzie's father was the chief of Clan Mackenzie, Francis Humberston Mackenzie (1754–1815), who was made Baron of Seaforth in 1797. He was elected Member of Parliament for Ross in 1784 and 1790. In 1793 he founded the 78th (Highland) Regiment of Foot (Ross-shire Buffs), which served in Ceylon from August 1826 to March 1837, and became a source of pioneer coffee planters. He was governor of Barbados from 1802–06. The Seaforth estate included the island of Lewis in the Outer Hebrides, which was in a state of economic decline. The harvesting of kelp to make barilla had produced a temporary prosperity in the eighteenth century, but the removal of the duty on imported barilla and the availability of alternatives lowered prices and caused the local market to fail.[19] Baron Seaforth endured financial difficulties in the early nineteenth century, but resisted evictions.[20] Poverty increased as the population continued to grow with insufficient opportunities for employment.

Baron Seaforth's four sons predeceased him; the title became extinct when he died, and his daughter was considered the chief of Clan Mackenzie. John Dalziel, who had been a Sergeant in the 78th Highland Regiment, welcomed her in full Highland dress when she arrived in Ceylon.[21] Dalziel was rewarded by appointment as Police Magistrate of Colombo.

Mackenzie took an active part in the administration of Lewis from 1817–31. He purchased the estate from his wife's family for £160,000 in March 1824, but the addition of his wealth did little to slow its decline.[22] In some respects his administration of Lewis paralleled his administration of Ceylon. In both periods, Mackenzie researched his plans carefully.[23] He was eager to try new experiments: he tried to establish a commercial fishing industry in Lewis, and when that failed he introduced sheep farming. Tenants were forced to move from any place suitable for fishing, and then to move away from pastureland. In 1825, he opened a distillery in Stornoway, which eventually failed because the grain had to be imported at a prohibitive cost.[24] He also made a quixotic attempt to circulate a private currency.[25] He introduced reforms in both careers; in Lewis he abolished the tacksmen (leaseholders) and let the land directly to the crofters, and granted a charter that allowed the landholders of Stornoway to elect magistrates and councillors.[26]

In both Lewis and Ceylon, Mackenzie found it difficult to complete his projects. A local historian wrote that his experiments in Lewis created hardship for the tenants.[27] Another has written that 'while J. A. Stewart Mackenzie seems to have been a man who had many ideas, and a great desire to do good, it also seems that he was largely incapable of executing his fine plans'.[28] In Ceylon, he tended to become distracted from his main objectives and to micromanage his tasks (for example, the repairs on his residence in Kandy)[29] instead of delegating them.

In Lewis, he was unable to resist the inexorable crisis of too many people and too few jobs. Lewis's most rapid decline took place after Mackenzie ceased to actively manage its economy.[30] The managers doubled rents, and 18,000 residents in 1838 were confronted with a demographic crisis. By 1839 the Mackenzies were in financial difficulties and discussed selling Lewis to avoid further debt. Mary Mackenzie finally sold Lewis to James Matheson in 1844 for £190,000.

Mackenzie was elected as a Liberal Member of Parliament for Ross-shire in 1831. He supported the Scottish Reform Act in 1832 and was elected for Ross and Cromarty from 1832 to April 1837. He supported Lord Melbourne when William IV dismissed him in November 1834, and was disappointed when his loyalty was not rewarded after the Liberals returned in April 1835. In April 1837 he was soundly defeated.

It was said that when his electoral defeat was imminent, he 'took time by the forelock, and popped himself into the Governorship of Ceylon'.[31] In fact he had been appointed to the post before October 1836. Ceylon was not Mackenzie's first choice. He had lobbied for the more lucrative post of governor of Bombay Presidency in 1834. In 1839 he wrote to T.B. Macaulay that 'Lords Grey and Althorp would have gladly given me that situation, but for the pretensions of Sir Robert Grant [Lord Glenelg's brother] at that time, to which I readily admitted that mine were second'.[32] He applied for the governorship of Madras Presidency in 1837. He was disappointed again that he was not made governor of Bombay Presidency after Robert Grant died on 9 July 1838.

Mackenzie sought out Alexander Johnston at the Royal Asiatic Society before leaving for Ceylon and joined its agricultural committee.[33] Johnston gave Mackenzie a copy of his 1809 proposals and conferred with him at length. Johnston encouraged him to promote cultivation (including coffee) by both Europeans and Ceylonese, and to establish 'a general system of education'.

GOVERNOR OF CEYLON

Mackenzie arrived in the island on 6 November 1837 with 43 pages of instructions from Glenelg.[34] Half of this dispatch was devoted to 'the moral and religious education of the people of Ceylon'.[35] De Silva leaves the impression that Glenelg intended Mackenzie to directly persuade Ceylonese to convert to Christianity, but Glenelg, another enlightened Scot, emphasised education, not proselytising, and both men expected conversion to be an inevitable consequence of the spread of education. The remainder of the dispatch discussed provisions of the Colebrooke-Cameron Reforms. Glenelg and the Colonial Office, however, had unrealistic expectations for the revenue. Horton's revenue was inflated by windfall revenue from the sale of cinnamon stocks and from two profitable pearl fisheries that were not repeated. In addition, in 1838 the Colonial Office levied a yearly charge of £24,000 to pay for the troops quartered there. Most of Glenelg's proposals for construction were abandoned owing to budget shortfalls. Glenelg seems to have been unaware of the emerging coffee economy.

For the first 18 months of his administration Mackenzie worked hard to carry out his instructions. In addition to his bitter confrontation with the Church of England establishment, he sought to increase the number of schools, to develop the economy of the colony, to improve the administration of justice, and to carry out the policy of opening government offices to capable Ceylonese candidates.

He had a broader view of the role of education than simply taking control away from the Church of England.[36] He subsidised mission schools, which provided education in Sinhala and Tamil as well as English. He revived the Colombo Academy, which provided a rigorous education for the local elite, although he was unable to find a qualified replacement when its founder, Joseph Marsh, was forced to leave the colony near death in December 1838. He attempted to hire an inspector of schools, a position first created in England to monitor grants to schools in 1837.[37]

Investors in plantation land, many of them civil servants, expected that Mackenzie would facilitate the sale and survey of land for plantations, build roads to the planting districts, and encourage the immigration of labourers from South India. Mackenzie was attacked mercilessly by the planting community for not doing more for them. For example, in April 1839 John Capper, a planter-turned-journalist, wrote a letter that was published in London promoting the coffee (and sugar) plantations of Ceylon, which he said were thriving 'in spite of the many obstacles thrown in its way by the narrow-minded policy of the local government'.[38] Mackenzie did encourage immigration from India with the resources available. He had a causeway built linking Mannar island with the mainland, and four rest stops placed along the road the plantation labourers walked from India. He also condemned the threat of planters from Mauritius evading Indian prohibitions by recruiting indentured labourers from India in Ceylon.[39]

Otherwise his economic policies did not favour the planters. He initiated a Ceylon Chamber of Commerce in March 1839, modelled after the one in Bombay, by encouraging merchants to get together to discuss grievances and then 'to come to him with united recommendations'.[40] He made the sale of crown land less susceptible to fraud.[41] He began selling the government cinnamon gardens in March 1838, which diverted the efforts of the survey department from coffee plantation development.[42] He tried to improve the efficiency of the survey department.[43] He complained that government employees left their posts to superintend their plantations and asked for instructions.[44]

Mackenzie attempted to reform the administration of justice.[45] The courts operating under the Charter of 1833 were unsatisfactory because of a huge and growing backlog of cases and a sense that judges' decisions neither upheld rights nor punished crimes effectively. The law was a jumble of Roman-Dutch law, English law, and special laws for Kandyan Sinhalese, Jaffna Tamils, and Muslims. The complex rules and orders written by Chief Justice Charles Marshall (1833–36)—some amounting to judicial legislation—added to the confusion. Mackenzie had the advantage of familiarity with the Scottish legal system's long history of contact with

Roman-Dutch law, and wrote that 'the very great influx of British settlers will make it absolutely necessary to assimilate the laws of the Colony to that of the Parent State'.[46]

John Frederick Stoddart (1805–39), the second puisne justice, allied with Mackenzie. Stoddart was Scottish on his mother's side; she was the daughter of Sir Henry Moncrieff. He was educated at the High School of Edinburgh and the Universities of Edinburgh and Glasgow. He was appointed to the Ceylon Supreme Court in 1836. Stoddart wrote a 200-page proposal for improving the administration of justice.[47] He argued that the greatest cause of difficulty was a failure to implement the charter fully and effectively, and suggested that the obvious way to improve the administration of justice was to employ the growing number of qualified Ceylonese lawyers. Mackenzie forwarded the reports to the Colonial Office in May 1839.[48] Stoddart unfortunately died on 29 August 1839 and reforms ended until some of his ideas were implemented after 1841.

Mackenzie's greatest difficulty came over his intention to appoint 'natives' to the civil service and the judiciary. Mackenzie, and governors before and after him, complained of the incompetence of the CCS. It had been modelled after the Indian Civil Service, but could not attract the quality of applicants that India did. Patronage appointments, nepotism, preoccupation with their coffee plantations, the infirmity of senior officials who refused to retire, and discontent from salary reductions in 1833 made it difficult to find capable Europeans to fill offices, at a time when the growing economy required more skilled administrators. As James Stephen euphemistically put it, the CCS had 'a certain amount of incapacity'.[49] In addition, Mackenzie had to cope with an unusually large number of deaths and resignations. Mackenzie announced his intention to appoint 'natives' to the CCS in January 1839,[50] and in April 1839 he appointed an Englishman whose wife was Sinhalese, a Dutch Creole with an English wife, and a man from an elite Sinhalese family as district judges.[51]

When the Chief Justice died in May 1838, Mackenzie promoted the queen's advocate to the Supreme Court—in spite of misgivings about his ability—and appointed John James Staples (1798–1852), a member of the English bar who was considered the best lawyer in the colony, acting queen's advocate. He then appointed Cyril Arnold Morgan to Staples' position as acting deputy queen's advocate. Both men were 'Burghers', a catch-all term that referred to Dutch creoles, Eurasians, and Europeans who married Ceylonese spouses, disparagingly called 'half-castes'. Burghers were English-educated and had been indispensable to the government up to 1830, but they were being systematically excluded from higher offices. Philip Anstruther (1802–62) and George Turnour (1799–1843), the two most influential officials, led the resistance to the Ceylonese appointments. Anstruther, the colonial secretary, was a man with a Scottish pedigree as proud as Mackenzie's. He was the third son of Colonel Robert Anstruther, a Member of Parliament. He joined the CCS in 1819 at the age of 17 and rose to become colonial secretary in July 1833, promoted over the heads of nine senior civil servants, and held the office until 1845. The phrase 'making of Ceylon' in the title of this chapter is from his statement in 1849, 'The public servants cultivating land, was, I believe, the making of Ceylon'.[52] Unlike Mackenzie, he has a favourable reputation in Sri Lanka. Anstruther married the Mackenzies' daughter Mary Frances on 27 August 1838. Despite their ideological differences it was a good match; Mackenzie wrote, 'there is but one life between him and an old Scotch Baronetcy and Estate'.[53]

Anstruther went on extended leave in October 1838, and was in London for two years and four months, during which he advised the Colonial Office.[54] Turnour replaced Anstruther as acting colonial secretary. He was a strong supporter of the Church of England establishment and quarrelled with Mackenzie in the Executive Council over its privileges. Turnour was increasingly preoccupied with the development of coffee plantations, especially his own.[55] He wrote that appointing members of the local bar to judicial posts would damage the plantation economy: 'Every ship almost now brings from Europe some Capitalist or representative of a Capitalist, to raise the commercial and agricultural importance of the Colony, and at such a juncture it is more specially necessary that the public services should be of the highest respectability and efficiency'.[56]

Anstruther convinced the Colonial Office not to confirm Staples' appointment and to deny him the seat on the Executive Council to which he was entitled. Turnour, referring to Burgher lawyers, wrote 'It is quite out of the question I suppose that such uneducated persons … can be competent either to define the construction of Laws or to be able to act for themselves in the various exigencies which must necessarily and almost daily arise in the execution of their complicated duties'.[57] Mackenzie told the Secretary of State that he had no other choice.[58]

Anstruther opposed the three Ceylonese appointments to the CCS on the grounds that none of them was 'qualified by Education or station in society for such elevation', and none was confirmed.[59] He objected to a civil service 'formed from Half Castes and Adventurers picked up in Ceylon. ... The natives who are close judges of character, ... only trust a pure native, but the half castes they both distrust and despise'.[60] He recommended that the Secretary of State stop 'allowing the Governor to give away the appointments in Ceylon'.[61]

Mackenzie contracted malaria soon after his arrival and had periods of illness throughout his term. In September 1838 he travelled to Nuwara Eliya to recuperate. On 6 September he wrote to his wife that rest and ten days of quinine 'will entirely overcome the shivering fits', signing the letter 'your worn out and rheumatic old husband'.[62] The incomplete letter refers to his 'mental torments', which may refer to difficulties they had with their sons rather than the opposition to his reforms. Thereafter he periodically left for Galle or Kandy to recuperate.

All these efforts were incomplete by mid-1839, when he decided to take several tours around the country. The most important was a tour to the east coast, where he hoped to meet the aboriginal Veddahs, with an eye to converting them to Christianity. He fell from his horse on the first day out, and suffered heatstroke, but continued for three days on to Trincomalee. He also slept in the open at night and exacerbated his malaria.[63] Thomas Skinner, who accompanied him on the trip, wrote that 'it was too apparent that his brain was affected by the sunstroke, for he talked occasionally very incoherently'.[64] He never recovered; there are many references to his illness in his correspondence.

Mackenzie's behaviour became erratic after this trip. For example, when C.A. Morgan was dismissed from his office on grounds of mental illness, Mackenzie also withdrew a scholarship to Calcutta that he had promised to Morgan's brother Richard. Richard Morgan, who had been an outstanding student at the Colombo Academy, in retaliation wrote three anonymous satirical articles for the *Ceylon Herald* newspaper, cruel but funny, on Mackenzie's trip to the east coast.[65] Rather than ignore the articles, as he had done many times previously, Mackenzie sued the editor, who was acquitted by a jury of planters and merchants.

By December 1839 Mackenzie had abandoned—other than his feud with Archdeacon Glenie—his reforms. In his first two years, he had met with the Legislative Council only once. In December 1839 he began holding sessions under strict controls.[66] He set the agenda; he required that amendments to the ordinances had to be submitted in advance and approved by him; and no dissent was included in the minutes. He publicly reprimanded members who deviated from these rules. In seven weeks the

Legislative Council passed 15 ordinances, most of which were designed to promote the plantation economy, to control the Ceylonese population, or both. The most notorious of these was Ordinance No. 5 of 1840, the Crown lands Encroachment Ordinance, which enabled the colony to sell forest land off to coffee planters without fear of litigation by Ceylonese claimants.[67] In October the Council passed Ordinance 16 of 1840, the Master and Servant law which effectively coerced immigrant labour from India to work as plantation labourers.[68] These two ordinances created the legal basis for a West Indian-style plantation economy. Other ordinances prohibited people from donating land to temples, required bullock carts (essential for transporting coffee and rice) to be registered, regulated the sale of landed property, and controlled the warehousing of goods.

Still other ordinances were designed to control the Ceylonese with whom the British came into contact: fiscals (tax collectors), lunatics, vagrants, prostitutes, drunks, gamblers, tavern keepers, beggars, labourers, porters, carters, and anyone loitering without 'giving a good account of himself'.[69] The effect of these ordinances was to give the ruling caste legal means to treat the Ceylonese as conquered subjects, reversing the intention of Colebrooke and Cameron. For example, freedom of the press was emphasised in their reforms, but Ordinance No. 5 of 1839 required that newspapers must be registered before a district judge and must submit copies of every edition to the government. The ordinances were poorly drafted; some were disallowed, others were amended or eventually repealed, and most did not operate the way they were intended, but that is beyond the scope of this chapter.

Mackenzie's swing from humanitarian reforms to legislation that undermined them is usually described as a means to build his own fortune as an investor in coffee plantations. He clearly hoped to recoup some of the money he had spent on Lewis and was disappointed when he did not, but this was true even at the beginning of his term. He envied the wealth Macaulay acquired in India.[70] The position proved less remunerative than Mackenzie expected. Mackenzie began acquiring coffee land in 1840.[71] His plantations were known collectively as the 'Horogalle Estate', and reportedly covered 2,264 acres,[72] a modest extent for a man who owned Lewis. His wife treated Mackenzie's coffee planting as a hobby: 'Your adventure in coffee land will amuse and interest you, your mind will be free from anxiety'.[73]

There is no evidence that the change in his politics were motivated by personal profit. K.M. de Silva has argued that the earlier reforms were a subterfuge by which Mackenzie consciously deceived the Colonial Office in order to slip the legislation past it by burying it in a number of documents in an unrelated dispatch.[74] This is not true. The dispatch was the one that forwarded C.A. Morgan's petition for reinstatement. Morgan had been the lawyer for the plaintiff in the case discussed, and thus it was directly related to it.

There were a number of events in 1839 that might have influenced Mackenzie: the dismissal of Glenelg, who was succeeded by secretaries of state less interested in reform; the antipathy of James Stephen at the Colonial Office; and dismay at the lack of success of his policies. It is most likely that Mackenzie's illness made him unable to resist the demands of the planters. The legislation was drafted in the Executive Council, all the members of which had interests in the coffee industry. Little is known of the Executive Council's proceedings.

Mackenzie's health deteriorated further in early 1840. Before leaving for England to resolve problems with their sons, Lady Hood Mackenzie wrote her husband a series of notes advising about his behaviour in her absence. Beginning on 27 April 1840 she asked him to rest more 'before you go again into the Lion's Mouth ... What is there to tempt you to do so? Is the whole Coffee land of Ceylon worth the sacrifice of a life & a life so [unbearable?]'[75] On 3 May 1840 he wrote a dispatch regarding his health, which is missing from the Colonial Office records.[76] He also asked the Colonial Office to consult Anstruther about pending issues.[77] On the basis of these dispatches Secretary of State Lord John Russell sanctioned a leave of absence for his health in August.[78] Mackenzie then moved to Galle to recuperate and the Colonial Office, unable to contact him, thought he might have left the colony.[79] Anstruther and Lady Hood Mackenzie met with Russell in September and convinced him that Mackenzie should be recalled. He was transferred to a healthier climate as Lord High Commissioner of the Ionian Islands. Mackenzie himself resisted the order, believing that his political rivals had engineered it.

In 1840 Mackenzie wrote fewer dispatches and instead wrote private notes to the Secretary of State with many attachments, even though he was ordered not to.[80] For example, he sent 78 pages of correspondence and clippings privately to Russell attacking the elder Glenie, in response to two letters Glenie sent him on 23 and 25 April.[81] Mackenzie wrote two private letters to Secretary of State Lord John Russell (8 June 1840), and James Stephen (15 June 1840) complaining about that 'scamp' Richard Morgan, whom he mistakenly calls 'Charles', who was in London protesting his brother's dismissal. Interestingly, Morgan, who eventually became the wealthiest and most powerful lawyer in the colony, came to appreciate Mackenzie's efforts. He wrote in his diary at the time of Mackenzie's departure, 'the island owes much to him. He has invariably had the public good for his object and in the pursuit of it displayed a liberality of mind and determination of purpose which cannot but elicit unmixed admiration'.[82]

Mackenzie's illness increased Anstruther's influence in the Colonial Office, where he wrote many memoranda.[83] It is clear that Anstruther was not representing Mackenzie but actually opposing Mackenzie's intentions. James Stephen wrote comments about Mackenzie that could only have come from Anstruther.[84] For example, Stephen wrote that Mackenzie was not satisfied with the 'fitness' of James Nicholas Mooyart, a Dutch creole, for the office of government agent of the Central Province and proposed to transfer him. There is no other evidence of this, but Anstruther's antipathy for Mooyart is well documented. In November 1840 Anstruther wrote two long memoranda on the administration.[85] In a letter accompanying his memorandum on the civil service he requested that he be given a commission as Lieutenant Governor in the event of the death or absence of the Governor.[86]

One of Mackenzie's last acts was to lay the foundation stone for the Scots Presbyterian Church in Colombo. A farewell dinner was held on 30 March 1841, and he left the island on 7 April for Bombay on the steamer *Seaforth* that he had purchased for the colony. As Lord High Commissioner he attempted to codify the colony's law, but was recalled in 1843 for refusing to reappoint the President of the senate.[87] He returned to London and died on 24 September 1843.

CONCLUSION

J.A. Stewart Mackenzie did not create the plantation economy; the legislation of 1839 and 1840 would have passed in some form in any case. He did shape the evolution of colonial society in Ceylon. The planters thought of themselves as a gentry class, claiming in the words of one 'a rank and authority such as would naturally have devolved upon them had they employed their means in the purchase of landed property at home'.[88] Plantations retained their authoritarian character throughout the coffee era, particularly in regard to their control over labourers,[89] but the dream of a West Indian-style plantocracy was short-lived.

From 1842 to 1845 the government of Ceylon passed some of Mackenzie's reforms.[90] The Colonial Office gave the governor more power to modify the charter and the governor created justices of the peace and additional police magistrates, as Stoddart had proposed. The Colonial Office continued to resist employing the local bar as judges, however. The long overdue reform of the CCS, including appointing Ceylonese candidates, took place in 1845. In 1844 members of the CCS were forbidden to own plantations and were asked to dispose of their holdings within a year.

Mackenzie's greatest influence was in education, as young men educated to a high standard in the schools he encouraged filled up the positions of lawyers, doctors and others required by the more complex society. For better or worse, Ceylonese elites became very highly Anglicised. In the 1840s Ceylon became a hybrid, a plantation colony with a growing and influential local elite. Although Mackenzie did not live to see these changes take place, his efforts made the changes after 1841 possible.

James Alexander Stewart Mackenzie was one of a legion of Scottish governors and high officials who held office throughout the British Empire in its heyday. This case study of a single member of that elite illustrates the difficulty in determining how far Scottish ideas and background were significant in their policies. Partly this is because Mackenzie was only in post for a limited period of time. Also, there is little evidence in his correspondence of overt borrowing in theory or practice from his homeland of the kind demonstrated in Chapters 8 and 9. Like most educated Scots of his generation, he was certainly aware of the thinking of some of the major figures of the Scottish Enlightenment and he also pursued wide-ranging attempts to expand education in Ceylon for the Ceylonese. It is well known that Scots had a special interest in schooling as a source of moral and social amelioration. But by the middle decades of the nineteenth century they were not alone in thinking along those lines. All in all, therefore, the records only allow scepticism. The significance of the Scottish factor in the governorship of James Alexander Stewart Mackenzie in Ceylon must remain indeterminate.

NOTES

1. The Mackenzie–Glenie confrontation is examined in detail in K.M. de Silva, *Social Policy and Missionary Organizations in Ceylon, 1840–1855* (London: Longmans, 1965), ch. 4, and in Sujit

Sivasundaram, *Islanded: Britain, Sri Lanka, and the Bounds of an Indian Ocean Colony* (Chicago and London: University of Chicago Press, 2013), 299–305. Department of National Archives Sri Lanka (hereafter SLNA), 10/44, contains documents regarding the School Commission.

2. De Silva, *Social Policy and Missionary Organizations*, 77.
3. See R. Spence-Hardy, *The British Government and the Idolatry of Ceylon* (Colombo: Wesleyan Mission Society, 1839).
4. For example, K.M. de Silva, 'Buddhism and the British Government in Ceylon 1840–55', *Ceylon Historical Journal* 10 (1960), 103.
5. V.L.B. Mendis, *British Governors and Colonial Policy in Sri Lanka* (Dehiwala, Sri Lanka: Tisara Prakasakayo, 1984), 130.
6. H.A. Hulugalle, *British Governors of Ceylon* (Colombo: Associated Newspapers of Ceylon, 1963).
7. K.M. de Silva, 'Buddhism and the British Government', 103.
8. Mendis, *British Governors*, 130.
9. For the influence of the Scottish Enlightenment on Indian administration, see Martha McLaren, *British India and British Scotland, 1780–1830: Career-building, Empire-building, and a Scottish School of Thought on Indian Governance* (Akron, OH: University of Akron Press, 2001).
10. L. Coltheart and P. Bridges, 'The Elephant's Bed? Scottish Enlightenment Ideas and the Foundations of New South Wales', *Journal of Australian Studies*, 68 (2001), 19–33, 220–223.
11. Glenelg to President of the Privy Council, 20 March 1837, The National Archives of the UK (hereafter TNA), Privy Council, 1/1929.
12. His 1809 report and note to Mackenzie are reprinted in G.C. Mendis (ed.), *Colebrooke-Cameron Reports*, 2 vols (Oxford: Oxford University Press, 1956), II: 221–226.
13. Barnes to L.H. Hay, 22 January 1831, TNA, Colonial Office (hereafter CO), 54/112, quoted in E.F.C. Ludowyk, *The Modern History of Ceylon* (New York: Frederick A. Praeger, 1966), 50.
14. Private letter from Glenelg to Horton, 15 December 1836, SLNA, 25.5/8.
15. For an outline of the early years of the coffee plantation economy see P. Peebles, *The History of Sri Lanka* (Westport CT: Greenwood Press, 2006), 58–60.

16. D. Macdonald, *Lewis—A History of the Island* (Edinburgh: Gordon Wright Publishing, 1978), 37.

17. Miscellaneous Reports Education Missions 1838–39, SLNA, 10/6.

18. Hulugalle, *British Governors*, 63.

19. W.C. Mackenzie, *History of the Outer Hebrides* (Paisley: Alexander Gardener, 1903), 548–549.

20. Eric Richards, *The Highland Clearances: People, Landlords and Rural Turmoil* (Edinburgh: Birlinn, 2008), 402.

21. J. Perry Lewis, *List of Inscriptions on Tombstones and Monuments in Ceylon, of Historical or Local Interest* (Colombo: n.p., 1913), 57.

22. Mackenzie, *History of the Outer Hebrides*, 493.

23. His correspondence on Lewis is contained in National Records of Scotland (hereafter NRS), Gifts and Deposits (hereafter GD), 46/1. The files he collected as governor form the basis of Record Group 10 in the SLNA. His other papers from Ceylon were initially included in the Seaforth papers in the Scottish Record Office. In the 1950s those on Ceylon (other than those referring to Mrs Stewart Mackenzie) were transferred to the SLNA, where they form Record Group 25.5.

24. Macdonald, *Lewis*, 190.

25. P. Symes, 'James Alexander Stewart Mackenzie: Portrait of a Private Note Issuer', *International Bank Note Society Journal*, 37, 1 (1998). (Accessed 28 January 2015 from http://www.pjsymes.com.au/articles/JASM.htm)

26. Mackenzie, *History of the Outer Hebrides*, 492–493.

27. Macdonald, *Lewis*, 81–83.

28. Symes, 'Portrait of a Private Note Issuer'.

29. For example, a three-page letter enclosed in Mylius to Skinner, 8 June 1840, SLNA, 18/2568. See also N. Karunaratna, *From Governor's Pavilion to President's Pavilion* (Colombo: Department of Government Printer, Sri Lanka, 1983), 54.

30. Richards, *Highland Clearances*, 402–404.

31. *The Times*, 21 April 1837, 4.

32. Mackenzie to B. McAulay, 5 February 1839, NRS, GD46/9/6 (72).

33. Proceedings of the Committee of Agriculture and Commerce, *The Journal of the Royal Asiatic Society of Great Britain and Ireland*, 4, 2 (1837), 11–12, 21–37.

34. Glenelg to Mackenzie, No. 18 of 2 October, 1837, TNA, CO 55/79. See also de Silva, *Social Policy and Missionary Organizations*, 30–41.
35. De Silva, *Social Policy and Missionary Organizations*, 16. See also K.M. de Silva, 'The Government and Religion: Problems and Policies, c.1832 to c.1910', in K.M. de Silva (ed.), *University of Ceylon, History of Ceylon,* Volume III (Peradeniya: University of Ceylon, 1973), 187–192.
36. L.A. Gratiaen, *The Story of our Schools: The First School Commission 1832–41* (Colombo: Ceylon Historical Association, 1927).
37. Mackenzie to Glenelg, No. 137 of 20 August 1838, TNA, CO 54/164/119.
38. J. Capper, 'An Outline of the Commercial Statistics of Ceylon', *Journal of the Statistical Society of London* (January 1840) 2, 6, 424–425.
39. *Colombo Observer*, 4 July 1838.
40. S.S. Jayawickrama, *The Ceylon Chamber of Commerce, 1839–2004: A Historical Review* (Colombo: Ceylon Chamber of Commerce, 2005), 2.
41. Mackenzie to Normanby, No. 65 of 2 May 1839, TNA, CO 54/170/235. The new regulations were published in the *Government Gazette,* 13 April 1839.
42. The cinnamon plantations are discussed at length in Mackenzie's dispatches to Glenelg for 1838, TNA, CO 54/161. See also P. Peebles, *Social Change in Nineteenth Century Ceylon* (New Delhi: Navrang, 1995), 202–204.
43. Ian J. Barrow, *Surveying and Mapping in Colonial Sri Lanka 1800–1900* (Oxford: Oxford University Press, 2008), 69–75.
44. Mackenzie to Russell, 12 May 1840, TNA, CO 54/180/140.
45. See P. Peebles, 'Unchartered Justice: Revising Ceylon's Charter of Justice 1833–45', paper presented at the Annual Conference on South Asia, Madison Wisconsin, October 2009. Documents, including Stoddart's report and correspondence between Mackenzie and the judges, are compiled in SLNA, 10/140 and in NRS, GD46/9/13.
46. Quoted in Michael Roberts, 'Land Problems and Policies c.1832 to c.1900', in de Silva (ed.), *University of Ceylon History of Ceylon, Vol. III,* 120. Roberts does not cite a source, and I have been unable to date it.

47. Report on the Charter of Justice, SLNA, 10/142.
48. Mackenzie to Normanby, No. 91 of 30 May 1839, TNA, CO 54/170.
49. James Stephen, Minute to Anstruther's Memorandum of 8 October 1840, TNA, CO 54/185/31.
50. Mackenzie to Glenelg, No. 14 of 18 January 1839, TNA, CO 54/169. Sujit Sivasundaram in *Islanded*, 291, is mistaken when he writes that 'Mackenzie wrote to London endorsing the view of Anstruther'. The private letter Sivasundaram cites endorses Anstruther's application to extend his leave of absence, not his views on the civil service.
51. *Ceylon Government Gazette*, 15 June 1839.
52. Testimony of Anstruther, Great Britain, Parliament, *Parliamentary Papers* (hereafter *Parl. Pap.*), 1849, 36 (1018), 'Papers Relative to the Affairs of Ceylon', 741.
53. Private Letter from Mackenzie to Lord Glenelg, 11 October 1838, SLNA, 25.5/15.
54. Anstruther's letters, minutes and memoranda are compiled in TNA, CO 54/185/13–194.
55. T.J. Barron, 'George Turnour and British Land Policy in the Kandyan Provinces, 1823–1841', *University of Colombo Review*, 1, 2 (December 1982), 1–16.
56. Turnour to Talbot, 15 July 1839, SLNA, 10/3.
57. Turnour to Assistant Government Agent Matale, 27 February 1837, SLNA, 18/2738.
58. Report by Turnour, 15 April 1839, enclosed in Mackenzie to Normanby, No. 91 of 30 May 1839, TNA, CO 54/170.
59. Anstruther's minute of 21 March 1840 in Mackenzie to Russell, No. 42 of 27 August 1839, TNA, CO 54/172/31.
60. Anstruther Memorandum of 23 November 1840, TNA, CO 54/185/138.
61. Ibid.
62. Letter from Mackenzie to Lady Hood Mackenzie, 15 September 1838, NRS, GD46/9/11.
63. See T. Skinner. *Fifty Years in Ceylon* (London: W.H. Allen, 1891), 201.
64. Ibid., 202.

65. W. Digby (ed.), *Forty Years of Official and Unofficial Life in an Oriental Crown Colony* (Madras and London: Higginbotham and Co. 1879), 86–89.
66. The minutes of the Legislative Council for this period are in SLNA 3/4 and were extensively reported in the Ceylon newspapers.
67. Peebles, *Social Change in Nineteenth Century Ceylon*, 121–123.
68. P. Peebles, *The Plantation Tamils of Ceylon* (London and New York: Leicester University Press, 2001), 86–91.
69. 'Suppression of Vagrancy', Ordinance No. 3 of 1840, in *A Collection of Legislative Acts of the Ceylon Government from 1796: Distinguishing Those Now in Force. Vol. II. Containing Ordinances, Orders in Council, and Letters Patent; from 1833 to 1852* (Colombo: W. Skeen, Government Printer, 1853), 94.
70. Mackenzie to B. McAulay, 5 February 1839.
71. There is a statement of the extent of his plantations in NRS, GD46/9/41. Mary Mackenzie also purchased coffee plantations. See NRS, GD46/9/21.
72. Mooyaart to Anstruther, 30 April 1841, SLNA, 10/26/304–306.
73. Letters from Mary Elizabeth Mackenzie to J.A. Stewart Mackenzie, NRS, GD46/9/23.
74. K.M. de Silva, 'Studies in British Land Policies in Ceylon—I. The evolution of ordinances 12 of 1840 and 9 of 1841', *Ceylon Journal of Historical and Social Studies*, 7, 1 (1964), 30. The dispatch is Mackenzie to Russell, No. 121 of 31 July 1840, TNA, CO 54/180/443.
75. Letters from Mary Elizabeth Mackenzie to J.A. Stewart Mackenzie, NRS, GD46/9/23.
76. Russell, Anstruther and Vernon Smith in the Colonial Office all mention this dispatch, and it is listed in the index.
77. Mackenzie to Russell, No. 75 of 9 May 1840, TNA, CO 54/180/91.
78. Russell to Mackenzie, No. 109 of 1 August 1840, TNA, CO 55/81/102.
79. Anstruther to Vernon Smith, 1 August 1840, TNA, CO 54/185/27.
80. Many but not all of these were copied in TNA, CO 54/180.
81. Mackenzie to Russell, unnumbered of 6 May 1840, TNA, CO 54/180.

82. Diary entry for 27 March 1841, quoted in Digby (ed.) *Life of Sir Richard F. Morgan,* 117–118.

83. All of these have been compiled in TNA, CO 54/185/13–194.

84. For example, Mackenzie to Russell, No. 90 of 8 June 1840, TNA CO 54/180.

85. Cf. K.M. de Silva, 'Two Unpublished Memoranda', *University of Ceylon Review,* 21, 2 (October 1963), 153.

86. Letter accompanying memorandum on the civil service, TNA, CO 54/185/137.

87. M. Pratt, *Britain's Greek Empire: Reflections on the History of the Ionian Islands from the Fall of Byzantium* (London: Collings, 1978), 110, 130; 'The Ionian Islands and Their Government', *Fraser's Magazine for Town and Country,* 46, 275 (November 1852), 603.

88. *Parl. Pap.,* 106 of 1850, 136.

89. Peebles, *Plantation Tamils of Ceylon,* 87–91.

90. T. Nadaraja, *The Legal System of Ceylon in Its Historical Setting* (Leiden: E.J. Brill, 1972), 99–100.

CHAPTER 8

Scots and the Coffee Industry in Nineteenth Century Ceylon

T.J. Barron

It has long been suggested that Scots played a major role in the development of the coffee industry in nineteenth century Ceylon (Sri Lanka). Their work is thought to have helped ensure the success of the early estates in the 1830s and 1840s and to have been of continuing importance throughout the rest of the century.[1] Yet while there is a recognition of a Scots role, there have been few attempts to explain it or to assess its significance. To do so requires a consideration of why Scots were present in numbers and in positions which allowed them to influence the industry's development. A helpful concept here is that of the bridgehead. Coffee first took off as an estate-based enterprise in the 1830s with the colonial government's decision to identify and then put up for sale so-called waste or crown lands.[2] By that time, it is clear, Scots had established a number of occupational bridgeheads which enabled them to seize the opportunities which then arose.

A key factor, for example, seems to have been the movement of skilled and experienced planters from the West Indies to Ceylon. As slave emancipation undermined the West Indian economy, a number of Scots who had been engaged in the sugar and coffee industries there decided to make

T.J. Barron (✉)
Edinburgh, Scotland

© The Author(s) 2017
T.M. Devine, A. McCarthy (eds.), *The Scottish Experience in Asia,
c.1700 to the Present*, DOI 10.1007/978-3-319-43074-4_8

163

the move. The one who became best known is Robert Boyd Tytler from Inverurie, who had been in Jamaica from the age of 15 (Fig. 8.1). Three years later, in 1837, he took up a post in Ceylon. Like most of the others from the West Indies, Tytler had been a superintendent.[3] But we also know of proprietors, like Sir William Reid from Barra, who abandoned their Caribbean estates and purchased a place in Ceylon.[4] Scots, of course, were not alone in making this transition, but it is clear that in terms of numbers they were particularly well established in the West Indies and that the knowledge they had gained and the capital they had acquired inspired and enabled them to move.[5]

The principal importance of this migration lies not in the numbers but in the cultivation skills which it introduced. It was by using what they called 'the West India method of cultivation' that British planters claimed superiority over the native producers of coffee. Coffee had been grown and probably traded in Ceylon for centuries before the British arrived, but the West Indian planters brought new methods of cultivation and processing which, they claimed, produced a better quality product.[6] Before 1830, the earliest British coffee planters (who were largely English or Welsh) had generally followed native methods. The methods which arrived from the West Indies with the Scots were quite different in mode of operation.[7] Strikingly, they owed a great deal not only to acquired experience, but also to a planting guide, *The Coffee Planter of Saint Domingo*, published in 1798 by a French West Indian planter, P.J. Laborie. Laborie's work was designed to pass on the secrets of French agricultural success as a reward for British support of the French planters in the struggle against the slave rebellion led by Toussaint L'Ouverture. But the instructions in Laborie's guide, though comprehensive and detailed, and still consulted by planters in Ceylon half a century later, had, of course, to be adapted for use elsewhere, and the techniques he described had to be tested, further developed and refined once the planters had moved there.[8]

In making adaptations, Scots seem to have been notably active. All commentators agree that planters in Ceylon almost obsessively concerned themselves with the task of surmounting the problems which arose in trying out the methods in a different environment. R.E. Lewis, a Scots coffee planter of the 1840s, describes how in his day planting was 'the one predominating topic of conversation':

> In every form and in every place, men argued, dogmatised and conversed on soils and elevation, on planting with or without shade, on the merits

ROBERT BOYD TYTLER, Esq.

Tropical Agriculturist Portrait Gallery,
No. III.

Fig. 8.1 Robert Boyd Tytler (*Source:* Image from the Biodiversity Heritage Library. Digitised by Natural History Museum Library, London. www.biodiversitylibrary.org)

of Forest, Chena and Patena lands, and the superiority of particular districts, more especially the one of their own selection, for coffee planting. The mode of forming nurseries, the mysteries of holing and a thousand other topics arising out of the simple idea of planting were discussed, in season and out of season, wherever men met and had three minutes to converse.[9]

Even 50 years later, one informed commentator suggested, 'the subject of "agricultural development" is one that may be regarded as a continuous permanent topic of conversation in Ceylon'.[10] But if Scots like Tytler clearly did do something by their espousal of Laborie's work and by their championing of debate to initiate and focus this discussion, it is not suggested that only they participated in it.

A second bridgehead grew out of the refinements made. Initially, planters were expected to command a variety of skills, not only in agriculture but in civil and mechanical engineering. In addition to cultivation, they had to supervise the erection of estate buildings, the creation of estate roads and drains and the design and construction of machinery for processing the crop.[11] Engineering was the first of these planter's tasks to be professionalised. Even before 1850, engineering workshops and companies were being established in the colony, and, to a marked extent, it was to Scotland that the industry looked for specialists. One of the earliest firms was Affleck and Gordon, started in the 1840s by the Affleck brothers from Ayrshire with John Gordon as a partner. A decade later, by which time two of the brothers had died, the Affleck family withdrew from the business and Gordon moved to London. His intention was obviously to aim at a wider market. He took out a patent on their most successful design, a coffee pulper, and began to achieve sales across the tropical Empire.[12]

Amongst several engineers who took the Afflecks' place in the colony, John and William Walker from Doune in Stirlingshire, who had worked in the Deanston cotton mills, one of Scotland's early industrial enterprises, became even more successful. They stole a march on their competitors in Ceylon by setting up small workshops throughout the planting area. They, too, soon sought an outreach beyond the island and again established headquarters back in the UK, first in Glasgow and then in London, eventually becoming one of the best known engineering firms of the Victorian age: John Walker and Sons.[13] Some other Scots engineers, though confining their work to the colony, also became more widely known. John

Brown, from Udny in Aberdeenshire, designed and helped commission irrigation works for the estates, using equipment built in Scotland (turbines, sluices and pipes) for projects which were thought ambitious enough to require an expansion of the then current frontiers of the profession. Even the UK press took an interest in his activities.[14] Amongst other developments, the use of wire shoots, to convey the coffee berry from the fields to the factory processing units, was another West Indian procedure familiar to Scots which was adopted and further developed in Ceylon.[15]

The emergence of an engineering profession in Ceylon did nothing, however, to discourage individual planters from making their own experiments, particularly with new designs for their machinery. On the contrary, the workshops made it easier for them to get their ideas tried out. One contemporary noted 'the adoption of mechanised appliances' which, it appeared to him, 'intelligent and scientific planters are continually inventing'.[16] What was aimed at was ease and economy of operation and the introduction of new, more durable materials, metal parts for wood, turbines and steam engines for human, animal or water power.[17] Some of these inventions appeared on the market, some patented, some not. William Clerihew produced a famous coffee dryer which replaced laborious and costly manual efforts to keep the beans, once pulped, from fermenting. Unluckily, his machine was so widely copied that it was some years after his retirement to Aberdeen that he managed to establish his claim to have been the first to devise the method.[18] John Brown invented a combined crusher and pulper which was held to more effectively remove the coffee's outer skin, a key element in the processing. But such inventions, though often adopted by others, were not the exclusive achievement of the Scots. English planters like Samuel Butler and George Wall were also successful in making improvements to the coffee processing machinery and most manuals which assessed the various local models were disinclined to suggest that any had universal applicability.[19]

Adaptations of West Indian methods were not, of course, confined to machinery. Many practical planters were aware of the improvements which could be achieved by trying out different agricultural processes, too, and at least in one area they got far beyond individual effort. Scots planters were notable in wishing to put the perceived need for manuring on a scientific basis. In a celebrated case, Robert Boyd Tytler brought in the assistance of a professor of Chemistry at the University of Aberdeen to try and find an elixir which would bring permanent felicity to his soils. Although that effort failed, an interest in the subject took root, both academically and practically, so that, at the end of the century, Aberdeen became the first university in the UK to offer scholarships in tropical agriculture on the basis of funds provided by one of its graduates who had made his wealth in part from his experiments in chemical engineering in Ceylon.[20]

A third bridgehead emerged from the decision of the government in Ceylon in 1833 to encourage civil servants to invest in land in an effort to inject capital into agriculture. Scots who had sought a career in the service of the crown, from governors to assistant government agents, now had an opportunity to buy land at a price (five shillings an acre) widely regarded as guaranteeing them a profit from re-sales alone.[21] The policy lasted only until 1844 when it was rescinded in the face of much public opposition since it was felt to compromise the impartiality of civil servants and to distract them from their duties.[22] But in this crucial period one of the more active of the colonial governors and the colonial secretary (head of the civil service) were Scots and both, like many Scots in lesser administrative ranks, became proprietors.[23] After 1844 the officials were required to divest themselves of the properties, but they were then allowed to put them in the name of relatives so that a family stake in planting could survive.[24] Moreover, if they did decide to cultivate rather than to re-sell the properties, they invariably sent home for relatives, friends or suitable recruits from their locality to superintend the estates for them. In this way, more Scots from outside the landed classes found their way to Ceylon.[25]

A fourth bridgehead was provided by the Scots who sought careers in the army. It has been largely overlooked that the colonial government in the early 1840s, perhaps alarmed by the growing signs of disaffection provoked by their land-sales policy, tried to encourage army men to purchase coffee estates and provided for them the inducement of a remission on the purchase price (which had in 1844 risen to £1 an acre), the amount varying according to their length of service and seniority of rank.[26] Many contemporaries and many more recent commentators have remarked on the large number of colonels, majors and other high-ranking former officers amongst Ceylon planters, and have speculated that the explanation must be found in the fondness of military men, once in civilian life, to inflate their rank the better to impress the neighbours. In fact, most of the ranks, even if some were from volunteer units, appear to be perfectly genuine.[27]

It was a stroke of luck, perhaps, that two regular Scottish regiments were on garrison duty in Ceylon at the time when these coffee estates were first on offer (though not fortunate from the point of view of their health—European soldiers were notoriously prone to tropical diseases).

The 78th Highland Regiment (the Ross-shire Buffs) was there between 1826 and 1842 and the 90th Light Infantry, recruited in Perthshire, between 1835 and 1846.[28] Not everyone in these regiments, of course, was Scots, especially not in the latter case, but a great many were. One of the leading Scots military planters was Colonel Martin Lindsay of the 78th Highlanders. He took leave from his regiment even before the remission rules were in place, went home to Scotland, sold his commission, and returned in 1837 to become co-owner of one of the best estates on the island, Rajawella.[29] But not only officers were involved. Sergeant Davidson from Bonner in Caithness and Sergeant Dalziel from Stuartfield in Buchan are examples of other ranks who left the 78th and tried planting. Neither, alas, seems to have enjoyed much success, though they did find other related employment locally.[30]

A fifth bridgehead was formed by the mercantile firms in Ceylon, many of which had Scottish connections. Nearly all of them began life as businesses working in the coastal trade between the Indian presidencies and Ceylon, particularly the private trade. The largest before 1848 was Acland and Boyd, which became one of the first to transform itself into an estate agency.[31] It was founded on the initiative of William Smith Boyd, who was a relative of Robert Boyd Tytler and like him hailed from Buchan. Boyd was said to have made a fortune in Brazil, after which he set up a mercantile firm in London with a branch in Calcutta. He then persuaded a nephew, George Hay Boyd, to open an office in Colombo in collaboration with George Acland (whose origins are less clear—he may even have been English) who, like his partner, had been in the East India Company mercantile marine. It was the Acland and Boyd company which is said to have bought up copies of Laborie's book for distribution in Ceylon, and which began to acquire a vast amount of land suitable for coffee for re-sale to clients in the UK and India. They were also behind the recruitment of large numbers of potential planters, many from north-east Scotland, to work on the estates.[32]

Boyd died in 1837 and the firm of Acland and Boyd vanished in the disastrous recession of 1846–49 when many of the early estate agencies (like estates in private hands) collapsed. But their place was rapidly taken by those who managed to survive the recession, such as Keir and Dundas (founded by Simon Keir and G.H. Dundas), an entirely Scottish agency, and Gavin and Pitts, which was an Anglo-Scottish one (John Gavin came from Strichen, Charles Pitts was a Londoner). These two firms amalgamated in 1851 under Gavin's leadership, retaining the Keir and Dundas name, to become Ceylon's biggest estate agency of the day. A decade later, in 1862, Gavin relinquished his chairmanship and was succeeded by two Englishmen, G.D.B. Harrison and Martin Leake (both Londoners), though it was said that the firm retained a strong Scottish constituency in its ranks.[33]

Estate agencies were largely responsible for the rapid spread of the coffee industry in the middle decades of the nineteenth century. They devised a system (known as 'creeping') for training estate managers and rapidly moving them on to positions of responsibility, and then requiring them in turn to train the next generation. In this way an exponential growth was achieved in the spread of coffee cultivation.[34] They also enlisted as clients many of the capitalists seeking land for development since the government's own procedures for land sales were regarded as cumbersome, complex and uncertain. Above all, the agencies succeeded in bringing together investors and planters by setting up credit streams from Britain and India to Ceylon which involved finance houses and banks.[35] The pioneer house here was the Madras firm Arbuthnot and Company. Its origins were not Scots, but in 1823 its chairmanship was assumed by George Arbuthnot from Edinburgh, later known as Arbuthnot of Elderslie, and he brought out from Scotland numerous members of his extended family to assist in running the business. Their commercial activities were numerous and spanned much of South India and beyond, and one service they provided was that of making financial advances to planters in Ceylon.[36]

As elsewhere, planters were always in need of finance to tide them over the long period between planting and crop (it took three years for an estate to produce a crop, five for it to be fully in bearing and there was then a further gap of around nine months for the crop, unless sold locally, to be moved to the London market and auctioned).[37] Here again, Scots, with their recognised interests in banking, were often prominent. The first chartered bank in Ceylon (the Bank of Ceylon), which broke the East India Company's monopoly in exchange banking, opened in 1840.[38] In origin, it was not particularly Scottish. When it foundered in the great recession of 1846–49, however, a substitute was already available which was very largely a Scottish concern. The Bank of Western India, begun in Bombay in 1842, opened branches in Ceylon as early as 1843. Its directors from the first were Scottish, the Ceylon offices being run by George Smyttan Duff from Banff, a relative of the Bombay founders. In 1845 the bank created new headquarters in London and became the Oriental Bank Company.[39] Surviving the recession, it amalgamated in

1851 with the Bank of Ceylon and changed its name to the Oriental Bank Corporation (OBC). Within ten years, it then became Asia's premier bank, the one which paid the highest dividends and boasted the largest paid-up capital and deposits. Its contribution to extending the coffee industry in the 1850s and 1860s, though not unique (Barings, Coutts and a number of other major houses were involved), is immense. In the 1870s, however, when its businesses in other countries suffered some setbacks, it began a reckless policy in Ceylon of allowing loans on the strength of mortgages on property (instead of on crop futures), even though its constitution forbade this. The policy coincided with the spread of a coffee leaf disease (hemelia vastatrix) which brought crisis to the industry and would ultimately largely destroy it. The bank was forced to foreclose on its loans and found itself encumbered with unsellable Ceylon estates. It finally stopped payments altogether in 1884, and many a planter's private nest-egg savings, along with investors' capital, went with it.[40]

Nor was it the only bank in trouble at this time. It has been suggested that a serious financial crisis occurred in Ceylon almost every ten years.[41] As a largely monocultural economy operating mainly on borrowed capital, it was sensitive to every ripple of financial discontent in the homeland. One such ripple (or perhaps wave) was the collapse of the City of Glasgow bank in 1878. Founded in 1839 and appealing particularly to small investors, the bank had taken a hand in financing the Ceylon estates. When it got into difficulties and experienced a run on the bank (the last major such occasion in the UK before the recent fall of Northern Rock), its difficulties, like those of the OBC, were blamed on troubles elsewhere, not on its Ceylon investments. But its collapse still contributed to a downturn in the Ceylon economy, too. The bank's directors went to jail for falsifying accounts, just as the last surviving member of the Arbuthnot banking family was to do when that firm, after several crises, finally collapsed in 1906.[42] Clearly not all bridgeheads were entirely secure.

If these bridgeheads offer some explanations of why Scots were able to find roles within the planting industry in Ceylon, there is still a need to account for why individuals responded to the opportunities provided. Scholars of imperial emigration suggest that family networks and chain migration often lie behind the decisions to move, and this certainly seems to apply to Ceylon.[43] It is evident from any list of planters that sons followed fathers, brothers brothers and relations relations into the industry. With landed proprietors, inheritance alone might explain the process. But it was by no means limited to them. Lists of superintendents show precisely the same family bias. There is evidence, too, that one family member choosing to take up an opportunity abroad was sometimes enough to encourage other members to do so, even when the choice of destination was very different. Family support mechanisms and familiarity with the place chosen may not have been the only factors involved.[44]

Equally, chain migration, whereby one individual in a community, by migrating and reporting home on his experiences, could persuade others from the same area to seek to follow him, is also evident. There are two striking examples involving Ceylon planters. In the 1840s and 1850s, the area of East Aberdeenshire with the small village of Crimond as its centre produced a large number of recruits for the estates; and in the 1850s and 1860s the process was once again in operation, with Laurencekirk in the Mearns serving as the focus. In both cases, a prominent Ceylon planter (Robert Boyd Tytler and Peter Moir, respectively, whose home areas these were) seems to have been a key figure in the recruitment. Perhaps predictably, also, more than one member of a family was often persuaded to go. The density of recruitment from these regions may explain why Aberdeen was chosen as the venue for a famous Ceylon planters' reunion dinner in 1875.[45]

Though recruitment to the estates seems to follow familiar lines, it also included a strong element of commercial recruitment, which adds another dimension to what appealed to Scots. It is clear that agencies, public and private, preferred using established planters as recruiters, sending them back to their home areas to spread the word. This enabled them to evoke local patriotism in making their appeals. Alexander (Sandy) Brown, who had enjoyed great success as a planter, when addressing an audience in his home town of Banff in 1873, began by asserting that 'Ceylon has been facetiously called an outlying dependency of Aberdeen and Banffshire', though he didn't go on to explain why this was a joke.[46] Some offered an even narrower definition: 'Tak awa Aberdeen and twal miles roon and faur are ye' was one comment. When applied to the Ceylon planting industry, this meant: if you were to remove Aberdonians and those who came from 12 miles round Aberdeen, there would be no-one of any significance in the enterprise left. Though no evidence was offered for the assertion, the intention was obviously to suggest that for north-east Scots Ceylon was certain to seem a home from home.[47]

If much exaggerated, there were grounds for the suggestion. Scottish clannishness did manifest itself strongly in Ceylon. When, for example, one recruit intent on a planting career arrived in Colombo from

Inverness, knowing no-one in the island, he was immediately provided with accommodation and advice by two Scots who knew the Highland capital well and whose wives were at that moment residing there.[48] The tradition of hospitality, whereby planters were expected to offer to put up any member of the planting fraternity who found himself passing near their estates and in need of accommodation (there were, of course, no hotels or boarding houses in the more remote districts), may also have provided support for the notion that Scots could universally expect a welcome in Ceylon, though the practice was widely observed and not exclusive to Scots.[49] But even the occasion of a Christmas or New Year's celebration could seem to some an expression of Scottish solidarity. One planter called his comradely seasonal get-togethers 'the gathering of the clans'.[50]

The local press must also be seen as a major source for such ideas. It was dominated by what was popularly called the Observer Press, more formally A.M. & J. Ferguson's, an uncle and nephew pair of editor/proprietors, who hailed from Ross-shire.[51] The firm had actually been started in the 1830s by an Englishman and first gained celebrity in the 1840s under an Irish owner and editor, but it was the Fergusons who brought it international attention as publishers of a whole series of books, guides, directories and gazettes which highlighted the achievements of the Ceylon plantation industry.[52] They also ran the best-known Ceylon newspaper, *The Observer*, which, though meant to appeal to all communities, they made into an organ which Scots would find peculiarly congenial. A good many poems in Scots were accepted for publication and not a few literary pieces, satires and squibs as well as serious analyses of planting life, in which Scots words or phrases and Scottish stories and reports found a place. The senior editor, Alistair Mackenzie Ferguson, was himself something of a poet in Scots, and his nephew and junior, John, was one of the admirers of his talent.[53]

Their work culminated in the launch of *The Tropical Agriculturist* in 1881 for which John later commissioned what amounted to a history of the Ceylon coffee industry through biographical studies of its leading proponents. In all, there were no fewer than four series of articles produced between 1893 and 1901 and, helpfully, John Ferguson, as editor in chief, drew attention in his introduction to the series to the national origins of his chosen subjects.[54] Though his categories are not entirely clear, the following table is one interpretation of what he intends to suggest:

Native-born English and Welsh	English descent born elsewhere	Native-born Scots	Scots descent born elsewhere	Irish	German
21	1	23	3	1	2

This gives the Scots a clear majority, but as the three Scots born elsewhere were actually born in England, the figures could also be presented as

Native-born English and Welsh	English descent born elsewhere	Native-born Scots	Scots descent born elsewhere	Irish	German
24	1	23	0	1	2

in which case the English are in the majority. Ferguson is not, of course, suggesting that these figures accurately reflect the proportions of each nation within the coffee planting community at any point in its history. He is dealing only with those he regards as making the most distinguished early contributions. Since most contemporary estimates of the numbers of planters (supervisors and assistants) in the middle of the coffee era suggest a total of around 500–800, with a maximum of 1,000, his sample is also too small to be used comparatively.[55]

Statistics on the relative proportion of national groups within the coffee industry are not yet available. But it is possible to get some indications or hints from the censuses of Ceylon which are available for 1871, 1881 and 1891. They are not easy to use.[56] Most authorities regard them as unreliable in various ways, especially the first; and, unfortunately, in the second, instead of being asked for their nationality, everyone was asked to provide their race and the country to which they belonged. The returns suggest facetious or perhaps political responses, some facile enough to evoke a rebuke from the editor about 'imbecile jocosity'.[57] Identifying Scots in the list is consequently not entirely easy: they may be contained within any of the following entries: 'Scotch', 'British', 'European', 'American-descended', 'American-Scotch', 'Anglo-Saxon' and 'Kelt'. If we count only those specifically designated English, Irish, Scotch and Welsh (though remembering these are figures for the total population, not just planters), the Scots are 23 per cent of the group and 25 per cent if only men are included. If only the population of the Central Province is considered (which is where most of the planters were based), Scots are 24 per cent of the English, Irish, Scotch and Welsh and 28 per cent if only men are included. These proportions are well above those of Scots in the UK domestic population, but well below the percentages which Ferguson's accounts seem to indicate.[58]

One difficulty is to know what dates and what categories of planters are being considered. Initially, even the Fergusons were critical of those who asserted Scottish superiority, but later they became less cautious.[59] In his book *Ceylon in 1883,* published that year, John suggests that 'the rough work of pioneering in the early days before there were district roads, villages, supplies, doctors, or other comforts of civilisation, was chiefly done by hard-headed Scots'. Opportunities for such work, he judged, still existed in the 1880s but by then had become a fringe activity, and gentlemen-planters (never predominantly Scots, he implies) were now the norm.[60] It is an image of the Scot as frontiersman which clearly had for him and others a plausibility and an appeal, though it would be difficult to prove its validity. The English/Welsh planter George Byrde, a key figure in the early period of planting, told Ferguson pointedly that he felt he had every bit as much of a claim to the appellation as anyone else.[61] Yet, in giving a vote of thanks at an event in the 1890s, John Ferguson congratulated the chairman, Lord Aberdeen, on hailing from the country (Scotland) which, he said, had once produced two-thirds of all Ceylon coffee planters at some earlier (undisclosed) time.[62] Was this pure hyperbole?

It would be hard to deny that in the first few decades of Ceylon coffee planting, particularly the 1840s and 1850s, Scots did achieve some prominence within the industry. When the Planters Association (PA) was formed in 1854, for example, its chairman and its secretary (both elected posts) were Scots (though replaced by Englishmen only two years later) and Scots often reappeared in one or other—or both—of the leading positions throughout the rest of the century.[63] It is also true, of course, that PA membership waxed and waned over time and never included all the planters. But there is no doubt that the organisation was regarded by the colonial authorities as the voice of the planting community and it was given the right to nominate to a place on the legislative council. All planters must at least have been aware of its activities.[64]

In a publication of 1907, Arnold Wright, like John Ferguson, included potted planter biographies in what he intended to be a general survey of life in the colony.[65] Wright deals with late nineteenth century planters. Unfortunately, his survey is even more problematic to use as a source of statistical evidence, the entries being apparently, to some degree, self-solicited. The biographical details do, however, display one clear difference from those in Ferguson's lists. Whereas Ferguson's Scots, who almost all first arrived in Ceylon between 1830 and 1860, are generally from rural backgrounds and are parish-school educated, Wright's Scots, who arrived from 1860–1900, are largely from an urban background and are public-school educated, and many more of the latter have been to University.[66] It is also clear that this social change marks a change in the skills planters were expected to command.

Before 1870, planters needed to be literate and numerate simply because most employers and investors wanted a careful record kept of the work performed (and particularly the costs) on the estates.[67] After 1870, improved communications, the arrival of the railway, better housing, a richer social life, particularly marked by the presence of more women, were indicative of a change which had also seen an alteration in the nature of employment. More of the planter's routine work was being passed on to those lower in the pay-scale ranks, assistants or conductors (quite often locally recruited) or even to canganies (the labour bosses), and much was now done by contract work, performed (at a cost) by local and coolie labour.[68] Even as early as 1865, when Andrew Hunter, from the Carse of Gowrie, took ill and went home, one of his friends suggested telling the caretaker left in charge 'that a great deal more can be done on a Coffee Estate by head work than by absolutely sticking behind a lot of coolies all day long'.[69] With basic tasks of supervision left to others, the role of the planter began to attract not frontiersmen but a more highly educated and more consciously managerial class.

Estate agencies, which once had provided the advances for recruits whom they trained as planters, after 1870 were more characteristically asked to provide a training for those who already had capital and the intention to purchase a property but who lacked a knowledge of the business. For this, of course, they were willing to pay.[70] The expectation grew that a planter should be able to supervise more than one estate and, to ensure that professionalism was not lost by this, there emerged out of the ranks of the best superintendents the new role of visiting agent (VA).[71] He had the responsibility of travelling round all the estates serving one particular agency (and others willing to pay for the privilege), offering guidance and advice on any problems which might arise. For the agency, his key function was that of making an evaluation of the likely crop from the first appearance of the berries, so ensuring that closer financial supervision over the individual planter could be achieved.[72]

These changes may have introduced a greater element of stability into the industry, but, for most of the nineteenth century, coffee planting could be a challenging career. Scots from the humblest backgrounds were often content with little, and contrasted their comfortable life in Ceylon (they all had servants, of course) with the rigours of farm labour at home.[73] But most aimed higher with very mixed results. Several both made and lost great fortunes and even the titled were not immune to the general instability. The Elphinstones, lairds of Logie, in 1876 controlled 32 estates, totalling over 14,000 acres, but in the 1890s Sir Graeme (the surviving son) was driven to asking their Tamil estate manager for financial assistance to enable him to move elsewhere.[74] Sandy Brown by the 1860s was proprietor or lessee of 21 estates and had become a pillar of the PA. But by the time of his death in 1876, he had lost everything and was living in penury.[75] Andrew Nicol from Banff made his wealth from buying and selling estates which he supplemented with mercantile work. By 1854, when he first went home, he was able to purchase Auchintoul House in Marnoch in Banffshire. But those he left in charge of his Ceylon enterprises soon succeeded in driving him into debt. It took a total of 23 further journeys to Ceylon before his finances recovered (Fig. 8.2).[76]

Those working in ancillary positions tended to fare rather better. Arthur Sinclair, another planter from Aberdeenshire, found a route to wealth through becoming a VA for several agencies. By his retirement, he was supervising around 100 estates, for which he was paid over £2,000 per year.[77] Estate agency headships also offered good prospects. John Gavin of Keir and Dundas went home in 1862 to a comfortable retirement.[78] William Duff Gibbon, from Lonmay, did even better: he moved from planting and VA work to become the UK agent for a number of Ceylon planting companies (by grouping together in companies, estates found they could obtain limited liability status for themselves). When nearly 80, he was knighted for his services to the industry.[79] John Lewis Gordon, from Moray, took over George Steuart and Company, one of the biggest agencies in the colony and one which barred its directors from owning estates. Perhaps in consequence, he also did well.[80] But there are exceptions here, too. Captain Keith Jolly, whose father had been lord lieutenant of Stirling and Dunbartonshire, enjoyed mixed success as a planter before securing a partnership in George Wall's agency, yet he still struggled. When he died in 1865 the *Observer* recorded that he had finally succeeded in earning what all planters sought—'a small independence'.[81]

Sir James Elphinstone amongst the Planters.

Fig. 8.2 Sir James Elphinstone amongst the planters (*Source*: Image from the Biodiversity Heritage Library. Digitised by Natural History Museum Library, London. www.biodiversitylibrary.org)

Some, including the most distinguished, like Robert Boyd Tytler, failed to achieve even that. The only option for most was eventually to move on. *The Tropical Agriculturist*, a journal for 'the practical planter', had features aimed especially at 'retired colonists and planters in other lands who owe their training to Ceylon'.[82] A few years on from the launch, the editor was claiming a circulation in India, Burma, the Straits, Java, Sumatra, Borneo, Northern Australia, Queensland, Fiji, Mauritius, Natal, the West Indies, South America, Central America, the southern states of the USA and the UK as well as Ceylon.[83] Sadly, this more or less precisely lists where one or other of the Scots planters would next find himself. By 1900, it was Ceylon which, in its turn, had become the new bridgehead.

Notes

1. Despite its title, D.M. Forrest, A *Hundred Years of Ceylon Tea* (London: Chatto & Windus, 1967), 62–66, 105, 121–122, 194–197, offers *inter alia* some helpful comments on Scots in the Ceylon coffee industry. A more specific account, though limited in coverage, is provided in Ranald C. Michie, 'Aberdeen and Ceylon: Economic Links in the Nineteenth Century', *Northern Scotland*, 4 (1981), 69–82.
2. I.H. vanden Driesen, 'Plantation Agriculture and Land Sales Policy in Ceylon, Part I' and 'Land Sales Policy and Some Aspects of the Problem of Tenure, Part II', *University of Ceylon Review*, XIV (1956), 6–25, and XV (1957), 36–52, is still the main source.
3. Tytler's career is outlined in 'Pioneers of the Planting Enterprise in Ceylon from 1830s Onwards' (hereafter 'Pioneers ... '), *Tropical Agriculturist* (hereafter *TA*), 13, 4, 2 October 1893, 217–222.
4. For Reid, see P.D. Millie, *Thirty Years Ago* (Colombo: A.M. & J. Ferguson, 1878), chapter VI, editor's footnote (no pagination) and A.M. Ferguson, *Ceylon in 1837–46* (Colombo: A.M. & J. Ferguson, 1886), 32.
5. Recent research on Scots in the Caribbean is summarised in T.M. Devine, *To The Ends of the Earth: Scotland's Global Diaspora, 1750–2010* (London: Allen Lane, 2011), 19–20, 43–7, 49–50.
6. An early account of 'the West Indian system' is given in *The Observer and Commercial Advertiser* (Colombo), 6, 21 February 1834, 3. The term became the established one: John Ferguson, *Ceylon in 1883* (London: Sampson Low, Marston & Co., 1883), 56.

7. In an autobiographical account by a witness, Henry C. Byrde, in 'Pioneers ...', *op. cit.*, 16, 9, 1 March 1897, 7–8, Scots are specifically identified as the instigators of the change.

8. P.J. Laborie, *The Coffee Planter of Saint Domingo* (London: T. Caddell & W. Davies, 1798), reissued Colombo 1845 (publisher W.J. Van Geyzel). Subsequent developments can be traced in Aliquis, *Coffee Planting in Ceylon* (London: Taylor & Francis, 1861), 1–36, and in A. Brown's contribution to J. Ferguson (ed.), *The Coffee Planter's Manual* (Colombo: A.M. & J. Ferguson, 1894), 1–62.

9. R.E. Lewis, 'Some Recollections of Early Days in Ceylon', *Monthly Register and Notes and Queries for Ceylon*, III, 12, December 1895, 284.

10. John Ferguson, editorial, *TA*, 17, 2, 1897–98, 83.

11. The work is described in Charles Pridham, *An Historical, Political and Statistical Account of Ceylon and its Dependencies* (London: T & W. Boone, 1849), I, 377–82.

12. J.P. Lewis, *A List of Tombstones and Monuments in Ceylon* (Colombo: H.C. Cottle, 1913), 64, discusses the Afflecks, as does Thomas Villiers, *Mercantile Lore* (Colombo: Observer Press, 1940), 236. For Gordon, see E.C.P. Hull, *Coffee Planting in Southern India and Ceylon* (London: E & F.N. Spon, 1877), 192–193, 198–199. Gordon's patent, dated 9 January 1858, is in the PRO: BT45/21/4043.

13. There are sketches of John and William Walker in 'Pioneers ...', *TA*, 13, 9, 1 March 1894, 575–581, and 17, 5, 1 November 1897, 297–302.

14. John Brown (and press comment) is also included in 'Pioneers ...', *TA*, 16, 11, 1 May 1897, 735–738.

15. Tytler to Planters Association, 14 December 1855, *Proceedings of the Planters Association* (Colombo: Observer Press, 1856), 52–53.

16. A.M. Ferguson, *The Ceylon Directory ... for 1866–68* (Colombo: Observer Press, 1868), 180.

17. Hull, *Coffee Planting*, 187–194.

18. Clerihew established his claim in correspondence with the PA: Clerihew to PA, 31 May 1858, *Proceedings of the Planters Association* (Colombo: Examiner Press, 1859), 71.

19. Brown and Butler's inventions are discussed in Hull, *Coffee Planting*, 189–190 and in A.M. Ferguson, *The Ceylon Commonplace Book* (Colombo: Observer Press, 1860), 74–76.

20. John D. Hargreaves, *Academe and Empire* (Aberdeen: University Press, 1994), 67–69.

21. Department of National Archives Sri Lanka (SLNA), 6/1839, Government Advertisement, 11 July 1833. For an example of a quick re-sale, SLNA, 38/59, AGA Kurunegala to GA, 31 July 1834.

22. C.W. Payne, *The Eastern Empire, Crown Colonies: Ceylon* (London: G. Odell, 1847), 8; Pridham, *An Historical, Political and Statistical Account*, I, 213; Thomas Skinner, *Fifty Years in Ceylon* (London: W.H. Allen, 1891), 222–223.

23. Stewart Mackenzie Manuscripts, National Records of Scotland (hereafter NRS), GD 46/9/38 and GD 46/9/39.

24. Mackenzie's and Anstruther's names still survive in the lists in A.M. Ferguson, *The Ceylon Common Place Book* (Colombo: Observer Press, 1861), section XXX, 'Yakdessa'.

25. Mackenzie used Mr McGregor as his first planting superintendent: Mackenzie MS, NRS, GD 46/9/19, Mackenzie to James Stewart, 5 April 1841; and estate expenses, entries for January to March 1841, GD 46/9/8 item 1. The fullest account of supervision of a civil servant's estates is by an Englishman in the R.B. Naish collection, newspaper clipping, 'Planting in 1843: Pioneering Eighty Years Ago: Letters from a Kegalle Clearing', Centre of South Asian Studies, Cambridge University.

26. J.W. Bennett, *Ceylon and its Capabilities* (London: W.H. Allen, 1843), appendix, xxv, Adjutant to General Macdonald, 16 April 1840.

27. The suspicion is voiced in Forrest, *A Hundred Years*, 36–37, which repeats the charge and identifies some of its sources.

28. A.M. Ferguson, *Ceylon in 1837–46*, 42–9; William Sabonadiere, *The Coffee Planter of Ceylon* (Guernsey: Mackenzie Son & Le Patourel, 1866), 3.

29. For Lindsay, 'A Pioneer's Plantation in Ceylon and a Soldier Planter', *TA*, 17, 12, 1 June 1898, 799–803; William Boyd, 'Ceylon and its Pioneers', *Ceylon Literary Register*, 29, 3 February 1888, 225.

30. For Davidson, SLNA, 6/1415, J. Davidson to Colonial Secretary, 13 December 1837; for Dalziel, see Boyd, 'Ceylon and its Pioneers', *Ceylon Literary Register*, 35, 16 March 1888, 273.

31. Acland (alias Ackland) and Boyd feature in Lewis, *A List of Tombstones*, 446–447 and in Thomas Villiers, *Mercantile Lore*, 240 (entry for Whittall & Co). See also SLNA, 6/1150, A&B to Col. Sec., 13 September 1835.

32. Boyd, 'Ceylon and its Pioneers', *Ceylon Literary Register*, 25, 27 January 1888, 217–218.

33. There are biographical sketches of the main figures in 'Pioneers …', entries for John Gavin, Keith Jolly, and William Martin Leake: 13, 10, 2 April 1894, 647–650; 18, 4, 1 October 1898, 229–231; and 17, 4, 1 October 1897, 223–229.

34. 'The Creeper', *TA*, 17, 1, 1 July 1897, 53.

35. Stewart Mackenzie to John Stewart, 6 May 1839, Mackenzie Papers, SRO, GD 46/9/6, item 138; *The Ceylon Calendar* (Colombo, 1841), 69–70; James Steuart, *Notes on the Monetary System* (Colombo: Examiner Press, 1850), 25–26.

36. R.S.M. Arbuthnot, *Memoirs of the Arbuthnots of Kincardineshire and Aberdeenshire* (London: Allen & Unwin, 1920), 328–423; Villiers, *Mercantile Lore*, 5–23; SLNA, 6/1473, no. 172, Turnour to Col. Sec., 17 May 1837.

37. Lieut. de Butts, *Rambles in Ceylon* (London: W.H. Allen, 1841),180–184.

38. *The Ceylon Almanac … for 1846* (Colombo, 1846), 113.

39. Ibid., 114–115; see also James Steuart, *Notes on Ceylon and its Affairs* (London: privately printed, 1862), 23–25; entry for G.S. Duff in 'Pioneers …', *TA*, 16, 10, 1 April 1897, 661–663.

40. Toshio Suzuki, 'The Rise and Decline of the Oriental Bank Corporation, 1842–84', http://www.oxfordscholarship.com/view/10.1093/acprof:oso/9780199646326 (accessed 12 May 2016).

41. George Wall made the theory his own: Speculum (alias Wall), *Ceylon: Her Present Condition* (Colombo: Observer Press, 1868), *passim*, especially p. 17. It was further developed by Ferguson, *Ceylon in 1883*, 76–78.

42. R. Srinavasan, *The Fall of Arbuthnot and Co* (Madras: EastWest, 2005), *passim*.

43. Marjory Harper, *Emigration from North-East Scotland* (Aberdeen: Aberdeen University Press, 1988), I, 348–349.
44. For example, John Smith casually chose Ceylon after his sister had emigrated to Australia and his two brothers to the USA: John Smith to James Willox, 26 November 1859, McIntosh-Smith family papers in possession of Lady Roberts.
45. Boyd, 'Ceylon and its Pioneers', *Ceylon Literary Register*, 218–219 (for Crimond), and Lewis, *A List of Tombstones*, 314 (under Hugh Blacklaw, for Laurencekirk). For the reunion, see Harper, *Emigration from North-East Scotland*, I, 333.
46. Alex Brown, *Ceylon: A Lecture* (Colombo: Observer Press, 1873), 1.
47. John Gavin in 'Pioneers ...', *TA*, 13, 10, 2 April 1894, 647–650.
48. McIntosh-Smith Papers, John Smith to Elsie Willox, n.d. (August 1859?) and John Smith to Maggie, 14 September 1880.
49. Mostly this company was welcomed but not always: e.g. Hunter of Glencarse Papers, National Library of Scotland (hereafter NLS), MS19724, Hunter's Diary, entry for 20 October 1869.
50. McIntosh-Smith Papers, John Smith to Elsie, 17 January 1863.
51. There are biographies of the Fergusons in 'Pioneers ...', *TA*, 13, 3, 1 September 1893, 145–149 and 24, 3, 1 September 1904, 141–142.
52. The Englishman was George Winter and the Irishman Dr Christopher Elliott. There is a brief history, uneven in quality, of the Ceylon Press by Francis Bevan in Arnold Wright (ed.), *Twentieth Century Impressions of Ceylon: Its History, People, Commerce, Industries, and Resources* (London: Lloyd's Greater Britain Publishing Company, 1907), 301–319.
53. There is an example of A.M. Ferguson's verse in his entry in 'Pioneers ...', *TA*, 145–149.
54. John Ferguson provides calculations of national origins only for the first two series. His classifications, never certain, have therefore to be deduced.
55. James Taylor, for example, suggested in 1859 some 300 superintendents and 150 assistants. See James Taylor to Michael Taylor, 27 May 1859, in Papers of James Taylor, planter in Ceylon, NLS, MS 15908.
56. Patrick Peebles, *The Plantation Tamils of Ceylon* (London: Leicester University Press, 2001), 9–10.

57. Lionel Lee (ed.), *Census of Ceylon, 1881* (Colombo: Government Printer, 1882), xxxii, 4 and table, 140.

58. Scots are generally thought to have constituted between 10 per cent and 11 per cent of the UK population in this period: Devine, *To the Ends of the Earth*, 14, 271.

59. P.D. Millie, '*Thirty Years Ago*' *or Reminiscences* ... (Colombo: A.M. & J. Ferguson, 1876), ch.17 (no pagination). Millie argued that Scots were better planters than the English: a Ferguson editorial footnote disputes this.

60. Ferguson, *Ceylon in 1883*, 97.

61. Entry for Lieut-Col. Henry C. Byrde, 'Pioneers ...', *TA*, 16, 9, 1 March 1898, 588–591.

62. John Ferguson, *Ceylon in 1893* (Colombo: A.M. & J. Ferguson, 1893), appendix 1, 230.

63. *Report of the Proceedings of the Planters' Association* (Colombo, 1855), Minutes, 17 February 1854, 1–2.

64. *Jubilee of the Planters' Association of Ceylon, 1854–1904* (London: Miller & Co., 1904), 1–10.

65. Wright, *Twentieth Century Impressions*, 711–892, especially 'The Planting Interest', 875–892.

66. This was noted earlier by Ferguson, *Ceylon in 1883*, 98.

67. For a detailed account of the work, see Hunter of Glencarse Papers, NLS, MS 19726-31.

68. These developments were first noted in the late 1860s by George Wall, Martin Leake and others in A.M. Ferguson, *The Ceylon Directory* (Colombo, 1868), 94–119. They are further explored in A.M. Ferguson, *Supplement to Ferguson's Directory* (Colombo, 1869), iii–v.

69. Hunter of Glencarse Papers, NLS, MS 19722 (f. 322–339), Ryan to Hunter, 6 November 1865.

70. Ferguson, *Ceylon in 1883*, 98.

71. Peter Moir's letter of 20 November 1865 in A.M. Ferguson, *The Ceylon Directory*, 102–103.

72. F.E.F.P., *Fickle Fortune in Ceylon* (Madras: Addison, 1889), 36. Reginald Downall, an Englishman and one of the most famous VAs, often urged his planters to 'ca canny' (Scots for 'proceed cautiously'), surely evidence of Scottish influence on the industry: Hunter of Glencarse Papers, NLS, MS 19722 (f. 79), Procter to Hunter, 11 April 1865.

73. A good example is Alex Cushny Mortimer in 'Pioneers...', *TA*, 23, 5, 2 November 1905, 297–301.

74. Frederick Lewis, 'A Few Pioneer Estates and Early Pioneers in Ceylon', *Colombo Historical Association Pamphlets*, 10 (Colombo, 1927), 16–18 (quoting from the *Jaffna Weekly*).

75. Entry for Alexander Brown, 'Pioneers ...', *TA*, 14, 3, 1 September 1894, 149–154.

76. Entry for Andrew Nicol, 'Pioneers ...', *TA*, 13, 8, 1 February 1894, 503–507.

77. Entry for Arthur Sinclair, 'Pioneers ...', *TA*, 19, 11, 1 May 1900, 723–730.

78. Entry for John Gavin, 'Pioneers ...', *TA*, 13, 10, 2 April 1894, 646–50.

79. J. Ferguson (ed.), *W.D. Gibbon* (offprint, *Tropical Agriculturist*), (Colombo 1905), 1–4.

80. Entry for J.L. Gordon, 'Pioneers ... ', *TA*, 23, 1, 1 July 1903, 79–81.

81. Entry for J.K. Jolly, 'Pioneers ...', *TA*, 18, 4, 1 October 1898, 229–231.

82. John Ferguson, editorials, *TA*, 1,1 June 1881, 1 and 13, 1 July 1893, 1.

83. Title page, ibid., 21, 1901/2.

CHAPTER 9

Ceylon: A Scottish Colony?

Angela McCarthy

In 1796 Ceylon (known as Sri Lanka since 1972), excluding Kandy until 1815, became a British crown colony. More than 90 years later, in 1887, John Ferguson, planter and publisher, announced, doubtless somewhat tongue-in-cheek, 'the blight to the former great enterprise of Ceylon was due to the mistaken policy of sending English and Irish Governors to rule this really Scotch colony!'[1] Declared at a St Andrew's Day dinner, Ferguson's remark was clearly designed to appeal to his fellow Scots. The term 'Scotch colony', however, is usually applied to organised group settlements such as at Darien in 1695 and Otago in the 1840s. But Scottish migration to Ceylon was characterised by individual flows to family and friends rather than organised group schemes. So why did Ferguson deploy the term, and did his claim have any merit?

A companion piece to the preceding analysis by Tom Barron, this chapter sets out to examine the evidence for the depiction of Ceylon as a Scottish colony, and to suggest why this characterisation was propagated.

I am grateful to Tom Devine and Tom Barron for their comments on an earlier version of this chapter, and to the Royal Society of Edinburgh and the University of Otago for funding towards research on the Scots in Sri Lanka.

A. McCarthy (✉)
University of Otago, Dunedin, New Zealand

© The Author(s) 2017
T.M. Devine, A. McCarthy (eds.), *The Scottish Experience in Asia, c.1700 to the Present*, DOI 10.1007/978-3-319-43074-4_9

187

It spans the nineteenth century and moves beyond a focus on coffee to also incorporate the tea economy. In addressing this depiction, three specific issues merit comment: the Scottish presence in Ceylon; the success and influence of Scots in Ceylon's planting enterprise; and the Scottish sense of ethnicity. Consideration is also given to an assessment of this legacy in Sri Lanka in the early twenty-first century. It concludes by considering broader issues of ethnocentrism and exceptionalism in the Scottish diaspora, and debates about Britishness and the diverse ethnicities of the four nations.

THE SCOTTISH PRESENCE IN CEYLON

The first factor to consider is the presence of Scots in Ceylon. Despite recognised difficulties with the Ceylon census data, extant figures indicate that they were among a small British contingent in Ceylon, with the majority of the population comprising Sinhalese, Tamils, and Moors (see Table 9.1). In 1881, for instance, these ethnicities contributed 98.5% of Ceylon's recorded population of 2,759,700. Nevertheless, ten years later

Table 9.1 'Nationality/Race/Birthplace' of British and Irish Migrants in Ceylon, 1871–1911

	Scotland	Ireland	England	Total Ceylon
1871	667	260	1,776	2,400,380
1881	930	375	1,747	2,759,738
1891	613	254	1,609	3,007,789
1901	728	272	2,199	3,565,954
1911	767	333	3,183	4,106,350

Sources: Figures were extracted from Anthony John Christopher, '"Ariane's Thread: Sri Lankan Census Superintendents' Reports as Guides to Identity Data', *Asian Population Studies* (2015), 8; *Times of Ceylon Weekly Summary*, 1130, British Library microfilm, July–December 1892; *Census of the British Empire, 1901: Report with Summary* (London: HMSO, 1906), Table 7, 119 (online at https://archive.org/stream/cu31924030396067#page/n3/mode/2up); S.N. Breckenridge, *The Hills of Paradise: British Enterprise and the Story of Plantation Growth in Sri Lanka* (Colombo: Stamford Lake Publication, 2012), 95, 128. The statistics exclude the military, shipping, and prisoners of war populations. For discussion about the problems with the census, see Christopher's article and the chapter by Tom Barron in this volume

the 1891 Ceylon census generated the following comment in the Ceylon press: 'That English should outnumber the Scotch nearly three to one is rather unexpected, seeing that Ceylon was once called a Scotch colony'.[2] The remark is an intriguing one. It may refer back to a period when Scots were dominant in the coffee enterprise, but, alas, no rigorous statistical evidence exists to support this.

Nevertheless, contemporaries and later commentators, including Englishman Thomas Lister Villiers, testified to a robust Scottish presence in Ceylon. In 1951, Villiers recollected that 'it was largely from Scotland that the original settlers came out' with the English 'following up the pioneer work of the Scotch' about 40 years later.[3] The weight of previous scholarship endorses this chronology, but also emphasises a strong north-eastern Scottish dynamic in Ceylon's coffee planting enterprise between the period 1830s to 1875.[4] No statistics exist to verify such claims, but statements from non-Scots endorse this perception. In 1889, an 'Old Sydney College Boy' wrote to the editor of the *Bath Chronicle* to attest that:

> every imaginable species of mankind is to be found engaged in tea-planting, from the best families of the upper middle classes to the Scotch country bumpkin. Scotchmen, as is usual in all colonies, preponderate in numbers, and Aberdeenshire 'takes the cake', so much so that our present Governor, Sir Arthur Gordon, once remarked at a public gathering, that he saw so many familiar faces from his own country around him, that he looked upon Ceylon as an outlying district of Aberdeen; many of us felt sad at this, but not because we were unfortunate enough to come from south of the Tweed.[5]

Several factors have been suggested to explain this penetration, including the importance of Scottish networking. Although this practice was not unique to the Scots, the north-east presence in Ceylon was facilitated by early and ongoing migration from that region, sometimes with a sojourn elsewhere. Such ties were vital for Ceylon as emigration there was not facilitated by assisted passages and widespread advertising as with other imperial destinations.[6] The early north-east Scottish presence in Ceylon likewise owed much to contact with India, with early ties emerging through the over-representation of north-east migrants among the country's administration, military, and trading partnerships.[7] Scots also played key roles in the Indian tea enterprise which developed links with

Ceylon. The Scottish Bruce brothers, for instance, discovered the tea plant while Scots 'laid the foundation of fortunes' in Cachar. Indeed, Assam was described 'as a Scoto-Irish colony'.[8]

Yet it is important to give due attention to the Scottish presence in Ceylon beyond those from the north-east. In 1855, a planter's dinner was observed to be attended by many Highlanders from Scotland.[9] Almost 25 years later a recent Scots arrival wrote home to Inverness declaring, 'The number of Scotchmen out here is extraordinary. I met a nice young fellow from Inverness last week, Urquhart, his father is or was in the Caledonian Bank. He is agent for the Oriental Bank in Dimbulla'.[10] John Walker, an engineer, inventor, and planter, and his brother William, merchant and engineer, hailed from Doune, near Stirling.[11] Charles Shand, the planter and merchant, was born in Liverpool to an Edinburgh-born father and Aberdeen-born mother.[12] Captain John Keith Jolly was the son of Stewart Jolly, JP and Deputy-Lieutenant of the Shires of Stirling and Dumbarton.[13] And W.B. Lamont, another planter, was 'a Galloway man'.[14] Tain-born John Ferguson, meanwhile, was declared 'a Scotsman by birth, which goes at once to prove what an admirable colonising race our friends beyond the Tweed are. And more than a Scotsman – Mr. Ferguson is also a Highlander, which is a synonym for grit, and pluck, and energy, and staying power'.[15] Indeed, it was Ferguson, editor of the *Tropical Agriculturalist, Ceylon Observer*, and the *Ceylon Handbook and Directory*, who acknowledged at a St Andrew's Day dinner at Hatton that at one time Ceylon was considered 'an outlying dependency of Aberdeenshire' but further emphasised its broader Scottish flavour:

> The hills and valleys of Ceylon had echoed to the accents of the tongues spoken and the classic songs sung on the banks of the Spey and the Ness as well as on the shores of the Dee, the Deveron and the Tay, while that night the souls of all of them had been cheered by the sounds of the Highland bagpipe. Names too, associated with the dearest recollections of Scotland had been reproduced in the nomenclature of the plantations.[16]

The naming of coffee and tea estates which reproduced place names from all parts of their country also suggests the possible dominance of Scots in planting activities. As one commentator writes, somewhat romantically:

> The Scottish immigrants to the coffee enterprise in Ceylon brought with them their frugality, their work ethic and above all their love of the

Highlands. They terraced the highlands of Ceylon like their beloved sheep country. The term estate was a Scottish term which became implanted during the period. The roads, the landscape and the bungalows that became distinctive of the plantations reflected their culture. The Hunnasgiriya and Matale sides of the expansion were pioneered by many Scots stalwarts. Their tradition was later carried over to the Upper Dimbula region where estates were given typical Scottish names, Edinburgh, Glasgow, Tillicou[*l*] try, Hatton, Blairthol, Dunkeld, Ythanside, Caledonia, Waverly, Balmoral, Sandringham [sic]—to name a few.[17]

Scottish plantation place names were, indeed, widespread in Ceylon including, for instance, Caledonia, Glen Alpine, Fassifern, Ettrick, Lochnagar, Craigie Lea, Devon, Glencairn, Holyrood, Eildon, and Dunsinane.[18] Ceylon therefore resembled other parts of the world where Scots and other migrants settled and named areas, towns, and streets after their homeland districts. Yet although no study has yet traced the changing nomenclature of estates in Sri Lanka, Ferguson's *Ceylon Handbook and Directory* and contemporary maps of Ceylon indicate that Scottish names were less extensive than native names. Furthermore, Scottish estate names were most prevalent in the Dickoya, Dimbula and Maskeliya districts. Even so, this replication of names from Scotland was more extensive than from elsewhere in Britain, further demonstrating the broader Scottish factor in Ceylon. As the *Tropical Agriculturalist* declared in 1887, 'The traditions and the associations connected with the imported names given to estates in Ceylon, traverse the whole domain of the history and topography of the British Isles, ... —and more especially Aberdeenshire and the Channel Islands'.[19]

A more rigorous and reliable indicator of the number of Scots in Ceylon might be derived from prosopographical investigation of the number and location of planters. Such an endeavour is, however, problematic as no authoritative directory exists from which to pursue record linkage. One possible avenue is to trace the owners and managers of estates in Ceylon as listed in Ferguson's *Ceylon Handbook and Directory*, but this cohort will inevitably be a significant underestimate. Regardless of numbers, however, and whether the English did outnumber the Scots in earlier as well as later periods, the key point is that this did not obviously detract from the perception of Ceylon as essentially a Scottish colony.

One possibility is that Ceylon was termed a 'Scotch colony' to reflect the sense in which the Scots were present in Ceylon in numbers disproportionate to their representation in the UK. For instance, for most of the nineteenth century, Scots generally numbered around 1 in 10 of the UK's population; in Ceylon, by contrast, it was usually 1 in 4. This over-representation meant that Ceylon was one of the most Scottish possessions in the British Empire.[20] Overall, however, the presence in Ceylon of Scots from within and beyond the north-east of Scotland only takes us so far in considering why Ceylon was declared a Scottish colony. Factors other than sheer numbers were more likely to shape the portrait of Ceylon as Scottish. One such factor to examine is the considerable success and influence of Scots in Ceylon's planting enterprise.

SUCCESS AND INFLUENCE IN THE PLANTING ENTERPRISE

In the previous chapter, Tom Barron highlighted Scottish influence in a range of diverse careers during the coffee planting period. To Barron's occupational 'bridgeheads' we might add those Scots who were said to occupy 'prominent positions in this country at the bench, at the bar and at the public service'.[21] This chapter, however, further contends that we must incorporate Scottish success and influence in Ceylon's varied planting endeavours to explain the country's characterisation as a Scottish colony. In 1870, Lancashire born George Wall, chairman of the Planter's Association, claimed that 'The prosperity in the island was due in a very measure [sic] to Scotch enterprise and Scotch labour'.[22] Admittedly, Wall was speaking at a St Andrew's Day gathering and he would have been conscious that Ceylon's coffee exports peaked that year.[23] Indeed, by 1875 Ceylon was considered the 'third largest coffee growing country in the world'.[24] Having been in Ceylon since 1846, Wall would have been privy to developments in the planting enterprise including the role of Robert Boyd Tytler from Inverurie, 'the father of coffee and cacao *cultivation* in Ceylon'.[25]

Ranald Michie drew attention to the north-east Scottish influence on Ceylon's coffee enterprise but limited it to the period between the 1830s and 1870s. At first glance, there is much to support Michie's claims that the impact ended in the 1870s. This was a time of disaster for coffee with the crop infested by disease, resulting in bankruptcies, the sales of estates, and the migration of many planters to other parts of the world. Other evidence is also suggestive of this apparent waning of Scottish influence. Scots churches founded in 1841 in Colombo and in 1850 in Kandy were disestablished in 1881 'Owing to the change in the personnel of the planting community (Scotch proprietary planters having sold their interests to English Companies)'.[26] There is substantial evidence, however, that the Scottish impact in Ceylon extended beyond the 1870s well into the era of the tea economy, which in terms of acreage replaced coffee from the mid-1880s onwards.[27] And at the forefront of that transition was James Taylor, 'father of the Ceylon tea enterprise', to whom we now turn.[28]

In 1852, 16-year-old James Taylor (see Fig. 9.1) from Auchenblae in north-east Scotland arrived in Ceylon. He was appointed to work as an assistant superintendent on the coffee estates of George Pride in the Hewaheta region. Taylor eventually became superintendent of Loolecondera and its neighbouring estates and never returned to Scotland. Initially cultivating coffee, by the early 1860s Taylor began to experiment successfully

Fig. 9.1 James Taylor and an unidentified friend, Ceylon, 1863 (Courtesy of T.J. Barron)

with cinchona (a medicinal plant, the bark of which was used to produce quinine to treat malaria) and China tea. He collected tea seeds from the Peradeniya Gardens and planted them along the estate's roads and paths.[29] As he reminisced in 1878, he was making China tea 'from old bushes in the garden and from roadside planting years before Mr. Jenkins, the Ceylon Company's tea manager, came to Ceylon. Some of what I made then was fairly good tea though I could not believe it was right because it did not taste like the China tea of the shops'.[30] In 1867, a year after a com-missioned report on tea cultivation and preparation in India, a position for which Taylor applied unsuccessfully, his managers (G. Denis B. Harrison, and William Martin Leake) ordered a consignment of hybrid Assam tea seeds. They placed them under 'the care of that ever watchful nurse, Mr. James Taylor (who had already by his success with cinchona, and more recently with China tea earned the complete confidence of his employ-ers for experimental work), formed the beginning of the now famous Loolcondura estate'.[31] Taylor's first clearing of 20 acres was made that year 'decidedly the earliest planted field of Assam-hybird tea in Ceylon'.[32] The first crop, however, failed. A successful crop was planted in 1869, the same year as the Ceylon Company planted theirs.

Of course, Taylor was not the first to introduce tea to Ceylon. This was attributed to the Dutch, while further attempts to grow tea were made by Mr Llewellyn and the Worms brothers on the Rothschild estate. But these and previous attempts were deemed failures. Taylor, it is acknowledged, was 'the first to make good tea on an appreciable scale'.[33] As the 'sage of Hewaheta' commented in 1879, 'I do not admit the Messrs. Worms' old tea experiments into the matter, as they were failures; and long ago given up when we began. The plants were allowed to remain, but there were many tea plants in gardens, and so on, over the coffee districts besides them'.[34] It was, then, the successful commercial cultivation of tea that made Taylor's name.

By 1872, Loolecondera tea samples were manufactured separately by Taylor and Mr Jenkins of the Ceylon Company, and were valued in London at higher prices than tea from Calcutta.[35] The very first packages of Ceylon tea sent to London for sale in 1873 were Taylor's and five years later George Thwaites, director of the Royal Botanical Gardens at Peradeniya, reckoned Loolecondera tea 'A.1. in my estimation'.[36] Press reports fea-tured the success of Loolecondera tea at exhibitions including Melbourne in 1881, where it was pronounced 'as near perfection as possible'.[37] Such achievements meant Taylor was among those declared as 'the back-bone of our country; such men as these ought to be the guiding stars of our young planters'.[38] Early acknowledgement of Taylor's influence on tea came from none other than Governor William Gregory who in 1884 declared Taylor the 'founder of the tea enterprise'.[39] In 1890, two years before his death, Taylor was publicly acclaimed for his contributions to the Ceylon tea and cinchona enterprises and presented with a Mappin and Webb silver tea and coffee set and a sum of money. According to one commentator, the transition from 20 acres of tea planted in Ceylon in 1869 to 384,000 acres producing 150 million lb of tea for export by 1900 'constitutes one of the most remarkable instances of rapid development in the history of the tea trade'.[40] This achievement in such a short space of time 'made the tea industry of relatively tiny Ceylon nearly as big as that of India'.[41]

James Taylor's role in developing tea in Ceylon is therefore undeniable. But how important was the involvement of other Scots in the tea enterprise? Taylor acknowledged the influence of several individuals who helped him develop his abilities as a teamaker, including William Cameron from Mull who, Taylor recounted:

> started finer plucking than I had been doing, and began to top the sale lists which I think we began to get about that time or very shortly before. When I found this I also took to weekly plucking, and topped the sale lists for a time. That finer plucking largely increased the selling prices of my tea and still more largely the profit per acre. So I was greatly indebted to the example of Mr. Cameron, though I only met him two or three times casually about Kandy and Gampola.[42]

According to Frederick Lewis in his book *Sixty-Four Years in Ceylon*, it was Cameron 'who really aroused the keenest interest in tea cultivation'.[43]

Further Scottish endeavour in Ceylon's tea economy emerges from consideration of the names of planters Taylor is credited with instructing. Ascertaining the birthplace of many of these individuals is difficult but among them were George Maitland of Edinburgh[44] and Gilbert F. Traill from Orkney.[45] Hugh Blacklaw from Laurencekirk, close to Taylor's origins, went to Loolecondera in the 1880s to learn tea making from Taylor.[46] Henry Kerr Rutherford from the Mariawatte plantation was another who paved 'the way for Ceylon to be known as the home of the best of all tea'.[47] Rutherford's origins were connected to his acclaimed *Ceylon Tea Planters' Note Book*.[48] As stipulated in 1892, 'although Englishmen have doubtless done their part, the author of the most generally useful and comprehensive book on tea and the greatest and most successful tea machinery engineers are Scotchmen!' The author went on to state:

There is no more mistake about Mr. Rutherford than there can be about Messrs Reid and Loudoun Shand or our good friend and everybody's good friend 'Logie Elphinstone'. Then we might as well deny the existence of 'Aberdeen awa'' and the influence its sons have had on Ceylon estate culture and Ceylon estate English ('Wha's mammoty's yon?') as doubt that Mr. Jackson of 'Rapid roller' and 'Britannia drier' fame is a Scotchman, whose model rooms and laboratory are within hail of Balmoral, although his honest and solid machines are made by the Marshalls on the wrong side of the border.[49]

The comment suggests that Rutherford was born outside Scotland but was considered no less Scottish.[50] Linking him to those of definitive Scottish birth such as David Reid (Kinross-shire),[51] John Loudoun Shand,[52] Sir Graeme H.D. Elphinstone (Aberdeenshire), and William Jackson (Aberdeen)[53] reinforces this. John Loudoun Shand's brother Peter was likewise identified as a key figure in the development of tea. According to one contemporary: 'I do not think the great impetus given to the same industry by Mr. Taylor's pupils, Mr. C.S. Armstrong and Mr. P.R. Shand, should be overlooked. At the very least, it ought to be publicly acknowledged, that, after Mr. Taylor, they were undoubtedly the pioneers in the new enterprise'.[54] By contrast with those already mentioned, Charles Spearman Armstrong was English. Other names identified with the development of tea were also non-Scots. R.E. Pineo, a former Ceylon planter who moved to the USA where he promoted Ceylon tea, similarly reflected on a range of key figures in the Ceylon tea enterprise: 'Taylor at Loolcondera [sic], Armstrong at Rookwood, Agars at Agarsland, Rutherford at Mariawatte, Leechman at Carolina, Scovell at Strathellie and others whom I cannot now remember by name, were paving the way for Ceylon to be known as the home of the best of all tea'.[55] Only Taylor and Rutherford were certainly Scots. Agar was likely to have been from Ireland, Arthur Scovell was from London, while no origin for Leechman or Agar has been traced.[56] Absent from these contemporary reflections of Scots-born individuals associated with Ceylon tea, as he had not yet made his mark, was Sir Thomas Lipton, though he considered himself a 'Glasgow Irishman'.[57]

These few names, however, do not in themselves provide any rigorous statistical evidence concerning all those who were recognised as influential in Ceylon's tea enterprise, many of whom were undoubtedly English-born. As with coffee, however, broad assessments testify to Scots playing a key part in the tea economy. In 1888, a newspaper headline 'Scotchmen Lead Ceylon!' featured a letter from a 'patriotic Scot' who claimed that Ceylon's leading newspaper, lawyers, manufacturers, brokers, storekeepers, banks, tea estates, tobacco enterprise, and cacao cultivation were all run by Scots. The writer concluded, 'Our railway will never be properly managed until a Scotchman is at its head!'[58] The following decade, Scotsman Arthur Sinclair similarly emphasised the critical role of Scots in the planting economy:

> Justly famous for agricultural enterprise at home, under conditions not the most favourable to success, the patient, plodding Aberdonian has certainly shown well to the front in the tropics. Indeed, it may be safely enough said of Aberdeen, that no county in Great Britain had contributed more to the success of tropical agriculture generally, and, in particular, to making Ceylon what it is[.][59]

Scots also dominated the Ceylon Tea Plantations Company. As the article accompanying the images of David Reid, John Loudon-Shand, and Sir William Johnstone (see Fig. 9.2) put it: 'The directors are all Scotch, the chairman is a Scotchman, the secretary—a real live baronet, by the way—is a Scotchman, and the shareholders look Scotch to a man. It is queer to

MR. DAVID REID, SIR W. JOHNSTONE, AND MR. SHAND ENJOY THEIR TEA !

Fig. 9.2 Scottish Ceylon Tea Company (*Tropical Agriculturalist*, 1 April 1892, 742), courtesy of the University of Edinburgh Library.

find Scotchmen combining together to vaunt the virtues of tea ... in view of the insult which the fact offers to whisky'.[60]

As with testimony relating to coffee, such claims did not simply emerge from Scots. In 1893, Englishman Clement Scott, the travel writer and theatre critic, echoed Wall's comments but this time drew attention to tea which had replaced coffee as Ceylon's key product:

> The best colonists all the world over are Scotchmen, and it is needless to say that half the success of Ceylon tea planting is due to the thrift, energy, and resistless determination of the Scotch character. You cannot go a mile in Ceylon without finding what a Buchanan, a Morrison, or a Stuart has done for this magnificently prosperous industry.[61]

Two years later, in 1895, another Englishman, Giles F. Walker, spoke at a St Andrew's Day dinner at Hatton and declared 'that the planting community owed such a very large share of its prosperity to Scotchmen because it was mostly men of that race who initiated the enterprise of tea-planting and had the hardest work when the planting enterprise was started in this Colony'. He claimed to be the only Englishman of around 18 folk at breakfast when he first arrived in Ceylon; all the rest were Scots.[62] Such declarations, of course, were designed to appeal to the patriotism and nostalgia of the Scottish majority towards their homeland at events when considerable quantities of drink were taken. But they also underline the critical role that Scots were perceived to have played in the development of tea in its foundation years in Ceylon, an influence extending beyond a focus on the earlier years of the coffee enterprise. And of fundamental importance was that tea, in light of coffee's decimation, came to be the saviour of Ceylon's economy.

Any assessment of the presence and impact of Scots in Ceylon must, however, incorporate the role of the press in how such claims circulated. The Highlander John Ferguson, editor of the *Ceylon Observer* newspaper and other important publications in Ceylon, played a critical role in this respect. Born at Tain in 1842, Ferguson was a journalist at Inverness before joining his uncle Alistair Mackenzie (A.M.) Ferguson in 1861 at the *Observer* newspaper in Ceylon. John ran the paper from 1879 and became the sole proprietor in 1892 upon his uncle's death. From 1863 he took charge of the *Ceylon Handbook and Directory*, which had commenced three years earlier. By 1881 he founded the monthly *Tropical Agriculturalist*. Ferguson perceived himself and others as ethnically distinct, and boasted of Scottish achievements relating to Ceylon. Part of the reason for the Scottish character of Ceylon, then, may rest with the capacity of a highly literate ethnicity to write about their achievements in print to a remarkable extent. And important here were the perceived skills associated with an upbringing in Scotland.

ETHNICITY AND SKILLS

Scottish ethnicity, as publicly and privately expressed, has received considerable coverage in the scholarly literature on the Scottish diaspora. Around the world, it is clear that in many places where Scots settled their reputation and identity remained important.[63] In Ceylon we can see early expressions of this from Robert Arbuthnot, chief secretary to the government of Ceylon, who wrote to his mother from Colombo in 1801 to advise that 'All Scotch friends are well'. Arbuthnot's letters to his family also convey his views of other ethnicities, including the diverse Ceylonese peoples, the Dutch, and the English, 'the least sociable people in the world'.[64] Scottish attributes, by contrast, as evident in the extracts already featured in this chapter, highlighted thrift, energy, determination and hard work. But other ethnicities also articulated their identities and were viewed by others as distinctive. What becomes very evident in Ceylon, however, is not just a sense of Scots being different but the linkage of their ethnicity with particular skillsets that were desired in the colony. In 1838, for instance, Governor James Alexander Stewart Mackenzie wrote to an acquaintance in London to seek two good road overseers and added, 'shall I say I would prefer Scotch people?'[65] That Stewart Mackenzie identified certain areas of Britain with particular accomplishments was further elucidated in his request for 'an experienced Staffordshire working Brick and Tyle maker'.[66] Two years later he wrote to Alexander Bannermann at Aberdeen asking:

> Can you send me out a good ploughman (who can milk cows—is that quite out of the question?) build Dikes, bring out with him, and work a pair of Aberdeenshire Oxen—a plough & Harrow, such as he is in habit of using? He will have from 40 to 60 acres to manage, in a climate milder than Aberdeenshire … Soil like the boggy part of Aberdeenshire … He shall have what wages he would have in Aberdeenshire as a Ploughman in a Cottage rent free.[67]

Stewart Mackenzie's request demonstrates that Aberdeenshire had already by the 1840s established a foothold in Ceylon. Almost two decades later a striking extract from James Taylor similarly highlights how valued Scots were as planters in Ceylon:

> Really neither the English nor Irish in this part of the world are nearly so good as Scotchmen with few exceptions. Even English proprietors try to get Scotch superintendents as for example Pride my old master and his brother says he thinks them the most useful people in the world and the Messrs Hadden proprietors of the Moirs' places have found scotchmen serves them better than any other manager in the country perhaps of any class would have done. When ever any estate is doing well it is a Scotchman that is on it. If we speak with a Scotchman it is about estate matters and wives if with an Englishman his whole heart and soul is in dogs and horses and I think the few Irish that I know seem generally to give themselves precious little trouble about anything. I see little of the wit they are famed for and terrible little practical sense.[68]

Taylor's statement, while appearing as ethnocentrism, is buttressed by other evidence. In 1870, G.D.B. Harrison, chairman of the Planters' Association and James Taylor's employer, observed that coffee's success:

> was owing to Scotchmen, and those who had been trained in Scotland, more particularly in agricultural pursuits, had brought with them to the country a knowledge of what must be done to maintain the fertility of the soil ... they now brought home teaching and home practice to bear on the subject and were adopting a system of manuring in order to maintain the fertility of the land.[69]

A further remark from a novel of the time indicates that English planters, by contrast, 'were University men' who 'knew absolutely nothing of agriculture ... They knew nothing of manuring and draining, roading and planting ... There was no preparation in England, either at school or at home, for the colonist's life in Ceylon, and everything had to be learnt from the beginning'.[70] By contrast, Taylor's letters point to his construction of Scottish cross-drains, still evident at Loolecondera, which meant that his roads, according to him, were the best in the district and 'It is the same with all my work it lasts for ever'. His roof thatching, he attested, was good for five years without a drop whereas others only lasted a year 'and few can make a roof without drops'.[71] The dry stone dikes (walls) that he erected without mortar replicated practices in the Scottish lowlands and are still evident at Loolecondera. The son of a wheelwright, Taylor was raised on the Monboddo estate and his practices in Ceylon reflected the skills prevalent in Lowland Scotland where small farmers and tradesmen thatched their houses and devised their own tools and were the skill base of the improved farm economy.[72]

Taylor's claims inevitably raise the question of possible Scottish exceptionalism. Scholars have suggested a number of explanations for this including a Scottish tendency to advance themselves, their literacy and education, and their high skill levels.[73] These factors and others, as outlined in this book's Introduction, undoubtedly were influential in Scots achieving such prominence and acclaim in Ceylon. One key consideration, however, was the demand in Ceylon for young men with agricultural and educational skills. North-east Scots were especially renowned for their agricultural skills 'applied to Ceylon, though often in a modified form'.[74] The early migration of Robert Boyd Tytler from Aberdeen to Jamaica and then on to Ceylon proved critical. While he would have acquired knowledge from planting manuals, he undoubtedly learned from other Scots who were over-represented in Jamaica and their expertise likely intermingled with the tropical plantation economies there. Scots were important in this respect as the revolution of Scottish agriculture from subsistence to capitalism between c.1760 and c.1830 saw it become ever more 'precise and progressive';[75] parts of north east Scotland were among the epicentres of excellence in this regard. As Tom Devine has put it, as a result of this great leap forward 'the Scottish agricultural system was attracting international attention for its excellence' and 'was widely copied elsewhere'.[76]

In addition, the evidence suggests that north-east Scotland had the best literacy rates and schooling in nineteenth century Scotland. The Scottish education was democratic, open to all regardless of class and with a breadth of curriculum.[77] While the quality of education was variable and attendance sometimes poor, there remained notable differences to education in England and most other parts of Europe. This included a national system of schools, the professional status and high regard in which schoolmasters were held, and a cultural demand for education.[78] Of fundamental importance in this respect was that planters in Ceylon needed to be equipped with key numerical, surveying, and writing skills. In an account of the planter Alexander Campbell White it was declared, 'he had the privilege of being fitted for his work in life with that useful practical education for which the Parish Schools of Scotland ... have been specially famous'.[79]

In this way, Scots in Ceylon resembled those involved in the Caribbean where their literacy and numeracy skills stood them in good stead as planters and clerks, among other occupations, in the sugar, coffee, and cotton trades.[80] As Devine argues, Scottish penetration of empire was not simply due to 'limited opportunities at home but it was also facilitated by the training they had received in basic numeracy, literacy and often in an impressively wide range of vocational skills'.[81]

LEGACY

Scots continue to migrate to Sri Lanka in small numbers in the twenty-first century. The Scots Kirk at Colombo, the last Scottish church in Asia, is still administered by an appointment from Scotland, while a Scots kirk at Kandy similarly functions to this day. Today, however, the congregations are predominantly Sinhalese and Tamil.[82] Expatriate Scot Gordon Kenny, meanwhile, is the current chief of the Caledonian Society of Sri Lanka, which has existed for at least 100 years. The Society's membership is approximately 10 per cent Scottish, and its annual Burns Night ball attracts more than 200 people, most of whom are Tamil and Sinhalese.[83] A descendant of the Stoneywood Moirs of Aberdeenshire, members of whom were integral to Ceylon's Victorian planting economy, also lives and works in Colombo. Elizabeth Moir initially established the Colombo International School in 1982 and then the British School. She now runs the Elizabeth Moir School, which educates around 4,000 children from 70 different nationalities.[84]

Echoes of Scotland's nineteenth century involvement in Sri Lanka also remain visible. Scottish estate names testify to an early influence, most striking in the highland tea district. Scottish names are likewise inscribed on many gravestones in both well-tended and over-run cemeteries, with some containing declarations of place of birth. Most recently, a new hotel in Colombo, The Steuart by Citrus, has opened in the former premises of Steuart House, the headquarters of Sri Lanka's oldest mercantile establishment, the George Steuart Group. The hotel bedrooms are named after places in Scotland (Edinburgh, Glasgow, Aberdeen, and Dundee), clan shields adorn the walls, the interiors are tartan, and Scottish fare features in its Scottish-themed pub.[85]

In one individual case, the Scottish legacy remains especially strong and unambiguous. James Taylor, the father of Ceylon tea, is commemorated to this day in the Sri Lankan tea industry. His grave at Mahaiyawa cemetery near Kandy is a place of interest while at Loolecondera a small patch of his original tea plants are still plucked. Visitors can inspect the remains of what is believed to be his cabin, a well, and his granite seat with stunning vistas across the beautiful interior highlands of Sri Lanka where he spent most of his life.[86] The current superintendent of Loolecondera, Lalith Abeykoon, also commissioned a local man, Milton Perera, to construct a monument to Taylor. Unveiled on 29 November 2013, it depicts Taylor with a teapot and teacup and a garland around his neck as a visible token of respect.[87] So too is Taylor commemorated at the Ceylon Tea Museum near Kandy with exhibits of photographs, a grinding stone, the wheel of his rickshaw, and his tobacco pipe.[88] In 1992, the 125th anniversary of Sri Lanka's tea industry, Taylor was remembered with a postal stamp, while in 2013 the British High Commissioner in Sri Lanka, John Rankin, unveiled a plaque and a 16-foot-high James Taylor monument at the St Clair tea estate at Talawakelle (see Fig. 9.3).[89] This imposing bust

Fig. 9.3 Scottish Baronial Tea Castle at Talawakelle, Sri Lanka (copyright Angela McCarthy)

is situated at the entrance to a mock Scottish baronial castle, made of Sri Lankan granite. Both are a strongly visible testament to Taylor's legacy from Anselm Perera, the managing director of the Mlesna tea company. As Perera explains:

> From the beginning we all knew that James Taylor was the father of Ceylon tea and I always realised that we don't give enough prominence to the man who gave us a business, the man who gave us a livelihood. This country has two million people working in the tea trade and all of us in the new genera-tion are forgetting the fact that one man was responsible for creating this trade in this country. And that made me think of doing a castle here because the Scottish love this area the mountains and highlands[.][90]

With the forthcoming 150th anniversary of Ceylon tea in 2017, and the ongoing importance of Ceylon tea to the Sri Lankan economy, it is unlikely that acknowledgement of the distinctive Scottish influence on Sri Lanka in the nineteenth century will disappear anytime soon.

CONCLUSION

A focus on the Scots in Ceylon facilitates insight into the debated issue of the distinctiveness of the four nations within the broader British impe-rial world. While migration scholars are alert to the diverse ethnicities of migrant groups, imperial historians, with some exceptions, are more con-cerned with the ethnic differentiation of the various peoples encountered by the 'British' abroad during the imperial project rather than the variety of peoples of the UK who moved outside its borders. That approach there-fore emphasises a sense of Britishness which it is said enabled migrants from the individual nations of the UK to 'transcend their internal divi-sions'.[91] Yet Scots saw themselves (and others) as distinctive; in that sense, ethnicity mattered.[92] These issues are also relevant to the study of Sri Lanka's ethnic history which has largely focused on Sinhalese and Tamil identities and relationships.[93] Perhaps, however, recognition by contem-poraries in Ceylon of the diverse ethnicities of its UK component helps explain the British imposition of ethnic divisions in Ceylon after the 1830s when ethnicity came to replace caste classifications.[94]

In the absence of detailed comparative studies with other ethnicities, it is of course important to sound a note of caution in relation to the evidence presented in this chapter. English migrants, as Tom Barron indicates, were more numerous than the Scots in Ceylon and many also made successful careers. Statistical analysis, then, is still required before we can ascertain to what degree, if any, Scots disproportionately occupied and influenced numerous professions and industries in Ceylon and elsewhere compared with other ethnicities. The key point, however, is that, although anecdotal, the evidence identified to date testifies unambiguously to the perception of a profound Scottish presence and influence in Ceylon, especially in the planting community. It is argued that this construction of Scottish Ceylon was facilitated through ethnic networking and Scottish boosterism, particularly, but not limited to, the publications of John Ferguson. Most especially, however, Ceylon was portrayed as a Scottish colony because Scots possessed skills which put them at the forefront of the two key global planting economies of coffee and tea that had such enormous resonance for Ceylon's economy. As John MacKenzie put it, 'Scots had a tendency to colonise certain key economic activities associated with the environment in the Empire'.[95] Indeed, today, Sri Lanka is the world's fourth largest tea producer and second largest in relation to global tea exports. In this way, the phrase a 'Scotch colony' as attached to Ceylon is conceptually different from its usage in efforts to organise group settlements as at Darien and Otago. And, as Iain Watson shows in Chapter 13, some parts of Scotland's diaspora, notably Hong Kong, continue to express such parlance in the twenty-first century.

NOTES

1. *Overland Ceylon Observer* (hereafter OCO), 1 December 1887, 1064–1067.
2. Census, *Times of Ceylon Weekly Summary*, 25 August 1891, 1130.
3. Sir Thomas L. Villiers, *Some Pioneers of the Tea Industry* (Colombo: The Colombo Apothecaries' Co. Ltd, 1951), 6–7.
4. Ranald C. Michie, 'Aberdeen and Ceylon: Economic Links in the Nineteenth Century', *Northern Scotland*, 4 (1981), 69–82.
5. 'Ceylon Tea Planter's Life', by Old Sydney College Boy, *Bath Chronicle*, 15 March 1889, in Major J.A. Forsythe Papers, 1860–1933, Box 1, Centre of South Asian Studies, University of Cambridge.
6. Marjory Harper, *Emigration from North-East Scotland: Volume One. Willing Exiles* (Aberdeen: Aberdeen University Press, 1988), 330; Angela McCarthy (ed.), *A Global Clan. Scottish Migrant*

Networks and Identities since the Eighteenth Century (London and New York: Tauris Academic Studies, 2006).

7. Michie, 'Aberdeen and Ceylon', 70; Andrew Mackillop, 'Locality, Nation, and Empire: Scots and the Empire in Asia, c.1695–c.1813', in John M. MacKenzie and T.M. Devine (eds), *Scotland and the British Empire* (Oxford: Oxford University Press, 2012), 66, 70. See also Barron's chapter in this volume.

8. 'Assam and its Tea Planters', *Tropical Agriculturalist* (hereafter TA), 12, 4, 1 October 1892, 238.

9. *Ceylon Times*, 23 February 1855, 126, The National Archives of the UK, CO 59/9.

10. A. Mackintosh (Kabragalle, Maturata) to Allan Macdonald (Inverness), 19 February 1879, Kabaragala Estate Correspondence, National Records of Scotland (hereafter NRS), GD176/2576.

11. TA, 13, 9, 1 March 1894, 575; TA, 17, 5, 1 November 1897, 297.

12. TA, 17, 6, 1 December 1897, 371.

13. TA, 18, 4, 1 October 1898, 229.

14. TA, 18, 2, 1 August 1899, 76.

15. TA, 12, 4, 1 October 1892, 227.

16. *Weekly Ceylon Observer* (WCO), 6 December 1884, 1009a.

17. S.N. Breckenridge, *The Hills of Paradise: British Enterprise and the Story of Plantation Growth in Sri Lanka* (Colombo: Stamford Lake Publication, 2012), 42. Blairthol (sic) is Blair Athol while Sandringham is in Norfolk, England.

18. OCO, 4 December 1869, 478–480. Devon is typically associated with England but may refer to the River Devon in Scotland. A computer print-out of plantations in Sri Lanka with a Scottish connection can be found in Special Collections and Archives, University of Aberdeen Library, MS 3813/4.

19. TA, 6, 8, 1 February 1887, 531.

20. David Fitzpatrick, 'What Scottish Diaspora?', in Angela McCarthy and John M. MacKenzie (eds), *Global Migrations: The Scottish Diaspora since 1600* (Edinburgh: Edinburgh University Press, 2016), 249.

21. OCO, 3 December 1870, 428.

22. OCO, 3 December 1870, 428. Wall's birthplace is taken from the *Jubilee of the Planters' Association of Ceylon, 1854–1904: Illustrated Souvenir of the "Times of Ceylon"* (Colombo: Capper & Sons, 1904), 3.

23. Roland Wenzlhuemer, *From Coffee to Tea Cultivation in Ceylon, 1880–1900: An Economic and Social History* (Leiden: Brill, 2008), 2.

24. 'Scottish Enterprise in Ceylon', *Aberdeen Journal*, 15 September 1875, British Newspaper Archive.

25. TA, 13, 4, 2 October 1893, 217.

26. Typed article about the presbytery of Ceylon, c.1924, Papers and Photographs of John Faulds, minister in Ceylon, University of St Andrews Special Collections, ms38419/28, 3.

27. A.E.J. Emmet, 'Ceylon Tea—100 Years and Now', *Journal of the Royal Society of Arts*, 115, 5133 (1967), 727.

28. An overview of Taylor's life can be found in D.M. Forrest, *A Hundred Years of Ceylon Tea, 1867–1967* (London: Chatto and Windus, 1967), especially ch. 3.

29. 'The Oldest Regularly Cropped Tea in Ceylon still Thoroughly Vigorous', OCO, 16 May 1890, 503.

30. 'Tea and Cinchona in Ceylon', OCO, 23 June 1890, 651.

31. 'The Tea Enterprize in Ceylon', WCO, 21 July 1885, 593. Taylor's work with cinchona began in the 1860s. His influence was such that it was noted: 'Mr. Taylor may claim to be the inventor of the sowing and seedling system'. See 'The Great Sale of Ceylon Cinchona, and Cinchona Cultivation in Ceylon', OCO, 13 September 1878, 642.

32. 'Tea and Cinchona in Ceylon', OCO, 23 June 1890, 651; 'The Oldest Regularly Cropped Tea in Ceylon still Thoroughly Vigorous', OCO, 16 May 1890, 503.

33. 'Notes and Comments', OCO, 16 June 1890, 624. An instructive account of the experiments can be found in 'The Tea-Planting Enterprize in Ceylon', OCO, 20 June 1890, 643.

34. 'Tea and Cinchona in Ceylon', OCO, 23 June 1890, 651. Taylor's letter was dated 16 February 1878 but not published until 1890. He is referred to as the 'sage of Hewahette' in 'The Extra-Labour Population of Coffee Estates', OCO, 23 November 1872, 468.

35. 'Ceylon Tea', OCO, 20 September 1872, 392. See also 'Tea', 30 July 1873, 14.

36. 'The First Tea Exported from Ceylon', CO (Weekly Edition), 11 October 1905, 1480; George Thwaites (Peradeniya) to Sir William Gregory, 27 September 1878, General Correspondence concerning

Ceylon, August 1877–December 1878, W.H. Gregory Papers, Bodleian Special Collections, University of Oxford, Dep d. 979.

37. 'Ceylon Tea in the Australian Colonies', WCO, 20 December 1880, 1192.

38. 'Estate Weeding: A Protest Against the Contract System', OCO, 21 November 1872, 3.

39. Supplement to the *Ceylon Observer*, 31 March 1884, 1.

40. William H. Ukers, *All About Tea*, vol. 2 (New York: Tea and Coffee Trade Journal Company, 1935), 132.

41. Roy Moxham, *A Brief History of Tea: The Extraordinary Story of the World's Favourite Drink* (London: Constable & Robinson, 2009), 173.

42. James Taylor (Loolecondera) to the Secretary, Planters' Association (Kandy), 28 September 1891, Papers of James Taylor, planter in Ceylon, National Library of Scotland (hereafter NLS), MS 15908.

43. Frederick Lewis, *Sixty-Four Years in Ceylon: Reminiscences of Life and Adventure* (Ceylon: Colombo Apothecaries Co Ltd, 1926), 194.

44. http://ghgraham.org/georgemaitland1854.html (accessed 5 October 2016).

45. http://www.thepeerage.com/p52845.htm (accessed 5 October 2016).

46. 'Another Ceylon Planter Retiring', CO (Weekly Edition), 9 April 1915, 651; CO (Weekly Edition), 24 October 1917, 1638.

47. 'Tea for America', OCO, 23 April 1888, 382.

48. Henry K. Rutherford and John Hill, *Ceylon Tea Planters' Note Book of Useful Memoranda*, 4th edn (Colombo: Times of Ceylon Press, 1902–3). Online at http://storage.lib.uchicago.edu/pres/2014/pres2014-1196.pdf (accessed 5 October 2016).

49. 'Some Thoughts about Tea', TA, 11, 11, 2 May 1892, 845.

50. Rutherford's birthplace is unknown but his father was born at Kelso. See: www.geni.com/people/Henry-Rutherford/6000000023953083125 (accessed 5 October 2016).

51. http://www.gracesguide.co.uk/David_Reid_(1841-1892) (accessed 5 October 2016).

52. https://en.wikipedia.org/wiki/Eric_Loudoun-Shand (accessed 5 October 2016).

53. http://www.gracesguide.co.uk/William_Jackson_(1849-1915) (accessed 5 October 2016).

54. 'Mr. James Taylor and Ceylon Tea', OCO, 18 June 1890, 640. Charles Spearman Armstrong was born in England.
55. 'Tea for America', OCO, 23 April 1888, 382.
56. I am grateful to Tom Barron for this information.
57. Sir Thomas J. Lipton, *Leaves from the Lipton Logs* (London: Hutchinson & Co, n.d.), 180.
58. 'Scotchmen Lead Ceylon!', OCO, 11 December 1888, 1166.
59. Sinclair's book, *In Tropical Lands: Recent Travels to the Sources of the Amazon, the West Indian Islands, and Ceylon* (Aberdeen: D. Wyllie & Son, 1895), 160, is online at: https://archive.org/details/intropicallandsr00sincrich (accessed 5 October 2016).
60. 'The Ceylon Plantations Tea Company', TA, 11, 10, 1 April 1892, 742.
61. 'A Cup of Tea' by Clement Scott, TA, 20, 11, 1 May 1893, 694.
62. OCO, 3 December 1895, 1289–1293.
63. See, for example, Angela McCarthy, *Scottishness and Irishness in New Zealand since 1840* (Manchester: Manchester University Press, 2011).
64. See, for instance, Robert Arbuthnot (Colombo) to his mother (Edinburgh), 22 September 1801, 115–16; Robert Arbuthnot (Colombo) to his father (Edinburgh), 16 November 1801, 138, Ceylon: Letters of George and Robert Arbuthnot, NLS, MS 5208.
65. James Alexander Stewart Mackenzie (Colombo) to James McAdam (London), 28 March 1838, Papers of the Mackenzie Family, Earls of Seaforth, NRS, GD46/9/6, No. 99.
66. James Alexander Stewart Mackenzie (Galle) to James McAdam (London), 1 July 1840, in Ibid., No. 102.
67. James Alexander Stewart Mackenzie (Galle) to Alexander Bannerman (Aberdeen), 7 July 1840, in Ibid., No. 11.
68. James Taylor (Loolecondera) to his father Michael Taylor (Mosspark), 21 February 1859.
69. 'The St Andrew's Dinner', OCO, 3 December 1870, 428.
70. FEFP [Fanny Emily Farr Penny], *Fickle Fortune in Ceylon* (Madras: Addison and Co, 1887), 36.
71. James Taylor (Loolecondera) to his father (Mosspark), 9 September 1860, Taylor papers.
72. Gavin Sprott, 'The Country Tradesman', in T.M. Devine (ed.), *Farm Servants and Labour in Lowland Scotland, 1770–1914* (Edinburgh: John Donald, 1984), 144; Angela McCarthy, 'The

Importance of Ethnicity? James Taylor and Ceylon Tea', in McCarthy and MacKenzie (eds), *Global Migrations*, 125–126.
73. John M. MacKenzie and T.M. Devine, 'Introduction', in MacKenzie and Devine (eds), *Scotland and Empire*, 10–11.
74. Michie, 'Aberdeen and Ceylon', 73.
75. Laurence James Saunders, *Scottish Democracy, 1815–1840: The Social and Intellectual Background* (Edinburgh: Oliver and Boyd, 1950), 38.
76. T.M. Devine, 'Introduction: Scottish Farm Service in the Agricultural Revolution', in Devine (ed.), *Farm Servants*, 1, 4.
77. Lindsay Paterson, 'Traditions of Scottish Education', in Heather Holmes (ed.), *Scottish Life and Society: Institutions of Scotland: Education* (East Linton: Tuckwell, 2000), 23.
78. R.D. Anderson, *Education and the Scottish People, 1750–1918* (Oxford: Clarendon Press, 1995), 23.
79. TA, 16, 8, 1 February 1897.
80. Douglas J. Hamilton, *Scotland, the Caribbean and the Atlantic World, 1750–1820* (Manchester: Manchester University Press, 2005), 4, 18.
81. T.M. Devine, *The Scottish Nation 1700–2000* (London: Penguin Books, 2000), 99–100.
82. Interview with Revd. Norman and Elizabeth Hutcheson, 9 February 2014.
83. Ibid., and interview with Gordon and Michelle Kenny, 10 February 2014. No early records exist to confirm the establishment of the Society but its earliest item is a cup that Sir Hugh Clifford, the colonial secretary of Ceylon, presented to the Society in 1907.
84. Interview with Elizabeth Moir, 12 February 2014.
85. All of this is supposedly redolent of the Scottish ancestry of James and George Steuart. The Stuearts were, however, born in England and no mention of a Scottish ancestry is made in George Steuart & Co Ltd, *The George Steuart Story* (Colombo: n.p., 1985).
86. http://trips.lakdasun.org/lulkandura-loolecondera-few-hours-with-the-pioneer-of-tea-planters-in-sri-lanka.htm#pictures (accessed 5 October 2016).
87. Discussion with Lalith Abeykoon, 25 January 2015.
88. www.ceylonteamuseum.com; www.sundaytimes.lk/070513/TV/tv_1.html (accessed 5 October 2016).

89. http://collect.ceylanka.net/itempage.asp?olditm=v92022; www.sundayobserver.lk/2013/01/27/new40.asp. See also http://exploresrilanka.lk/2013/03/tribute-to-the-father-of-ceylon-tea/ (accessed 5 October 2016).

90. Interview with Anselm Perera, 4 February 2014.

91. Andrew Thompson, 'Empire and the British State', in Sarah Stockwell (ed.), *The British Empire: Themes and Perspectives* (Maiden, MA: Blackwell, 2008), 50.

92. John M. MacKenzie, 'Irish, Scottish, Welsh and English Worlds? A Four-Nation Approach to the History of the British Empire', *History Compass*, 6, 5 (2008), 1244–1263. See also McCarthy and MacKenzie (eds), *Global Migrations.*

93. See, for instance, Nira Wickramasinghe, *Sri Lanka in the Modern Age: A History of Contested Identities* (London: Hurst and Company, 2006).

94. Sujit Sivasundaram, 'Ethnicity, Indigeneity, and Migration in the Advent of British Rule to Sri Lanka', *American Historical Review*, 115, 2 (2010), 430.

95. John M. MacKenzie, 'Scotland and Empire: Ethnicity, Environment and Identity', *Northern Scotland*, 1 (2010), 17.

CHAPTER 10

Addicting the Dragon? Jardine, Matheson & Co in the China Opium Trade

T.M. Devine

This is a study in the history of reputations. The characters featured are two Scottish merchants who traded with great profit in the eastern seas during the first half of the nineteenth century. William Jardine (1784–1834) and James Matheson (1796–1878) were little different from many of their fellows who left Scotland at the time with the aim of making fortunes in the British Empire. They, like a minority of other adventurers, having become very rich, were then able to return to their native land with the spoils of empire and establish themselves as landed gentlemen and respectable pillars of Victorian society.

Long after their deaths, however, the hard-earned status of influence and privilege eventually disintegrated as their reputations became at first undermined and then comprehensively destroyed in both academic and popular writing from the later twentieth century. The crime for which they were publicly condemned was that their wealth had been generated in the opium trade to China. Their misfortune was that from the later nineteenth century and thereafter, Western attitudes to opium were radically trans-

I am grateful to my co-editor, Angela McCarthy, for her valuable comments on an early draft of this chapter.

T.M. Devine (✉)
University of Edinburgh, Edinburgh, Scotland

© The Author(s) 2017
T.M. Devine, A. McCarthy (eds.), *The Scottish Experience in Asia, c.1700 to the Present*, DOI 10.1007/978-3-319-43074-4_10

213

formed. The substance now became widely redefined as a repellent moral evil and a dangerously addictive drug. Even those families in Scotland who had become very rich on the profits of Caribbean chattel slavery and the generous compensations offered for their 'property' in black slaves after emancipation in 1833 did not suffer anything like the same fate of popular opprobrium from posterity as Jardine and Matheson.[1]

Why their reputations collapsed so completely from the public status they had both enjoyed during the middle decades of the nineteenth century is the central question of this chapter. It is hoped that the answer given might cast some light not only on their role in the China trade but on the broader issues of how historical analysis relates to changing moral values over time.

CONTEXT

In summer 2015 *The Economist* published a flattering report on what it termed the 'grand old trading house' of Jardine Matheson Holdings. The article showed in full detail the remarkable scale and success of the enterprise globally in the early twenty-first century, with flourishing businesses across the world in China, North America, Europe, Australia, the Middle East and parts of Africa. This mighty conglomerate also had interests in many sectors of the international economy, from hotels to supermarkets, vehicle manufacture to palm oil production and much else. 'The Firm', as it was popularly known, employed over 430,000 people in five continents and in its traditional home, Hong Kong, only the government had more workers.[2]

Unusually, Jardine Matheson is still controlled by the Scottish descendants of William Jardine, one of the two original partners who first set up the company in 1832. The Keswick family, who currently run the vast enterprise, can trace their ancestry to William's sister, Jean. Jardine himself came from tenant farming stock in the parish of Lochmaben in Dumfriesshire, while his partner, James Matheson, was born into a small landed family in the parish of Lairg in Sutherland. In many ways they were at least as materially successful in their own day as their successors of the twenty-first century.

Jardine Matheson & Co became by far the dominant force in the highly lucrative opium trade from India to China and at the same time emerged as the most powerful trading house in the 1830s along the South China coast, although in competition at the time with over 130 European and

American companies, together with untold numbers of Chinese intermediaries, all vying for commercial supremacy.[3] In little more than a decade
or so, the two men became fabulously wealthy. William Jardine was able
to retire to Britain from Canton in 1837 with an accumulated fortune
reckoned then to be over £300,000. Matheson returned five years later
with riches of £225,000.[4] In today's values, they were millionaires many
times over. The partners went on to ostentatiously display their success
by buying up landed property in their native Scotland. Jardine acquired
the estate of Lanrick in Perthshire while Matheson built up an even more
impressive territorial empire in the Highlands and Outer Hebrides. He
became the proprietor of the Island of Lewis in 1842 and then went on
to purchase further estates in Rosshire and Sutherland.[5] Both men, but
especially Jardine, also managed to gain trusted access to the highest levels
of the British government as advisers on the China trade and relations with
the Chinese Empire.[6]

History, however, has been much less kind to both of them. The pages
of both academic texts and popular accounts from the later twentieth
century onwards are peppered with vitriolic condemnation of their roles
in the opium trade and the origins of the first Opium War of 1840–42.
'Utter rascals', 'drug smugglers', 'drug dealers', 'criminals', and 'leading
Sinophobe warmongers' are just some of the many claims in the literature.[7] For the historian Saul David, for instance, Jardine and Matheson
were deeply involved 'in one of the blackest episodes in the imperial story:
capitalism and mercantilism [sic] at its worst'. He asserted that British
merchants bore much of the blame for the outbreak of the first Opium
War and the 'largest and most powerful among the traders were Jardine,
Matheson'.[8] One of Britain's most distinguished scholars of Chinese history, John King Fairbank, characterised the opium trade which made the
two men rich as 'the most long-contrived and systematic intentional crime
of modern times'.[9] The opprobrium is not confined to academic circles.
In recent years attempts have been made in Scotland to have the portraits
of James Matheson and his nephew, Alexander, also very active in the
China trade, summarily removed from the walls of Dingwall Sheriff Court
in Rosshire where they have hung for many years. The reason given was
that 'the pair were no better than drug lords whose wealth was created
by inflicting misery on thousands of people in nineteenth century Asia'.[10]

This chapter argues that these recent denunciations primarily reflect
the context of different times and different attitudes in history, especially
between the mid-Victorian era of the opium trade and the modern period

when postcolonial studies and perspectives have flourished. It suggests also that some writers have failed to take into full account three aspects of the story of Jardine, Matheson & Co. First, no scholar has yet considered why the firm failed to attract such searing criticism when active in the opium trade, during the lifetimes of the two partners and for many years after their deaths. Favourable press comment about Matheson, as indicated below, was in fact still being published in Scotland as late as the 1950s. Second, why did such condemnation only start to surface in the more recent past, generations after the company had severed all connections with opium trading from 1864? Third, even some modern studies have failed to take account of new and innovative scholarship written on the basis of Chinese language sources and important reappraisals of the place of opium in Chinese society and culture in the nineteenth century.[11] This chapter seeks to grapple with the first two of these issues, in part at least, on the basis of material drawn from the third.

CONTEMPORARY REPUTATIONS

Far from being treated as social pariahs because of distaste at the origins of their wealth, both Jardine and Matheson were able to gain easy and rapid access to the highest levels of British society on their return from China, even though this was a time when Britain had become increasingly sensitive to the moral and legal issues associated with the governance of empire. Those who were thought guilty of plundering India in the later eighteenth century had been widely denounced in Parliament, the judiciary and the public sphere in the later eighteenth century. The campaign to secure the abolition of the slave trade in 1807 and then slavery itself in the British Empire in 1833 had also made both politicians and the public more aware of the great evils that had been committed overseas in the nation's name. Yet, despite such sensitivities, little odium seems to have been directed at those who were in later times so passionately condemned for their preeminent role in the China opium trade.

William Jardine, for instance, returned to a hero's welcome from the East India merchants of London and was hosted as the principal guest at a glittering public dinner held in his honour.[12] He was elected to Brooks's, the highly fashionable London club, a year later. Matheson joined him as a member and was also nominated to the Reform Club on Pall Mall. In 1841, Jardine was elected unopposed to the parliamentary seat of Ashburton in Devon. After the death of his partner in 1842, Matheson stood for election successfully and retained the same seat in 1843. The voters of Ashburton later elected another member of the dynasty, James's brother Thomas, who served as MP from 1847–52. In the meantime, James Matheson became the Member for Ross and Cromarty in 1847, a constituency which included his own estate in Lewis, and which he represented for two decades until 1868. His London mansion was in the much sought after district of Westminster, close to Buckingham Palace.

Matheson went on to receive several accolades in his lifetime, including a baronetcy, awarded for his generous support of the poor, destitute and distressed of the Island of Lewis during the failure of the potato crop in the Highlands between 1846 and 1855.[13] Further honours and appointments also came his way: Fellowship of the Royal Society in 1846, chairman of the Peninsular and Oriental Steam and Navigation Company (P&O) and lord lieutenant and sheriff principal of the county of Rosshire. In 1843, Matheson wed Mary Jane Perceval, the daughter of Sir Charles Flower, a former lord mayor of London.[14] Sir James and Lady Matheson soon became familiar figures during the fashionable London social season.[15]

Tributes flowed in fond remembrance of Matheson after his death in 1878. The pro-landlord Highland newspaper *Inverness Courier* unctuously recorded that 'a more kind-hearted and generous landowner never owned property in the Highlands'.[16] School boards in Lewis also proclaimed their heartfelt thanks for his support in advancing education on the island. As late as 1950, the *Stornoway Gazette* published articles recalling the benign support given to the island by 'Sir Seamus', as it was suggested he was affectionately known by the people in his day. This was despite Matheson's highly controversial role and that of his estate chamberlain John Munro MacKenzie in 'encouraging', by various methods of coercion, the 'assisted' emigrations of over 2,200 'surplus' inhabitants from the island to Canada in the early 1850s, near the end of the potato famine.[17]

After his death, Matheson's widow erected an impressive monument to her late husband in the grounds of Lews Castle on which he had lavished a fortune building a home of splendour and distinction for himself and his spouse. Inscribed on it are words from *Matthew 25:21*: 'Well done, thou good and faithful servant ... Enter now into the joy of thy Lord'. Matheson himself was buried in the family plot at Lairg in Sutherland, beneath a raised structure which recalled the architecture of imperial India and the East, where he had made his fortune. Bizarrely to modern eyes, the tomb is garlanded with opium poppies set in stone, which hardly suggests that Matheson's name at his death was yet tainted with the nefarious reputation which it attracted in later times.

Perhaps, the most telling confirmation of the social standing and political influence of Jardine, Matheson & Co is to be found in the several discussions which William Jardine held with Lord Palmerston, the foreign secretary, in the weeks before the outbreak of the First Opium War with the Chinese Empire in March 1839. The significance of these talks has long been the subject of historical debate but as a result of recent research a much clearer picture has now begun to emerge of the realities at the time. Before the evidence is considered, however, a brief sketch of the background to the Opium War is outlined.[18]

THE OPIUM WAR

From the mid-1830s the enormous scale and growth of opium imports to China gave rise to increasing concern within the imperial government in Peking. The anxieties had several foundations. Some officials feared the threat that the massive export of silver to pay for the drug might have on the economy of the empire; others thought the extent of the contraband trade was causing endemic corruption among the bureaucracies in Canton and other coastal areas. The importation of opium to China had first been declared illegal in 1729 and the law was reiterated on several occasions thereafter. Some of the Emperor's advisers also regarded the spread of opium smoking among the lower orders as a potential threat to social control and state authority. The practice had traditionally been the exclusive leisure pastime of rich Chinese and the administrative elites, and it was only when opium started to appeal to the lower strata of society that it began to be stereotyped as a pernicious influence. Two factions then emerged within the imperial court as the debate intensified. One side favoured the legalisation of the drug; the other, led by Lin Tse-Hsu (Commissioner Lin), advocated its complete eradication from the empire.[19]

This hawkish group eventually won the day and Lin was authorised by the Emperor to take rigorous action to end opium consumption and destroy the trade which fed it. On 18 March 1839 he demanded that all foreign merchants in Canton surrender their opium stores and sign a bond declaring they would withdraw from selling the drug in the future under penalty of death. The traders were also forced into confinement in Canton for a period of two months. The superintendent of British trade in Canton, the Scot Captain Charles Elliot (1801–75), then agreed that all

British opium should be delivered to the Chinese authorities. In return, Elliot provided the traders with 'opium receipts', which in effect made the British government the guarantor of financial compensation for any losses they might sustain from punitive action imposed by the Chinese. Opium valued at £2 million—£2.5 million sterling was surrendered to Lin. On Lin's orders, the confiscated stock was soon consumed in its entirety by fire and the ashes washed into the sea.[20]

As a result of Elliot's actions and promises, the involvement of the British government in the developing crisis was now inevitable. London had a number of anxieties. The cessation of the opium trade, the only major commodity in demand among the Chinese, threatened the supply of tea which had become the national drink of the British masses by this time. Apart from a few minor items, the Chinese only wanted Indian opium or silver in exchange for tea, of which they possessed a virtual world monopoly in the 1830s. The finances of the East India Company and hence British governance of the subcontinent might therefore be undermined by the ban on opium, the most lucrative export to China on which the entire tea trade depended. In addition, some ministers were outraged that Britain's national honour had been impugned by a remote, archaic and despotic empire and Lin's haughty and high-handed actions against British subjects. Retaliation was therefore likely. Great Britain regarded itself as the most powerful nation on earth at the time and wounded national pride and prestige demanded speedy retribution. The government was also determined to seek compensation for the confiscated opium, which it now legally owned as a result of Elliot's initiative.

A motion to go to war against the Chinese was debated in Parliament on 7 and 8 April 1840 and eventually carried by a mere nine votes. The Tory opposition voted *en bloc* against, not for reasons of moral disapproval of the opium trade *per se*, but because the view was taken that the whole episode had been very badly mismanaged by the government. In a passionate and eloquent speech, the future prime minister, a young William Gladstone (1809–98), denounced 'this infamous and illegal traffic' and bitterly condemned the government for its threat to use force in defence of criminal smugglers conducting an illicit trade. In taking the moral high ground at this time on the contraband commerce, he was virtually a lone voice in the House of Commons.[21]

The arrival of a British fleet in Chinese waters was the opening act in a grossly unequal contest between obsolete Chinese war junks and the firepower of the most formidable navy in the world. The result of the conflict was never in any doubt and in August 1842 the Chinese accepted British peace terms and signed the Treaty of Nanjing. Four additional 'Treaty ports' were to be opened for foreign trade in addition to Canton. The Qing government was, in addition, required to pay Britain a total of $21 million for the opium confiscated by Commissioner Lin, together with war reparations and debts in Canton owned to British merchants there. China also agreed to cede Hong Kong to the British crown. Thus began what China later came to regard as the 'Century of Humiliations' during which the empire was by turn invaded, plundered and exploited by foreign forces and external economic influences until after the Second World War and the victory of the Communist Revolution in 1949.

The Opium War, as indicated above, came about for fundamental political and economic reasons but the influence of William Jardine and James Matheson on the tactics of the British government is still undeniable. Both lobbied hard in influential circles, exploited their commercial contacts in London and other cities to the full, organised petitions and authorised that articles be drafted for circulation to the press advocating the justice of military intervention in China. The key role was played by Jardine, who had three meetings with Lord Palmerston during the emerging Chinese crisis. At the first on 27 September 1839, he and his associates provided the Foreign Secretary with charts of the China coast and discussed in detail how a successful British punitive expedition might be launched against the Chinese if the government decided to seek redress. Palmerston retained the maps and charts at the end of their meeting. A few days later the government decided that military action was indeed necessary. Jardine met Palmerston again on 26 October when he presented him with a 'shopping list' of the Canton merchants' demands. In outline its terms were close to those later agreed in the Treaty of Nanjing. He then prepared a long memorandum of advice to the government on the best way forward, which included a plea for the annexation of some Chinese territory as a safe future refuge for British opium merchants. A final discussion with the Foreign Secretary took place on 6 February 1840. Jardine stressed the need for repayment of debts to British merchants at Canton that had been incurred as a result of the interruption of trade, a demand later incorporated in the Treaty of Nanjing.[22]

The most recent student of these negotiations has concluded:

> Unquestionably, Jardine and Matheson played a great role in the development of a situation that led to the Opium War of 1840–42. However, the

specific occasion of the war and the very fact that there was a prolonged war were largely outside their initiatives.[23]

After the war ended in British victory, Palmerston admitted that Jardine and his associate John Abel Smith were key to the planning of British military strategy for the conflict. As he later wrote to Abel Smith:

> To the assistance and information which you, my dear Smith and Mr Jardine so handsomely afforded us, it was mainly owing that we were able to give to our affairs, naval, military and diplomatic, in China, those detailed instructions which have led to these satisfactory results.[24]

Smith was based in London and had little direct knowledge of Chinese affairs. The crucial source of information was William Jardine, Palmerston even declaring that his advice was so comprehensive and accurate that it was embodied without amendment in the directions sent to British naval forces before the onset of war.[25]

The harsh invective and censorious opprobrium visited on Jardine and Matheson in more recent times hardly surfaced, therefore, when they were alive. There was indeed unease and even criticism about the opium trade in some quarters after the end of the war with China, but not much evidence of personal attacks on the two partners because of their involvement in it. The future prime minister Benjamin Disraeli, in his novel, *Sybil* (1845), famously satirised William Jardine as 'A Scotchman, richer than Croesus, one McDruggy, fresh from Canton with a million of opium in each pocket, denouncing corruption and bellowing free trade'. It has to be remembered, however, that these men came from opposite ends of the political spectrum of the day. Jardine was an ardent and vocal Whig, while Disraeli was a loyal and distinguished Conservative.

In April 1843 a motion was introduced in the House of Commons by the eminent Anglican evangelical Lord Ashley, later Earl of Shaftesbury (1881–85), advocating the suppression of the opium trade. Petitions in support were received from the Baptist, Wesleyan and London missionary societies. The initiative came to nothing, however, when the motion was withdrawn on the advice of Prime Minister Robert Peel on the grounds that it might interfere with tariff negotiations then ongoing with the Chinese authorities.[26] As will be shown later, the missionary societies did eventually became a powerful element in the anti-opium lobby of the later nineteenth century. But before then they had little impact. In the

1830s there were probably only a half dozen or so Christian missionaries active in China and the numbers thereafter increased only slowly, as shown in Chapter 3 above. Indeed, far from exhibiting open hostility to the trade, some missionaries were wont to use the distribution channels of the opium merchants as a means of ensuring the circulation of their biblical tracts. The gospels translated into Chinese regularly went out packed alongside chests of the drug. The most famous exponent of this unusual commerce was the expert German linguist Dr Karl Gutzlaff (1803–51), who was profitably employed by Jardine, Matheson as their translator of Chinese dialects. Other missionaries, such as the American E.C. Bridgman (1801–61), were initially deeply hostile before eventually advocating the legalisation of opium in China, but even they did not attack the trading houses directly. After all, Jardine, Matheson and the other big British opium company of that time, Lancelot Dent, were major contributors to the philanthropic endeavours of the missionaries, including support for the Medical Missionary Society, the Morrison Educational Society and the Society for the Diffusion of Useful Knowledge in China.[27]

THE OPIUM CONTROVERSY

In today's world, when some mind-changing substances are shown to have devastating physical and social consequences, most governments maintain a high-profile war against drugs. But to see opium in the nineteenth century as little more than a lethal narcotic enslaving millions in China and reducing vast numbers of its population to chemical dependency is both simplistic and unhistorical. As Dikötter, Laamann and Xun have recently shown in their pioneering study, the conventional narrative today, especially as fostered by the Chinese communist state, reads thus:

> Britain, in its merciless pursuit of financial gain, trampled on the sovereign rights of China to enforce a shameful trade which reduced the country to a state of opium slavery ... the emperor of China was alarmed by opium's devastating impact on his people, and tried to ban the substance and bar foreign smugglers from the country. The British government decided to send an army to fight for the opening of China to foreign trade; it crushed the imperial army, enforced the opium traffic with gunboats, burnt down the Summer Palace in Beijing and imposed several unequal treaties during the 'Opium Wars' in the 1840s and 1850s ... the evil of opium turned China into a nation of hopeless addicts, smoking themselves to death while their civilisation descended into chaos.[28]

Over the last two decades or so, however, examination of Chinese sources and a more thorough engagement with the medical evidence has done much to challenge this stereotypical view of the nefarious effects of opium on the Chinese.[29] The following insights are instructive.

Opium's bad name in Britain mainly originated from the later nineteenth century and after, not from the heyday of William Jardine and James Matheson in earlier decades. The substance was not illegal in Britain and only from 1868 were any controls imposed on sale to ensure it would only be available in dispensaries. Before then opium could be bought over the counter in any number of shops across the country. Throughout South Asia, the Middle East and Europe, the drug was known primarily as a popular painkiller, unique in its palliative effects before the discovery of aspirin in the twentieth century. It was regarded as a medical panacea, not only providing pain relief but a means to fight fever, abate dysentery and other ailments. Laudanum, produced by mixing the substance with alcohol or water, was widely used in Victorian Britain and was the most popular analgesic of the age. The curative effects of opium inevitably gave it a much more positive public image than today and ensured that early campaigners against the drug, such as Lord Ashley, the prominent leader of the evangelical group in the Church of England, were still few and far between in the middle decades of the nineteenth century and had limited impact on public discourse.

Exports of Indian opium to China, especially from Patna in Bengal, the highest quality product, did rise spectacularly from the 1790s, despite the importation of the drug long being illegal in China. In 1809 shipments totalled 12,700 chests (each containing 120 lb of opium). By 1817 the figure stood at 21,600 and nearly doubled again to 40,000 chests in 1824.[30] British, American, European and Parsee traders eagerly delivered these increased supplies to a booming market. Among them Jardine, Matheson & Co reigned supreme. But the multiple transactions of the opium trade also involved countless numbers of Chinese, whether pirates who swarmed around the eastern sea lanes in their junks, coastal merchants, the inland distributors of the drug, or corrupt officials in Canton who turned a blind eye to the imperial prohibitions against importation.[31]

Despite attempts by several scholars over the years, an answer to the central question of the number of consumers or addicts by the 1830s in China still remains elusive. All that can be said is that opium was no longer only being smoked by the elites at that time and the habit was becoming much more common among the masses, especially in the eastern regions of the country closest to the source of imports. Serious scholarly doubt has, however, now been cast on the old belief that the impact of the drug on the native Chinese was always as lethal as later accounts have claimed. New evidence from Chinese sources suggests that few users could have been compulsive addicts as opium, like nicotine, is a psychotropic 'which is usually taken in determined amounts rather than ever-increasing ones'.[32] For some, opium smoking was a pleasurable recreation. But for many others it was a necessary support, in the way that alcohol was consumed in heroic quantities by manual workers in Britain, for hard and unrelenting physical labour. It was taken especially by Chinese coolies to sustain them during their long hours of backbreaking toil. Opium allowed the muscles to relax and recuperate. One British witness, Violet Cressy-Marcks, noted that 'the men always worked harder after they had smoked, and, obviously took a pipe before doing a strenuous job'.[33]

The most thorough and far-reaching British social and medical investigation of the nineteenth century on the effects of opium in Asia was launched in 1893 by the then prime minister, William Ewart Gladstone. The Royal Commission on Opium of 1895 was the British government's answer to the growing criticism from evangelical and Quaker groups which had become increasingly vocal about the moral impact of the drug. The Commission focused on the consumption of opium in India and on India's opium exports to China and elsewhere. It was asked to determine whether the export trade should be ended, poppy growing and consumption of opium in India prohibited and only uses for medicinal purposes permitted. There was universal agreement that the nine members of the Commission—seven British and two Indians—composed a fair and impartial tribunal. Some commissioners were anti-opium at the beginning of deliberations; others were not. But those who favoured prohibition in the country agreed that it was an objective and expert commission, even after a verdict was delivered which was unhelpful to their cause.[34]

Indeed, the Society for the Suppression of the Opium Trade, whose foundation reflected radically changed attitudes to the drug in the late nineteenth century, commented in its journal after members had listened to the early hearings of the Royal Commission in London: 'The Commission is as fair-minded and impartial as could have been desired to hear our case'.[35] Evidence was gathered from traders, missionaries, physicians and civil servants, who were selected for their experience and knowledge of China and India. The Commission released its final report after an extended enquiry in early 1895. It ran to around 2,000 pages and was accompanied by several appendices and annexes.[36] All Commissioners were agreed on their conclusions, except for one dissenting voice, H.J. Wilson MP, a long-standing anti-opium campaigner. They firmly rejected the view that 'opium caused moral or physical degradation', concluded that its use was little different from the consumption of alcohol in Europe and argued that the concerns of the Chinese empire were based not on proven medical evidence but on commercial vested interest.[37]

The *British Medical Journal* (BMJ) in April 1895 then published its own gloss on and interpretation of the Commission's conclusions.[38] It placed great emphasis on the diseases from which the people believed opium provided some relief, including malaria, dysentery, diarrhoea and cholera. In a devastating critique, the BMJ asserted that Europeans who drank alcohol and to which many were addicted had no moral right to condemn those who consumed another drug whose side effects by comparison were relatively benign and which for certain maladies had palliative compensations:

> A perusal of the addendum written by one of the native Commissioners makes it clear that an alcohol drinking people can, but with evil grace, protest against a habit for which there is much more excuse, and which produces so much less evil results than would follow what many consider the alternative, namely the spread of alcohol or ganja (marijuana).[39]

However, the verdict of the medical establishment of the day did not in the long run stop the growing chorus of condemnation of the drug in wider society. Opium became increasingly regarded as a lethal and dangerous narcotic.

CRUMBLING REPUTATIONS

Between 1839 and 1841 William Jardine and James Matheson had, in the view of Lord Palmerston, foreign secretary at the time, rendered signal service to the British state in helping to ensure victory in the conflict with China. If prohibition of the opium trade had been enforced by the Chinese, the finances of the Indian empire would have been placed in serious jeopardy. Only the massive export of silver could have compensated for the drug in the purchase of tea which was so much in demand by British consumers and for which China was the only source of plentiful supply at the time. Jardine died in February 1843 but Matheson lived until 1878 as a respected member of the nation's governing classes and was honoured when he died with effusive obituaries and enduring memorials. He ended his life as the owner of vast estates in the Highlands and Western Isles reaching over 406,000 acres in extent.[40]

Since then, however, the reputations of the two partners have been fundamentally revised in the most vituperative terms. They may have been aggressive adventurers and utterly ruthless in pursuit of profit and fortune, but in that they hardly differed much from so many of their fellow traders who were also on the make across the global British Empire in the eighteenth and nineteenth centuries. What marked out Jardine and Matheson, however, was their intriguing and singular metamorphosis from Victorian gentlemen of standing to disreputable drug barons and unscrupulous imperialists, an image that persists to the present day.

It will be argued that this reputational change reflected in part and in microcosm a radical reappraisal of Western relationships with China in the nineteenth century. Opium was also redefined in negative terms while the Opium Wars of the Victorian era were reinterpreted as especially brutal exemplars of European greed and exploitation in the Orient. In the view of Chinese nationalists, they were the catalyst for the many later miseries imposed by foreigners on the victimised peoples of China.

From the 1870s professional and political attitudes in the West to opium also began to change. As one writer has argued, opium did not alter in itself but the world around it slowly did.[41] A key aspect was the growing professionalisation of medicine. Doctors began to enforce exclusive legal rights to practise and regulate the use of pharmaceutical substances in an increasing number of European countries. Theories of addiction which were emerging at the same time presented a new image of the opium smoker as a victim of chemical dependency. Professional groups combining both medical and moral convictions, such as the China Medical Missionary Association, represented opium as a narcotic which inevitably led to compulsive behaviour.[42] Opium was transformed in the process 'from a folk remedy into a controlled substance'. Notions of 'opium plague' began to proliferate and pedlars of the drug were vilified as a result.[43]

Missionary societies added religious fervour and moral outrage to the attacks of the medical intelligentsia. The time was now long gone when the opium traders and their networks of distribution were regarded as useful channels through which scriptural readings and gospel tracts might be circulated to the vast populations of the Chinese interior. By the 1880s that approach by Protestant missionaries was effectively turned on its head. Far from being allies in the international campaign to Christianise China, the opium traders became reviled as evil distributers of a substance which rendered smokers sluggish, passive and languid and so incapable of absorbing the good news of Christ's message. In essence, opium was now portrayed in missionary propaganda as satanic because it helped to perpetuate the paganism of China. Bodies such as the Anglo-Oriental Society for the Suppression of the Opium Trade, founded in 1874, which received generous financial support from wealthy Quaker businessmen in Britain, also became vocal and influential. The Society enthusiastically adopted the radically new position that opium was a cause of moral cancer in the Chinese people. In his capacity as the Society's president, Sir Joseph Pease attempted to pass a motion in the House of Commons in 1891 to declare the opium trade was 'morally indefensible'. His intervention and its response were confirmation of changing opinion among the political classes in Britain. The motion attracted majority support in the House, though it eventually failed to pass into law because of an amendment calling for financial compensation to India in the event of the prohibition of the drug.[44]

Nevertheless, the image of an empire of over 300 million souls enslaved to a pernicious drug was a powerful propaganda tool for missionary societies. Equally as active as the Society for the Suppression of the Opium Trade was the China Medical Missionary Association. As its title suggests, the Association's attack combined Christian moral zeal with 'scientific' argument. The ubiquitous opium habit was the devil's way of ensnaring the Chinese in his embrace and preventing a heathen people from accepting the Word of Christ.[45] The decision of Gladstone's government in 1893 to convene a Royal Commission on Opium was in large part a response to the growing impact of the missionaries' campaign. As already noted, their arguments were comprehensively rejected by the Commission. However, in 1906 the motion proposed by Pease in Parliament was finally accepted. Finally, in 1913 Britain ended the opium trade to China from India. The age of narcophobia had dawned.

Long before this, however, the Chinese Empire had itself begun to redefine opium-smoking as no longer a leisure pursuit or a medical panacea but a criminal activity threatening the entire fabric of society. Increasingly, Chinese scholars and commentators in the later nineteenth and early twentieth centuries drew a correlation between the humiliations of the opium wars of the 1840s, the opening up of the opium trade on a much larger scale and the subsequent decline of the Chinese Empire. After

1895 the drug was represented by nationalist thinkers as 'a racial poison spread by white people', and by seducing the population into addiction, opium smoking threatened 'racial extinction'.[46] After the Empire's defeat by Japan in 1894–95, opium was identified as a leading cause, though modern research has shown that this was an attempt to provide a public scapegoat in order to conceal deeper internal military and political weaknesses. Nevertheless, the government then tried to enforce a policy of strict prohibition of the drug.

After the Communist Revolution of 1949 a new official narrative of Chinese history was developed and disseminated. The modern history of the country was depicted as starting with the First Opium War, which was then followed by over a century of humiliations until a national renaissance finally began with the victory of communism. The facts were set out in such texts as *A Century of Humiliations* and the one-and-a-half inches thick *Dictionary of National Humiliation*, a detailed catalogue of infamy and shame which recounted the decline of a once proud civilisation to the sorry plight of 'the sick man of Asia' by the time of the Second World War. At the heart of this narrative was the key role played by opium in the decline of China. The villains were unscrupulous British traders who were condemned for forcing large quantities of the drug on the hapless masses who then became addicted in huge numbers. The arch-villain was Lord Palmerston, who prevented the efforts of the Chinese state to prohibit the marketing and sale of the drug by British force of arms in the First Opium War. Even in the emerging superpower of the early twenty-first century sensitivities about that history remain very real. David Cameron and four British Cabinet ministers were reported to have caused offence to their hosts when they wore commemorative red poppies on their visit to China in November 2010.

It is a view of the Chinese past which is recounted and repeated to the present day in museums, school textbooks, television documentaries and popular films such as *The Opium War*, a new version of which was released on the eve of the British handover of Hong Kong to the Chinese People's Republic in 1997.[47] The refurbished National Museum of China opened in Tiananmen Square, Beijing, in spring 2011, boasting the latest in technology, but still repeating the established tale of Chinese victimhood. At the centre of the story are the wicked opium merchants, including the most infamous of them all, 'the grand old trading house' of Jardine, Matheson & Co, merchants from Scotland.

But it is not only the continuing patriotic propaganda of the Chinese government which ensures that the early history of Jardine, Matheson is remembered in notoriety when that of virtually all of their contemporaries in the China trade has been long lost to history.

As the books and articles in the Notes for this chapter amply confirm, the opium trade and the Opium Wars of the nineteenth century continue to have a fascination for scholars of today. The influence in the academy of postcolonial studies, which has mushroomed over the last few decades, has served to draw even more attention to the darker aspects of the history of European empires. In such discourse, the saga of opium and China predictably attracts researchers and maintains a high profile in historical scholarship. The popular narrative seems to display in especially stark terms many of the stereotypes of imperial exploitation: rapacious merchants, gunboat diplomacy, racism and plunder, all culminating in military violence against native peoples followed by their humiliating defeat and dominance at the hands of foreign powers. Jardine and Matheson always loom large in texts which either support or oppose this interpretation. In the words of one scholar writing in 1981, 'A familiarity with the early history of Jardine, Matheson & Co is critical to an understanding of the old China trade, the Opium War and of early East–West relations in general'.[48]

The fact that the name of the original nineteenth century company remains the designation of one of today's world-renowned conglomerates when the names of its nineteenth century rivals have long vanished from history is perhaps another reason for its immortality in the public domain. But in addition, since the 1960s, the story of 'The Firm' has also generated exceptional interest among modern novelists, filmmakers and television producers. Their work has in turn given the two partners a dark celebrity status as the emperors of the drug trade in South Asian seas, consumed with a lust for profit and gain and brutal indifference to the human costs of their transactions. These exploits, although Jardine and Matheson may not feature by name, inspired the bestselling books of James Clavell, especially *Tai-Pan* (1966) and *The Noble House* (1981), together with an associated film and television series. The distinguished Indian novelist Amitav Ghosh completed his magnificent and compelling trilogy of opium in Indian and Chinese culture in 2015 with *Flood of Fire*, after *Sea of Poppies* (2008) and *River of Smoke* (2011). They are set in the period of the opium trade before 1850 and fictionalise characters associated with the events of that era.

Thus has the tale endured of two Scots merchants trading to China nearly two centuries ago, even if their names are now only recalled by posterity in infamy.

NOTES

1. T.M. Devine, 'Lost to History', in T.M. Devine (ed.), *Recovering Scotland's Slavery Past: The Caribbean Connection* (Edinburgh: Edinburgh University Press, 2015), 21–40.
2. 'Return to China: Jardine Matheson', *The Economist*, 4 July 2015.
3. The most recent and thorough study is Richard J. Grace, *Opium and Empire: The Lives and Careers of William Jardine and James Matheson* (Montreal and Kingston: McGill-Queen's University Press, 2014). See also Robert Blake, *Jardine Matheson, Traders of the Far East* (London: Weidenfeld and Nicolson, 1999) and Maggie Keswick (ed.), *The Thistle and the Jade* (London: Octupus, 1982). Some of the firm's vast archive in Cambridge University Library has been published in Alain Le Pichon (ed.), *China Trade and Empire: Jardine, Matheson and Co. and the Origins of British Rule in Hong Kong* (Oxford: Oxford University Press 2006).
4. Le Pichon (ed.), *Trade and Empire*, 23, 26.
5. T.M. Devine, *Clearance and Improvement: Land, Power and People in Scotland 1700–1900* (Edinburgh: John Donald, 2006), 215–216; T.M. Devine, *The Great Highland Famine: Hunger, Emigration and the Scottish Highlands in the Nineteenth Century* (Edinburgh: John Donald, 1988, 2004), 212–225.
6. Julia Lovell, *The Opium War* (London: Picador, 2011), 24–25.
7. Michael Fry, *The Scottish Empire* (Edinburgh: Birlinn, 2002), p. 307; Lovell, *Opium War*, 24.
8. Saul David, 'The Opium Wars: How Scottish Traders Fed the Habit', *Scotsman*, 6 September 2005.
9. John K. Fairbank, 'The Creation of the Treaty Systems', in Denis Twitchett and John K. Fairbank (eds), *The Cambridge History of China* (Cambridge: Cambridge University Press, 1978), vol. 10, 213.
10. Gavin D. Smith, 'The Family Business', *Scotland Magazine*, No. 57, June 2011. The article is about James Matheson. It begins, 'This is the story of a drug dealer but not one who ended his days behind prison bars, shot by rivals, or hooked on his own merchandise'.

11. Grace's *Opium and Empire*, published in 2014, does not draw on these sources.

12. For these biographical references, see Richard J. Grace's articles 'William Jardine, 1784–1843', and 'Sir James Matheson, Bart., 1796–1878', in Lawrence Goldman (ed.), *Oxford Dictionary of National Biography* (Oxford: Oxford University Press, 2004), Index Numbers 101037595 and 101037746 respectively.

13. Devine, *Highland Famine*, 212–216. Later, however, the Matheson estate imposed a policy of 'compulsory emigration' on selected crofting and cottar communities in Lewis. Some 2,337 men, women and children were 'emigrated' across the Atlantic to Canada at a cost of £13,000 to the landowner. Direct and indirect methods of coercion were employed.

14. *Inverness Courier*, 15 November 1843; *Scotsman*, 15 November 1843.

15. Grace, *Opium and Empire*, 306.

16. *Inverness Courier*, 2 January 1879.

17. *Stornoway Gazette and West Coast Advertiser*, 29 September 1950.

18. See Lovell, *Opium War*; Robert Bickers, *The Scramble for China* (London: Allen Lane 2011); Peter W. Fay, *The Opium War, 1840–42* (Chapel Hill, VA: University of Virginia Press, 1975).

19. Lovell, *Opium War*, 35–54. For a different view to what follows see Chapter 13 by Iain Watson.

20. Fay, *Opium War*, 368; James Matheson (Canton) to William Jardine (London), 1 May 1839, in Le Pichon (ed.), *China, Trade and Empire*, 357–370, gives a detailed account from Matheson's perspective of the punitive action taken by the Chinese and the background to the Opium War.

21. Hansard, Parliamentary Debates, vol. 43, House of Commons debate on war with China, 7–10 April 1840.

22. Evidence for all the meetings can be found in Blake, *Jardine Matheson*, 93–94; Fay, *The Opium War*, 194–195; Maurice Collis, *Foreign Mud: The Opium Imbroglio at Canton in the 1830s and the Anglo-Chinese War* (New York: Faber, 1946, 1948), 257; Kenneth Bourne, *Palmerston: The Early Years* (London: Macmillan, 1982), 587–588; Grace, *Opium and Empire*, 248–258.

23. Grace, *Opium and Empire*, 258.

24. Lord Palmerston to John Abel Smith, 28 November 1842 in Michael Greenberg, *British Trade and the Opening of China* (Cambridge: University Press, 1954), 214–215.

25. Ibid.
26. David E. Owen, *British Opium Policy in China and India* (Newhaven, CT: Yale University Press, 1968), 230–231.
27. Michael C. Lazich, 'American Missionaries and the Opium Trade in Nineteenth-Century China', *Journal of World History*, 17, 2 (2006), 198–202.
28. Frank Dikötter. Lars Laaamm and Zhou Xun, *Narcotic Culture. A History of Drugs in China* (Chicago, IL: University of Chicago Press, 2004), 1.
29. The information summarised in the paragraphs which follow is mainly derived from: Dikötter et al, *Narcotic Culture*; Virginia Berridge, *Opium and the People: Opiate Use and Drug Control Policy in Nineteenth and Twentieth Century England* (London: Free Association Books, 1999); Richard K. Newman, 'Opium Smoking in Late Imperial China: A Reconsideration', *Modern Asian Studies* 29 (1995), 765–794; John F. Richards, 'Opium and the British Indian Empire: The Royal Commission of 1895', *Modern Asian Studies*, 36, 2 (2002), 375–420; Herbert Giles, *Some Truths about Opium* (Cambridge: Heffer, 1923); Jack Gray, *Rebellions and Revolutions: China from the 1800s to the 1980s* (Oxford: Oxford University Press, 1990); Zheng Yangwen, *The Social Life of Opium in China* (Cambridge: Cambridge University Press, 2005). The interpretation of the material is of course the responsibility of this author.
30. Cheong Wang Eang, *Mandarins and Merchants* (Atlantic Highland, NJ: Humanities Press, 1980), 21.
31. Leslie Marchant, 'The Wars of the Poppy', *History Today*, http://www.historytoday.com/Leslie-marchant/wars-poppies (accessed 30 October 2015).
32. Peter Lee, *The Big Smoke: The Chinese Art and Craft of Opium* (Bangkok: Lamplight Books, 1999), 129.
33. Violet Cressy-Marcks, *Journey into China* (London: Hodder and Stoughton, 1940), 72.
34. Richards, 'Opium and the British Indian Empire', 375–420.
35. J.B. Brown, 'Politics of the Poppy: The Society for the Suppression of the Opium Trade, 1874–1916', *Journal of Contemporary History*, 8, 3 (1973), 97–111.
36. *First Report of the Royal Commission on Opium: With Minutes of Evidence and Appendices* (London: HM Stationary Office, 1895).

37. Ibid.
38. *British Medical Journal*, 13 April 1895, 836.
39. Ibid., 837.
40. *Inverness Courier*, 2 January 1879; Grace, *Opium and Empire*, 333, 431. On the island of Lewis, at least, respectful articles about Matheson were still appearing in the local press in the 1950s.
41. Mike Jay, *Emperors of Dreams: Drugs in the Nineteenth Century* (Sawtry: Daedalus, 2002), 69.
42. Florence Bretelle-Establet, 'Narcotic Culture', *China Perspectives*, http://chinaperspectives.revue.org/554 (accessed 29 October 2015).
43. Dikötter et al, *Narcotic Culture*, 95.
44. Brown, 'Politics of the Poppy', 97–111.
45. Kathleen L. Lodwick, *Crusaders Against Opium: Protestant Missionaries in China, 1874–1917* (Lexington: University Press of Kentucky, 1996), *passim*.
46. Dikötter et al, *Narcotic Culture*, 94, 107–110, 206.
47. Lovell, *Opium War*, 9–10, 29.
48. Review of W.E. Cheong, *Mandarins and Merchants: Jardine, Matheson & Co. A China Agency of the Early Nineteenth Century* (1980) by Jacques M. Downs, *Business History Review*, 55, 2 (1981), 271. For a recent view of postcolonialism in Scottish writing see Carla Sassi and Theo van Heijenbergen (eds), *Within and Without Empire: Scotland Across the (Post) Colonial Borderline* (Newcastle: Cambridge Scholars, 2013).

CHAPTER 11

The Shanghai Scottish: Volunteers with Scottish, Imperial and Local Identities, 1914–41

Isabella Jackson

Scots were integral to the British presence in Shanghai, as elsewhere in China, from the beginning. Shanghai was opened to British and other foreign settlement in 1843, after the conclusion of the First Opium War (1839–42) when British warships blasted open the most advantageous ports on the China coast. It was, of course, the Scottish traders William Jardine and James Matheson who had persuaded the British government to go to war to protect the lucrative opium trade in China.[1] Scots contributed to the military victory over China in the Cameronian Regiment, and fought in the Second Opium War (1857–60) and Boxer War (1900–01). Their primary work in Shanghai, however, was as merchants and bankers.

My thanks to the editors and organisers of the 'Scots in Asia' symposium on 26–27 June 2015, where this work was first presented, and to all those who attended and gave helpful comments, particularly John MacKenzie. I would also like to thank Robert Bickers and Graham Thompson for their assistance in tracking down some of the sources consulted.

I. Jackson (✉)
Trinity College Dublin, Dublin, Ireland

© The Author(s) 2017   235
T.M. Devine, A. McCarthy (eds.), *The Scottish Experience in Asia,
c.1700 to the Present*, DOI 10.1007/978-3-319-43074-4_11

Scots migrated overseas, including to parts of the British formal and informal empire, in greater numbers than their counterparts from the United Kingdom's other constituent nations. Two million people migrated from Scotland in the long nineteenth century, a higher proportion of the population than migrated from England, Ireland or Wales.[2] This pattern was reflected in Shanghai: although the censuses did not disaggregate British subjects by nation, the St Andrew's Society was the largest of the national societies, with over 700 members by 1912, and it hosted the largest annual ball in the Shanghai calendar, the Caledonian Ball each December.[3] There were also two Scottish Masonic lodges in Shanghai.[4] Census figures for Hong Kong suggest that around 15 per cent of the British population were Scottish,[5] greater than the 10 per cent of the United Kingdom's population living in Scotland, and if Shanghai had a similar proportion of Scots (as is likely) their number would match the membership of the St Andrew's Society. The total foreign population in the International Settlement at Shanghai was 15,000, of which 4,500 were British, including British subjects of the colonies. It was the largest foreign grouping until some point between the 1910 and 1915 censuses when the Japanese first outnumbered Britons in the Settlement.[6] Britons remained, however, a privileged group, at the top of the social and racial hierarchy of Shanghai society—at least in their own eyes.[7] Scottish migrants were particularly adept at retaining and capitalising on their national identity through the regular practice and performance of traditional customs together,[8] and Shanghai was no exception.

In October 1914, as the First World War was taking hold in the Asia-Pacific region, the Scottish community in Shanghai came together to establish a Scottish company of volunteers. The Shanghai Volunteer Corps (SVC), which provided the first line of defence for the foreign community, was considered too low in recruits: a long-term problem exacerbated by the exodus of European men to their home nations to join up to their respective national armies. Appealing to the national loyalty of the residents of the city's International Settlement was seen as a way of winning more volunteers. The SVC was an international body of men and the Shanghai Municipal Council (SMC), which managed the Settlement and oversaw the corps, expressed some concern that national companies undermined the principle of internationalism that was crucial to the status of this anomalous outpost of imperialism in China. The British dominated the council, Settlement and volunteer corps, but all were explicitly international, ensuring a large degree of autonomy from control by any imperial authority.[9] But the Scottish Company of volunteers was a success, more national companies were established, and the Shanghai Scottish were prominent in parades and military action for the next 30 years, symbolising British imperialism in an international context.

The First World War was a boom period for Scottish military recruitment. Scots enlisted during the volunteering phase of the war (1914–15) in much higher numbers than other Britons, to the extent that agencies in some areas were so overwhelmed with volunteers that recruitment had to be temporarily halted.[10] As is well established, Scotland had a strong military tradition, dating to at least the late medieval Scottish mercenaries seeking a living around Europe. Scottish service in the armies of the crown dates back to the late seventeenth century, but increased from the 1760s. In the years following the Battle of Culloden (1746), Scots were recruited to the British Army in large numbers to fight the wars with France, the American Revolutionary War and wars of imperial conquest. Dozens of Highland regiments were established, though most were short-lived.[11] Volunteering was also highly popular in Scotland, where the image of the citizen soldier was promoted in newspapers.[12] Twice as many Scots per capita than other Britons joined volunteer companies in the late Victorian period, which T.M. Devine attributes both to the 'military spirit' of Scots and the inducement of the allowance given to British volunteers.[13] No such financial incentive was offered to Shanghai's volunteers, where appeals to a combination of local and national pride were the main method of recruitment, but the tradition of volunteering was familiar to Britons and especially Scots before their arrival in Shanghai.

The military tradition in Scotland was matched, if not exceeded, by the perception among both Scots themselves and other Britons that they were exceptionally formidable on the battlefield. Highlanders in particular were perceived as a martial race. Highland regiments were first singled out for popular praise at the culmination of the Napoleonic wars, as noted by Devine, with kilted battalions taking 'pride of place' in triumphal marches.[14] Yet Heather Streets argues that the reputation of the Scottish as effective military servants of empire was cemented in the British imagination by the role of Highland regiments in crushing the Indian Rebellion of 1857, alongside Sikhs and Gurkhas.[15] The Scots' heroic image then mingled with late-Victorian notions of biological racial determinism to support the belief that these groups were uniquely well-suited for military service. Streets identifies the connotations of what were believed to be characteristically British manly virtues of 'valour and loyalty', embodied in the idea of martial races.[16] The rugged environment of the Highlands was believed to instil these virtues, and although the army and the public were well aware that most recruits to the Highland regiments were in fact Lowlanders, all Scots came to be associated with these qualities. Scots as Highlanders symbolised an idealised vision of Britishness, despite being peripheral within Britain.

The kilted regiments in particular were bound up in the British imagi-nation with empire-building: John M. MacKenzie identifies them as being among 'the principal icons of the imperial enterprise'.[17] Highland regiments were critical in establishing, expanding and defending colonies throughout the empire and their role was avidly reported. Streets finds that connections between Scottish officers and influential newspaper writ-ers ensured that the Scottish contribution to military success was well-reported.[18] Soldiers in Highland military dress were instantly recognisable to all nations, not just the British, and their iconic value helped make the Shanghai Scottish successful in recruitment and projected the image the British wanted to promote in China. The British in Shanghai, though not formally part of the British Empire, were nonetheless keen to demonstrate their imperial ties. They employed Sikhs as police to capitalise on Indians' supposed martial qualities and to remind foreigners and Chinese alike of the extent of the British Empire through these exotic and visually striking men.[19] There was a preference for Scots when recruiting for the foreign branch of the Shanghai Municipal Police (SMP) in Britain, particularly men from rural areas, as their perceived martial qualities were valued in the quasi-military police force.[20] But the volunteers of the Shanghai Scottish brought the additional benefit of being just as visually exotic in their Highland regalia as the Sikh police in their red turbans, and they performed a similar function to the Sikhs in parades as symbols of British imperial and military strength.

The Shanghai Scottish Company was established late in the history of the SVC, which itself dated from 1853, just ahead of the wave of new volunteer forces emerging around the empire during the Crimean War (1853–56) to provide defence in the absence of the regular British mili-tary. The foreign community (which numbered only 373 at the time) felt threatened by rebels in Shanghai and mobilised British and US civilians to help the regular forces defend the Settlement. The following year the volunteers clashed with Qing forces who encroached on the Settlement in their efforts to recapture the walled city of Shanghai from the rebels.[21] The skirmish became glorified in the local foreign memory as the Battle of the Muddy Flat and was always given as the founding date of the SVC. The volunteers next organised in 1860 and were thereafter considered available for action at any time, though the force was not formalised with regular annual inspections until 1883.[22] Volunteers attended training most weeks of the year to keep them ready for another battle. There were almost always British, US, French and other naval vessels in the port of Shanghai, to ensure the safety of foreign lives and property should the need arise, but the civilian volunteers were intended to provide a rapid response to threats, alongside the militarised SMP, until the regular troops arrived.

In its early years, the SVC's companies were largely British and named by function: the Mounted Rangers (forerunners of the Light Horse Company), the Rifle Brigade, a Field Battery, and infantry companies. The first company named for the nation of its members was the Portuguese Company, consisting largely of Macanese living in the International Settlement and established first in 1884, though it was disbanded several times due to a perceived lack of discipline before it became a permanent fixture in 1906.[23] A German Company was formed in 1891, but the first major expansion came at the time of anxiety over the Boxer Rebellion in 1900, when Japanese and American companies were established and the corps grew from 350 to over 1,000 volunteers.[24] After the end of the Boxer War, when Shanghai was not in fact threatened, the American Company disbanded and the corps shrank down to around 500 men. The council rejected a suggestion by Chinese merchants that they should form a company of volunteers in 1900, but from 1907 they were accepted into the corps, initially only under the command of British officers.[25] The Chinese volunteers, like the Americans, Germans and Portuguese, initiated their company in order to assert their place within the Settlement community by volunteering to defend it.

The Scottish Company arose not from such bottom-up pressure but in response to criticism of the SVC by Major-General Kelly from Hong Kong, who came to inspect the volunteers in spring 1914 and found the force too small. According to Kelly, 'There are far too many men in Shanghai who appear content to let others defend them'.[26] His criticism was discussed avidly in the pages of the *North China Daily News*, the most widely circulated English-language newspaper in Shanghai, and it was a letter to the editor from a self-styled 'Old Volunteer' that first suggested national companies. The correspondent's proposal was for English, Irish, Scottish and Welsh companies, each sporting the uniform of a famous regiment from their home nation: he suggested 'some Fusilier uniform, say, for the English Company, 42nd or Black Watch for the Scottish Company, Royal Irish Rifles for the Irish Company and Royal Welsh Fusiliers for the Welsh Company'.[27] His argument was based on capitalising on both patriotic spirit and 'the power of a smart uniform'. As he predicted, the idea was met with a barrage of further letters to the editor, most in favour, although 'Light Horseman' cautioned that while 'a gay uniform has been found to be no mean recruiting agent, I would venture to suggest that the class of recruit that takes the "King's shilling" on the strength of this future picturesque appearance alone, is usually of inferior intellect and standing'.[28] He continued, 'I think it would take more than a kilt or a Fusilier's busby to bring the slacker and scoffer into the S.V.C. fold'. Most correspondents, however, agreed with the suggestion that an attractive uniform would enhance recruitment, 'Fusilier' going so far as to rebut the views of 'Light Horseman' on the basis that 'I fear he has never had the honour of wearing such a [dress uniform]'.[29] The patriotic appeal of national companies was not discussed in the paper: the primary appeal was thought to be the use of an attractive uniform.

The SMC took up the suggestion for national companies from the exchanges in the pages of the *North China Daily News* and approached leading members of the Scottish, Irish and American communities to investigate the chances of successfully forming such companies. The Irish and Americans doubted that sufficient numbers from their communities would join, but the Scots took up the idea. The recruitment drive was led by Charles McLeod Bain, a prominent Scottish businessman (general manager of Maitland and Company, a Manchester-based trading firm) originally from Strathpeffer, a Highland village, who had served as a lieutenant in the Reserve Company of the SVC.[30] Bain may have written the initial letter to the *North China Daily News*, and the articles in the paper boosting the idea of national companies were later claimed to have been written by the journalist Harry Kendle Strachan, a son of Montrose in East Scotland, who had served as a piper in the London Scottish and went on to join the new Shanghai Scottish Company.[31] Many of the new recruits had experience in the London Scottish, and the Company's badge was based on the thistle design used by that territorial battalion.

Scottish companies were established elsewhere in China and East Asia. The Hong Kong Volunteer Defence Force and the Tianjin Volunteer Corps both had Scottish companies. A Scottish Company was added to the Singapore Volunteer Corps in 1922.[32] The Federated Malay States Volunteer Force had two Scottish platoons, one of which, like the Shanghai, Singapore and Calcutta Scottish, opted to wear the Stewart Tartan because, as the royal tartan, it favoured no particular clan. The Calcutta Scottish unit of the Auxiliary Force, India, was established, like the Shanghai Scottish, in 1914 and was open explicitly to 'Scots by birth or ancestry', as were the Scottish units in the Canadian Army Reserve Unit.[33] Elsewhere, colonial armies included numerous regular Scottish troops. The Shanghai Scottish were thus following an empire-wide trend by volunteering to a specifically Scottish unit, but what made them unique was that they did so within an explicitly international corps.

The SVC was known in Chinese as *wanguo shangtuan*: 'the militia of the merchants of many nations'. From the founding of the Shanghai Scottish on, the corps as a whole typically numbered between 1,000 and 1,500 men, although at its peak in 1938 the corps boasted 2,320 members, with American, British, Chinese, Italian, Japanese, Jewish, Philippine, Portuguese, Russian, Scandinavian and Scottish companies. In addition, Germans, Austrians, Czechoslovakians and others volunteered, particularly in the Field Battery, Transport and Intercommunication companies, bringing the total number of nationalities represented in the Corps to 32.[34] But Britons dominated the SVC, from the commandant on secondment from the British Army to British volunteers, the largest single nationality in the corps: 583 in 1938. And it was the Shanghai Scottish that represented the corps in the local media and imagination. It was one of the larger companies of the SVC, with 120 members in 1938, a peak of 148 in 1925, and averaging 95 members: typically, only the Machine Gun, Portuguese, and Chinese companies were larger. The Light Horse and Armoured Car Companies were the only ones to rival the Scottish in visual appeal, frequently appearing in newspaper photographs in the same way, but they lacked the exoticism offered by the kilt and pipes, and did not share the prestige of belonging to a so-called martial race.

The Scottish volunteers, almost as soon as they appeared publicly in their dress uniforms for the first time, came to symbolise the SVC and the British presence in Shanghai and therefore, to a large extent, in China as a whole, at least in Western eyes. Photographs of the volunteers on parade and newspaper accounts of its manoeuvres featured the Scottish Company prominently. Their kilts and pipes became a highlight of the annual SVC parades and inspections. The Company guarded the British Consulate-General during the First World War, providing a service to the British state that the ostensibly international corps as a whole could not.[35] The Shanghai Scottish also featured prominently in celebrations of Empire Day and the King of England's birthday, representing the whole SVC at the King's Birthday Parade in June 1927. They marched alongside all the British battalions that remained in Shanghai after the defence of the Settlement from Chinese troops during the establishment of the Nationalist state. Thereafter, the King's Birthday was celebrated with all the predominantly British companies of the SVC, but the Scots always drew the most attention. It was not only the British community that admired the Scots. The internationally oriented *China Press* (traditionally American, but by now Chinese-owned) published a front-page report of the 1931 King's Birthday Parade, describing the Shanghai Scottish as 'the smartest looking outfit participating in the parade'.[36] The Company was positioned penultimately in the parade, after the British navy and army units, which that year included the Royal Scots Fusiliers, and all the other British companies of the SVC—the Light Horse, Armoured Car, and A Companies—with the Sikh branch of the municipal police bringing up the rear. According to the reporter, 'These loyal sons of the British Empire all drew rounds of applause from the spectators but the lion's share went to the Shanghai Scottish, S.V.C., who, in their khaki uniforms and tartan kilts, were most picturesque'.[37] The positioning of the two supposed martial races together in the parade and in the apparent appreciation of the crowd underlines the symbolic value of the Shanghai Scottish to the visual projection of British military power in Shanghai. The cheers for the Shanghai Scottish were reportedly not matched by those for the Royal Scots Fusiliers, so it was important to the spectators that these manifestations of British imperial force were drawn from the population of the Settlement and belonged to it. Moreover, the Royal Scots Fusiliers did not sport kilts, so did not provide the same 'picturesque' appearance as the Shanghai Scottish (Fig. 11.1).

In the 1933 King's Birthday Parade, the Shanghai Scottish paraded alongside the Royal Navy and eight regular British Army companies as well as other British companies of volunteers, but the photograph accompanying the newspaper's report showed only the Scottish Company.[38] These celebrations were major events with thousands of spectators, the *China Press* reporting that 'long before the hour set for the parade, all available parking space near the Race Course was occupied, and the trackside stands were filled'.[39] Robert Bickers stresses the importance of such regular celebrations in the competitive imperial world of Shanghai, where

Fig. 11.1   The Shanghai Scottish at the King's Birthday Parade, 1933 (*Source: Virtual Cities Project*, Institut d'Asie Orientale, Lyon)

each nation marked its state holidays with pomp to demonstrate its local and global position.[40] Such festivities were a normal part of imperial life, but in Shanghai the different nations could show off to one another in close proximity. The use of British forces demonstrated that the British community could draw on a vast army and navy if threatened, but the use of Scottish soldiers in particular drew on the associations of manliness and hardiness that the martial race symbolised. When these Scottish forces on display were Shanghai's own volunteers, the British community felt its own manliness and military prowess to be burnished all the more.

Chinese observed and participated in these events to varying degrees, from ignoring them to turning out in large numbers and participating.[41] Some Chinese were struck by the unusual uniforms of the Scottish volunteers, typifying the otherness of the foreigners who controlled the heart of Shanghai. A sketch of typical sights of Shanghai in *Guo Yi* (National Art) magazine in 1940 showed a Sikh policeman, a Scottish volunteer and a French police inspector to illustrate the city (see Fig. 11.2). The cartoonist's eye was drawn to the iconic visual appearance of the Highland uniform. On the whole, however, Shanghai's Chinese took little notice of the Scottish volunteers, unlike the Sikh police who took root in the popular imagination of the city's residents as emblematic of imperial oppression.[42]

Fig. 11.2   A Sikh policeman, a Scottish Highlander and an English inspector (*Source:* 'Shanghai', *Guo Yi* (National Art), 1, 5–6 (Shanghai, 1940), 80)

The SVC rarely came into direct contact with the city's inhabitants—only on the occasional mobilisations were they likely to interact directly with Chinese or foreign residents—whereas the Sikh police were a daily presence, directing traffic and patrolling the streets. The volunteers were most visible in their various annual parades, but Chinese reports of these events did not make special reference to the Shanghai Scottish. It seems that the SVC's attempt to project imperial power through the image of the Highlanders was more effective in impressing the foreign community than the Chinese.

Recruitment was an ongoing concern for the SVC, and the strength of the Shanghai Scottish varied as did that of the other companies of European volunteers—the Chinese, Japanese and Russian communities were more consistently enthusiastic, and the Americans were the least ready to volunteer. But national companies were accepted as a positive force in aiding the recruitment and retention of volunteers. Their appeal was attributed to a combination of the desire to parade in an attractive uniform (the main reason cited in the pages of the *North China Daily News* for establishing national companies in 1914) and national loyalty.

The Shanghai Scottish boasted the most striking uniforms, although it was reported that those at the initial meeting to organise the Company had debated at length whether or not it should feature a kilt, this still being considered specifically Highland garb rather than representing the whole of Scotland as it came to do later. It would be crucial to the popularity of the new Company in Shanghai that the iconic kilts were chosen. The chosen uniforms were elaborate, with Hunting Stewart tartan imported from Scotland, a shoulder-plaid and silver-mounted dirk for officers, and sporrans modelled on those in the London Scottish (or on those of the Black Watch for officers). It was intended that the volunteers would cover the cost of the Highland uniform themselves, however: the SMC provided only the same funds as required by other companies for their simpler summer and winter uniforms, approximately £30 per volunteer.[43] It seems, however, that the volunteers did not cover the remainder of the cost and the Scottish Company amassed a debt to the SMC of 1,340 taels for uniforms between 1927 and 1932. The SMC hoped the St Andrew's Society would pay the debt, but was instead forced to cancel it. Thereafter the SMC decided to provide khaki uniforms to the Company and an additional 20 taels towards the costs of each member's dress uniform, the volunteers to cover the rest themselves.[44] As most of the community was well-heeled, the cost of uniforms did not apparently deter recruitment: volunteers joined the Company not for a free uniform but for the right to wear the uniform and to be seen to do so.

The Highland uniforms helped the SVC tap into Scottish self-perceptions of their national strength as soldiers. Devine stresses the appeal of the martial tradition, symbolised by the kilt and tartan, in recruiting Scots to fight in the First World War.[45] Just as Streets found that regular Scottish soldiers internalised the values attributed to the martial races to serve the interests of the British state,[46] so did volunteering Scots in Shanghai, in seeking to display their Scottish identity through the new Company, serve the interests of the SMC in gaining more volunteers. When it was first established, more than 50 local Scots volunteered for the Company, the majority of whom had not volunteered to the corps before there was an explicitly Scottish section. The SMC's criteria for establishing new national companies included that they must recruit at least 30 new members who had not previously joined the SVC: there would be no point establishing a new company if volunteers simply transferred to it from a pre-existing one. But there were also many who transferred from other companies to the Shanghai Scottish, including Arthur Ernest Stewart, a stockbroker, said to be the only member of the Corps entitled to wear both the SVC Jubilee Medal, issued during the 1893 celebrations, and the China Medal issued for service during the Boxer Rebellion. He was still volunteering at the age of 56 in 1932, when he committed suicide (due, it was believed, to 'financial embarrassment').[47] The Scottish Company thus had an undoubted appeal to old and new volunteers alike, though the uniform and appeal to a sense of national identity alone do not explain its popularity.

The transient community of Shanghai meant that it was not seen as a permanent home by many employees of large expatriate firms, making them less likely to volunteer to defend it and ensuring a steady turnover of personnel, so it was always necessary to attract new volunteers to replace those who left. There was, however, a strong sense of local loyalty among those who settled in the city. Old stalwarts repeatedly stated that young men should join the SVC out of a sense of duty to Shanghai: the Shanghailander spirit explored by Bickers that ensured settlers in the city mixed local identity with national and imperial identity.[48] Except in times of clear external threat, however, local loyalty was insufficient to entice enough men to choose volunteer service over the many diversions on offer in Shanghai, famous for its races, clubs and nightlife. The Shanghai Scottish, however, met the desire for socialising opportunities with its annual Company dances, Highland games, and regular sporting fixtures. All volunteer companies played one another at cricket, rugby, football and other sports, but the Scottish Company afforded additional opportunities to compete and socialise. The Highland games, with caber tossing, putting the shot, piping and dancing, were considered by the self-styled 'Sutherlander', writing in the *North China Daily News*, to be a major boost to recruitment in the early days of the Company.[49] The sociability of the Company was evident when the festivities at the gala dinner to celebrate the 21st anniversary of the Company went on until the early hours:

> Towards breakfast-time, speeches still were being made simultaneously in a half-dozen different places, toasts quaffed, reels danced, the pipers were playing retreats, gatherings, and anything else that came into their heads, and for a half-mile around could be heard the joyous 'hooches' of a hundred Scottish revellers.[50]

Little wonder that the esprit de corps of the Shanghai Scottish was singled out for praise by the commandant in his annual reports.[51] This was a crucial part of the appeal of the Company.

The Shanghai Scottish Company's association with the St Andrew's Society ensured a ready-made social network for volunteers. The St Andrew's Society was the cornerstone of Scottish associational life in Shanghai, as Tanja Bueltmann has shown such societies to be in sites of Scottish settlement around the world.[52] Celebrating a shared national identity helped migrants meet the demands, psychological and material, of life far from the support available at home, and both the St Andrew's Society and the Scottish Company of volunteers met this need. Although the Society did not itself organise the establishment of the Shanghai Scottish, at the annual meeting of the society in October 1914, Bain, the Company's founder, was made president of the Society and the assembled members agreed that the Company should come under its patronage. Thereafter the two organisations were very close: the Shanghai Scottish pipers performed at every St Andrew's Society ball, the society provided prizes in various categories of shooting for the Company's annual competitions, and the Company's officers and men were the members and leaders of the Society. Alister Campbell, who served in the Argyll and Sutherland Highlanders during the First World War, was asked to command the Shanghai Scottish on his return to Shanghai and was simultaneously elected president of the St Andrew's Society. He was promoted to major by the SMC shortly before his death in 1927 and the Shanghai Scottish turned out in force at his funeral. His brother, the chief mourner, wore the Company uniform.[53] In Scotland, family and friendship connections greatly increased men's propensity to volunteer for military service, and it seems there was a similar pattern of relatives and friends joining the Shanghai Scottish. Through its social events and connections, therefore, the support of the St Andrew's Society was crucial to the success of the Shanghai Scottish.

Despite the foreign community's pride in them, however, the Shanghai Scottish did not live up to the hopes of its founders. The members wanted a full piping band, but generally had only one piper.[54] It was initially hoped that two companies might be formed, but the Shanghai Scottish suffered from the same slumps in recruitment in periods of peace as the rest of the corps and recruits were never sufficiently high to consider establishing another company. Even during the Sino-Japanese hostilities of 1932, when recruitment increased dramatically, there were bitter mutterings that 'there are a thousand or so more Scotsmen here who don't seem to care to come into' the conflict.[55] The SMC repeatedly issued calls for more volunteers, and Scots were no more likely to respond than others. The appeal of the Shanghai Scottish Company to local Scots should not, therefore, be overstated. But the SMC and the wider foreign community did appreciate the Company for providing a visual focus at public events and as effective soldiers in times of crisis.

The Shanghai Scottish were mobilised on at least six occasions, along-side the other companies of the corps. Each time they were given a signifi-cant and highly visible role in the defence of the International Settlement, which 'Sutherlander' attributed to the large number of former regular soldiers in the Company.[56] Their eye-catching uniforms also allowed the foreign community to see and show off their defence force, helping them feel safe and, they hoped, intimidating those who threatened them.

In the early 1920s civil war raged in eastern China and the SVC were called out from September to October 1924, when the Shanghai Scottish defended North Railway Station just outside the Settlement from Chinese fighting. In January 1925 the Scottish Company guarded the internment camps hastily opened for Chinese troops at the end of the fighting to pre-vent them from causing disorder. The *North China Herald* (the weekly digest of the *Daily News*) called for sympathy for the Scottish volunteers: 'Standing in thick sticky mud under drizzling rain throughout the night is not pleasant and the men deserve high praise for the cheerful way in which they carried out their duties'.[57] Members of the Company were despatched at 1am to disarm 2,000 or 3,000 retreating Chinese soldiers (depending on whether the commandant of the corps or the *North China Herald* journalist is believed) at Jessfield Railway Bridge in the north of the city. This was easily accomplished as the defeated soldiers 'were per-fectly willing and laid down their arms at once', and they joined the other troops in internment. The Chinese Chamber of Commerce provided food to the internees, but conditions in the camps were poor, with little shelter or space and no sanitation, and the internees' tempers were reported to be 'ugly'. After a day and a night of guarding the camps, the Shanghai Scottish were relieved from duty by US marines, and later French sail-ors guarded them. As conditions worsened, attempts were made by the internees to escape and it was reported that a US marine shot at escap-ees, killing one and wounding five other Chinese soldiers.[58] The interned soldiers were soon after removed on boats and taken as far as Qingdao, where they were left to find their way home as best they could. The Sikh branch of the SMP guarded the camps alongside the Shanghai Scottish, but no other SVC companies were engaged in camp guard duty. The Sikh police and Scottish volunteers enabled the SMP and SVC to perform their primary function of providing the initial protection of the Settlement prior to the arrival of foreign forces.

Later in 1925, the SMC called upon the SVC to give a display of force to help restore order following major protests in the wake of the municipal police shooting and killing peaceful protestors in the International Settlement on 30 May 1925: what would become known as the May Thirtieth Incident.[59] The Shanghai Scottish, with the other companies, 'made a demonstration march round the Chapei Boundary' of the Settlement the day after the shooting and then they moved into billets (the Scots in the Cricket Club) to be available at short notice. They remained on duty for 13 weeks.[60] The Scottish and American Companies were the first to be deployed, clearing protestors from Nanjing Road, the main thoroughfare through the Settlement. The Scottish volunteers also guarded the town hall with the American Company and regular US troops. Alongside the Light Horse Company and SMP, the Shanghai Scottish occupied buildings used by Chinese gunmen to attack US troops. The violence was soon contained but a general strike lasted the rest of the summer, bringing most Settlement business to a halt, and the repercussions were long-lasting. During the crisis, however, the Shanghai Scottish were consistently deployed in important and dangerous positions, contributing both their manpower and the element of military display that they brought to the municipal efforts to contain the protest. Predictably, in the *North China Herald*'s review of the year, a photograph of the Shanghai Scottish was used to illustrate the May Thirtieth Incident story.[61]

The next major threat to the International Settlement came in early 1927, when Chiang Kai-shek's nationalist troops claimed Shanghai during their Northern Expedition to unite China after more than a decade of warlord rule. Chiang targeted the local warlord forces and seized the Chinese-run city outside the foreign settlements only, but fighting encroached on the International Settlement. The foreign community, which saw the Nationalist Party, with its links to Soviet Russia, as a dangerous Bolshevik force, were frightened that the Settlement itself would be attacked. As the Nationalists claimed the nearby cities of Nanjing, Hankou and Wuhan, recruitment to the SVC surged, with 50 men signing up to the Shanghai Scottish in the first weeks of January.[62] A record 1,200 volunteers paraded in early February, reassuring residents that their local defences were strong.[63] The Shanghai Scottish were among those stationed at the boundary of the Settlement in case fighting came too close, until the duty could be handed over to regular soldiers. The British troops of the Shanghai Defence Force arrived from India to defend British life and property, filling the Settlement with soldiers.[64] They were not deployed but served their purpose: Chiang Kai-shek did not attack the settlements. The British Admiralty was impressed by the service of the SVC and recommended its numbers be increased.[65] The SVC were next called upon to face not a military threat but a threat to business: a general strike was called affecting major Chinese and foreign employers, including Butterfield and Swire and British American Tobacco - 5,000 employees of the latter downing tools.[66] The SMC primarily served foreign business interests, so used its volunteer corps to contain the strike. The Shanghai Scottish stood guard with the other volunteers and were not demobilised for ten weeks.

Following the Japanese occupation of Manchuria in 1931, Japan turned its attention to Shanghai, attacking the city in an undeclared war in January 1932. The SMC declared a state of emergency and mobilised the SVC to defend the International Settlement's perimeter. The Settlement was now highly militarised, with blockhouses, pillboxes, and gates at the Settlement boundaries.[67] The volunteers erected barbed wire barricades and constructed sandbag redoubts in what was their first real military action. The Shanghai Scottish were stationed first at North Honan Road and then at a blockhouse dubbed 'Windy Corner' opposite North Railway Station, a point of strategic importance for both the Chinese and Japanese.[68] 'Sutherlander' reported regularly (and light-heartedly) on their activities, revealing to readers of the *North China Herald* that the Company had gained a dog as a mascot (named Winnie) and had stolen a bus from the Cathay Hotel to use as transport: the man allegedly insisted it would only be released in return for '"so many" cases of "so-and-so"'.[69] Residents of the Settlement gave gifts, primarily food and drink, to the volunteers at their posts to show appreciation of their services. The Company played a football match for a crowd in the Race Course 'in full war regalia', the winning side getting a case of beer.[70] Morale was high. 'Sutherlander' also claimed, however, that 'a night at any of our posts would convince anyone that a real danger to the Settlement still exists, for, apart from stray rifle bullets, shells pass continually over our heads, and it is difficult to believe they can all clear Settlement territory'.[71]

The Shanghai Scottish suffered no casualties, but they were in potential danger. The SMC sought to demobilise the volunteers in early February when British and US military reinforcements reached Shanghai to defend the Settlement, but Brigadier Fleming, the British commander of the combined international defence force, including the SVC, insisted they were performing essential duties and could not be spared. The volunteers were gratified, he pointed out, to be defending the Settlement's perimeter and their employers would have to do without them for the duration of hostilities.[72] It was perhaps the most significant contribution the volunteers made to the defence of the Settlement.

The SVC again mobilised to defend the centre of the Settlement in August 1937 when the Sino-Japanese War engulfed Shanghai. This time the Settlement experienced heavy gunfire and bombing, although neither side was targeting it. The Shanghai Scottish were removed from their posts on 16 August after just two days due to the heavy bombing, and returned to their billets at the Race Course for 'internal security duty'.[73] For the rest of August they contributed to volunteer guards and street patrols, including breaking up minor disturbances, and evacuation and rescue work.[74] More foreign troops were stationed in Shanghai than in 1932 and the volunteers were less integral to the defence of the Settlement. The Japanese forces took most of the city, barring the principal districts of the International Settlement and the French Concession, by late October, and thereafter the foreign settlements had to keep an uneasy peace within occupied China. British and US troops remained in the Settlement until August 1940, when SVC companies including the Shanghai Scottish were called out to replace them.[75] In subsequent years the Shanghai Scottish were mobilised with the rest of the SVC and the SMP to maintain law and order during the frequent anniversaries of contentious events, such as 9 August (the date on which Japanese hostilities broke out in Shanghai in 1937).[76] The SVC was finally disbanded in early 1942 after the Japanese seized control of the International Settlement, by which time the Scottish volunteers had mostly been interned, along with other Allied nationals in the Settlement.

The commitment to volunteer was thus a real one, involving time spent training and on mobilisations and the risk of physical danger. Volunteers joined the corps to defend the International Settlement from tangible threats, demonstrating a sense of loyalty to the Settlement that was their temporary or more permanent home. The national companies allowed volunteers to serve these ends with an additional patriotic twist, as they asserted their ties to home as well as to Shanghai. For British volunteers, including the Scots, there was also a sense of imperial duty being performed, defending the empire in the tradition of Highland regiments defending the British Raj from mutiny in 1857 or in other celebrated imperial conflicts. The Scots once again performed their perceived role as a nation of empire-builders with a specific ethnic contribution to make to British imperialism. This imperial performance allowed the ambiguous status of Shanghai to be brought closer to the protection afforded by the

British Empire, which proved essential in times of trouble for the defence of the Settlement. As John Darwin notes, 'all imperial communities were extensions of the military systems on which they ultimately depended'.[77] The foreign community in Shanghai depended first on the combined strength of the SMP and SVC and second on the protection of foreign, primarily British, forces. The Shanghai Scottish contributed to the first and, through its evocation of empire, boosted claims to the second.

The Shanghai Scottish played a prominent part in the various mobilisations of the SVC, but their role was primarily one of display. The conspicuous visual spectacle offered by the Shanghai Scottish in their kilts offered the British in Shanghai the same opportunity as the Sikh police branch to advertise their imperial strength to foreign and Chinese onlookers. These so-called martial races represented the image of military might that the British wanted to project. Like the Highland regiments—visibly Scottish but also British imperial soldiers—Scottish volunteers symbolised militarily the dual identity of Scottishness and Britishness within the union state. The Shanghai Scottish, however, had the additional benefit of being a clearly designated British company in a corps defined otherwise by its internationalism. The Scottish Company could be used alongside regular British troops to guard the British consulate-general or parade in celebration of the King's birthday. They therefore represented Britishness in a polyglot community. Despite being perceived by other Britons as exotic due to their striking Highland regalia and geographically peripheral position in Britain, the Shanghai Scottish became emblematic of British imperialism and indeed all foreign imperialism in China.

Notes

1. Julia Lovell, *The Opium War: Drugs, Dreams and the Making of China* (London: Picador, 2011), 24, 67.
2. John M. MacKenzie and T.M. Devine, 'Introduction', in John M. MacKenzie and T.M. Devine (eds), *Scotland and the British Empire* (Oxford: Oxford University Press, 2011), 3.
3. Andrew Field, *Shanghai's Dancing World: Cabaret Culture and Urban Politics, 1919–1954* (Hong Kong: Chinese University Press, 2010), 22.
4. 'Lodge St Andrew in the Far East', *The Skirret*, 493 [2] (2012), http://www.skirret.com/papers/dgl/lodge_493_2.html (accessed 2/1/2016).

5. Tanja Bueltmann, *Clubbing Together: Ethnicity, Civility and Formal Sociability in the Scottish Diaspora to 1930* (Liverpool: Liverpool University Press, 2014), 166, using figures from *Census of the British Empire: Report with Summary* (London: HM Stationary Office, 1906), 106, 119, 126, 129, 134.

6. Shanghai Municipal Council (hereafter SMC), *Report for the Year 1940 and Budget for the Year 1941* (Shanghai: Kelly and Walsh, 1940), 339.

7. Robert Bickers, *Britain in China: Community, Culture and Colonialism 1900–1949* (Manchester: Manchester University Press, 1999), 73, 77 and passim.

8. John M. MacKenzie with Nigel R. Dalziel, *The Scots in South Africa: Ethnicity, Identity, Gender and Race, 1772–1914* (Manchester: Manchester University Press, 2007), 5–7 and *passim*.

9. Isabella Jackson, 'Who Ran the Treaty Ports? A Study of the Shanghai Municipal Council', in Robert Bickers and Isabella Jackson (eds), *Treaty Ports in Modern China: Law, Land and Power* (London: Routledge, 2016), 87–116.

10. T.M. Devine, 'Soldiers of Empire, 1750–1914', in MacKenzie and Devine (eds), *Scotland and the British Empire*, 193.

11. Andrew Mackillop, 'For King and Country? The Highland Soldiers' Motivation and Identity', in Steve Murdoch and Andrew Mackillop (eds), *Fighting for Identity: Scottish Military Experiences, 1550–1900* (Leiden: Brill, 2002), 199.

12. Edward M. Spiers, *The Scottish Soldier and Empire, 1854–1902* (Edinburgh: Edinburgh University Press, 2006), 182–183.

13. T.M. Devine, *To the Ends of the Earth: Scotland's Global Diaspora, 1750–2010* (London: Allen Lane, 2011), 227; *Scotland's Empire 1600–1815* (London: Allen Lane, 2003), 302.

14. Devine, *To the Ends of the Earth*, 210.

15. Heather Streets, *Martial Races: The Military, Race and Masculinity in British Imperial Culture, 1857–1914* (Manchester: Manchester University Press, 2004), 18.

16. Streets, *Martial Races*, 6, 8.

17. John M. MacKenzie, 'Essay and Reflection: On Scotland and the Empire', *International History Review*, 15, 4 (1993), 726.

18. Streets, *Martial Races*, 12–13.

19. Isabella Jackson, 'The Raj on Nanjing Road: Sikh Policemen in Treaty-Port Shanghai', *Modern Asian Studies*, 46, 6 (2012), 1672–1704.

20. Shanghai Municipal Archives (hereafter SMA), U1-1-82: SMC Watch Committee minutes, 10 April 1902; Robert Bickers, 'Who were the Shanghai Municipal Police, and Why were They There? The British Recruits of 1919', in Robert Bickers and Christian Henriot (eds), *New Frontiers: Imperialism's New Communities in East Asia, 1842–1953* (Manchester: Manchester University Press, 2000), 187.

21. 'The Battle of "Muddy Flat", 1854, Being an Historical Sketch of that Famous Occurrence, Written Specially for the Jubilee Commemoration Thereof at Shanghai, April 1904; with some Added Particulars Relating to the Shanghai Volunteer Corps' (Shanghai: North China Herald, 1904), 1–12.

22. 'Shanghai's Volunteers: An Eightieth Anniversary History of Settlement's Unique Corps', *North China Herald* (hereafter *NCH*), 28 June 1933, 515.

23. Edbert A. Hewitt, Chairman of the SMC, to J.M.T. Valdez, Consul-General for Portugal, 7 July 1900, in SMC, *Report for 1900*, 33.

24. 'The Battle of "Muddy Flat"', 15–16.

25. Xu Tao, 'The Chinese Company of the Shanghai Volunteer Corps', in Toby Lincoln and Xu Tao (eds), *The Habitable City in China: Urban History in the 20th Century* (forthcoming: Palgrave Macmillan, 2017).

26. 'Our Volunteers; Inspecting Officer's Report: Some Practical Suggestions', *Shanghai Times*, 11 June 1914, 5.

27. 'Correspondence' from 'Old Volunteer', *NCH*, 27 June 1914, 988.

28. 'Correspondence' from 'Light Horseman', *NCH*, 4 July 1914, 40.

29. 'Correspondence' from 'Fusilier', *NCH*, 4 July 1914, 41.

30. George F. Nellist, *Men of Shanghai: A Standard Biographical Work* (Shanghai: Oriental Press, 1933), 15–16.

31. Carroll Lunt, *The China Who's Who: A Biographical Dictionary* (Shanghai: Kelly & Walsh, 1922), 254.

32. Jonathan Moffatt and Paul Riches, *In Oriente Primus: A History of the Volunteer Forces in Malaya and Singapore* (Coventry: J. Moffatt and P. Riches, 2010), 9.

33. J.B. Kirkwood, *The Regiments of Scotland: Their Histories, Badges, Tartans, etc.* (Edinburgh: Moray Press, 1949), 137, 140–142.
34. SMC, *Report for 1938*, 44, and *Report for 1939*, 77.
35. 'Shanghai Scottish Silver Jubilee: History of Kilted Unit of S.V.C. Shows Record of Unstinted Service', *NCH*, 24 January 1940, 130.
36. 'Britons Observe King's Birthday', *China Press*, 4 June 1931, 1.
37. Ibid.
38. Wei Fong, 'At the King's Birthday Parade', *NCH*, 7 June 1933, 374.
39. 'Britishers Celebrate King's 68th Birthday', *China Press*, 4 June 1933, 9.
40. Robert Bickers, 'Incubator City: Shanghai and the Crises of Empires', *Journal of Urban History*, 38, 5 (2012), 869–870.
41. Bryna Goodman, 'Improvisations on a Semicolonial Theme, or, How to Read a Celebration of Transnational Urban Community', *Journal of Asian Studies*, 59, 4 (2000), 889–926.
42. Jackson, 'The Raj on Nanjing Road', 1691–1692.
43. SMA, U1-1-89: SMC Watch Committee minutes, 13 November 1913.
44. SMA, U1-1-89: SMC Watch Committee minutes, 18 November 1932; U1-1-89: SMC Watch Committee minutes, 17 July 1933.
45. Devine, 'Soldiers of Empire', 93–94.
46. Streets, *Martial Races*, 6.
47. 'Deaths', *NCH*, 19 April 1932, 119; 'Stewart Inquest Not Yet Finished', *China Press*, 16 April 1932, 3; 'The Late Mr A.E. Stewart', *NCH*, 26 April 1932, 143.
48. Robert Bickers, 'Shanghailanders: The Formation and Identity of the British Settler Community in Shanghai 1843–1937', *Past & Present*, 159 (1998), 161–211.
49. 'Sutherlander', 'Shanghai's Volunteers: Shanghai Scottish: "Chunghwa Jocks"', *NCH*, 6 September 1933, 396.
50. 'The Shanghai Scottish Gala Dinner', *NCH*, 20 November 1935, 315.
51. SMC, *Report for 1923*, 6.
52. Bueltmann, *Clubbing Together*.
53. 'Death of Mr A.S. Campbell', *NCH*, 5 February 1927, 195; 'Funeral of Major Alister Campbell', *NCH*, 12 February 1927, 242.
54. 'Sutherlander', 'Shanghai's Volunteers', 396.

55. 'Sutherlander', 'Tall Tales from a Tin Hat', *NCH*, 16 February 1932, 256.

56. 'Sutherlander', 'Shanghai's Volunteers', 396.

57. 'Interned Soldiers in Shanghai', *NCH*, 17 January 1925, 82.

58. 'Death Takes Toll of Two in Crowded Refugee Camp', *China Press*, 16 January 1925, 1.

59. On the May Thirtieth Incident and subsequent anti-imperialist movement, see Robert Bickers, *Empire Made Me: An Englishman Adrift in Shanghai* (London: Allen Lane, 2003), 163–201.

60. 'Volunteer Commandant, In Report, Says Corps Have Played The Game', *China Press*, 4 April 1926, 1.

61. O.M. Green, 'China in 1925: A Retrospect', *North China Trade Review*, a supplement to the *NCH*, 20 March 1926, 4.

62. 'Americans Are Asked to Join Volunteer Corps', *China Press*, 23 January 1927, 1.

63. 'S.V.C. Route March Cancelled: Simple Inspection Held Instead', *NCH*, 5 February 1927, 192.

64. Nicholas R. Clifford, *Spoilt Children of Empire: Westerners in Shanghai and the Chinese Revolution of the 1920s* (Hanover, NH: Middlebury College Press, 1991), 195.

65. The National Archives, FO 371/13206: 'Memorandum of the Commander-in-Chief, China Station, of the Defence of the International Settlements at Shanghai in the Absence of Regular Troops' and accompanying correspondence.

66. 'The Strike in Shanghai', *NCH*, 26 February 1927, 317.

67. Isabella Jackson, 'Expansion and Defence in the International Settlement at Shanghai', in Robert Bickers and Jonathan J. Howlett (eds), *Britain and China, 1840–1970* (London: Routledge, 2015), 199.

68. I.I. Kounin (compiler), *85 Years of the Shanghai Volunteer Corps* (Shanghai: Cosmopolitan Press, 1938), 214. Kounin copied his material from the *NCH*.

69. 'Sutherlander', 'The Predatory Race: Cathay Hotel is Held to Ransom', *NCH*, 9 February 1932, 215.

70. 'Torry Wilson's Men Forget War to Play Football', *China Press*, 21 February 1932, B1–4.

71. 'Sutherlander', 'Tall Tales from a Tin Hat', 256.

72. Zhang Qian (ed.), *The Minutes of Shanghai Municipal Council* (Shanghai: Shanghai guji chubanshe, 2002), 25, 5 February 1932, 163.
73. 'Shanghai Scottish Silver Jubilee: History of Kilted Unit of SVC Shows Record of Unstinted Service', *NCH*, 24 January 1940, 130.
74. SMC, *Report for 1937*, 47.
75. 'S.V.C. Takes Over Sector', *NCH*, 28 August 1940, 324.
76. Robert Bickers, 'Incubator City: Shanghai and the Crises of Empires', *Journal of Urban History*, 38, 5 (2012), 862–863.
77. John Darwin, 'Afterword: A Colonial World', in Bickers and Henriot (eds), *New Frontiers*, 257.

CHAPTER 12

Ethnic Associationalism and Networking among the Scots in Asia: A Longitudinal Comparison, c.1870 to the Present

Tanja Bueltmann

I was recruited from the UK, bumped into a friend of my uncles who happened to be our CEO … it was during the recession, so there wasn't a huge amount of jobs when I graduated. Erm, yeah, had a conversation in the bar … and he, sort of, came up and said, 'You should think about Asia, essentially, because the recession hasn't hit really anywhere near as bad, things are still pretty good' … in the other jobs I went for … apart from one or two that I think I identified and sorted out, they were all through family, friends, networks and extended groups.[1]

Networks have long played a critical role in the lives of migrants—the quote above by a Scottish expatriate in Shanghai making a case in point about their potential utility in establishing a career abroad. As historians

The research underpinning this article was funded by the Economic and Social Research Council, Future Research Leaders Grant, ES/K008161/1, 'European, Ethnic and Expatriate: A Longitudinal Comparison of German and British Social Networking and Associational Formations in Modern-day Asia'.

T. Bueltmann (✉)
Northumbria University, Newcastle, England

259
T.M. Devine, A. McCarthy (eds.), *The Scottish Experience in Asia, c.1700 to the Present*, DOI 10.1007/978-3-319-43074-4_12

and sociologists have shown, networks are tools that migrants readily employ for a number of reasons, such as: the desire to counteract a sense of dislocation post-migration; safety nets during times of crisis; and the provision or facilitation of patronage and opportunities, including, as we have seen, for work.[2] Historically, networks were more locally confined given the practical limitations of communication and travel: the development of the Internet generally, and social media and online network platforms specifically, have added a broad range of new means for making connections that extend far beyond the immediate contact circle. Portals for professionals such as LinkedIn (over 300 million users) provide entirely new ways to connect, while services specifically designed for expats continue to thrive.[3] Within this context of change it is the purpose of this chapter to examine the role of networks among Scots in Asia over time and in comparative context, focusing in particular on the role of ethnic associations in facilitating and sustaining such networks.

Asia, as other chapters have already demonstrated, has long since been characterised by a high level of transience in Western migrant communities. This is one reason why ethnic associations have always played an important role in the Far East: they facilitated a network-rich environment by providing an organisational platform that could anchor connections as well as opportunities, with the shared denominator—ethnic origin—in place by default. From the earliest examples of members of Jardine, Matheson & Co drawing on Scottish networks and associational structures to enhance business[4] to the still thriving Scottish groups in many Asian centres today, Scottish clubs and societies have long since been an important component of expat life. Historically, it was along the China coast that Scottish ethnic associations became an integral part of what Robert Bickers has called the 'web of China coast communities'.[5] To untangle that web, and examine the associations' role for networking, this chapter explores the development of Scottish ethnic societies, their activities and membership. Examples from other ethnic groups— English and Germans—are considered to establish more fully to what extent developments in the Scottish community were distinctive. The English offer the most pertinent comparator: as a fellow British Isles group, they had a similar cultural background, as well as migratory trajectories in Asia, while including Germans permits exploration of the role of language and external factors, especially the First and Second World Wars, in shaping associational life.

The Development of Scottish Ethnic Associations in Asia

Tracing the early development of Scottish ethnic associations in Asia is complicated by the absence of discrete manuscript evidence. Newspaper accounts do, however, provide key pointers. Reports suggest that in Asia, as in many other sites where Scots settled, celebrations for St Andrew's Day preceded the official formalisation of ethnic societies. In tune with patterns of migration and contact with the Far East, the earliest references come from India, where dinners were a common affair and widely reported by the mid-nineteenth century.[6] They became prominent quickly, developing, as Elizabeth Buettner rightly concludes in relation to St Andrew's Day events at the end of the nineteenth century, 'social and political dimensions that went far beyond the celebration of a romanticised vision of Scotland'.[7] From India such annual festivities made their way further east in the cultural baggage of Scots as the British imperial sphere of influence extended. In Singapore the earliest evidence can be found for St Andrew's Day dinners from the mid to late 1830s. In 1837 the dinner brought together 'the Scottish gentlemen of the Settlement', being formally organised and with proceedings led by a chairman; this role fell to Dr William Montgomerie, government surgeon in Singapore, who was supported by a croupier and stewards.[8] It was also at this point that the first evidence can be found for Canton, where William Jardine of Jardine, Matheson & Co hosted St Andrew's Day dinners as early as 1835.[9] What makes both the Singapore and Canton dinners particularly interesting is that they document that these were not exclusively Scottish affairs: while organised by Scots, they were open to others. This is indicative of the events' wider role as networking and engagement platforms for purposes that had little to do with maintaining a sense of Scottishness. Jardine's dinner, for example, counted prominent hong merchant Hingtae among the guests. He was a hong merchant chiefly involved in trading with foreigners, his presence therefore emphasising that he was viewed as an important connection, and one worth nourishing a link with at the social level too.[10] This nourishment of connections through more informal channels of sociability was, for many migrants, a key means to generate social capital,[11] with ethnic associations serving well as a vehicle for it.

Out of these early roots of St Andrew's Day dinners, more formalised ethnic organisations developed in many sites. Designed to promote the maintenance of Scottish traditions, they also gave an organisational home to the kind of sociability that we have seen above. These ethnic clubs and societies of the Scots were part of a plethora of associations that were formed in Asia from the late eighteenth century onwards, including sporting, recreational and social clubs. Some of the new associations were a direct response to local needs, such as the Simla Winter Amusement Club, which was established for those British expats who decided not to return to Delhi after the summer break in Simla, while others were set up as part of existing transnational associational networks, including the Freemasons and Rotary.[12]

The earliest traceable Scottish ethnic association, and the one this chapter will utilise as a principal case study, was the St Andrew's Society of Shanghai established in 1865.[13] The Society appears to have done well as, by the end of the first decade of the twentieth century, it reportedly had nearly 800 members.[14] While details on the full membership are not available, evidence suggests that the majority were Scots, but that the Society was not exclusively Scottish.[15] Its success in attracting a strong membership base is particularly noticeable because the Society was plagued by internal turmoil, contributing to a period of inactivity, for a short time in the 1880s. The comparatively high level of transience among members, which was a direct result of the association's location in Asia, was, at a minimum, a contributing factor for this. Any association could struggle for lead figures, but that possibility is compounded by high transience in the community—a factor that affects Scottish ethnic associations in Asia to this day. As one current expat interviewee explained, the ideal scenario is that association leaders move up the ranks, 'a year on the Committee, a year as Vice, a year as Chief, minimum, ideally two years on the Committee, that's four years. Keep in mind that a lot of people come here on two-year contracts, so even if they wanted to commit, they couldn't necessarily commit'.[16] Asia was never a principal settlement destination: for the vast majority of nineteenth and early twentieth-century migrants, as for the 'nabobs' of the eighteenth century, Asia was intended to be a sojourn. Whether for want of acquiring wealth or as a work posting, the number of those who remain in Asia permanently is small. While, on the one hand, that very fact made ethnic associations all the more important as an anchor in this high-flux society, it could still mean that ethnic associations in Asia were sometimes less stable than those elsewhere: with the frequent departure of lead members, organisations could, at least temporarily, lose their footing.

It is also such factors that explain why the Singapore St Andrew's Society was not formalised until the early twentieth century. While celebrations of St Andrew's Day had taken place since the 1830s, the establishment of an organised society was only mooted at a meeting in 1908.[17] The evening's chair, Sir Arthur Henderson Young, noted that 'there was no regular body of Scotsmen in Singapore to take the lead in arranging St Andrew's Day celebrations or other events', a result in part of the high turnover of members in the community. Surely, therefore, Singapore should follow the 'example of Hong Kong, Calcutta and other places in the East' which already had St Andrew's Societies.[18] There clearly was transnational awareness: Scots in Singapore and throughout Asia knew of the existence of ethnic associations elsewhere, exchanged rules when forming groups and dispensed greetings after their formation. This transnational awareness was one factor that strengthened networks, especially for members who moved between locations.

In Shanghai the knowledge of activities in Hong Kong contributed to changes when the Society was reconstituted in 1886: it used the Hong Kong St Andrew's Society's rules as a framework in the hope of establishing as successful a base—while it had only been formed in 1881,[19] it was thriving. Another motivation may have been that Hong Kong Scots were, certainly going by reports also published in Shanghai, more united in their associational endeavours. While it is difficult to establish for certain the exact reasons behind the hiatus in Shanghai, evidence relating to some of the activities of Scots that continued during that period reveals frictions in the Scottish community, particularly questions over the ownership, as it were, of the association, with claims and counterclaims as to the membership and role of the St Andrew's Society being made.[20] The mode of admitting members, and who actually made up Shanghai's St Andrew's Society, was certainly a point of discussion within the context of the Society's reconstitution.[21] In any case knowledge and use of the Hong Kong Society's rules as a framework for reconstitution provides evidence of a network in itself: the transplanting of ideas between colonies was not unusual; from merchants and colonial administrators to sports and architectural styles,[22] many forms of capital and ideas were transferred throughout the British Empire, and the sharing of association rules happened often as part of such exchange processes. What it meant practically in Shanghai was that the St Andrew's Society was now concentrating its activities on a mixture of social and philanthropic pursuits, giving particular importance to the hosting of an annual St Andrew's Ball.[23]

We will explore the background of members in more detail below. Suffice it to note that, as was the case in North America where philanthropy was the foundation of Scottish ethnic associations, it was the high socio-economic status of St Andrew's Society members that provides the key to understanding the inclusion of charity in the rules. With members generally coming from an upper or middle class background, the belief that patrician benevolence was their duty was critical in shaping ethnic associationalism: there was a clear sense of responsibility towards those who had 'fallen on evil days'.[24] Based on available annual reports from St Andrew's societies throughout Asia, provisions were most substantial in Shanghai (see Table 12.1), consisting of different types of relief that ranged from covering expenses for onward journeys to cash disbursements.[25]

The First World War had a notable impact. As the entry for 1915 highlights, the War directly changed the nature of charitable endeavours, donations now being directed towards groups in Scotland. This was a common occurrence around the world, uniting ethnic and other associations in their efforts to contribute to the war effort from afar. At times these initiatives were triggered by appeals from home, as was the case in Shanghai in 1917, when the St Andrew's Society was sent an appeal by the Soldiers' and Sailors' Help Society of Edinburgh; the Shanghai Society collected £500 in response.[26] In Hong Kong special fundraising activities were developed, often drawing on Scottish traditions to generate inter-

Table 12.1   Examples of relief provided by the Shanghai St Andrew's Society

Year	Money spent	Use
1890	Tls. 226	Provision of relief for one 'distressed Scotchman', including expenses at Shanghai, passage to Vancouver, and a cash advance
1895	Tls. 17.11	For fares to other destinations, e.g. to Hong Kong
1901 (no report for 1900)	Tls. 432.76	'Cash, disbursed in relief'
1905	Tls. 185	Put into 'Charity Reserve Account'
1910	Illegible, but clearly a designated sum	N/A
1915	N/A	Funds collected for the Scottish Red Cross
1920	$590	N/A
1925	$6,277.46	Help provided for 30 cases

Source: established from newspaper reports of annual meetings and Society reports in *North China Herald* (Shanghai), 24 October 1890, 25 October 1895, 23 October 1901, 13 October 1905, 14 October 1910, 19 October 1915, 30 October 1920

est, but with the distinct civic purpose of generating funds for war relief projects. Hence, in 1916, the Society launched Heather Day to collect donations, also issuing calls for the purchase of war bonds.[27] The funds sent back home to Scotland were gratefully received: acknowledgements were sent directly from the front and from Regimental societies. For the recipients of financial aid in Callander, the creation of the Scottish Soldiers Comfort Fund was 'a striking testimony to the close bond of fellowship which unites Scotsmen all the world over.[28]

Despite these laudable support initiatives—which document a very practical form of diasporic consciousness and supply further evidence of the degree to which ethnic associations served to connect Scots across the globe and not just locally—it is clear from the figures presented that the aid dispensed by Scots in Asia pales compared to provisions made elsewhere, particularly in North America.[29] It was by the Shanghai St Andrew's Society's own admission that 'the claims on the Charity of the Society' were often small.[30] Critically, some of the disbursements made were paid back by those 'in distress who had accepted money as a temporary loan'.[31] What this confirms is that the majority of the Asian Scots supported were not generally in distress: they were more likely to be facing a temporary problem with their funds or business, from which a loan from the St Andrew's Society offered them respite. Consequently, ethnic associations gave them a practical means to re-establish themselves during a period of hardship, enabling them to better their situation themselves. While certainly charitable—there were no fees or interest charges—this was a very different type of benevolence than the large-scale provision of aid to poor immigrants in distress that Scots made in North America.

The differences in the types of charity dispensed reflects the circumstances of Scottish migration to Asia, particularly the migrants' socioeconomic background, but also the timing of their arrival. While there were a number of working-class migrants, by and large those Scots who went to the Far East were in the military, were businessmen, merchants, diplomats or bankers. In short, they came from a privileged socio-economic background, and their number was always comparatively small. In terms of the latter, it is difficult to establish precisely how many Scots there were as available records do not tend to distinguish national origins or are, for the present day, largely absent as there is no requirement to register. Figures for Hong Kong and Shanghai by Bickers do, however, provide a yardstick for the early period. The number of British residents in Hong Kong rose from 785 in 1881 to 3,761 in 1911, while there were 1,057 British residents in Shanghai in 1880, and 4,465 by 1910; Scots will obviously only have made up a fraction of them.[32] As a result of these small numbers and the prevalent background of arrivals, they did not require the types of philanthropy that we can find in the large settlement centres of North America. The charity provided there was designed to relieve immediate distress, consisting of cash disbursements, meal tickets or advice relating to employment; some societies set up homes for old people and even offered free burial plots. Such provisions in the USA and Canada were a direct response to non-existent or minimal state-run poor relief support: its absence increased the need for alternative mechanisms to help those in need, with ethnic clubs and societies frequently filling the void. What the divergent developments in Asia and North America underscore is that ethnic associations always develop in response to local circumstances. While the same traditions underpin activities, and societies may have shared the same name, local needs determined what exactly groups were offering and how they operated. As a result, in Shanghai and other Asian centres, the principal focus was on sociability rather than charity—and this, as the earliest examples have already indicated, was a sociability designed primarily to foster social capital and patronage systems.

St Andrew's Balls in Asia

[F]or the ball given by the St. Andrew's Society on Friday ... something like fifteen hundred people were invited. Not only was the resident community of Shanghai well represented, for, as we have often said before, the hospitality of the Scots among us is absolutely unbounded, but there were the officers of the garrison and of the warships in harbour, whose uniforms brightened what the decorations and the frocks of the ladies made already a most brilliant scene ... [T]he walls were hung with garlands and feathery bamboos, and the shields of the clans; while the Saint himself, illuminated, smiled benignantly on the revels.[33]

This vivid account of the 1901 St Andrew's Day Ball in Shanghai immediately highlights that the balls were by no means exclusively Scottish: they were the 'leading event of the social calendar',[34] often the nexus of social life. Given Shanghai's status as an International Settlement, balls, which also included the English St George's Society's Ball, the Russian Ball and Washington's Birthday Ball in the US community, annually projected 'Anglo-American authority of the civil body of the International Settlement'.[35] In that sense Bickers is right to point out that balls offered a 'forum for integration'[36] as opposed to putting in place boundaries between communities.

The Scottish community balls, in both form and scale, were notable departures from the celebratory dinners that shaped earlier activities. While dinners were, as newspaper accounts document, enjoyed by many members and friends, they were confined in their reach. It was partly as a result of the desire to widen that reach that Shanghai Scots decided to switch to hosting St Andrew's balls in 1878, a change that was well-received.[37] The first balls held thereafter drew crowds of 300, and once the Shanghai St Andrew's Society was reconstituted in 1886 we find a steady increase in the number attending so that, by the early twentieth century, it reached around 1,500 guests.[38]

While Scottish balls were part of a wider social scene, they were often the largest: St Andrew's Day balls in Shanghai, Hong Kong and Singapore, for instance, could easily attract a combined total of 3,000–4,000 guests in the early twentieth century. They were elaborate and well-planned affairs, looked after by committees with responsibilities that ranged from dancing and music to decorations. The chosen venue's decoration was especially important, serving to effectively transmit memory and invoke a sense of homeland heritage.[39] At the 1910 Scottish ball in Singapore, for instance, 'some never-to-be-sufficiently thanked person had inserted a few little blocks of peat that brought a whiff of Caithness bogland or Hebridean marsh'.[40] This sensory experience, apart from invoking memories, was a unifying force, an encounter which, for expatriates, could 'indicate sameness and belonging'.[41] Balls were combined with a dinner, which was usually arranged in multiple sittings to accommodate all guests. Smoking rooms gave male guests a more intimate setting for informal conversations—some of which undoubtedly also concerned wider networking and business discussions.[42] The First World War put a temporary halt to celebrations, with societies abandoning balls altogether, or replacing them with the types of fund-raising activities we have already explored above. In Shanghai as elsewhere, balls were, however, soon re-instituted after the War, and continued to flourish, attracting up to 2,000 guests in the 1920s.[43]

Balls of different national groups were arranged in such a way that—in combination—they made up a proper ball season: this reflects the balls' civic role, even if their roots were, in most cases, ethnic. In Shanghai the ball season began, each year, with the St Andrew's Society's Ball. All

balls served a broad range of wider purposes that ranged from allowing businessmen to informally discuss collaborations and projects to
offering opportunities for socialisation between the sexes.[44] Balls were
successful platforms for this because they brought together the elite
of the migrant community at regular intervals—the Scots were, therefore, not exceptional in using their St Andrew's Ball in this way, but
they were usually the first and among the most adept in pursuing this
route, certainly in terms of attendance numbers and longevity of events.
The civic reach was, however, always restricted as the local population
usually only featured in the margins. While Chinese merchants or local
officials could be spotted attending, the balls were, by and large, meant
to bring together resident Westerners, thereby consolidating colonial
hierarchies.

ACTIVE ASSOCIATIONALISTS AND NETWORKS

We have already broadly established that those who joined Scottish clubs
and societies came from a generally well-to-do background, a key point
also raised by Buettner in her exploration of St Andrew's celebrations in
India.[45] A closer examination of those we may suitably describe as active
associationalists is, however, important to fully understand the extent of
ethnic networking. Overall, the profiling of members is not a straight-
forward undertaking. In part this is the result of the absence of manuscript records, but, again, the relative transience of the Scots in Asia plays
a critical role too. By utilising newspaper reports of association events
and annual gatherings, as well as early Shanghai directories, it has been
possible to put together a membership database that lists the names of
133 members of the Shanghai St Andrew's Society, covering the period
between 1890 and 1905—a period chosen primarily because it offers the
strongest source base. Biographical details could be established for 93 per
cent of the Shanghai members. The vast majority (over 90 per cent) were
Scottish, with all but one, who was born in England, born in Scotland—a
fact again reflecting Asia's nature as a sojourner rather than settler society; among the other members recorded were a few Englishmen and one
German, thus confirming that ethnicity was not exclusionary. The high
match rate for establishing biographical details tells a story in itself as it
reflects the Shanghai members' relatively high status in society: for many
it was a status elevated enough to ensure that records about their life and

activities are more likely to exist, and have survived. On the basis of the details extracted, the members' socio-economic profile can be measured by an analysis of occupations (see Fig. 12.1); classifications have been used in line with the most common profile headings adopted in contemporary directories.

What united many of the Scots captured in the database was not only their membership of the St Andrew's Society but also that they were joiners: nearly everyone was a member of at least one other club or society, with recreational and sports clubs such as the Shanghai Yacht Club and the Shanghai Rowing Club being prominent. Critically, this also included the Shanghai Club which, as a contemporary directory noted, was the 'centre of the business and social life of the Settlement'.[46] Founded in 1861 as an all-male and white-only club for British/European residents in the city, membership included reciprocal belonging to similar clubs in Hong Kong, Singapore, Bengal, Yokohama and Kobe. These clubs were openly elitist and exclusive, vetting members and implementing strict membership rules to ensure that exclusivity remained—though it was not necessarily impenetrable in terms of 'race'.[47] Nevertheless, being part of one (or several) of these clubs was certainly essential for white society: they provided entry to a circle that was akin to a colonial aristocracy,

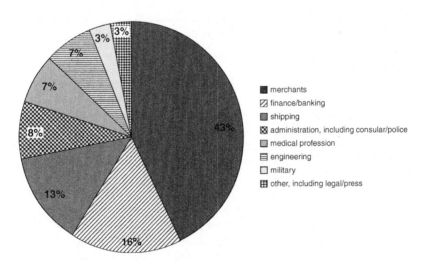

Fig. 12.1 Socio-economic profile, Shanghai St Andrew's Society members, based on data from 1890–1905 (*Source*: the author)

and that brought with it many privileges and benefits, aiding the social capital generation many migrants were so keen on. Moreover, it was a club that facilitated 'transnational imperial linkages'[48] given the extent to which colonial clubs were connected, and membership overlapped. More importantly for this study, there certainly was significant overlap with the St Andrew's Society membership—one factor that explains why interstices between the Shanghai Club and Scottish associational activities were significant, to the degree, in fact, that early celebrations of St Andrew's Day were held 'at the Club'.[49]

The fact that members of the St Andrew's Society were active in other associations should not be seen as evidence of the ethnic association's lesser role. Rather, it confirms the importance of layered networking: to maximise opportunities and generate social capital, networks best rest on a broad range of associational activities. Those channelled through ethnic associations were critical for many, and, as the membership database for the Shanghai St Andrew's Society reveals, often the initial locus through which connections were formed. This point is strongly borne out by a network case study of connections relating to the Shanghai Ice, Cold Storage and Refrigeration Co Ltd. Not only does the Company itself connect at least six St Andrew's Society members in business but there is also evidence that initial contact among them was through the Society, with ties later cemented in other associations.[50] As noted at the beginning, the simple fact that shared origin was a common denominator that did not have to be established, but was in place by default, could give ethnic associations the edge. They were a principle anchor in a very transitory world. It was a world characterised by comparatively short-term stays in specific locations, often with no family members around. This was not a world for planting roots. Membership in ethnic associations could compensate for that absence of 'rootedness', offering stability and familiarity regardless of location. In general terms this is a characteristic common to Scottish ethnic associations around the world, but the specific setting of Asia as a sojourner society amplified the power of ethnic associationalism and networks in this respect. We can see this documented in the Shanghai St Andrew's Society membership: at least 23 per cent took out membership of more than one Scottish society simultaneously, making the associations pan-Asian link hubs. For many Scots such transnational associational links were underpinned by personal connections, reaffirming networks.[51]

A COMPARATIVE VIEW ACROSS ETHNIC GROUPS

While the examples explored so far demonstrate the sustained value Scots saw in ethnic association and its role in the wider matrix of associational life and networking in Asia, it is important to recognise that the Scots were not exceptional in their associational behaviour. Globally as well as in Asia specifically, they were, certainly from among British and Irish groups, often the first, usually the most prolific, but by no means the only migrant group drawing on their ethnicity to formally organise in societies. When considering the activities of migrants from across the British Isles, the most immediate comparator group, the English, offer important insight into the variations and similarities of ethnic association. While established scholarship tends to view the English, certainly in the North American context, as 'invisible migrants' lacking strong ethnic expression,[52] new research has successfully questioned that view and enhanced our understanding of the ways in which the English too made use of essentially the same responses and strategies as other ethnic groups.[53] At times they were motivated by a sense of ethnic competition. In Singapore an 1836 communication sent to the editor of the *Singapore Chronicle* certainly lays bare the sense of rivalry. Sent only a few months after the Scots' first celebration of their patron saint, the letter-writer asked upon what day St George's Day would fall that year for, according to the correspondent, 'our countrymen from the South of the Tweed will not be "backward in coming forward" to treat the Sons of Caledonia to the roast beef and plumb [sic] pudding of old England on that occasion'.[54] Still the competitive spark was not quite enough for the letter does not appear to have incited a public celebration of St George's Day. It took until the 1880s for the English in Singapore to celebrate their ethnicity in a formalised and public manner.

The later consolidation of English activities in Singapore was mirrored elsewhere in Asia, where English clubs and societies proliferated from the late nineteenth century in particular. The significant increase of activity at that point was a direct result of developments at home in England, and marks a critical point of difference between the ethnic associationalism of the English and the Scots. It was then, in 1894, that the Royal Society of St George was founded specifically to 'strengthen and encourage the instinctive patriotism of the English people, and to develop the race consciousness of all of English birth or origin throughout the world'.[55] This objective was critical in promoting the establishment of new St George's societies, also providing the necessary stimulus in Singapore and other Asian centres.[56] Scottish ethnic associations never had that kind of 'homeland head' organisation, while for the English the Royal Society of St George became the heart of a functioning, communicating, global movement of over 40 imperial centres.

In the German community the motivation for forming ethnic associations was always, at least in part, the result of a very immediate practical consideration: the simple fact of speaking a different language made clubbing together with fellow kin particularly appealing. Prior to German unification in 1871 language was an even more important identifier for German-speaking peoples as national categories did not work well to achieve coherence. In Asia, as elsewhere, the German associational scene was characterised by diversity, there being a number of associational formations that became prominently associated with the Germans: there were traditional ethnic associations—usually called German Club (Deutscher Club), though names like Club Germania or Concordia were common—but also a very prolific associational branch of musical/singing clubs.

In Hong Kong a German Club was initially established in 1859 and, after expanding significantly, eventually occupied a beautiful club building near the Peak that offered amenities such as a library and a billiard room. This Club was intended only for elite members, however, with Germans in Hong Kong distinguishing along class lines by opening the Captain's Club for lower-class residents.[57] In Shanghai the German Club Concordia held its inaugural meeting in January 1866, with 70 members present.[58] The evening was an enjoyable affair, displaying too the amicable relations between Germans and other ethnic groups—to the point that an Englishman was among those delivering a toast in praise of the Club's inauguration, stating that 'Germans and Englishmen are led to regard one another as more closely related than are the nationals of any other two countries'.[59] These sentiments continued at the annual celebrations of the Kaiser's birthday, which became common from the late nineteenth century. In 1902, 'the day passed in patriotic observances and in jollies', the German flag being visible all over Shanghai. There was a religious service in the morning, with a reception and parade held later in the day in which 'officers of other nationalities' took part; similarly, the representatives of numerous foreign missions were present.[60]

Despite the history of such joint celebrations, Germans in Asia faced their greatest challenge—in terms of their community status—during the two World Wars. The Scots and English, like many others in Asia and elsewhere, soon began echoing the prejudices of their kinsmen at home.

During the First World War, where once Germans and nationals from other countries would join hands at celebratory dinners, there was animosity. All over the world, Germans faced prejudice and backlash.[61] In the summer of 1917 both the German Club and the *Deutsche Zeitung für China* (German newspaper) were closed by the Shanghai Municipal Police—at the Club German members present 'finished their drinks, transacted whatever business they desired' and then left Club for it to be closed.[62] Suggestions were made by some locals to turn the Club over to the Shanghai Volunteers Corps, or, as someone using the alias 'Anti-Hun' recommended, to turn it into a club for the Allies.[63] Germans were deported from China in 1919, which put a complete stop to activities. Once they were allowed to return, community ties had to be rebuilt and it took a good while for attitudes to normalise,[64] only for the Second World War to disrupt that normalisation process completely. What this highlights is that while wartime united British Isles migrants to their home nations, it also united them in shared opposition against the German 'other'. Neither Scots nor English ever had to address being outcast from the wider expat community; there was never a need to respond to the external ascription of identifiers that were entirely negative. Within the context of associational life and wider expat networking this often meant that Germans were less integrated than other groups, certainly after the First World War.

THE CONTINUED IMPORTANCE OF ETHNIC ASSOCIATIONS AND NETWORKING AMONG TWENTY-FIRST CENTURY SCOTTISH EXPATS

Scottish ethnic associations and networks—as with those of English and German migrants—have been enduring in Asia, and continue to play a vital role for expats to this day. Many of the earliest Scottish societies in Asia still exist, and as the example quoted at the beginning of this chapter has already highlighted, the dispensation of patronage and use of networks for employment opportunities certainly remains a notable aspect. But there have been significant changes, too, initiated in particular by modern technology. While transnational communication networks have played a critical role in facilitating an imagined community of Scots—for instance through the printing of telegram greetings on St Andrew's Day—new social media and networking services have made that community significantly more real than imagined by connecting expats broadly, and members of particular associations more specifically, in new and instantaneous ways.[65] It is also thanks to these new technologies that the transition to life in Asia can be much easier now than ever before: many questions a migrant may have can now easily be answered prior to departure—ranging from practical concerns of house hunting to questions about where one might find Marmite, expat forums abound and offer answers to exactly such questions.

Still, ethnic networks and associations have not become superfluous, with high transience continuing to provide a critical reason for their continued relevance in twenty-first century expat life in Asia. As one interview respondent explained, life in Shanghai is 'more transient' and 'you don't have the same depth of connection with the country or the people or family, whatever it might be', so people are very social and look to connect in other ways. The high level of mobility also means that:

> you can have a good mate but then a year later they'll be gone. And so the, sort of, social dynamics of groups are constantly changing. Erm, whereas you go back to the UK and, you know, your group of friends … I'm thinking of my home village, I walk in there at Christmas time and it's the same guys on the same stools drinking the same drinks. Nothing really changes … Whereas year to year, the, the social group dynamics, erm, of the foreign crowd in Shanghai changes significantly.[66]

Ethnic societies remain critical in this environment because they continue to provide a home, a constant, in a fast-changing world. And so fast-changing is that world that it can appropriately be referred to as an environment of hyper-mobility, with the term 'flexpatriate' now often applied to those who travel around the world in search of opportunities.[67] As one expat currently living in Beijing explained, people 'flit around'.[68] Sometimes, this may be the result of very practical concerns about immigration rules and residency permits: 'You just don't know what's going to happen with immigration. The rules change every five minutes'.[69] All the while the environment remains alien, with language being a critical factor, particularly in China, where it is especially difficult to acquire a working knowledge. As one Scottish woman resident in Shanghai noted, joining an ethnic association was not something she had done in the past despite having lived abroad for a long time.[70] But in China she chose to do so because there were more, and entirely new, challenges.

Expats continue to put up with challenges and uncertainties life in Asia can bring for the same reasons that have long since been a principal motivation for a sojourn in the Far East: the potential—certainly perceived potential—to better one's position: 'their [expats'] whole reason for doing it [spending some time in Asia] is a financial gain … and really they're always looking for their next hit, for their next port of call … So to move up the ladder'.[71] Networks can help with that. At the same time, however, there continues to be a strong sense that relationships promoted through networks and associations are not a one-way enterprise. This is expressed now as in the past, through benevolent activities—now usually directed towards the host community—but also through continued engagement in ethnic associations themselves, which is a critical factor in keeping them going strong. As one Scottish expat in Singapore noted when talking about being actively involved in the St Andrew's Society, 'the Society had done a lot for me and given my girls a sense of identity, erm, and on a personal basis, lots of the St Andrew's Society members gave me their business … so it was really I felt that I had benefited from it so it was my time to give back'.[72] As in the nineteenth and early twentieth centuries, these benefits rest, in large part, on shared cultural roots and norms, and their unifying power. That is why people 'tend to congregate with those that are most culturally similar'. After all, 'we'll get the same jokes, we'll know the same rhetorical references to when you were a kid, or whatever it might be'.[73] As one expat aptly concluded, 'I laugh loudest with Scots'.[74]

The biggest challenge to ethnic associations has come from other organised activities: from Toastmaster meetings to leisure-focused clubs, there is now an even broader range of choices for expats in terms of associations. Given the changing characteristics of the expat—we now find larger numbers of families and also significantly more women—it comes as no surprise that traditional activities offered by ethnic clubs and societies have lost some of their appeal. Now the pull stems not only from potential networking opportunities and sociability, but often primarily from the facilities on offer.[75]

CONCLUSION

This chapter has documented a number of persistent features as well as changes in the nature of ethnic associationalism and networking in the Scottish community in Asia. Historically, from the earliest contact, sites in the Far East where Scots settled—albeit usually only for a comparatively short time—were largely a preserve for what we can aptly call the colonial elite. Many of the businessmen, merchants, also military personnel or those in the finance sector who went to Asia, did so at least in part because they were motivated by a desire to make money during their time in the East that would give them a better life back at home after their return. This has not changed significantly, with a majority of expats still seeing Asia as a springboard for their personal economic advancement. This has always resulted in a lack of commitment to permanent settlement, and meant that life in the Far East, for Scots and other Westerners, lacked many of the structures in place at home or in settler colonies. The void that consequently appeared was often filled by ethnic clubs and societies as shared origins provide a readily usable common denominator for establishing connections. While ethnic associations existed all over the world and among essentially all migrant groups, their role as an anchor for migrants was all the more important in Asia. In a transitory world in which expats are part of a minority, part of a limited white population, ethnic associations provide one of the most potent mechanisms that could provide a sense of rootedness and support. Their potential for social capital generation continues, as we have seen, to provide an additional pull.

Yet while ethnic associations of most groups were important for these reasons, there are key characteristics that distinguish the Scottish case and make it distinctive. Scots were, in Asia and elsewhere, often the first group to commence ethnic activities, also formalising associational structures at an early point. Certainly compared to their English counterparts this was a marked difference in Asia, where the English were much later in setting up formalised societies. This was because the motivation for their ethnic associationalism stemmed, in no small part, from home—it was the Royal Society of St George founded in London that drove developments from the mid-1890s. Scots had no such home connector, continuing to drive their ethnic associationalism in the diaspora. Compared to both the English and the Germans, the Scots were also placing their ethnic associationalism on a broader footing, one that linked their ethnic associations very firmly into civic life. As I have argued elsewhere, in Asia, too, the Scots were very much 'interlocked ethnics'.[76] This becomes especially clear when considering the German case. As a result of language difference and significant external developments (two World Wars), Germans were less able to utilise their ethnic associations to integrate or generate social capital, certainly after the First World War. Even before the outbreak of the war, however, they were a more fractured community, attaching more importance to reflecting class difference in associational life. Over time other factors continued to consolidate the prominent role of ethnic clubs and societies, especially as China was opened up further for Westerners—questions such as those about language barriers, which could make adjustment difficult, were a central concern. Ethnic associations adapted to these unique challenges of the local Asian environments, providing members with a temporary home, and did so transnationally throughout the region as communities were strongly connected. The interconnectedness of Scottish Asian networks is, in fact, especially significant: we have seen evidence of this in the membership of societies, as well as more personal links, that transcended borders or were mobile and moved from one location to another. The principal constant in this mobile environment was, and continues to be, fellow expats, making the expat community, ethnic networks and associations, all the more important in everyday life to this day.

NOTES

1. Interview 150601 with Scottish expat, Shanghai, June 2015.
2. See also Enda Delaney and Donald M. MacRaild (eds), *Irish Migration, Networks and Ethnic Identities since 1750* (Abingdon: Routledge, 2007), and Angela McCarthy (ed.), *A Global Clan: Scottish Migrant Networks and Identities since the Eighteenth Century* (London: Tauris Academic Studies, 2006). For contemporary evidence, see Part II in Frank D. Bean and Stephanie Bell-Rose (eds), *Immigration and Opportunity: Race, Ethnicity, and Employment in the United States* (New York: Russell Sage Foundation, 1999).
3. For example 'How to Find a Job and Network in Shanghai', 14 June 2013 http://www.cityweekend.com.cn/shanghai/article/how-to-find-job-and-network-shanghai (accessed 3 January 2016).
4. See also Geoffrey Jones, *Merchants to Multinationals: British Trading Companies in the Nineteenth and Twentieth Centuries* (Oxford: Oxford University Press, 2000).
5. Robert Bickers, 'Shanghailanders and Others: British Communities in China, 1843–1957', in Robert Bickers (ed.), *Settlers and*

Expatriates: Britons over the Seas (Oxford: Oxford University Press, 2010), 272.

6. See for instance *The Indian News and Chronicle of Eastern Affairs*, 22 January 1850. For later examples: St Andrew's dinner in Bombay in 1866, *The Pioneer* (Allahabad), 17 December 1866; in Calcutta in 1867, *The Pioneer* (Allahabad), 4 December 1867; in Colombo in 1869, *Ceylon Observer* (Colombo), 1 December 1869.

7. Elizabeth Buettner, 'Haggis in the Raj: Private and Public Celebrations of Scottishness in Late Imperial India', *Scottish Historical Review*, 81, 212 (2002), 221. See also Gordon T. Stewart, *Jute and Empire: The Calcutta Jute Wallahs and the Landscapes of Empire* (Manchester: Manchester University Press, 1998), 158.

8. *Singapore Free Press and Mercantile Advertiser*, 7 December 1837. There is no reference to attendance numbers nor to the location of the event, so unfortunately it is impossible to establish exactly the early extent of activities in terms of attendance numbers. However, reports are phrased in a way that suggests that these were smaller gatherings. Evidence from other locations suggests attendances of around 50 at this time.

9. Reported in *Singapore Free Press and Mercantile Advertiser*, 7 January 1836.

10. For details on hong merchants, see Weng Cheong, *Hong Merchants of Canton: Chinese Merchants in Sino-Western Trade, 1684–1798* (London: Curzon Press, 1997).

11. For example, Barbara A. Misztal, *Informality: Social Theory and Contemporary Practice* (London and New York: Routledge, 2000), 89–90. For a historical exploration see also Tanja Bueltmann, *Scottish Ethnicity and the Making of New Zealand Society, 1850–1930* (Edinburgh: Edinburgh University Press, 2011), ch. 4.

12. For details on some of the clubs that developed, their operations and activities, see Benjamin B. Cohen, *In the Club: Associational Life in Colonial South Asia* (Manchester: Manchester University Press, 2015); this is a valuable addition to the literature on associational culture, though it must be noted that Cohen, regrettably, fails to identify ethnic associational clubs as a discrete category in his assessment.

13. For its first Annual Report see *North China Herald* (Shanghai), 16 June 1866.

14. *Straits Times* (Singapore), 29 October 1909.
15. This assessment is based on all available newspaper accounts and directory entries that contain details on members.
16. Interview 150612 with Scottish expat, Singapore, June 2015.
17. *Straits Times*, 28 November 1908.
18. Ibid.
19. See *North China Herald* (Shanghai), 20 December 1881.
20. *North China Herald* (Shanghai), 20 October 1886.
21. Ibid., 27 October 1886.
22. John Mark Carroll, *A Concise History of Hong Kong* (Lanham: Rowman & Littlefield, 2007), 4.
23. *North China Herald* (Shanghai), 27 October 1886.
24. Ibid., 29 October 1902.
25. Reports suggest that other Scottish groups, certainly prior to the First World War, tended to be more restrictive in the charity provided, focusing largely on small donations. However, it is important to remember that there are no manuscript sources for this period, so this cannot be established for certain.
26. Ibid., 19 October 1917.
27. See posters for these initiatives, Imperial War Museum, Art.IWM PST 12273, Art.IWM PST 12270, and Art.IWM PST 12268.
28. *Callander Advertiser*, 8 March 1919.
29. For details on the extensive charity provisions made in North America, see Tanja Bueltmann, *Clubbing Together: Ethnicity, Civility and Formal Sociability in the Scottish Diaspora to 1930* (Liverpool: Liverpool University Press, 2014), ch. 2.
30. *North China Herald* (Shanghai), 2 February 1867.
31. Ibid., 23 October 1901.
32. Bickers, 'Shanghailanders and Others', 282–283, Table 10.2.
33. *North China Herald* (Shanghai), 4 December 1901.
34. Description of the Hong Kong St Andrew's Day Ball, *China Mail* (Hong Kong), 30 November 1901.
35. Andrew David Field, *Shanghai's Dancing World: Cabaret Culture and Urban Politics, 1919–1954* (Hong Kong: Chinese University Press, 2010), 22.
36. Robert Bickers, *Britain in China: Community, Culture and Colonialism 1900–1949* (Manchester: Manchester University Press), 84.
37. *North China Herald* (Shanghai), 5 December 1878.

38. Newspaper reports provide some detail on those in attendance, which confirms the elite nature of the events: local dignitaries, military leaders and the elite of the business world were always present.

39. See, for instance, A. Radley, 'Artefacts, Memory and a Sense of the Past', in D. Middleton and D. Edwards (eds), *Collective Remembering* (London: Sage, 1990), 54.

40. *Straits Times* (Singapore), 1 December 1910.

41. Emily Walmsley, 'Race, Place and Taste: Making Identities through Sensory Experience in Ecuador', *Etnofoor*, 18, 1 (2005), 43.

42. Capturing those within their historical contexts is very difficult, though personal papers can be illuminating. For an exploration of their role in the modern world, see Eelke M. Heemskerk, *Decline of the Corporate Community: Network Dynamics of the Dutch Business Elite* (Amsterdam: Amsterdam University Press, 2007).

43. *North China Herald* (Shanghai), 3 December 1921.

44. See also Cohen, *In the Club*, 54.

45. Buettner, 'Haggis in the Raj'.

46. Arnold Wright (ed.), *Twentieth Century Impressions of Hongkong, Shanghai and other Treaty Ports of China: Their History, People, Commerce, Industries and Resources* (London: Lloyds Greater Britain Publishing Company, 1908), 388.

47. For instance, within the context of India, looking in particular at the differences between private and public spheres, see Partha Chatterjee, *The Black Hole of Empire* (Princeton, NJ: Princeton University Press, 2012), 225–226.

48. Cohen, *In the Club*, 68.

49. For example, *North China Herald* (Shanghai), 6 December 1871.

50. See, for instance, *North China Herald* (Shanghai), 31 July 1899, 2 May 1900, 26 December 1900, as well as directory entries.

51. For instance, the connection between Addis and James Haldane Stewart Lockhart, see Shiona Airlie, *Thistle and Bamboo: The Life and Times of Sir James Stewart Lockhart* (Hong Kong: Hong Kong University Press, 2010), 59.

52. Charlotte Erickson, *Invisible Immigrants: The Adaptation of English and Scottish Immigrants in Nineteenth-Century America* (Coral Gables, FL: University of Miami Press, 1972).

53. See, for instance, Tanja Bueltmann, David Gleeson, and Donald M. MacRaild, 'Invisible Diaspora? English Ethnicity in the United

States before 1920', *Journal of American Ethnic History*, 33, 4 (2014), 5–30.

54. *Singapore Chronicle and Commercial Register*, 9 April 1836.

55. Lesley Robinson, 'Englishness in England and the "Near Diaspora": Organisation, Influence and Expression, 1880s–1970s' (PhD thesis, University of Ulster, 2014), 66.

56. For details see Tanja Bueltmann and Donald M. MacRaild, 'Globalising St George: English Associations in the Anglo-World to the 1930s', *Journal of Global History*, 7, 1 (2012), 79–105.

57. For a broader discussion of Germans in Asia, see also Stefan Manz, *Constructing a German Diaspora: The 'Greater German Empire', 1871–1914* (New York and London: Routledge, 2014).

58. *North China Herald* (Shanghai), 20 January 1866.

59. Ibid. There is ample further evidence of groups gathering together, for instance after the unveiling of the *Iltis* monument in November 1898, see *North China Herald*, 28 November 1898. The monument commemorated the 77 German naval personnel who died when the SMS *Iltis* shipwrecked off the coast of Shandong in 1896; see Heinrich Walle, 'Deutschlands Flottenpräsenz in Ostasien 1897–1914', in Markus A. Denzel et al. (eds), *Jahrbuch für Europäische Überseegeschichte* (Wiesbaden: Harrassowitz Verlag, 2009), 138.

60. *North China Herald*, 29 January 1902.

61. See for example Panikos Panayi, *The Enemy in Our Midst: Germans in Britain during the First World War* (London: Bloomsbury, 1991) or Andrew Francis, *'To be Truly British we Must be Anti-German': New Zealand, Enemy Aliens and the Great War Experience, 1914–1919* (Oxford: Peter Lang, 2012).

62. *North China Herald* (Shanghai), 25 August 1917.

63. Ibid., 25 August 1917.

64. *China Press*, 30 January 1936.

65. For the idea of an imagined community see Benedict Anderson, *Imagined Communities: Reflections on the Origin and Spread of Nationalism* (London: Verso, 1991); for more on the role of communication, see Bueltmann, *Clubbing Together*.

66. This and the previous quotations from interview 150601 with Scottish expat, Shanghai, June 2015.

67. H. Mayerhofer et al., 'Flexpatriate Assignments: A Neglected Issue in Global Staffing', *The International Journal of Human Resource Management*, 15, 8 (2004), 1371–1389.

68. Interview 150516 with Scottish expat, Beijing, May 2015.
69. Interview 150227 with Scottish expat, Kuala Lumpur, February 2015.
70. Interview 150603 with Scottish expat, Shanghai, June 2015.
71. Interview 150516 with Scottish expat, Beijing, May 2015.
72. Interview 150612 with Scottish expat, Singapore, June 2015.
73. This and the previous quotations from interview 150601 with Scottish expat, Shanghai, June 2015.
74. Interview 150612 with Scottish expat, Singapore, June 2015.
75. For examples, see Jonathan V. Beaverstock, 'Servicing British Expatriate "Talent" in Singapore: Exploring Ordinary Transnationalism and the Role of the "Expatriate" Club', *Journal of Ethnic and Migration Studies*, 37, 5 (2011), 709–728.
76. Bueltmann, *Scottish Ethnicity*, 210.

CHAPTER 13

The Right Kind of Migrants: Scottish Expatriates in Hong Kong Since 1950 and the Promotion of Human Capital

Iain Watson

INTRODUCTION

Sitting in the comfort of the American Club on the 49th Floor of Two Exchange Square on Hong Kong Island, overlooking the harbour with a hazy Kowloon skyline in the background, Alan Powrie, a Dundonian and a 40-year resident of Hong Kong, comments that:

> We're sitting in a building that was built by Scottish money, it's part of the Jardine Matheson/Hongkong Land [Group]. … We would not be here if it were not for Scots, and that's essentially the history of Hong Kong.

> The Scots were the most successful opium dealers and that was the financial foundation of Hong Kong. We were better drug smugglers than anyone else.

> Since the 1840s when that was started, Scots have always been prominent. Most of the trading houses here within the old British sphere with one or two exceptions are of Scottish history.[1]

I. Watson (✉)
University of Edinburgh, Edinburgh, Scotland

© The Author(s) 2017
T.M. Devine, A. McCarthy (eds.), *The Scottish Experience in Asia, c.1700 to the Present*, DOI 10.1007/978-3-319-43074-4_13

Powrie's interpretation is far from being an exception among Scots in Hong Kong, who appear to have developed a history of Hong Kong's founding as a British colony and its rise to a regional financial centre and bastion of capitalism as a significantly Scottish project. Typical of the promotion of such a narrative is Welsh sports journalist Huw Richards' article published on the eve of the 2007 International Hong Kong Rugby Sevens tournament:

> Scots made an immense impact across the entire extent and history of the British empire, but rarely more so than in Hong Kong.
>
> They were responsible for the island becoming British. It was taken over in 1841 under the Treaty of Nanking, the conclusion of the war against China which had been fought to safeguard the interests of British opium traders.
>
> The most important of these was Dumfriesshire [sic] native James Matheson – described by modern Scottish historian Thomas Devine as 'a drug dealer on a massive scale' – whose business partner Thomas Jardine [sic], also a Scot, successfully urged the British government into punitive action against the Chinese for seizing and destroying their opium.
>
> The company they created in 1832 was one of the key architects of Hong Kong's commercial success. The Hong Kong and Shanghai Bank was founded by another Scot, Thomas Sutherland.[2]

The piece is inaccurate, as Matheson was a Highlander and it was <u>William</u> Jardine who was from Dumfriesshire. Yet these inaccuracies are emblematic of how history can be distorted. For the Scots in Hong Kong such re-imaginings serve to enhance their social status as well as provide a cultural centre for their self-image in what is, for many, an alien and sometimes surreal world.

This chapter draws on oral history research into Scots sojourning in Hong Kong, which in turn is part of a larger study comparing those sojourners to predominantly settler Scottish migrants to New Zealand since the 1950s. The Hong Kong study and the interpretations of this chapter are derived from a survey completed by 100 sojourners and from 23 in-depth, semi-structured life-story oral history interviews, of which 14 interviewees were in Hong Kong with the balance being returned sojourners.

Thus far, this study has shown that both the Hong Kong and New Zealand cohorts evidence a propensity to preserve and promote Scottish human capital in their respective destinations. In other words, they promote Scots as the right kind of migrants. For those Scots in Hong Kong an historical narrative is central. This chapter seeks to validate this narrative and suggest reasons for its promotion, beginning with brief overviews of the origins of colonial Hong Kong and the Hongkong and Shanghai Banking Corporation, addressing the Scoto-centric narratives highlighted above. Thereafter, the chapter looks at sojourner perceptions of the Scottish impact on Hong Kong before turning to the reality of modern Hong Kong. The chapter concludes by considering how a lack of competing historical narratives may have contributed to the perceptions of Hong Kong's Scots and suggesting that the historical narrative combined with selected Scottish identity markers are used to promote Scottish human capital to a targeted audience.

COLONIAL HONG KONG'S ORIGINS

As suggested by Alan Powrie and Huw Richards, Hong Kong's founding as a British colony is indeed coloured by the involvement of Scots, most notably in the personas of Lord Napier, Captain Charles Elliot and the leading merchants James Matheson and William Jardine. However, despite their involvement this was a British project and ultimately it was Britain that went to war with China, not at the behest of Scottish traders in the South China Seas, but to protect wider British trading interests.

Early nineteenth century China was a difficult market for British merchants to penetrate, not only because of the East India Company's (EIC) monopoly but because of the terms of trade. By the 1830s European demand for Chinese products such as tea, porcelain and silk was high and showed no signs of abating. China was a closed society and officially wanted nothing from the Europeans and Americans other than silver bullion in exchange for their products. However, bullion was scarce with New World production declining and post-Napoleonic governments retaining reserves for potential military needs.

The EIC and the US trading company of Russell and Company (Russells) had sought to mitigate this demand for silver by encouraging demand for opium in China. The EIC, well aware that opium was illegal in China, had refrained from shipping the narcotic into that country directly. Instead, the EIC relied on independent merchants, known as *country traders*, to smuggle the drug into China in exchange for bullion, which could then be used to purchase Chinese goods for export to Europe and the USA. Chief among these country traders were the Scots-owned firm of Jardine, Matheson & Co. (Jardines) founded in 1832 and Dent & Co. (Dents). By 1842, the latter was an English-led partnership, having been established in 1824 after two early iterations, of which one had been Scottish, W.S. Davidson and Company (1813–24).

The EIC's monopoly ended in April 1834, opening the door to independent traders. Opium, however, remained illegal in China until the ratification of the Treaty of Tianjin in 1860. It 'took sixteen years, from 1809 to 1824, for opium shipments to double and reach close to 9,000 chests. From there, the quantities doubled every seven to eight years to reach over 40,000 chests at the start of the [First] Opium War [1839–42]' (see Fig. 13.1).[3]

The British government, recognising the need to protect British interests and fill the vacuum left by the EIC, despatched a mandarin of their own to treat with the Chinese. William Napier, a Scottish peer, the 9th Lord Napier and a friend of the foreign secretary, Lord Palmerston, was appointed to the role of superintendent of trade in Canton in 1833, arriving in the Portuguese enclave of Macau in July 1834. Despite his background, 'to the Chinese, Napier was a trader, however superior; and traders were held in low regard, [while] to Napier, every rebuff … was an insult to the Crown he served'.[4] Journeying with him as master attendant, effectively fifth in rank, was Captain Charles Elliot RN, an Anglo-Scottish diplomat with misgivings about the opium trade,[5] reservations he shared with another Anglo-Scot of the time, William Gladstone.

Napier's tenure was brief and he died in October 1834, just three months after arriving in Macau. Napier, faced with the slights of the Chinese, had first recommended that a British force 'should take possession of the island of Hong Kong'.[6] A little over six years later it was to be Elliot, as chief superintendent, who would make this recommendation a reality. In the interim, Napier's death presented an opportunity for the British merchants led by James Matheson to petition the British government for the 'appointment of a plenipotentiary … supported by a naval expedition'.[7] Napier's successor, Sir John Francis Davis, was opposed to any such intervention and so began a period of antipathy between the traders and the superintendents. Davis, who was to return as Hong Kong's second governor in 1844, was retired to England in 1835 and succeeded

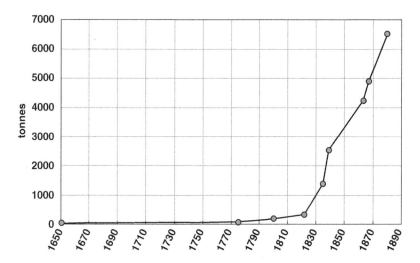

Fig. 13.1   Opium imports into China, 1650–1880 (*Source:* United Nations Office on Drugs and Crime, *A Century of International Drug Control*, https://www.unodc.org/documents/data-and-analysis/Studies/100_Years_of_Drug_Control.pdf (accessed 24 May 2015), 23. [Original data converted into metric tonnes using 1 chest = 140 lbs = 63.5 kg])

by Sir George Robinson, who 'was personally offended by the smuggling that surrounded him'.[8]

Briefly, a significant catalyst for the First Opium War was the Emperor's appointment of Lin Zexu as 'a special commissioner to extirpate the drug trade at Canton'.[9] This was something the incumbent viceroy, Deng Tingzhen, had failed to do as he 'was an active participant in the ... trade'.[10] Lin besieged the factories in Canton, took merchants hostage and destroyed impounded opium, which together with the ongoing slights to British diplomacy prompted military action. Clearly the flouting of Chinese law by Jardines, Dents, Russells and the other merchants was a pretext for war, but the war's prosecution and its outcomes lay largely outside their influence.

Of relevance to this chapter is Hong Kong's annexation, and it would appear that Jardines were not the prime movers with James Matheson describing Hong Kong as Elliot's 'pet child'.[11] Matheson had been a critic of Elliot, writing in 1840 that Elliot had 'adopted the novel course of assisting the [Chinese] Government against his own countrymen'.[12] Overall, the Canton merchants were not impressed by Elliot's acquisition of Hong Kong and their opinion was largely mirrored by that of Palmerston: 'a barren island with hardly a house upon it'.[13] That said, Jardines were quick to move their operations to Hong Kong despite their stated preference for Chusan (off Ningpo)[14] and other traders followed suit.

The clear evidence is that Charles Elliot was responsible for colonial Hong Kong's founding, yet, at the time he was vilified for annexing Hong Kong and was recalled in some opprobrium. His role in Hong Kong's founding has been largely forgotten. This amnesia extends to the physical, which in Hong Kong includes streets and places named after British royalty, governors, colonial secretaries, military officers and businessmen. There are no fewer than four streets and two places named after Jardine and Matheson, yet there is no mention of Elliot in Hong Kong save for in the government map book where:

> there is a small private pathway off Robinson Road ... marked as Elliot Crescent. However, on location there is no street sign or other physical evidence ... In fact, it is possible that Elliot Crescent was named after his cousin Rear Admiral George Elliot, who was the commander of the naval expedition to Canton in 1840.[15]

THE ORIGINS OF HSBC

Founded in 1865 as the Hongkong and Shanghai Banking Corporation (HSBC), much is made of the role of the Scot Thomas Sutherland. Yet the name of the lawyer and co-author of the Bank's prospectus, E.H. Pollard, has, like Elliot's, been largely forgotten. Sutherland was the Hong Kong superintendent of shipping company Peninsular and Oriental Steam Navigation Company (P&O) and the Bank's founding deputy chairman. He held this position for just a little over a year, resigning in April 1866 when P&O moved him to Shanghai. Bizarrely, HSBC's own abbreviated corporate history says of him that he 'never ... held a bank account'.[16] The Bank's founding chairman was not a Scot but an Englishman, Francis Chomley of Dents. Pointedly, Jardines declined to participate, which is attributed to their 'traditional feud with Dent & Co'.[17] Indeed, it was not until 1877, ten years after Dents' demise, that there was any Jardines representation on the Bank's court.

In his December 1909 speech at HSBC's annual dinner in London, Sutherland claimed to have written the 'prospectus with my own hand'.[18]

However, economic historian Frank King questions his account as 'how could the P&O agent, however brilliant, design a successful banking project in so short a time?'[19] That said, Sutherland was the catalyst, as it was intelligence acquired by him that capital for a Royal Bank of China to be established in Hong Kong was being raised in Bombay. This prompted action among Hong Kong's leading firms. Additionally, it was probably he, reputedly based on an article he had read in *Blackwood's Magazine*, who had included in the Bank's articles that it should be 'based on sound Scottish banking principles'.[20]

It is unlikely that those who read HSBC's literature see past the word Scottish or understand what it was Sutherland and Pollard had intended. The principles they referred to were: '(i) joint stock, (ii) a bank of issue, (iii) characterized by a branch system, (iv) granting interest on current accounts, (v) lending on the basis of cash credits'.[21] None of these would be unfamiliar to a modern banker, save the lending policy which is more conservative than the risk taken by banks today. Nor was the Bank's founding committee particularly Scottish as 'eight of the fourteen members were not from Britain and … for some four months in 1875, [the court] was without a single British director'.[22] The founding committee's non-British members included two Germans, two Americans, a Norwegian, two Parsees and a Jew.

The Bank's first chief manager, Victor Kresser, was Swiss, although his stewardship was marred by personal speculative investments and he was succeeded by 'the generally uninspired administration'[23] of James Greig, who may have been Scottish although of his 'early life … little is known'.[24] In 1875 he was succeeded by an Irishman, Thomas Jackson, whose tenures as chief manager in 1876–88 and 1893–1902 saw the Bank 'revive and … develop into the most formidable financial institution in the East'.[25]

Executive recruitment was not overtly Scottish and the first executive recruited from Britain was an Englishman, A.M. Townsend, who arrived in Hong Kong in 1870. That same year David McLean, a Scot and the Bank's Chief Manager in Shanghai, unimpressed by Kresser's speculations, had written: 'I don't want foreigners. I want English, or Scotch, nothing like sticking to one's colors'.[26] By 1872 he was in London where he could influence recruitment, and King suggests that McLean may have had a Scottish bias, being 'opposed [to] non-British [recruits] – he just preferred British, or, to read behind his letters, Scottish-trained lads'.[27]

The belief that HSBC is inherently Scottish, like the myth of the Jardines' founding of Hong Kong, is long-lived. As early as 1875,

Townsend, HSBC's English recruit, noted on his journey to Hankow that 'the American captain of the Yangtze River steamer [was] surprised that he was English. The captain had thought that all bank men were Scotch'.[28]

SOJOURNER PERCEPTIONS OF THE SCOTTISH IMPACT ON HONG KONG

In his article, Huw Richards claims that the Scots made an 'immense impact' on the British empire, 'but rarely more so than in Hong Kong'.[29] This view's currency is highlighted by Hong Kong government lawyer Stuart Stoker's evaluation that 'the Scots have been in the fabric of the place since day one ... There's been Scots judges, lawyers in government, in private practice, ... Hong Kong today reflects a fair amount of Scottish input over the years'.[30]

Of the 100 survey respondents, all bar 14 believe that the Scots have provided a cultural legacy to Hong Kong. To use a term borrowed from the advertising and media industry, their *Front-of-mind* responses are tabulated below. No tick-box choices were provided and respondents could mention as many areas of Scottish cultural impact as they wished (Table 13.1).

Trade and business (of which 20 per cent of respondents named Jardines) is considered to be the core Scottish influence on Hong Kong, with civil institutions and banking and finance sectors running close in the migrants' estimation. Surprisingly, despite 55 per cent of respondents coming from a financial services background, they account for just 44 per cent of the responses citing banking and finance as a Scottish legacy (this equates to just 27 per cent of this group). This holds true for other job sectors. For instance, none of those in the education sector cite education as a Scottish input. Yet among the Hong Kong migrants interviewed, only one made no mention of Jardines and one no mention of HSBC.

Hong Kong's Scots clearly see the Scottish story linked to the colony's founding and Scottish involvement in trade, finance and its civil institutions, although some tempering of these perceptions is evident in interviews. Educator David Bruce accepts that there may be some exaggeration of the Scottish contribution: 'I suppose, like any culture, the stories are overdone and ... it's probably more in the past, what we did, than the present'.[31] Additionally, retired police officer Ian Seabourne accepts that Hong Kong has had other competing cultural influences: 'we always called it a Scottish colony. I don't know why; there were more English expats.

Table 13.1 Perceptions of the Scottish cultural impact on Hong Kong

List areas in which Scottish culture has had an influence on Hong Kong in your opinion	Number of responses	%
Trade and Business	38	38
Civil administration, governance and policing	35	35
Banking and finance	33	33
Pipe bands	17	17
Scottish associations	14	14
Work ethic/character	15	15
Education	10	10
Community/philanthropy/meritocracy	11	11
Law	9	9
Sport	9	9
Heritage and history	8	8
Music, arts & media	7	7
Road & place names	5	5
Engineering	4	4
Religion	3	3
Medicine	2	2
Little or no influence	14	14

Sources: Scottish Migration to Hong Kong, Bristol Online Surveys, https://www.survey.ed.ac.uk/scotsinhk (closed 31 July 2014); The Scots of Hong Kong, Bristol Online Surveys, https://edinburgh.onlinesurveys.ac.uk/the-scots-of-hong-kong (closed 15 August 2015)

There were probably more Americans, but we always thought it was a Scottish colony'.[32]

THE REALITY OF LATE TWENTIETH AND EARLY TWENTY-FIRST CENTURY HONG KONG

Despite what Scots in Hong Kong may consider to be their legacy, this is not readily visible to the majority of Hong Kong's population. David Bruce observes that the Scots 'are a very small community in a Chinese city'.[33] Retired Senior Assistant Commissioner of the Hong Kong Police Mike Dowie takes this further:

> I think the majority of Hong Kong people, ... they're still quite naïve as regards what goes on outside of Hong Kong. It's changing ... – for example, the Chinese newspapers have very little international coverage.

I call Hong Kong the international city with the village mentality. ... The vast majority of people are still more interested in what's affecting them on a day to day basis really, than what's going on around the world.[34]

The reality is that Hong Kong was little more than a colonial backwater until events in China in the latter half of the twentieth century catapulted it into a regional financial and trading powerhouse. Indeed, the Second World War saw Britain commit more resources to Singapore's defence than Hong Kong's. Of its first 15 colonial governors up to 1918, seven were Irish and none was Scottish. It was not until 1958 with the appointment of Sir Robert Black that Hong Kong got its first of three Scottish governors. The other two were Sir Murray MacLehose (1971–82) and Sir David Wilson (1987–92). Significantly, MacLehose's tenure saw Hong Kong's rise from a conservative colonial entrepôt to a major Asian and international financial centre and this is best evidenced by Hong Kong's population growth.

It is estimated that of Hong Kong's 1845 population of 28,000, Europeans only numbered 595 or 2.5 per cent of the population.[35] This was probably the high point for white ethnics in per capita terms and as at 2011 white ethnics totalled just 55,236 or 0.74 per cent[36] of the population. Figure 13.2 shows that increases in population have largely been driven by the turbulent events of China's twentieth century history. Of particular relevance to modern Hong Kong is the Great Leap Forward and Cultural Revolution, which saw China's capitalists flee the mainland in large numbers, especially from Shanghai, with many starting new businesses in Hong Kong.

At the first full postwar census in 1961, Hong Kong's population had grown to just over 3 million but only 59 per cent (1.9 million) were aged over 15. The levels of education were very low; only 26 per cent of the population had attained at least secondary level education and only 2.4 per cent were university educated.[37] Consequently, managerial and professional sojourning opportunities were available to Britons to cope with the demands of the burgeoning colony's administration, infrastructure and service needs. Despite this, the absolute numbers of Britons in Hong Kong were never significant compared to the total population.[38] As at the 1971 census their numbers were an estimated 29,000, which represented just 0.74 per cent of the population.[39]

The most recent census has seen a demographic shift in age and educational attainment. By 2011, 88.4 per cent were aged over 15 and 73.8 per

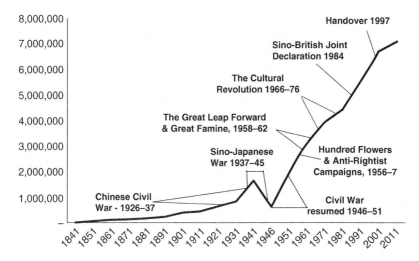

Fig. 13.2 Hong Kong's population, 1841–2011 (*Sources:* Fan Shuh Ching, *The Population of Hong Kong*, 1–2; Census and Statistics Department – Hong Kong, *Hong Kong Statistics, 1947–1967* (Hong Kong; Census and Statistics Department, 1969), 13–14; Census and Statistics Department – Hong Kong Special Administrative Region, *Demographic Trends in Hong Kong 1981–2011* (Hong Kong: Census and Statistics Department, 2012), 4)

cent of the population over 18 had attained secondary level qualifications, with a further 18 per cent being university educated.[40] The numbers of British citizens peaked in 1991 when 68,502 Britons were enumerated. Caution needs to be exercised with this number as uncertainty regarding the 1997 handover prompted many Hong Kong Chinese to seek citizenship elsewhere. Pointedly, 40,372 (59 per cent) of the 1991 British citizens were Hong Kong born and a further 2,987 China or Macau born.[41] In 2011, of the 33,733 Britons, just 10,486 (31 per cent) were born in Hong Kong and 20,689 elsewhere.[42]

White ethnics continue to supplement the ranks of the tertiary educated in Hong Kong, with 74 per cent of this group holding post-secondary qualifications as at 2011. More importantly, the change in the educational profile of the Hong Kong born has served to resource its establishment as a regional financial centre (Fig. 13.3).

In GDP per capita terms, Hong Kong has been a success and is now amongst the most affluent territories in the world. However, care should be taken with this number as income inequality is high (Table 13.2).

Hong Kong's economic miracle has come on the back of an influx of Chinese labour and entrepreneurial ability. Britain is often 'described as a relatively "benign" colonial ruler in Hong Kong'[43] and this provides the basis for the argument that this benign administration and its civil structures were intrinsic to Hong Kong's success. Significantly, there is no hint of Scottish exceptionalism here; rather, this was a British project. Such interpretations also ignore the fundamental irony that at the close of the twentieth century this supposedly benevolent colonial system did not guarantee personal liberties and operated in a globally connected city at a time when colonialism had long since been discredited. As Carole Peterson and Kelley Loper comment, 'the colonial system was inherently undemocratic and institutionalized racial inequality'.[44]

Hong Kong's Historiography

The preceding paragraphs show that Scottish influence on modern Hong Kong is limited, but this is not necessarily how Hong Kong's Scots see it, as David Bruce comments: 'in the 1800s they introduced the commercial infrastructure, for sure, and, obviously, you've got to talk about the

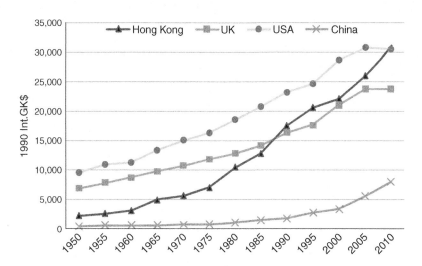

Fig. 13.3 Hong Kong GDP per capita comparison (*Source*: The Maddison-Project, http://www.ggdc.net/maddison/maddison-project/home.htm (2013 version))

Table 13.2 Gini coefficients of income inequality in UK, USA and Hong Kong

	1981	1991	2001	2011
UK	0.290	0.356	0.350	0.337
USA	0.406	0.428	0.466	0.477
Hong Kong	0.451	0.476	0.525	0.537

Sources: 'Statistical bulletin: Nowcasting household income in the UK: Financial year ending 2014', Office of National Statistics, http://www.ons.gov.uk/ (accessed 14 July 2015); 'Gini Ratios for Households, by Race and Hispanic Origin of Householder', *United States Census Bureau*, https://www.census.gov/ hhes/www/income/data/historical/inequality/ (accessed 14 July 2015); 'Hong Kong Economy, Half-yearly Economic Report 2012', *The Government of the Hong Kong Special Administrative Region*, http://www.hkeconomy.gov.hk/en/pdf/ box-12q2-5-2.pdf (accessed 14 July 2015)

Jardine Group and HSBC. And HSBC, as you know, stands for Home for Scottish Banking Clerks'.[45] Underpinning these constructions of Scottish Hong Kong are kernels of historical fact. For instance, Jardines was the largest British trading company on the Pearl River and did play a role in Hong Kong's colonial establishment. Thomas Sutherland was the first deputy chairman of HSBC and claimed to have written its prospectus, identifying it with 'Scottish banking principles'.[46]

Jardines is still prominent in Hong Kong and remains in business, whereas Dents folded in 1867 and Russells in 1891. The other British trading house synonymous with modern Hong Kong, John Swire and Company, has its roots in Liverpool and only moved into China physically in 1866 when it opened its doors in Shanghai and not Hong Kong. The field was therefore open for Jardines to suggest that it had been key to Hong Kong's story. This has been achieved through a number of corporate hagiographies and by controlling access to the company's archives, which are held at Cambridge University and where one of the access conditions is that: 'Nothing derived from or referring to the archives may be published without the prior consent of Matheson & Co. Ltd, ... Any publication using these sources requires the consent of Matheson and Company, London'.[47]

Histories derived from the Jardine archives unsurprisingly promote the roles of Jardine and Matheson in Hong Kong's founding. Author and colonial administrator Maurice Collis' 1946 book *Foreign Mud* is an example of a work derived from these archives. The book recounts the events that led to the First Opium War, culminating in the 1842 Treaty of Nanking and the cession of Hong Kong. It focuses on events in the Pearl River delta and largely ignores the wider conflict and the campaigns to the north at Amoy, Chingkiang and the Chusan archipelago, which were considered strategically more important. The hagiographic tone of the work is visible in Collis' evaluation of Jardine's 1840 meeting with Palmerston: 'The famous merchant prince saw the Foreign Secretary again in early February [1840] and almost immediately afterwards the Government's decision was communicated to its representatives in the East'.[48]

This meeting does not feature in Julia Lovell's 2011 history of the First Opium War, which places a very different spin on the Palmerston relationship, describing Jardine as 'snubbed' when his first attempts to meet Palmerston drew no response. Lovell also adds that when Jardine was granted an audience in September 1839, Palmerston 'kept him waiting for two hours before extracting as much information as possible … in exchange for no promises'.[49] In contrast, Richard Grace's 2014 history, which uses the Jardine archive, views the relationship much more favourably. It describes the February meeting as seeming 'to have had [a] strong influence on solidifying the intent of the cabinet'.[50]

Whatever the debates concerning Jardines involvement in Hong Kong's origins, this received history sits firmly within the school of colonial historiography characterised by the works of Eitel, Endacott and Welsh,[51] whose narratives generally celebrate Hong Kong's achievements under colonial rule. This historiography, supplemented by the corporate hagiographies, has only been challenged by Marxist historians from mainland China in the second half of the 1990s. Their narratives depict China as a victim of colonial aggression and Hong Kong as 'an inalienable part of the territory of China since ancient times'.[52] Even then, only Liu Shuyong's history has officially been translated into English.[53] In addition, both colonial and Marxist historiographies rarely evaluate the agency of Hong Kong's residents. This is changing and there is a growing body of work that has examined Hong Kong society in more detail, studying the interaction and divisions within the colonial, Chinese and Eurasian elites and the wider relationships within society like those of the plutocratic elite with labour and externally with mainland China.[54]

Limited competing historical narratives have left the field open to the moulding of a Scoto-centric interpretation amongst Scottish sojourners where the facts have been embroidered, although arguably not in a consciously deliberate way. Rather, they have chosen to promote a received history adopted and passed down by those who have preceded them, as Michelle McEwan experienced:

> I was at a night that was organised by the St Andrews Society ... Somebody was talking to me and saying ... "Scots have been integral in Hong Kong, have you not read such and such a book, and such and such a book?" And I went "No". And they said "Well, you know, Scots, where do you think Jardine House comes from, where did you think this came from? Scots are the backbone of Hong Kong." So I mean, I suppose ... Scots are the backbone of Hong Kong but I can't define how ... other people can do that.[55]

Yet, this is not the defensive narrative of a marginalised minority on the extremities of the host society, nor is history being used to create a victim diaspora or justification for departure. Rather, the narrative is one of engagement with the host society and importantly as an active and equal participant in a society where there is a perceived Scottish legacy. The narrative is integral to a combination of cultural identity markers that Scottish sojourners use to promote themselves to both local and expatriate populations.

Interpreting and Using Scottish Identity

The historical reality is that Hong Kong has, for much of its time since 1841, survived in limbo between its British colonial and Chinese cultural masters, and struggles to understand its identity. This remains unresolved and with 60.5 per cent of the population Hong Kong born as at the 2011 census[56] compared to 47.7 per cent in 1961,[57] a non-colonial Hong Kong identity has begun to emerge, as the protests of the 2014 *Umbrella Movement* highlight. Against this social backdrop, any Scottish historical legacy is background noise and few differentiate Scots from other *gweilos*.[58] Hong Kong is an homogenous Chinese city by ethnicity (93.6 per cent)[59] and language, where 88.2 per cent of the population speak Cantonese at home while 5.3 per cent speak other Chinese dialects.[60]

Mastery of Cantonese is difficult for sojourners and as a result language can be a source of social dislocation, as Fiona Donnelly describes of her frustration at not being able to use Cantonese: 'My Cantonese is rubbish. I've made a big effort over the years to really try, but ... I don't even hear the language, the nine tones ... I just don't get it'.[61] However, she is resigned to this sense of exclusion, concluding that 'it's been my volition to live in a town that I actually don't understand ... it's quite weird to live your life for 20 years in that kind of bubble'.[62]

In this Chinese environment there is a tendency for many sojourners, including the Scots, to become segregated and gravitate to affluent neighbourhoods, living in complexes in which there are expatriate communities. For many this may not be a conscious choice but one made by their employers and by necessity, as the sojourn may not be a long term one. Often referred to as *expat ghettos*, accommodation in these neighbourhoods commands rents comfortably in excess of what would be affordable for many in Hong Kong, where the average median monthly domestic household income in 2014 was HKD23,500 per month.[63] As only 4.7 per cent of Hong Kong's population earn in excess of HKD100,000 per month,[64] these are privileged ghettos (Table 13.3).

As the Gini coefficient (Table 13.2) implies, Hong Kong is an unequal society in terms of income. Scottish expatriates are, or have been, predominantly employed in managerial or professional roles in the higher end of the public, finance, legal and commercial sectors. Therefore, they tend to be amongst the top 10 per cent of income earning households in Hong Kong, which account for 41.2 per cent of monthly income.[65] This appears to be a global phenomenon reflecting Richard Alba and Victor Nee's research in the USA, which shows that professional immigrants are ordinarily employed in the upper-end of the labour market, 'where they hope to re-establish their middle-class lifestyle[s]'.[66] Yet, this is more than a re-establishment of lifestyle and includes the creation of a social niche based on a cultural identity. As Ernst Gellner argues, when an individual 'is not firmly set in a social niche, whose relationship as it were endows him with his identity, he is obliged to carry his identity with him, in his whole

Table 13.3 Hong Kong mid-range luxury apartment average rent per month

District	HKD
The Peak	96,000
Discovery Bay	89,000
Mid-Levels	88,000
Happy Valley	82,750

Source: Savills Research quoted in Edward Ngai, "Expat Cuts Hit Hong Kong Luxury Rentals," *Wall Street Journal*, http://www.wsj.com/articles/hong-kong-rental-market-suffers-as-expat-numbers-decline-1406809967 (updated 31 July 2014; accessed 15 January 2015). Price per 2,500 sq.ft. (gross) as at first quarter 2014

style of conduct and expression: in other words his "culture" becomes his identity'.[67]

For Hong Kong's Scots, the promotion of a cultural identity that adds value to the community is core to their privileged social position in Hong Kong society. To achieve this, the small community are willing to invest in the promotion of their identity despite its limited impact on the wider population. It is a real investment in Scottish identity as banker David Hamilton outlines when remembering his first leave in Scotland: 'something told me that having a kilt overseas would be better than wearing this dinner jacket that I had bought ... to go abroad with, because everybody had dinner jackets. So I bought a kilt on leave'.[68] Additionally, it is an investment in time and energy as Fiona Donnelly highlights, recounting her partner as saying, 'I've had my kilt on more often in Hong Kong than I have in Scotland'.[69]

Scottish migrants invest time in their Scottish identity so as to establish their social niche, but with Britons accounting for only 0.45 per cent of the population at the 2011 census,[70] British let alone Scottish culture can play only a small part. To have any appreciable effect, the promotion of Scottishness is targeted at specific social groups which include other wealthy minority ethnicities, potential employers and Hong Kong's plutocratic governing elite. Alan Powrie evidences the latter when outlining Scottish legacies:

> Most of the professions, even the law, which is a different legal system, had a very strong Scottish component, banking in particular and accountancy, and medical, everything, had a very strong component. The Chinese community, for those who were fairly well knowledgeable about it, know this as well, both here and up in Mainland China.[71]

It is a process of reiteration as Mike Dowie suggests: 'I think in the business area ... the Scots have had a tremendous influence. Now, speaking to many Chinese friends, ... many of them don't realise until you tell them, "These are all Scottish companies, Scottish things"'.[72] Migrants deploy their Scottishness as something that sets them apart from other ethnicities in adding value to Hong Kong, being apolitical and importantly non-colonial, despite the links with colonialism intrinsic to the Scoto-centric interpretation of history. Rather, they tend to distance themselves from the colonial past, leaving the English to bear the burden of colonial imperialism, as Calum Watson (CW) highlights:

CW: In an office environment, if I'm dealing with an American or a local
Chinese person, if they're typically dealing with an English person
and they're having a go, then it's great, just to start saying, "Yes, you
know, I'm Scottish and yes, they're always fussing and whiney and all
that." ...

IW: Do you find that using a Scottish identity means that you're not as
connected, say, with a British colonial identity?

CW: Yes. There seems to be a little less of a view that you're involved in
suppression. If you say you're Scottish, you're perhaps viewed as an
underdog as well.[73]

Ironically Scotland's role in Empire and colonial Hong Kong was reaf-
firmed in 1997, when it was the Black Watch who were the last British
regiment in Hong Kong and played a role in the handover ceremony itself.

Additionally, they promote their Scottishness as adding value to Hong
Kong and Asia by being better able to relate to the local community, as
Ian Seabourne comments:

I think generally speaking, if you meet the Chinese in Hong Kong, they say
the Scots are always a wee bit different. They're a wee bit more outspoken.
They don't rely on patronage so much ... I think the Scots are less up [them-
selves], and when they go there, they're more prepared to get involved and
not look at themselves as being superior. You get a lot of non-Scots in Hong
Kong who think that they're superior to Chinese people because they're
white or whatever. I never met anybody from Scotland who's like that.[74]

This opinion is pervasive throughout Scottish sojourning communities as
shipping executive Gordon Watson, a national serviceman in Hong Kong
in the 1950s and a sojourner in Singapore, Malaysia, Jamaica and Nigeria,
attests:

The Scots were respected out there. Even the locals also respected the Scots.

... I think it was because we were more down to earth. I think that was
something I learnt from ... an engineer friend ... he was teaching the
Chinese ... The Chinese thought he was terrific because he was just basically
a down to earth, good old Scots engineer. Once you were accepted by the
Chinese, you were asked to all sorts of weird and wonderful things. Yes, you
learnt a lot doing that. Being a Scot also helped.[75]

Gordon also outlines another aspect of Scottish sojourner identity creation: a perceived willingness to learn from and understand other cultures.

Again, this is a widely held belief and often combined with a perceived commitment to destinations and importantly being more adaptable than other ethnicities, as Alan Powrie argues: 'Some people didn't adapt and some people would get homesick. I would say from observation through the accountancy community, that [that] seemed to be more of an English thing than a Scottish thing. I didn't see many Scots being in the slightest bit homesick.'[76]

The central theme is one of concern for the wellbeing of the host community and this comes with an expectation and belief that Scots are involved in good works or philanthropy, as Gordon Lamb outlines: 'There's a lot of Scotsmen involved generally in community work here. It's not so much an expectation. It's more of an obligation, I think'.[77] Such expectations are supported by Scottish societies such as the Hong Kong St Andrew's Society, the Hong Kong Highlanders, the Hong Kong Scottish Piping and Drumming Association and Hong Kong Scottish Rugby Club. These societies provide networking forums for Scots in addition to a focus for the promotion of Scottish value to the host community, while providing philanthropic assistance under an explicitly Scottish umbrella. It is not that the Scots are any more exceptional or philanthropic than other wealthy minority communities. Rather, they are more adept at connecting identity to philanthropy through overtly ethnic associations, unashamedly utilising the physical iconography of Scotland together with a narrative of deep Scottish ties to Hong Kong.

Sojourners in Hong Kong are active promoters of their identity but because of their number their wider impact is low. Any real, embellished or imagined Scottish history or legacy pertaining to Hong Kong is largely unknown to the population where white ethnicities are not differentiated. While they may be segregated with other whites, and alienated linguistically and culturally from the majority of the population, theirs is a combative promotion of Scottish identity targeted at specific societal niches for a greater impact than the number of migrants warrants. Nor is the posture a defensive one but one that embraces and emphasises positive perceptions of the Scottish contribution to Hong Kong.

CONCLUSION

The historical narrative, together with perceptions of a significant Scottish legacy and the benefit of Scottish inputs, serves to preserve the social standing of Scots in Hong Kong and the human capital of that community in the eyes of those targeted. For migrants to invest time and capital in promoting Scotland and Scottishness, they must believe that the Scots are well received by the host society and those interviewed are of the almost universal opinion that they are. This is most clearly articulated in the testimonies of Gordon Watson, Ian Seabourne and Alan Powrie. It is not an obviously conscious process, nor is it formally structured by any of the Scottish societies, which provide a focus to Scottish notions of identity and human capital. Unfortunately, the parameters of the oral history project upon which this chapter is based did not envisage evaluating whether the investment in preserving Scottish human capital had produced the expected dividends. Perhaps this is unnecessary, as the perception that it does is sufficient enough for Hong Kong's Scots to invest capital, time and energy in the promotion of Scottish human capital.

Hong Kong's Scottish community is small and their human and cultural capital is not imbued in settler personas and thus needs to be recreated, reimagined, preserved and passed on by those living and sojourning there. Additionally, the message needs to be flexible and sympathetic to the host society, and this is evident in narratives that separate Scots from a British colonial past and focuses on the legacies of commerce and finance. This retelling provides Scots with both a focus for their identity in a Chinese environment, and more importantly serves to provide them with social status. This social standing cannot be assumed from the cultural capital they travel with, as that cultural capital is alien to the overwhelming majority of Hong Kong's population. Their promotion of their cultural and human capital is targeted at a narrow segment of Hong Kong's population, and leverages aspects of Hong Kong's past, which have been partially if unwittingly embellished to enhance the Scottish role. The consistent message is that the Scots are the right kind of migrants who will engage with and add value to the host society.

Notes

1. Alan Powrie, interviewed by Iain Watson, 31 July 2014, Hong Kong, held at The School of Scottish Studies Sound Archive, University of Edinburgh.
2. Huw Richards, 'Borders legend converted to global craze', *Financial Times*, 30 March 2007, http://www.ft.com/home/uk (accessed 3 December 2012).

3. Alain Le Pichon (ed.), *China Trade and Empire: Jardine, Matheson & Co. and the Origins of British Rule in Hong Kong 1827–1843* (Oxford: Oxford University Press, 2006), 18.

4. Susanna Hoe and Derek Roebuck, *The Taking of Hong Kong: Charles and Clara Elliot in China Waters* (Hong Kong: Hong Kong University Press, 2009; first pub. 1999), 21.

5. Charles Elliot, Dispatch, 16 November 1839, quoted in Hoe and Roebuck, *The Taking of Hong Kong*, 52.

6. E.J. Eitel, *Europe in China* (Hong Kong: Oxford University Press, 1983; first pub. 1895), 56.

7. Richard J. Grace, *Opium and Empire: The Lives and Careers of William Jardine and James Matheson* (Montreal and Kingston: McGill-Queen's University Press, 2014), 163.

8. Ibid., 178.

9. Ibid., 223.

10. Hoe and Roebuck, *The Taking of Hong Kong*, 67.

11. Michael Greenberg, *British Trade and The Opening of China 1800–42* (Cambridge: The University Press, 1969; first pub. 1951), 213.

12. James Matheson to William Jardine, 1 May 1840, quoted in Hoe and Roebuck, *The Taking of Hong Kong*, 86.

13. Lord Palmerston, 'FO 17/45', quoted in W.C. Costin, *Great Britain and China 1833–1860* (Oxford: Clarendon Press, 1937), 99.

14. Greenberg, *British Trade*, 213.

15. Andrew Yanne and Gillis Heller, *Signs of a Colonial Era* (Hong Kong: Hong Kong University Press, 2009), 42.

16. HSBC Holdings plc, *The HSBC Group: Our Story* (n.p., 2013), 2.

17. Maurice Collis, *Wayfoong: The Hongkong and Shanghai Banking Corporation* (London: Faber and Faber Ltd, 1965), 29.

18. Thomas Sutherland, 16 December 1909, quoted in Collis, *Wayfoong*, 22.

19. Frank H.H. King, *The Hongkong Bank in Late Imperial China, 1864–1902: On an Even Keel. Volume 1 of The History of the Hongkong and Shanghai Banking Corporation* (Cambridge: Cambridge University Press, 1987), 51.

20. HSBC, *Our Story*, 2.

21. King, *The Hongkong Bank, Volume I*, 76.

22. Ibid., 54–55.

23. Ibid., 44.
24. Ibid., 240.
25. Ibid., 43.
26. David McLean to W.H. Vacher (the Bank's London Manager), 9 June 1870, Early Letters (Shanghai), IV, 62; quoted in King, *The Hongkong Bank, Volume I*, 229.
27. King, *The Hongkong Bank, Volume I*, 231.
28. A.M. Townsend, quoted in King, *The Hongkong Bank, Volume I*, 218.
29. Richards, 'Borders legend'.
30. Stuart Stoker, interviewed by Iain Watson, 2 August 2014, Hong Kong, held at The School of Scottish Studies Sound Archive, University of Edinburgh.
31. David Bruce, interviewed by Iain Watson, 1 August 2014, Hong Kong, held at The School of Scottish Studies Sound Archive, University of Edinburgh.
32. Ian Seabourne, interviewed by Iain Watson, 10 July 2015, Edinburgh, Scotland, held at The School of Scottish Studies Sound Archive, University of Edinburgh.
33. David Bruce, interview.
34. Mike Dowie, interviewed by Iain Watson, 17 July 2015, Edinburgh, Scotland, held at The School of Scottish Studies Sound Archive, University of Edinburgh.
35. Fan Shuh Ching, *The Population of Hong Kong* (Hong Kong: The Committee for International Co-ordination of National Research in Demography, 1974), 1.
36. Census and Statistics Department—Hong Kong Special Administrative Region (CSD-HKSAR), *2011 Population Census: Ethnic Minorities* (Hong Kong: Census and Statistics Department, 2012), 27.
37. Census and Statistics Department—Hong Kong (CSD-HKGov), *Hong Kong Statistics, 1947–1967* (Hong Kong: Census and Statistics Department, 1969), 13 and 189.
38. Hong Kong's censuses do not differentiate between British ethnicities.
39. Fan Shuh Ching, *The Population of Hong Kong*, 2 and 18.
40. CSD-HKSAR, *2011 Population Census Summary* (Hong Kong: Census and Statistics Department, 2012), 5 and 42.

41. CSD-HKGov, *Hong Kong 1991 Population Census* (Hong Kong: Government Printer, 1993), 41.

42. 'Usual Residents by Place of Birth, Ethnicity, Sex and Nationality, 2011 (F105)' *2011 Population Census Office, CSD-HKSAR*, http://www.census2011.gov.hk/en/main-table/F105.html (last revision date: 30 March 2012).

43. Carole J. Peterson and Kelley Loper, 'Equal Opportunities Law Reform in Hong Kong: The Impact of International Norms and Civil Society Advocacy', in Michael Tilbury, Simon N.M. Young and Ludwig Ng (eds), *Reforming Law Reform: Perspectives from Hong Kong and Beyond* (Hong Kong: Hong Kong University Press, 2014), 176.

44. Ibid.

45. David Bruce, interview.

46. HSBC, *Our Story*, 2.

47. Archives of Jardine, Matheson & Co. Ltd. at the University Library, Cambridge, Janus, http://www.lib.cam.ac.uk/deptserv/manuscripts/applicationJM.html (accessed 2 December 2012).

48. Maurice Collis, *Foreign Mud: Being an account of the Opium Imbroglio at Canton in the 1830s and the Anglo-Chinese War that followed* (London: Faber and Faber Ltd., 1997; first pub. 1946), 265.

49. Julia Lovell, *The Opium War: Drugs, Dreams and the Making of China* (London: Picador, 2011), 100.

50. Grace, *Opium and Empire*, 254.

51. See Eitel, *Europe in China*; G.B. Endacott, *A History of Hong Kong* (London: Oxford University Press, 1958); Frank Welsh, *A History of Hong Kong* (London: HarperCollins, 1997).

52. Liu Shuyong, *An Outline History of Hong Kong*, translated by Wenjiong Wang and Mingyu Chang (Beijing: Foreign Languages Press, 1997), 1.

53. Lawrence Wang-chi Wong, 'Narrating Hong Kong History: A Critical Study of Mainland China's Historical Discourse from a Hong Kong Perspective', in Shi-xu, Manfred Keinpointer and Jan Servaes (eds), *Read the Cultural Other: Forms of Otherness in the Discourse of Hong Kong's Decolonization* (Berlin: Walter de Gruyter GmbH & Co., 2005), 198.

54. See John M Carroll, *A Concise History of Hong Kong* (Lanham, MD: Rowman and Littlefield Publishers Inc, 2007); John

M. Carroll, *Edge of Empires: Chinese Elites and British Colonials in Hong Kong* (Hong Kong: Hong Kong University Press, 2007); Wai Kwan Chan, *The Making of Hong Kong Society* (Oxford: Clarendon Press, 1991); Wing Sang Law, *Collaborative Colonial Power: The Making of the Hong Kong Chinese* (Hong Kong: Hong Kong University Press, 2009); Christopher Munn, *Anglo-China: Chinese People and British Rule in Hong Kong* (Richmond: Curzon Press, 2001); Jung-fang Tsai, *Hong Kong in Chinese History: Community and Social Unrest in the British Colony 1842–1913* (New York: Columbia University Press, 1993).

55. Michelle McEwan, interviewed by Iain Watson, 5 August 2014, Hong Kong, held at The School of Scottish Studies Sound Archive, University of Edinburgh.

56. CSD-HKSAR, *2011 Population Census Summary*, 35.

57. CSD-HKGov, *Hong Kong Statistics, 1947–1967*, 22.

58. Patrick J. Cummings and Hans-Georg Wolf, *A Dictionary of Hong Kong English: Words from the Fragrant Harbour* (Hong Kong: Hong Kong University Press, 2011), 69. **gweilo** (also **gwailo**): Definition: A Caucasian male (possibly derogatory, literally 'ghost man').

59. CSD-HKSAR, *2011 Population Census Summary*, 37; CSD-HKSAR, *2011 Population Census: Ethnic Minorities*, 27.

60. CSD-HKSAR, *2011 Population Census Summary*, 39.

61. Fiona Donnelly, interviewed by Iain Watson, 4 August 2014, Hong Kong, held at The School of Scottish Studies Sound Archive, University of Edinburgh.

62. Ibid.

63. Information Services Department – Hong Kong Special Administrative Region Government, *Hong Kong the Facts* (Hong Kong: Information Services Department—Hong Kong Special Administrative Region Government, 2015), 2.

64. Ibid.

65. CSD-HKSAR, *Thematic Report Household Income Distribution in Hong Kong* (Hong Kong: 2011 Population Census Office, 2012), 22.

66. Richard Alba and Victor Nee, *Remaking the American Mainstream: Assimilation and Contemporary Immigration* (Cambridge, MA and London: Harvard University Press, 2003), 48.

67. Ernest Gellner, *Thought and Change* (London: Weidenfeld and Nicolson, 1964), 157.
68. David Hamilton, interviewed by Iain Watson, 9 April 2014, Edinburgh, Scotland, held at The School of Scottish Studies Sound Archive, University of Edinburgh.
69. Fiona Donnelly, interview.
70. CSD-HKSAR, *2011 Census Summary*, 5 and 36.
71. Alan Powrie, interview.
72. Mike Dowie, interview. Major companies of Scottish origin operating in Hong Kong in 2015 include Jardine Matheson Holdings Ltd, Inchcape plc, A.S. Watson Group and Hutchison Whampoa Ltd.
73. Calum Watson, interviewed by Iain Watson (IW), 6 December 2014, Hong Kong, held at The School of Scottish Studies Sound Archive, University of Edinburgh.
74. Ian Seabourne, interview.
75. Gordon Watson, interviewed by Iain Watson, 13 November 2012, Blainslie, Scotland, held at The School of Scottish Studies Sound Archive, University of Edinburgh.
76. Alan Powrie, interview.
77. Gordon Lamb, interviewed by Iain Watson, 6 August 2014, Hong Kong, held at The School of Scottish Studies Sound Archive, University of Edinburgh.

INDEX

© The Author(s) 2017
T.M. Devine, A. McCarthy (eds.), *The Scottish Experience in Asia, c.1700 to the Present*, DOI 10.1007/978-3-319-43074-4

Printed in Great Britain
by Amazon

78232288R00193